THE SHAPING OF THE NAZI STATE

Peter D. Stachura is Lecturer in History at the
University of Stirling.

THE SHAPING OF THE NAZI STATE

EDITED BY PETER D. STACHURA

CROOM HELM LONDON

BARNES & NOBLE BOOKS NEW YORK
(a division of Harper & Row Publishers, Inc.)

© 1978 Peter D. Stachura

Croom Helm Ltd., 2-10 St John's Road, London SW11

British Library Cataloguing in Publication Data

The shaping of the Nazi state.

    1. National socialism 2. Germany – Politics and
government – 1918-1933 3. Germany – Politics
and government – 1933-1945
I. Stachura, Peter D
335.6'0943   DD240

ISBN 0-85664-471-4

Published in the USA 1978 by
Harper & Row Publishers, Inc.
Barnes & Noble Import Division

Library of Congress Cataloging in Publication Data

Main entry under title:

The Shaping of the Nazi state.

    Bibliography: p
    Includes index.
    1. Germany–Politics and government–1918-1933.
    2. Germany–Politics and government–1933-1945.
    3. National socialism. I. Stachura, Peter D.

DD249.S43   320.9'43'085   77–10038
ISBN 0-06-496492-2

Printed and bound in Great Britain by
Redwood Burn Limited, Trowbridge & Esher

CONTENTS

Introduction *Peter D. Stachura*   9

1. The Evolution of Hitler's Ideas on Foreign Policy, 1919-1925   22
   Geoffrey Stoakes

2. Gottfried Feder and the NSDAP *Albrecht Tyrell*   48

3. 'Der Fall Strasser': Gregor Strasser, Hitler and National   88
   Socialism 1930-1932 *Peter D. Stachura*

4. The Occupational Background of the SA's Rank and File   131
   Membership during the Depression Years, 1929 to mid-1934
   Conan J. Fischer

5. The Rise of the National Socialist Students' Association and   160
   the Failure of Political Education in the Third Reich *Geoffrey
   J. Giles*

6. The Nazi Organisation of Women 1933-39 *Jill Stephenson*   186

7. The Oldenburg Crucifix Struggle of November 1936: A Case   210
   Study of Opposition in the Third Reich *Jeremy Noakes*

8. Bureaucracy, Politics and the National Socialist State   234
   Jane Caplan

9. The German Film Industry and the New Order *Marcus S.   257
   Phillips*

Glossary and Abbreviations   282

Contributors   294

Index   298

For Marie, George and Michael

INTRODUCTION

Peter D. Stachura

National Socialism, as a historical phenomenon, continues to exert a
special kind of fascination among wide sections of the general public as
well as professional historians. Books, monographs, and learned papers
on the subject have accumulated to the point where even the specialist
is increasingly hard pushed to keep abreast of all the latest
developments and lines of enquiry. This compelling interest exists
despite the fact that National Socialism arose more than half a century
ago, and collapsed amidst the most ignominious circumstances
imaginable in 1945.

There are many good reasons, however, why this topic still attracts
such far-ranging attention. It is not just that National Socialism, and
particularly its *Führer,* Adolf Hitler, remain essentially enigmatic and
elusive of comprehensively satisfying and precise definition. The era
itself in which all this took place was so utterly extraordinary and
grotesque by any measurement. The circus-like atmosphere of the
Third Reich, the absurd antics of its leadership, the awesome sight of
disciplined marching columns, the frenzied mass rallies, all seem to
promote an aura of the unbelievable about the years 1933 to 1945. Yet
the prosaic and gargantuan evil of the Hitlerian epoch, epitomised by
the physical annihilation of millions of people, especially of Jews and
Eastern Europeans, will remain its indelible hallmark. Names like
Auschwitz, Buchenwald, Bergen-Belsen, and Dachau will be forever
synonymous with National Socialism. They bear lucid testimony to
its devastatingly destructive impact on the whole physical and ethical
fabric of European culture and civilisation. There are too many
people, uprooted and displaced as a direct result of the Second World
War—Hitler's War—who, having experienced the nightmare of National
Socialism at first hand, can never allow discussion and judgement of it
to rest. For them, above all, National Socialism can never be forgotten,
or forgiven.

Moreover, while all the answers to the critical problems of why
Germany should have been the first highly industrialised and advanced
country to witness the advent to power of an avowedly totalitarian
party, and why such a richly cultural nation could have succumbed to
nihilistic barbarism in the form of Hitler's dictatorship, have not been

supplied, searching examination of National Socialism must go on. Otherwise, the course of not only German but also European and world history in the twentieth century cannot be understood as deeply or as sensitively as it should be.

From a narrowly academic point of view, it must be borne in mind that a good deal of the literature on National Socialism which appeared in the decade or so after Germany's defeat, especially where it related to the era of the Third Reich, was inevitably and understandably influenced by the direct personal involvement of many authors in that calamitous period. Survivors of the Weimar political system, the concentration camps, and opponents from Germany and other countries certainly wrote much that was in detail useful and relevant. They unequivocally established and documented the cruelty and inhumanity of the National Socialists, but they naturally lacked that necessary detachment for their accounts and impressions to be regarded as entirely objective and sober appraisals. In consequence, it is only comparatively recently that dispassionate, scholarly perspectives have been brought to bear which allow National Socialism to be analysed within conventional criteria of historical enquiry.

Thus, notwithstanding the plethora of literature, there is considerable scope for new interpretations and reassessment of many basic questions, and for more probing scrutiny of still relatively unexplored aspects of National Socialism. While it would be quite inappropriate to suggest that the Nazi era as a whole requires thorough revisionist assessment, it is already the case that some areas, such as the relationship between the internal political dynamics of the Third Reich and its social and economic organisation, and the broad field of foreign policy development, have been the subject of much fresh re-evaluation in recent historiography. Further aspects which need more systematic consideration include the sociological typology of the National Socialist movement, and the nature and magnitude of links between the Nazi Party and big business. *The Shaping of the Nazi State* is designed as a contribution to these new avenues of approach to the study of National Socialism.

The nine essays, which are original and specially written for this volume, collectively present critical and often provocative analyses of a variety of significant themes pertaining to the evolution of National Socialism. Although a number of different methodologies and interpretative frameworks of reference are employed by the authors, every contribution is concerned with penetrating the innermost core of Hitler's movement and offers above all a serious and reasoned challenge to many traditional orthodoxies and assumptions. Based on an extensive and diversified array of predominantly German archival material, the essays produce a host of controversial arguments and conclusions. While it is not claimed that these ideas constitute a new and identifiable school of thought, they will, it is hoped, advance our knowledge of National Socialism and stimulate further discussion and research. In particular, the present volume is designed to convey the range and quality of the most up-to-date scholarship of a younger generation of historians in the field. The essays, which have been arranged with an eye to chronological order and thematic continuity, are primarily intended for a specialist audience but have been written in such a way as will also appeal, I believe, to non-specialists with a genuine interest in one of the most momentous periods in modern German and European history.

The development of National Socialist attitudes to foreign policy has aroused sustained scholarly comment in recent years, especially in the works of the West German historians Andreas Hillgruber, Klaus Hildebrand, and Jost Dülffer. It has been established beyond reasonable doubt that Hitler's ideas in this sphere are to be regarded as constituents of a coherent, if fundamentally irrational, programme. Andreas Hillgruber originally advocated the concept of a *Stufenplan* in Hitler's calculations, whereby German political and territorial power would expand in stages to the point where the Third Reich not only achieved hegemony in Europe and *Lebensraum* in the East, but also ultimately became poised for overseas global aggrandisement. Accepting this scenario, Geoffrey Stoakes, in the first essay in this volume, nonetheless takes issue with established interpretations of a central theme of Hitler's foreign policy, his attitude towards Russia and Britain.

Until now, it has been accepted that Hitler only conceived of creating a vast empire in Eastern Europe at Russia's expense in 1924, and that this was essentially the result of his espousal of the idea of an alliance with Britain two years earlier. Disagreeing with this view, Stoakes argues that for a combination of ideological, strategic, political, and personal reasons, Hitler had decided by late 1922 on a policy of hostility towards Russia, and a policy favouring alliance with Britain. This is despite the fact that these attitudes were expressed only privately by Hitler to Party colleagues and not made public until the writing and subsequent publication of *Mein Kampf* in 1924-6. Hitler was convinced, Stoakes continues, that Britain's support was vitally necessary if Germany was to be able to realise her territorial ambitions in the East. Indeed, extending this hypothesis, Stoakes states, against current opinion, that this spatial dimension had been added to Hitler's outlook well before he came into contact in 1924 with geopolitical theories as propounded, for example, by Professor Karl Haushofer. The latter's theses did not form the foundation of Hitler's imperialist ambitions because they were too restricted in scope for the Führer's liking, were not specifically directed against Russia and, in any case, came too late to influence Hitler's decision. In contrast to Haushofer's lack of influence, however, Stoakes underlines, within the limits of a general enquiry into the extent of ideological motivation behind the Führer's opinions, the important bearing of Alfred Rosenberg. He suggests that Rosenberg's conspiratorial view of history, which was moulded on the basis of a virulent anti-semitism and anti-Bolshevism, provided Hitler with attractive ideological justification for his estimate of both Russia and Britain. These views were not made public until the appearance of *Mein Kampf,* Stoakes explains, because of Hitler's fears that important supporters outside the NSDAP (for example, Russian émigrés) might be alienated by his Russian policy, and also because of his fears that opinion within the Party might be offended by his proposed alliance strategy towards Britain.

On a wider scale, Stoakes' paper re-emphasises the crucial significance of the very early 1920s for the development of the NSDAP. Although the Party suffered severely from the abortive Munich *Putsch,* it carried forward into the new phase after 1925 much of the ideology, organisational and propagandistic precepts, and of course, fanatical commitment to the Führer, which had been embedded in the National Socialist ethos during those turbulent incubation years. The NSDAP undeniably underwent profound changes after it was re-founded, particularly as regards the question of how to achieve power in the state, but the spadework completed before 1923 was indispensable to the Party's later success.

Stoakes' discussion of Alfred Rosenberg in his essay furnishes an appropriate connection with the following contributions by Albrecht Tyrell and Peter Stachura. Both authors consider the role and relative importance of subsidiary leaders in the NSDAP. Their choice of Gottfried Feder and Gregor Strasser respectively is apt if only because of the fact that of all Hitler's top leaders they are among the very few who have not yet been the subject of full-scale biographies. While studies of Hitler continue to swamp the academic and popular market, other figures like Josef Goebbels, Hermann Göring and Heinrich Himmler have succeeded in attracting a degree of interest which is in disproportion to their real significance in the NSDAP during the

Kampfzeit. There is plenty of scope, therefore, for investigating lesser
known and largely neglected leaders not merely to ascertain what each
of them actually did in the National Socialist movement, but also to help
illuminate still further the growth of the NSDAP as a totalitarian party
dependent on the autocratic and charismatic leadership of Hitler.

   In his essay, Tyrell probes beyond the undifferentiated image of
Gottfried Feder as the author or co-author of the 1920 Party programme,
and as the somewhat eccentric propagandist of the 'breaking of the slavery
of interest' theory. In attempting to define more accurately Feder's role
in the NSDAP before 1933 and in the few years following the
Machtübernahme, as well as the nature of his relationship with Hitler,
Tyrell describes, firstly, Feder's activities within and around the NSDAP
during the early 1920s, laying emphasis on the genesis and substance of
his economic theories. Tyrell sees them as representative of the anti-
liberal and anti-capitalist psychosis of the post-1918 German bourgeoisie,
and crystallising around the concept of a 'German Socialism'.
Nonetheless, Tyrell states, Feder's participation in the formulation of
the Party programme in 1920 was limited. In any case, much of his time
and energy were directed, not into the NSDAP, but into the *'Deutscher
Kampfbund zur Brechung der Zinsknechtschaft',* which Feder founded
in early 1920.

   Although Feder's economic and financial conceptions left a mark on
Hitler's political ideology during this early period, he never established
a close relationship with the Führer, nor did he create for himself,
despite his sense of personal importance, a substantial power base in the
NSDAP. Feder did not even acquire the status of the Party's official
financial expert, and his theories were not at any time formally adopted
as Party policy. His position during the 1920s therefore remained rather
ambivalent and insecure, and when during the early 1930s the depression
brought economic questions more to the fore in public debate, Feder
found his views even being vigorously challenged by others within the
NSDAP, including Otto Wagener and Walther Funk. In short, he failed
throughout the pre-1933 period to commit the Party wholeheartedly to
his financial and economic plans, while during 1933-5 his influence was
perhaps even less noteworthy. Tyrell concludes that since Feder never
realised his ambition of becoming the official Party spokesman on
economic and financial matters, it is quite misleading to argue, as most
historians have done hitherto, that Feder's standing in the NSDAP
suddenly declined in the early 1930s. Quite simply, he had never been a
personality of real importance in the Party. His role was that of a mere
propagandist.

Tyrell's study accentuates the point that in the vehemently anti-intellectual NSDAP, whose leader openly and repeatedly derided 'bourgeois intellectuals', theorists like Feder had little opportunity for self-assertion. Feder's failure to leave a decisive mark on the Party's ideological development reinforces the belief that in the NSDAP action, not ideas, was of paramount consideration. Those with ideas were looked upon with unyielding scepticism and kept at a safe distance from the machinery of decision-making and political power. After all, Hitler scarcely took ideology seriously as a factor in the battle for power. For him, the complementary and interdependent elements of disciplined organisation and adroit propaganda constituted the real substance of that overriding objective.

Concentrating on Gregor Strasser, with special reference to the resignation crisis at the end of 1932, Stachura calls into question a number of previous assumptions concerning the political orientation of this dynamic yet neglected Party leader. With the broad intention of clarifying the principal issues at stake in Strasser's final disillusionment with Hitler's leadership of the NSDAP, Stachura identifies and analyses the crucial changes which took place in Strasser's political and ideological outlook, and at the same time raises some questions about the character of the Party itself prior to 1933. It is argued that Strasser's alleged 'socialism' which had earned him the unofficial status of leader of the so-called Nazi Left, was notably tempered during the early 1930s as he established concrete ties with a variegated body of mainly moderate conservative-nationalist opinion outside his own party. To people like General Kurt von Schleicher and moderate leaders in industry and the trade unions, Strasser represented the acceptable face of National Socialism with which a degree of understanding could be reached. The quest for a coalition government at the end of 1932 came into the reckoning in this regard.

In progressively drifting away from an exclusively NSDAP perspective, Strasser effectively ceased being the Party's leading 'socialist' and, of course, the main inspiration of the Nazi Left. In any event, Stachura contends that the description 'Nazi Left' had no substantive ideological or organisational meaning. Disenchanted with Hitler's uncompromising stand vis-à-vis government participation, and apprehensive of what the NSDAP under Hitler signified for Germany's interests, the ambitious Strasser decided he could no longer remain in the Party. However, acknowledging that he lacked the requisite power-base and the personal courage to mount an open challenge to Hitler, Strasser simply made his protest a personal affair and retired quietly from active involvement in the NSDAP and Weimar politics altogether.

The episode brought into clear focus Strasser's undeniably complex personality and also stressed once again the limitations of protest in a *Führerpartei*. Throughout the early history of the NSDAP, Hitler was able to increase his hold on the Party in the wake of every instance of unsuccessful disaffection: the Bamberg Conference and the collapse of the northern *Arbeitsgemeinschaft* in 1925-6, the Otto Strasser affair in 1930, the Stennes Revolt in 1931, and finally the Gregor Strasser crisis. In the latter case, Hitler's speedy defeat of the dissenters helped smooth the way towards his uppermost aim, the Reich chancellorship. The intrinsic strength and pervasiveness of the Führer Myth doomed any resistance to him to abject failure. By 1932, the fortunes and political future of National Socialism hinged totally on Hitler. The Gregor Strasser crisis essentially reaffirmed, therefore, that the NSDAP was indeed the 'Hitler Movement' (*Hitler-Bewegung*).

When, in 1924-5, Hitler decided that the way to power was not by revolutionary but by quasi-legalistic, constitutional means, the resultant need to win mass support among the German electorate caused him to reconsider the place of ancillary organisations (*Gliederungen*) within the National Socialist movement. Before 1923 only the SA, or Stormtroopers, played a meaningful role in the Party's bid for power, while other auxiliaries, like the *Jugendbund der NSDAP* (Youth Association of the NSDAP), contributed very little. As part of his reassessment of the overall political situation in 1925, therefore, Hitler began to encourage the idea of a proliferation and strengthening of ancillary organisations and even professional interest groups connected with the Party. Although the initiative for such developments did not always come from central Party headquarters (*Reichsleitung der NSDAP*), the years after 1925 saw not only the setting up of a streamlined and more politically-conscious SA, but also a series of other groups, including the Hitler Youth, the National Socialist German Students' League (NSDStB), the National Socialist Schoolboys' League (NSS), and specialised women's formations. The basic task of each of these groups was initially to disseminate the National Socialist gospel as widely as possible among the German people, and to attract new adherents to the Führer's cause; later, in the Third Reich, they were meant to reconcile whole sections of the population to the National Socialist *regime* and to indoctrinate them in the Nazi *Weltanschauung*.

The performance of the ancillary organisations was generally uneven and their combined efforts on behalf of National Socialism did not surpass the Party's contribution. Nonetheless, they were a significant extra dimension of the movement's swift rise and consolidation of power. On this account alone, they are worthy of independent and detailed examination, and recent scholarship has already made a beginning in this direction. The three essays which form the central part of this volume pursue this trend by analysing the SA, the most powerful ancillary group, the NSDStB, and the *NS-Frauenschaft*, the women's auxiliary.

The SA's muscle power and usefulness as a terror and propaganda weapon to National Socialism is undisputed. But on one other vital aspect, the sociological composition of its rank and file membership, there is no such unanimity of agreement among scholars. They are heatedly divided over the question whether the SA was primarily a movement of the lower middle class or of the working class. Involved in the debate is the central issue of the relationship between the NSDAP and the class structure of Weimar Germany.

Conan Fischer tries to come to terms with the conflicting and often contradictory interpretations of this question on the basis of new archival evidence. By firstly defining class terms, particularly relating to the working class, and then analysing a comprehensive range of sociographic data, including parental background, occupational patterns and age. Fischer demonstrates that the overwhelming majority of the SA's rank and file in both urban and rural areas came from the working class. The independent lower middle classes were largely absent. At the same time, Fischer is able to confirm previous ideas that most ordinary SA men were unemployed (as many as 70 per cent) and belonged to younger age categories (under 30 years). Indeed this evidence, taken in conjunction with the age composition of the main occupational groups in German society before 1933, inevitably meant a preponderance of blue collar, and to a lesser extent, white collar employees in the SA ranks. The social composition of the SA ordinary members contrasted sharply, therefore, with that of the organisation's middle and higher leadership echelons which were largely staffed by the lower middle class. Although this pattern of class affiliation is not unique in mainly working-class movements and, indeed, is apparent in the Hitler Youth before 1933, Fischer rightly concludes that his findings raise broader questions about the social and class nature of the National Socialist movement in general, the more so as the NSDAP itself was a lower-middle-class organisation. A revision of standard generalisations about the class basis of National Socialism is obviously called fo   while other implications of this for wider aspects of Hitler's rise to power can hardly be discounted.

Geoffrey Giles and Jill Stephenson discuss the role of ancillary organisations within the power structure of the Third Reich, emphasising the extent to which the NSDStB on the one hand, and the *NS-Frauenschaft* on the other, managed to carry out a programme of political and ideological indoctrination among their respective clientèle.

Giles emphatically rejects the thesis that the NSDStB was in any way successful in this endeavour. The organisation, he contends, displayed in the years before 1933 impressive energy and dedication, as well as a capacity for skilful and ruthless politics. The NSDStB was thus able to emerge as an authoritative voice among Germany's university student population by 1931/32 but this, Giles maintains, represented in many ways the apotheosis of its achievement. After 1933 the group adopted a policy of permanent revolutionary activism more suited to the conditions of the *Kampfzeit* than the different ambience of the Third Reich. Beset by internal leadership struggles and confusion over aims, by stout resistance to its totalitarian schemes from the traditional fraternities, by the absence of support from a suspicious Party, and above all, by increasing apathy among students at large, the NSDStB failed in its fundamental task of politically educating the university sector. With the advent of war in 1939, the situation only deteriorated further. The record of the NSDStB was therefore one of unfulfilled adaptation to the demands of the National Socialist State.

Jill Stephenson comes to much the same conclusion about the role of the *NS-Frauenschaft* between 1933 and 1939, though in a few other respects its contribution to the Führer's work was more positive. Designed like other ancillaries to serve the interests of the NSDAP and later the Third Reich, and in no way meant to promote the cause of feminism, the *NS-Frauenschaft* under the leadership of Gertrud Scholtz-Klink (1934-1945) developed a formidable administrative apparatus which allowed it to pervade many spheres of concern to women. Often this was effected through subsidiary groups such as the *Reichsmütterdienst* and the *Kultur-Erziehung–Schulung*. Despite this sizable bureaucracy, however, which Stephenson describes in some detail, the *NS-Frauenschaft*, though able to bring about the nationalisation and nazification of the organisational life of women under its own leadership, never controlled more than a relatively small minority of them. The task of political indoctrination was therefore bound to be executed to only a severely limited degree. Stephenson explains why most women in National Socialist Germany were unwilling to become officially organised by referring to the voluntary basis of participation in the*NS-Frauenschaft,*the inherent difficulties of organising housewives and more important, the sheer indifference of women. Apathy, we have noted, was the principal stumbling block of the NSDStB. On the other hand, while active support for National Socialism was not forthcoming from most German women, Stephenson stresses that the vast majority of them were prepared passively to acquiesce in the régime.

Giles and Stephenson together add weight to the argument that nazification of German society did not go far beyond the immediate and overt, that it was in fact largely confined to institutional and organisational forms, while leaving relatively untouched in an ideological sense the hearts and mind of most Germans. This situation engenders further doubts about the efficacy of totalitarian regimes where the majority of people under their domination are able to avoid being sucked in entirely by the system, even if they refrain from offering open resistance to it. German resistance to National Socialism is a theme which has, of course, commanded wide attention. Historians have probed not only the actual physical manifestations of resistance but also the allied problem concerning the peculiar constraints and possibilities of mounting opposition in a totalitarian and closely guarded society. Considerable differences of opinion still exist on the scale of importance which the German resistance to Hitler merits. A somewhat underdeveloped aspect pertinent to the controversy is the state of public opinion in the Third Reich regarding the policies, actions, and objectives of the régime. How far the ordinary German supported the government, whether his support was active or passive, is a question which hitherto has been clouded by National Socialist propaganda and coercion. The consequent image of a Reich contented and unswervingly loyal to the Führer clearly requires critical scrutiny.

By making a case study of one particular example of public disaffection, the controversy aroused by the removal of crucifixes from schools and other public buildings in South Oldenburg in 1936, Jeremy Noakes comes to grips with the larger problem of measuring the level of public support for the Third Reich. He is concerned to delineate the limits of opposition to a totalitarian regime both from the point of view of the reaction of the regime to opposition, and from the point of view of the attitudes and behaviour of the population itself.

Noakes argues that groups bound together by either a common ideological, social, or religious identity, provided the strongest resistance to the Third Reich. This applies especially, he adds, to the two categories which had proved most resilient to NSDAP appeals before 1933, the industrial working classes and Catholics. In the case of the latter, the Catholic Church possessed social cohesion, a degree of protection due to its international character, and an independent organisational structure. The Church was thus better equipped than most other institutions to challenge the regime if its interests were being threatened. Applying this criterion to the overwhelmingly Catholic districts of South Oldenburg, Noakes states that the inner social and ideological vitality of the Catholic sub-culture there was primarily responsible for thwarting the efforts of the NSDAP and the State in the crucifix conflict. But although the Catholics of South Oldenburg scored a dramatic victory, Noakes cautions against reading too much of wider significance into the episode. The victory was ephemeral because within two years all denominational schools had been closed in even that staunchly Catholic region. It also has to be remembered that in 1936 the National Socialists were soft-pedalling on contentious religious issues for domestic and diplomatic reasons. Hence, generalisations based on the Oldenburg affair about the extent of Catholic hostility to the regime, and about hostility in general to the National Socialists, are not permissible. The 1936 crucifix scandal is to be seen specifically in the political and social context of that part of Germany and no more.

The deep consternation into which the state authorities were temporarily plunged as a result of the South Oldenburg struggle was a symptom of a more pervasive confusion in the agencies responsible for the administration of the Third Reich. A full and convincing picture already exists of the wasteful overlapping, lack of common purpose, and inefficiency of government during 1933-45. Many historians regard the regime as having been fundamentally unstable and held together only by the extraordinary charismatic force of Hitler in his role as Führer and supreme authority. Interpretations of the National Socialist State are also invariably of a dualist type, that is, they embody theories which see the state's dynamic as some kind of opposition between Party and State, between totalitarianism and authoritarianism, or between politics and administration, and so on. But in her discussion of the National Socialist State, Jane Caplan unfolds a trenchant critique of the traditional dualist approach.

Caplan contends that the dualist interpretations depend upon a particular view of the bureaucracy and administration as incarnations of stability, a view she criticises for applying an organisational insight to a political system. In exploring the specific weight of some basic components of civil service structure and policy in Germany before 1933, Caplan argues that these questions of state organisation were already politicised before the National Socialists came to power. Not only does this fact belie the idea that the Nazi State can be analysed primarily in terms of a dynamic assault by the Party upon an established and stable system of government, but it also underlines the importance of investigating the continuity of political problems and solutions across the dividing line of 1933. Caplan illustrates this continuity with reference to a number of the policies implemented after 1933 by the Reich Ministry of the Interior, the body mainly in charge of administrative affairs. She believes that especially after 1935 this Ministry's policy objectives and methods were themselves significant sources of the very incoherence which characterised the operation of the Nazi State.

In a concluding section, in which she attempts to examine the theoretical implications of her empirical critique, Caplan argues that it is incorrect to lift the bureaucracy as an institution out of its political situation. To do so tends to reduce political problems to their institutional or ideological locations, so that a concrete analysis becomes impossible. In other words, the administrative structure and civil service policy in the Third Reich furnish a basis for examining the political machinery of the Nazi State. Stressing that the vital problem of this state was its inability to reproduce itself as a functioning political system, Caplan outlines how the bureaucracy shared in and contributed to this incapacity. Her final and provocative conclusion is that the real polarities evident in this overall problem must ultimately be understood in terms of a crisis of class representation.

Further evidence of the ineffectiveness of National Socialist governmental policy in practice is provided by Marcus Phillips's consideration of the cultural side of the 'New Order' project which Hitler conceived for occupied Europe. The 'New Order' envisaged a Europe dominated by, and subservient to German political and economic interests, and also ensnared by National Socialist cultural tastes. Phillips examines the predominant influence of Goebbels in the latter sphere with special reference to the priorities he mapped out for the German film industry. The Reich Propaganda Minister was convinced that National Socialist cultural policies in occupied Europe should be used to consolidate Germany's military achievements, and he wanted the film industry to act as a vehicle for the twin purposes of propaganda and ideological indoctrination. The essence of the film industry's brief was to propagate German i.e. National Socialist *Kultur* in order to combat the alleged prodigious advance of American *Unkultur*. The policy was commercially profitable, but the film industry failed in its crucial mission as an agent of the National Socialist cultural revolution for a cluster of reasons which Phillips discusses in detail. He concludes by assessing the light thrown on the character of the 'New Order' and on National Socialist rule in general by the experience of the German film industry, suggesting that in the last analysis the industry's failures merely reflected the weaknesses and tensions of the Third Reich's political and administrative structures.

The underlying and coordinating idea of the essays presented here is to assess certain developments intimately associated with the emergence of a National Socialist State in Germany, and to examine some of the ways in which that state took shape. The volume treats only a small part of a complex historical process, but if it at least partially extends our awareness and comprehension of Adolf Hitler's National Socialism it will have served its purpose.

1 THE EVOLUTION OF HITLER'S IDEAS ON FOREIGN POLICY 1919-1925

Geoffrey Stoakes

Over the past few years the foreign policy ideas formulated by Adolf Hitler in the *Kampfzeit* have been subjected to intensive scrutiny. It is now clear that Hitler's ideas on foreign affairs, far from being a conglomeration of illogical ideological prejudice and crude predictions based on his reading of political history, actually formed part of a coherent and all-embracing *Weltanschauung*.[1] Particular aspects have been examined in exhaustive detail: Nazi attitudes to the acquisition of colonies;[2] the development of the navy;[3] the problem of Hitler's world ambitions;[4] and the origins of the 'alliance system' outlined in *Mein Kampf*.[5]

The aim of this essay is to re-examine current interpretations of the origins of Hitler's foreign policy with particular reference to the position of Russia and England in the Nazi foreign policy programme. For it seems to this writer that there is still a marked tendency amongst many historians to concentrate unduly on the figure of Adolf Hitler and to overlook the ideas of other party members who may well have made significant contributions to the formulation of foreign policy ideas.[6] The relative neglect of the writings of Alfred Rosenberg, probably Hitler's earliest adviser on foreign affairs, is a case in point; these writings are studied, if at all, only to illustrate his differences with Hitler.[7] For example, it is generally assumed that Rosenberg's ideas were characterised by ideological rigidity and Hitler's by the flexibility of the *Realpolitiker*. This is an oversimplification of the position resting on a study of their respective careers only after 1933 and ignoring their relationship in the 1920s. Only if Hitler's thought processes are studied within the context of the Nazi party as a whole is it possible to arrive at valid conclusions about the relative importance of Hitler's personal contribution to the development of Nazi ideology.[8] So far this has not been attempted.

A second aim of this essay is to reassess the relative importance of ideological factors and personal influences in the fashioning of the party's foreign policy. For it is curious how reluctant historians are to pay serious attention to ideological factors. Since Jäckel's brilliant synthesis appeared, everyone pays lip service to the view that a

combination of ideological considerations and *Realpolitik* forged
Hitler's outlook. But with the exception of Günther Schubert[9] no
historian has seriously considered the possibility that ideological
factors actually *determined* (and not merely reinforced) Hitler's
'alliance system'.

Klaus Hildebrand in his study of the foreign policy of the Third
Reich takes 1924 as a starting-point because 'Hitler's remarks on
foreign policy between the years 1919-23 seem far more conventional
and indeed resemble those indiscriminate pan-world aspirations of
the Wilhelmine policies of the conservatives in Germany and within the
Nazi party which he attacked so strongly in *Mein Kampf*.'[10] On the
contrary, in the years 1919-23 the Nazis were in fact developing —
behind a carefully nurtured facade of conventionality — many of the
ideas, which appear so novel in Hitler's autobiography. This is
particularly true of Hitler's plans for England and Russia. If applied
only to the years 1919-20, Hildebrand's judgement would have far
more validity. For it is perfectly true that in the first year of his
membership of the German Workers' Party, Hitler's speeches on
foreign affairs were mainly concerned with vitriolic attacks on the
Versailles settlement, and his view of the international powers was
coloured by his unfailing demand for the revision of this treaty.
England was castigated along with America and France as one of
Germany's 'absolute enemies'.[11] Hitler's hostility towards England
was based on the belief that she had been responsible for the seizure
of Germany's colonies, which, by robbing her of supplies of raw
materials, had destroyed her competitiveness in world markets.[12]
Hitler was more sympathetic towards Russia. He described her as one
of those states which 'became our enemies because of their
unfortunate situations or because of circumstances.'[13] According to
Hitler, Russia and Germany had no conflicting interests whilst Russia
followed 'an asiatic policy of conquest'; in fact, before the war only
'the international Jewish press concern' had prevented an alliance
between the two nations.[14]

As this last comment suggests, during the course of 1920 Hitler
began to apply his deep-rooted anti-semitic prejudices to foreign affairs
(he had already blamed Germany's internal disorder on the Jews in
1919). The development of this international dimension to Hitler's
anti-semitism has been attributed to the publication in January 1920
of the *Protocols of the Elders of Zion*, the famous tract which
purported to reveal the existence of a Jewish world conspiracy to
achieve global domination. It has been suggested that Hitler read the
'Protocols' between February and May 1920 and from that time on

applied anti-semitic observations to his foreign policy speeches.[15] This seems to be the likeliest explanation since Hitler was also being tutored in the machinations of the 'conspiracy' by Alfred Rosenberg, who quickly became the acknowledged party expert on Russian affairs and the conspiracy (and possibly also by Dietrich Eckart). In 1919 Rosenberg observed that the collapse of Russia into Bolshevism in 1917 completed the first stage of the Jewish conspiratorial plan, since Russian nationalism had been subverted and Russia was in the hands of several 'Jewish-Bolshevik' leaders; Germany would be next to suffer destruction by the Jews.[16] Whoever was responsible for revealing to Hitler the relevance of the conspiracy to the study of foreign affairs, the important point is that its impact on Hitler's assessment of Russia was immediate. The hitherto friendly attitude towards Russia was tempered by an aversion to her present rulers: 'an alliance between Russia and Germany', he pointed out, 'can only come into being when Jewry is deposed.'[17]

Were Hitler's reservations about a Russian alliance perhaps caused by considerations of *Machtpolitik* alone? Certainly Hitler quoted the physical weakness of Russia after the ravages of the civil war which raged from 1917-20 as a contributory factor.[18] Also important was the fact that Russia under Bolshevik leadership had adopted a policy of imperialist development. 'Bolshevism', Hitler declared, 'is only a cloak for the construction of a great Russian empire.'[19] Whether these political considerations or the ideological insights carried more weight with Hitler at this stage is frankly uncertain; there is certainly no evidence to justify the confident conclusion that 'the danger lay for Hitler not in Lenin's proposal to bring to fruition a world-wide revolution emanating from Germany, but in the strategic striving of the Soviet Union for an increase in her territory.'[20] If strategic factors really determined Hitler's foreign policy, why is there no evidence of Hitler's hostility towards the leaders of Bolshevik Russia *before* 1920? There was, after all, abundant evidence of Russia's territorial aggrandisement at this time — the Red Army's advance into the Baltic States in 1918-19 gave early warning of Russia's aggressive designs on Eastern Europe. Why, then, did Hitler only begin to express reservations about a Russian alliance in 1920? The explanation which cannot be ignored is that ideological 'insights' — that is, the revelation that the Jews were the force behind Bolshevism — led to a fundamental revision of Hitler's view of Russia.

It should be remembered that Nazi ideology, revolving as it did around the notion of 'international conspiracy of Jewry' had implications for the whole field of foreign affairs (not just for Russia). Under the influence of the *Protocols of the Elders of Zion*, Nazi anti-semitism became a universalist racialist ideology postulating a struggle for existence between the forces of good and evil, represented by the Aryan race and Jewry respectively. To the Nazi mind, this was the ultimate struggle and every state in the world would be the battleground. The struggle between capitalism and marxism described by Lenin was completely illusory in the opinion of the Nazis. As early as 1918, Rosenberg had pointed out that there was, in essence, no dichotomy between marxism and capitalism; the overt and apparently antithetical confrontation between the two was, according to Rosenberg, a deliberate deception — the Jews were in the vanguard of both camps, as leaders of the proletarian revolution in Russia and as bankers in the financial centres of capitalist Western Europe.[21] So despite apparent incompatibility, international marxism and international capitalism were manipulated by the Jews, whose real enemies were the forces of nationalism. In this struggle between Good and Evil, peaceful Western Europe was just as important a battlefield as war-torn Russia, where the two sides, represented by White Russian nationalists and the Bolshevik Red Army, were facing each other in the civil war. Rosenberg regarded the democratic regimes of Western Europe as, in fact, the first step towards Bolshevism. Put quite simply, world Jewry by propagating democratic and internationalist ideas in the West at the expense of nationalist aspirations, and by exploiting class conflicts in Russia, was attempting to lay the foundations for its own world domination.[22] Hence to Rosenberg's mind, the progress of the twofold machinations of the 'Jewish world conspiracy' materially affected the value of each and every European country as a prospective ally for Germany. If the triumph of Jewry in the guise of Bolshevism in Russia made a Russian alliance less attractive to the Nazis, would it not follow logically that the position of England would also be affected in Nazi eyes by similar ideological considerations? To this aspect of the problem we must now turn our attentions.

Rosenberg's view of England was initially jaundiced by his belief that London was the centre of the 'Jewish world union' which co-ordinated the plans of world Jewry[23] and that following the Balfour Declaration of 1917 which committed Britain to support the establishment of a Jewish state in Palestine, the British Empire had assumed the role of 'guardian angel' of Jewry.[24] On the other hand, Hitler's first recorded references to England in 1920 were full of righteous indignation at the severity of the Versailles treaty but even so his veneration for the British Empire could not be concealed: 'the English as a nation', he pointed out in one speech, 'have reason to be proud.'[25] Hitler soon began to recognise that the Jews were at work throughout Europe and not just in Bolshevik Russia: 'The Jew is sitting in Russia exactly as he does in Berlin or Vienna, and so long as capital remains in the hands of this race, there can be no talk of reconstruction because the Jews are working hand-in-glove with the international capitalists, who are also Jews, and sell out us Germans.'[26] However, even though Hitler appears to have adopted Rosenberg's conspiratorial world view, anti-semitic arguments still do not appear in 1920 to have affected his view of England.

On the other hand, Rosenberg's attitude towards England was undergoing a distinct modification. Initially he had interpreted the espousal of the zionist cause evident in the Balfour Declaration as an example of how the interests of British imperialism might coincide with those of the Jews. 'England', he wrote in 1920, 'possessed India, Egypt and footholds on the Persian coast, and lacked only a territorial connection between these lands and here Palestine fell into place as part of a chain.'[27] Almost immediately, however, Rosenberg began to differentiate between the interests of Britain and those of world Jewry. The reason for the change is unknown, but henceforth Rosenberg's animosity towards England was curbed by the realisation that in fact true British national interests did not coincide with the plans of world Jewry. The British failure to give adequate support to the White Russian nationalist forces in the Russian civil war did not represent 'true' British policy, but was an aberration attributable, in Rosenberg's view, to Jewish influence on government policy.[28] From now on any subsequent action taken by the British government which appeared to advance the cause of Jewry or hinder that of nationalism could be conveniently explained away as evidence of Jewish subversion of British national interests. He had already started to 'unmask' Jewish figures in foreign governmental circles to back up his thesis. Even non-Jewish leaders were not immune; Lloyd George, whose association with the treaty of Versailles damned him in Nazi eyes, was alleged to be in the pay of the Jews.[29]

The fact that Rosenberg went out of his way to think up 'plausible' explanations of British diplomatic manoeuvres suggests either a certain predilection for England on his part, or alternatively, a determination to minimise the gulf between *actual* British policy and Rosenberg's preconceived notions of what that policy *should be*. Whichever explanation is more acceptable, Rosenberg clearly believed that a more favourable treatment of Germany would be in accord with 'true' British interests. In August 1921, he stressed that English 'national' policies, as advocated by the strong nationalist party (Conservative Party), were not compatible with the complete ascendancy of either France or Germany in Europe, but only with 'a balance of power in Europe.'[30] The complete destruction of Germany (the aim of the Jewish faction) would not be to the advantage of the English nationalists because it would make certain French hegemony in Europe.

The resurrection of the outmoded strategy of the 'balance of power' in Europe as the (supposed) rationale behind a foreign policy dictated by genuine British interests was to be the basic assumption behind Hitler's concept of an English alliance after 1922. Rosenberg was not advocating an Anglo-German alliance in 1921 because, as far as he was concerned, the Jews, and not the English national party, were in control of British government at that time and, therefore, an alliance would not have been forthcoming. It is interesting to note that Hitler felt the same way. In May 1921, he rejected Lloyd George's conciliatory speech over the question of Upper Silesia* as a mere trick. 'An intrinsic change in England's attitude towards Germany is however impossible, because the same society of Jewish press bandits directs the state there as does here.'[31] Hitler clearly felt that the removal of Jewish influence would increase the possibility of a favourable change in England's attitude towards Germany, but whether an Anglo-German alliance would result when traditional British policy reasserted itself is uncertain. Hitler did not feel inclined to explain away British policy solely by reference to Jewish influence[32] despite paying lip-service to conspiratorial anti-semitic theories. Neither Hitler nor Rosenberg was prepared to advocate an English alliance in 1921. The indications are that Rosenberg felt the effects of such an alliance would be beneficial to Germany. His frequent resort to the 'Jewish world conspiracy' to explain British policies may have been a conscious attempt to use ideology to explain away discrepancies between his interpretation of British interests and the actual course of British

---

* The ultimate fate of Upper Silesia was to be decided according to the terms of the treaty of Versailles by a plebiscite in the area. This took place on 21 March 1921, the majority voting in favour of a return to German rule. France and Poland opposed the return of the whole area to Germany, which caused uproar in Germany. In May 1921 Lloyd George made known his disagreement with the Franco-Polish decision.

policy. But even assuming that Rosenberg were cynically using anti-semitic ideology to correct his own basic misconceptions (and at this stage he could surely have changed his little-known views without losing too much face), this is no reason why historians should ignore his ideological arguments. At the very least, they reflected the prevailing current of Nazi opinion and are thus invaluable; in this case, the use of the 'ideological corrective' shows that one leading Nazi at least believed in the possibility of a future alliance with England.

But did ideological factors affect Hitler's decision to advocate an English alliance late in 1922? The Ruhr crisis is generally considered to be the turning-point in Hitler's alliance policy, because, in his own words, 'for the first time, [the Ruhr crisis] really alienated England basically from France.'[33] The physical occupation of the Ruhr industrial area in January 1923 by French and Belgian troops was, in fact, incidental to Hitler's decision (he announced the alliance in the late autumn of 1922).[34] Much more important, so it is argued, was the evidence of Anglo-French friction caused by Poincaré's threat to extract German reparation payments by force. This, it is believed, was sufficient inducement for Hitler to adopt his new line in foreign policy. But was that the only reason for the change? After all, Hitler had ignored signs of Anglo-French disagreement over Upper Silesia only a year earlier. It is possible that personalities played some part. Just as Hitler's attitude towards Italy must have been modified by the seizure of power by Mussolini's Fascists in October 1922, so Lloyd George's resignation as Prime Minister of England in the same month may have contributed to Hitler's decision to announce to his party colleagues this new facet of his foreign policy programme. In view of Lloyd George's intimate association with the treaty of Versailles and, in Nazi propaganda, with the interests of international Jewry, it is difficult not to see a synchronisation between Hitler's first recorded support for an English alliance and the resignation of the man who seemed to represent Jewish influence in British affairs of state. Lloyd George's departure would at least have provided a convenient, ideologically acceptable, pretext for a change in policy.

Rosenberg certainly relished the moment of Lloyd George's fall from power. It offered, he felt, an opportunity for the traditional aim of British policy — the maintenance of a European balance of power — to reassert itself and to replace Lloyd George's Jewish plans.[35] British diplomacy might now be dictated by the instinct for self-preservation in the face of possible French hegemony in Europe and 'as a result support for Germany would necessarily emerge.'[36] Rosenberg did,

however, express doubts about the ability of the national party in
England to defeat the entrenched power of the Jewish capitalists, but
he still regarded Lloyd George's resignation as a step in the right
direction.[37] Whilst changes in the political scene may have influenced
Rosenberg's attitude towards England, there is little evidence about
Hitler's reasons for introducing the English alliance concept into the
party programme. But in view of his previous comments about the
British Prime Minister, Lloyd George's political eclipse ought not to be
overlooked. This is not, of course, to suggest that the event was in any
way decisive — he may have been considering the English alliance for
some time, but it could have precipitated his decision. Taken in
conjunction with the breach in good relations between France and
Britain and the emergence of Fascist rule in Italy, Lloyd George's
resignation added up to a diplomatic revolution which may have
encouraged Hitler to reassess Germany's position in Europe.

Axel Kuhn argues that 'Hitler's change-over to an alliance with
England occurred as a solitary decision against the opinion of the
party.'[38] But there is good reason to doubt this interpretation, which
is based mainly on the belief that Rosenberg — the main party
spokesman on foreign affairs — opposed the alliance. Kuhn quotes
several articles from Rosenberg's pen in 1923 during the Ruhr crisis,
in which he expressed bitter disappointment that Britain's verbal
condemnation of the French occupation had not been converted into
more concrete support for Germany: 'England does not think at all
about making a serious break with France.'[39] Did this mean that
Rosenberg opposed Hitler's projected alliance strategy? Not necessarily.
Several points must be borne in mind. Firstly, Rosenberg as editor of
the *Völkischer Beobachter*, the Nazi party's newspaper, was obliged
to comment on current events, in this case, on the fading hopes of
Anglo-German cooperation in 1923. A clear distinction must be drawn
between such comments and Rosenberg's fundamental beliefs. Indeed
on one occasion, Rosenberg showed an awareness of this important
distinction when he wrote that 'we want to hold back our positive
appraisal (of foreign affairs) for the time being . . . and we will wait
reservedly on future events and not lapse into daily cackle over every
piece of news.'[40] In fact, Hitler expressed similar sentiments to
Rosenberg's in March 1923: 'Help from abroad? Foolish hopes,'[41]
he observed. He, too, denied that England (or America) would lift
a finger to help Germany.[42] No one would suggest on the basis of
these comments that Hitler had abandoned his programmatical
allegiance to England, so why should Rosenberg be regarded as an

opponent of the alliance because of not dissimilar comments? Rosenberg was not obediently 'toeing the party line', against his earlier opinions[43] when he pointed out in July 1923 that England had always been the opponent of the strongest state on the continent and was, therefore, liable to support Germany against France.[44] Rosenberg, as we have seen, had reached this conclusion much earlier. He did not oppose the English alliance; indeed he may even have recommended it to Hitler.

One may conclude that the interest in an English alliance was not a response to any lasting change either in the field of international relations or in British domestic politics. Neither Anglo-French friction over the Ruhr nor the resignation of Lloyd George proved to be a turning-point. Four years later, in 1927, Rosenberg still maintained that true British interests had not replaced the preponderant Jewish influence in the corridors of power,[45] but since the proposed alliance was only to be formed between a National Socialist Germany and a future nationalist government in Britain, it was quite consistent with the party's anti-semitic ideology. Whether for reasons of ideology, power politics, or personal predilection, by late 1921 Rosenberg had begun to look favourably on the prospect of an English alliance. Hitler's attitude towards England changed from hostility to friendship between 1921 and autumn 1922. And it is difficult to ignore the fact that the only noticeable change in the Nazi view of England was the tendency to distinguish between true English interests and those of Jews in control of government policy.[46] The adoption of an English alliance cannot be explained solely in ideological terms but clearly it would be an error to dismiss ideological motivation altogether. The fact that in late 1922 British policy, by opposing French aims in Europe, appeared to be adhering to the balance of power strategy (which Rosenberg had outlined) may have influenced Hitler.

II

If the Nazi party's ideas on an English alliance matured earlier than has been commonly assumed, can the same be said of the rest of its foreign political programme? In the years 1920-22, Hitler's attitude towards Russia appeared to harden. He continued to criticise the suggestion that Germany should reach an understanding with Soviet Russia, even though it might act as a counterweight to the pressure from the Entente powers over reparations payments. At the time of the London conference on reparations in March 1921, Hitler dismissed the idea on the grounds that 'Russia represented in real political terms a mere cripple',[47] since the Bolshevik leaders had lost the support of the Russian working class. Hitler's reaction to the Rapallo agreement signed between Germany and Russia in April 1922 made it clear that his rejection of friendship with Soviet Russia rested on ideological grounds:

> In Russia the Jews and their Chinese-Latvian protectors rule . . .
> Amongst us preparations are being made for the same thing . . .
> Soviet Russia is not the last straw which Germany can clutch like
> a drowning man, but a lead-weight which pulls us further down into
> the depths.[48]

It has been argued that if the Russian nationalists had been successful in the civil war, then a Russia purged of Bolshevism would have been a suitable ally for Germany. According to this interpretation, only in 1924 when the Bolsheviks were firmly installed in power and all hopes of a national Russian victory had been dissipated, did Hitler finalise his diplomatic strategy and relegate Russia to the ranks of Germany's foes.[49] In other words, the hopes pinned on Russian nationalist forces held up the finalisation of Hitler's programme for two years. This last point seems dubious for several reasons. Firstly, since the Bolshevik victory had been secured by the end of 1922 at the latest, Kuhn's argument would only hold water if Hitler had remained totally uninformed about events in Russia (which is unlikely) or if he allowed himself to be misled by reports exaggerating the extent of continued White Russian resistance within Russia. The latter is a more feasible, though still unlikely, explanation because Rosenberg in particular continued to look for signs of life in the Russian nationalist elements long after the Bolsheviks had established control.[50] In 1924 the prospect of a national Russia may have receded but Nazi policy remained unchanged. An interesting question however is whether, if the national Russian forces had defeated the Bolsheviks in the civil war, Hitler would have regarded the new Russia as a possible ally? To attempt to answer this difficult and hypothetical question, one has to ask how seriously the Nazi party took the possibility of an alliance with a national Russia.

The concept of an alliance with 'national Russia' received considerable support in the Nazi party and brought the party into contact with powerful and influential supporters — in particular, the Russian émigrés who settled in Bavaria. Rosenberg was the only Nazi to explain what was meant by a 'national Russia'. Rosenberg drew a

distinction between, on the one hand, Muscovite Russia, in which
various non-Russian nationalities had been linked in a federation
loosely controlled from Moscow, and, on the other hand, the Czarist
Russian Empire, which by ruthlessly centralising political power had
tightened its hold on subject nationalities and created a *Grossrussland*
'a Russian world empire'.[51] By 1917 Czarism was seen according to
Rosenberg as an obstacle to the development of a truly 'national
Russia', in which the various nationalities would enjoy self-
determination.[52] The Bolsheviks had, of course, set about suppressing
nationalist aspirations so that it seemed as if only a truly national Russia
would grant independent statehood to the Poles, Ukrainians and
other national minorities within the Russian Empire. All that would
remain of the Russian empire, one presumes, would be a state
equivalent in size (and nature) to the old Muscovite state.

Hitler's support for the principle of national self-determination
in Russia may have been implicit in his criticism of Russian imperialism
in 1920. He blamed the Russians themselves for their failure to pacify
their own country; 'if they were to bother only about the purely
Russian areas, then no Ukrainian, Pole or Latvian would dare to take
a stance against Russia.'[53] Hitler certainly recognised the strength of
non-Russian separatist movements in Russia, but he also sought to
mobilise anti-Bolshevik feelings *in the Russian people themselves.* In
April 1922, criticising the Rapallo agreement, Hitler urged Germans
'not to negotiate with those who were destroying Russia, but to call
on the Russian people to shake off their tormentors, in order that we
can become friendly with them.'[54] The appeal of the Nazis' anti-
Bolshevik campaign was, therefore, two-pronged: Hitler, on the one
hand, was appealing to the Russian nationalists and Rosenberg, on the
other, to the separatists. Although both could and did unite against
their common enemy — Bolshevism — the aims of the two groups were
ultimately incompatible and the Nazi party, as we shall see, tried to
avoid committing itself firmly to the separatist cause.

It is interesting to speculate on the relevance of the two strategies
for Nazi alliance policy. If, first of all, Rosenberg's ideas were
implemented (on lines indicated above), the Russian state would
be broken up and a small Muscovite state recreated. An alliance with
this truncated 'national Russia' would scarcely be an effective
counterpoise to the Anglo-French entente in international affairs, so
it is extremely unlikely such a consideration held up formulation of
Nazi foreign policy strategy between 1922 and 1924, as has been
suggested. On the other hand, the dismemberment of the Russian Empire

into national units would greatly diminish the danger of Germany's
ever having to face a war on two fronts with France in the West and
Russia in the East as she had done in 1914-18. This was exactly the
argument that General Erich Ludendorff had used early in 1918 to
persuade a reluctant German foreign office to adopt his more
expansionist peace terms for the armistice with Russia.[55] Ludendorff
had pressed not only for the cession of several of the Baltic States
and Poland to Germany in order to increase German security in the
East but had also supported Finnish and Ukrainian independence.[56]
In 1922 and 1923 Ludendorff came increasingly to collaborate with
the *Kampfbund* and through the mediation of its organiser, Dr Max
von Scheubner-Richter, with the Nazi party.[57] Clearly, Rosenberg's
plans for Russia with their emphasis on national self-determination
would have satisfied Ludendorff and the need to keep the support
of the still-prestigious hero of Tannenberg may have prevented the
abandonment of the separatist solution to the Russian question, a
solution, which was, of course, unpopular with exiled Russian nationals.

Rosenberg's support for separatist movements, which he sustained
throughout the 1920s, would never (even if the movements had been
successful) have been a realistic alternative to the proposed Anglo-
German alliance against France. Can the same be said of Hitler's
vague talk of an alliance with the Russian nationals – the second
possible participants in his anti-Bolshevik crusade? It would seem so.
In 1921 Hitler had reduced his strategy for a German alliance policy
to a simple formula: either Germany allied with England against Russia
or with Russia against England.[58] In Kuhn's view, though, Hitler did
not immediately realise that his decision in favour of an English
alliance directed against *France* necessarily entailed enmity towards
Russia.[59] In 1924 Hitler repeated the England-Russia alternative –
proof, according to Kuhn, that he was still undecided about his final
stance on the Russian question. Only later did Hitler grasp the possible
connection between Anglo-German cooperation against France and his
anti-Bolshevik policy and in *Mein Kampf* he accordingly eliminated
Russia from his alliance considerations.

This ingenious interpretation is implausible for several reasons.
It is unlikely, first of all, that a man of Hitler's undoubted political
acumen would not realise that by choosing one alternative (England) he
automatically ruled out the other (Russia). After all, the unspoken
assumption behind the above equation was that Britain and Russia were
irreconcilable enemies. This fact alone gave Germany a free choice
between the two alternatives. Hitler's approach to foreign affairs was

already characterised by an eagerness to exploit friction between the foreign powers; when the English alliance finally emerged it was at a time of Anglo-French disagreement, whilst the notion of an Italian alliance emerged during the Franco-Italian clash over Fiume.[60] In all probability, Hitler took note of Anglo-Russian enmity when he decided on the English alliance — he was, evidently, fully aware of the long history of conflict of interest between the two powers over Afghanistan and the Bengal Lowlands.[61] It is difficult to believe, therefore, that Hitler failed to appreciate the significance of possible British support for his anti-Bolshevik policy when he announced the English alliance in 1922.

This impression is corroborated by a secret report on the Nazi party dating from December 1922. In that month Eduard Scharrer, the co-owner of the Munich daily *Münchener Neueste Nachrichten*, and the rich proprietor of Schloss Bernried in Bavaria, submitted three reports on the Hitler movement to the Reich Chancellor, Wilhelm Cuno.[62] One of the reports (the other two were written by Nazi party 'sympathisers') was Scharrer's account of an interview he had arranged with Hitler in December 1922.[63] In the course of their discussion, Hitler reviewed his ideas on foreign policy, pointing out that of the major powers only England had an interest in the future existence of the German people.[64] 'England,' he explained, 'has an interest in seeing that we do not go under, since, otherwise, France would become the greatest continental power in Europe, whilst England would have to be satisfied with the position of a third-rate power.'[65] English assistance against France, he felt, would only be forthcoming when Germany showed herself to be a reliable economic proposition and an effective counterweight to France in Europe and provided, of course, 'she posed no threat to England herself.'[66] Significantly, Hitler was already counting on exploiting an English alliance for his policies against both Russia and France:

> The destruction of Russia with the help of England would have to be attempted. Russia would give Germany sufficient land for German settlers and a wide field of activity for German industry. Then England would not interrupt us in our reckoning with France.[67]

This document, the authenticity of which there seems little reason to doubt,[68] suggests a picture very different to the one drawn by Kuhn. From the start, it seems, Hitler realised that the English alliance could be turned not only against France but also — in line with his formula — against Russia. Scharrer recorded no reference to Russian nationals in

Hitler's conversation so one can conclude that the promise of support to this group did not hamper the development of Hitler's aggressive designs on Russia.

Scharrer's report is in many ways an exceptional find, answering as it does several intriguing questions. Of course, some of the answers could have been pieced together from a careful study of the scattered articles and pamphlets of Alfred Rosenberg, which do confirm much of what Scharrer reported. Rosenberg recognised the twofold relevance of an English alliance. As early as August 1921, he had predicted that true British (as opposed to Jewish) interests would dictate a more friendly attitude towards Germany.[69] Elsewhere, Rosenberg explained that these self same interests would necessitate russophobic policies: 'the real Great Britain would have every cause to fight tooth and nail against supporting a rebellion (Russian Revolution?) which was reaching Afghanistan and India.'[70] Characteristically, Rosenberg identified international Jewry as the villain of the piece, being behind the threat to Britain's position both in Europe and the Empire: 'the Jewish stock exchange works openly with the Soviet Jews not only for the annihilation of Germany but also for the destruction of the English world empire, in India, in Egypt and at the Bosphorus. France is the gendarme of the Jewish bankers.'[71] England was clearly a suitable ally for Germany in the struggle against Jewish internationalism – the above quotation certainly shows that an English alliance against France and Russia would be given an ideological stamp of approval by Rosenberg.

To sum up: the relegation of Russia to the ranks of Germany's foes in *Mein Kampf* cannot be seen as a belated consequence of the English alliance first announced to a Nazi audience two years previously. The reverse may even have been true, namely, that since Russia's decline into Bolshevism ruled her out as a possible ally for Germany, Hitler looked to Russia's long-time imperial rival, England, for support. However, in view of Hitler's respect for the British, evident as early as 1919, it would be misleading to interpret the English alliance simply as a reaction to the disappointment of hopes of an eastern alliance. The really important point is that Hitler had finalised his alliance strategy by the end of 1922. What we must always bear in mind here is that Hitler had spoken of these new developments only in party circles and confidential interviews; there was no explicit public statement of these foreign policy ideas before *Mein Kampf* was written. Several reasons for this secrecy will be suggested shortly but first we will examine the connection between the new orientation in foreign policy and Nazi plans for territorial aggrandisement.

III

The new light shed on Hitler's policy towards Russia has important implications when one attempts to assess the role of geopolitical ideas — and in particular, the doctrine of *Lebensraum* (living space) — in the development of expansionist policies in eastern Europe. Klaus Hildebrand feels that whilst anti-semitism and anti-Bolshevism pulled Hitler away from a rapprochment with Russia, one essential element in his policy was missing in 1923 — *Raumpolitik* — the policy of territorial expansion.[72] Two years later in *Mein Kampf*, Hitler incorporated this final ingredient in his programme to make Russia not only the ideological arch-enemy but also the source of the space so necessary for Germany's future development. Since Hitler had designated Russia as the prime target of his alliance strategy as early as 1922, one must ask again whether, in fact, Hitler had still to add a spatial dimension to his policy after 1922?

The imperialist tendency which ultimately produced the synthesis of ideological and spatial requirements in Hitler's programme is generally attributed to the influence of the leading exponent of German geopolitics, Professor Karl Haushofer, who visited Landsberg gaol during Hitler's imprisonment there in 1924. Actually, it seems likely that Haushofer had little direct contact with Hitler and that his ideas were transmitted to Hitler only indirectly through the young Rudolf Hess, whom Haushofer visited as friend and geopolitical mentor.[73] Haushofer remembered taking several geopolitical books to Landsberg for Hess to read at the very time when Hess was helping to type Hitler's autobiography.[74] However, if Hitler first became conversant with geopolitical arguments in 1924, the need to extend German *Lebensraum* can have played no part in Hitler's estrangement from Russia evident long before 1924. Is it possible to go one step further and to say that geopolitical ideas were not even the original inspiration behind Hitler's desire for territorial expansion at Russian expense?

This question raises several problems because it is difficult to identify with any certainty or precision geopolitical influences on the Nazi party's foreign policy. The original party programme of 1920 demanded 'soil and land (colonies) for the nourishment of our people and the settlement of our surplus population.'[75] The need for land to settle 'surplus population' was a faithful echo of the Pan-German League's plea for *Ellenbogenraum* (elbowroom) in 1914 and the underlying assumption that Germany was overpopulated was one shared by the geopoliticians. As a result, it is not easy to determine whether the arguments used by the Nazis were the legacy of pan-germanism or the result of geopolitical teaching. Even so, ideas on overpopulation, colonial settlement and Germany's need for increased *Lebensraum* were not the exclusive preserve of these two groups. Moeller van den Bruck and the intellectuals of the Ring Movement in Berlin had long talked in semi-mystic terms about German *Lebensraum* and the problem of German overpopulation; Hitler may have discussed such topics when he came into contact with this group in 1922.[76] Hitler was thus exposed to several, though by no means unrelated, schools of thought on the future extension of Germany's territory.

However, since Hitler did not meet Haushofer or Moeller before 1922 (and it seems fair to assume that their ideas had no real influence on his before that), it may be possible by studying Hitler's earliest speeches to determine his original views on the solution to the problem of overpopulation in Germany. Reflecting on pre-war politics in a speech in May 1921, Hitler spelt out the possible solutions as he saw them:

> There are only three ways for a progressive nation to maintain itself as long as it does not want to become the plaything of the other progressive nations through a policy of deliberate birth-control. Colonization. Germany came too late, she found no room in which to exert her excess energies. Emigration. Which land wants to give away her children as cultural fertilizer for other lands? Since the first two possibilities were denied to the German nation, she proceeded to secure her existence by the development of industry and the export of goods. Social Democracy deliberately rejected all national power politics.[77]

Hitler would clearly have favoured the pursuit of a power political solution – one which involved territorial expansion along the lines indicated by the treaty of Brest-Litovsk in 1918:

> Through the peace with Russia the sustenance of Germany as well as the provision of work were to have been secured by the acquisition of land and soil, by access to raw materials, and by friendly relations between the two lands.[78]

It may seem surprising that Hitler was willing to accept friendly relations between Germany and Russia – it was, after all, Lenin's Bolshevik government which had no alternative but to sign the treaty of Brest-Litovsk. This Hitler either forgot or felt was a worth-while price for territorial arrangements which would secure Germany's future needs and would leave Russia dismembered (the treaty recommended national independence for the Ukraine and Finland). Evidently Hitler's mind was already attuned to the possibility of territorial gains in Eastern Europe before he came into contact with geopolitical ideas.

The territorial arrangements of the Brest-Litovsk treaty clearly whetted Hitler's appetite for expansion in Russia. But Hitler's interest in the treaty may have other roots. Both General Ludendorff and Max von Scheubner-Richter had been involved at different levels in implementing Germany's *Ostpolitik* in 1918, Ludendorff as Germany's war supremo and Scheubner-Richter in his capacity as assistant to the Reich Plenipotentiary for the East, August Winnig. Under the influence of both men after 1921, the idea not only of territorial expansion but also of the settlement of Germans in Russia may have taken root in Hitler's mind.[79] Scheubner-Richter had helped to negotiate a treaty with the Latvian government in December 1918, whereby German volunteers were to protect Latvia against the advancing Red Army in return for German control of all the military in the province and a guarantee of the right of every German volunteer to citizenship and the ownership of land.[80] The idea of German settlement in the East (*Ostsiedlung*) obviously appealed to Scheubner-Richter as a Baltic German. After narrowly escaping execution at the hands of the Soviets when they captured Riga, he established an economic and political information service in Königsberg in East Prussia, which provided Germans with information on (amongst other things) settlement in the Baltic provinces.[81] Two years later, his interest in *Ostsiedlung* undiminished, he addressed the congress of exiled Russian monarchists in Bad Reichenhall:

> Russia can only be built up through the excess of intellectual and technical resources which we have in Germany. For the intelligentsia in Russia is either no longer alive or banished . . . Everywhere resources are lacking and, therefore, we in Germany must lead the stream of emigration to Russia.[82]

Scheubner-Richter's plans were designed to facilitate the economic recovery of Russia after the collapse of Bolshevism (which he abhorred) and it is noticeable that German settlers in all his schemes were to contribute to Russia's recovery, not to exploit Russia's potential for Germany's own use. He would have fully endorsed Hitler's talk of an alliance with the 'Russian people' — Scheubner-Richter's negotiations with the Russian émigrés had this very end in view.

However, at the end of 1922, whilst Hitler was still paying lip-service to the idea of aiding Russian nationals against Bolshevism, he was talking in private about the destruction of Russia and the conquest and forcible settlement of Russian territory. In December 1922 he described to Scharrer the type of foreign policy Germany should adopt:

> Germany would have to adapt herself to a purely continental policy avoiding any damage to English interests. The destruction of Russia with the help of England would have to be attempted. Russia would provide sufficient land for German settlers and a wide field of activity for German industry.[83]

Obviously Hitler did not share Scheubner-Richter's concern for the recovery of the Russian economy after the removal of the Bolsheviks. Russia was to provide Germany's future needs, no more. Clearly Hitler had completed the transition from aggressive revisionist to territorial imperialist by the end of 1922 — two years earlier than is usually assumed.[84] The basis of Hitler's foreign policy alliance with England for war against France and Russia already clearly implied territorial expansion at Russian expense. Hitler hoped that this purely continental policy would not offend his ally, England, whose opposition to the rise of a naval or colonial power on the continent was well known.

It is therefore very likely that Hitler's imperialism was derived from his rejection of pre-war policies of economic and commercial expansion and from the example of German *Ostpolitik* in 1918, which showed the potential of a territorial policy at Russian expense. His imperial ambitions were then reinforced by his anti-Bolshevism. This interpretation seems to coincide with Hitler's own account in *Mein Kampf*:

> At long last we break off from the colonial and commercial policy of the pre-war period and shift to the soil policy of the future. If we speak of soil in Europe today, we can have primarily in mind only Russia and her vassal border states. Here fate itself seems desirous of giving us a sign. By handing Russia to Bolshevism, it robbed the Russian nation of that intelligentsia which previously brought about and guaranteed its existence as a state.[85]

Clearly though, the last ingredient in Hitler's recipe for the restoration of German power — territorial imperialism — was in his mind some time before Haushofer's ideas began to influence the Nazi party. It seems that geopolitical arguments were brought in to bolster up Hitler's case for a new *Ostpolitik*. The acquisition of land was described as necessary for reasons of politico-military expediency since 'the size of the area inhabited by a people constitutes in itself an essential factor in determining its natural security.'[86] Such arguments merely reinforced decisions already taken; far from inspiring Hitler's call for eastward expansion,[87] geopolitics did not even provide the original basis for his *Bodenpolitik*. Haushofer's theories gave Hitler's programme only a veneer of pseudo-scientific respectability. But did Hitler pervert Haushofer's ideas for his own ends, as the geopolitician claimed in 1945? There is some justification for the view that Haushofer's talk of German expansion was irresponsible and invited perversion or misinterpretation because of the virulence of his attack on the territorial provisions of the Versailles treaty and his ambivalence about the direction of the proposed German expansion. Nevertheless, a close study of Haushofer's work shows that he would not have backed a policy of expansion in Russia. On the contrary, Haushofer spoke of the need for 'intelligent cooperation with the spatial requirements of the Russian area.'[88] Germany was to expand, Haushofer wrote in a rare moment of self-revelation, into the 'borderlands', which he identified as 'North Schleswig, Eupen-Malmedy, the Saar, the Palatinate, Lorraine, Alsace, Vorarlberg and Tyrol, Carinthia, Styria, Burgenland, Moravia, the Austro-Hungarian diaspora, the old duchies of Auschwitz and Zator, Eastern Upper Silesia, Austria (Ostmark), Danzig and Memelland.'[89] All these areas, though under foreign rule, did have German communities and past ties with Germany and this adds conviction to Haushofer's later claim that he 'never approved of annexations of territory alien to our people and which had no German settlements.'[90] The suggestion that Haushofer was behind Hitler's plans for Russia is, therefore, totally without justification; Haushofer's talk of expansion into the border areas around Germany was far too limited for Hitler. In 1928 Hitler wrote critically of such a 'border policy':

> The foreign policy of the national bourgeois world has in truth always been only a border policy; as against that, the policy of the national socialist movement will always be a territorial one. In its boldest plans, for instance, the German bourgeoisie will aspire to unification, but in reality it will finish with a botched-up regulation

of the borders.[91]

Such a criticism would surely apply to Haushofer's schemes. So it would seem that geopolitics was not an essential ingredient determining the nature of Hitler's foreign policy programme; it merely provided the icing on the cake.[92]

IV

If Hitler had already decided by the late autumn of 1922 that his foreign policy programme should seek to use an English alliance against Russia in order to secure large areas of Russian territory for settlement and exploitation by Germans, why did he nevertheless suggest in an article in 1924 that Germany still had a free choice between Britain and Russia as allies? In another retrospective analysis of German policy in 1914, Hitler observed that:

> In foreign affairs, Germany had to choose: either she decided to win farm land by renouncing overseas trade and colonies, and by renouncing over-industrialization, etc., in which case the German government had to recognize that this was only to be achieved in alliance with England against Russia; or she wanted sea-power and world trade, in which case only an alliance with Russia against England could be considered . . . '[93]

Since Hitler did not state his own preference even in 1924, this has been taken to mean that he had not decided between England and Russia, between colonial or territorial policy in his own programme.[94] Scharrer's document is surely conclusive proof that this view is mistaken. But we are still left with the question of why Hitler did not reveal his own preference in 1924 and why, indeed, the Nazi party avoided discussing their party programme in public at this time? Hitler, of course, was always reticent about allowing discussion of the party programme, feeling that any discussion would weaken the party's absolute faith in it. Scharrer had learned of Hitler's schemes for Russia only in a confidential interview. During 1923 the *Völkischer Beobachter* seemed reluctant to discuss its foreign policy platform; Rosenberg spoke of 'holding back our positive appraisal' of foreign affairs (though admitting it could be ascertained by 'reading between the lines').[95]

The obvious explanation of the party's reluctance to announce its foreign policy programme was its fear of losing powerful and influential supporters. Hitler's plans for the destruction of Russia presented a

special problem. Ludendorff, as we have seen, had been an
enthusiastic advocate of the reorganisation of Russia along the lines of
nationality in 1918 and even though he wanted to increase German
security in the east by acquiring territory in Eastern Europe, it was no
part of his plans to destroy Russia entirely. 'It was no desire of mine,'
he wrote in his memories, 'to destroy Russia or to weaken her so that
she could no longer exist. I hoped rather that the restoration of the
Empire would be the work of the Ukraine.'[96] Clearly then, there was a
danger that Ludendorff might oppose Hitler's plans for Russia.

A more important limitation on Nazi policy was the need to keep
the financially lucrative support of the Russian émigrés living in
Bavaria. Max von Scheubner-Richter was primarily responsible for
establishing this contact with the rich and influential refugees from
Russia. In 1920 he had travelled to the Ukraine in an attempt to
establish trading links between the White Russian forces under General
Wrangel and Munich industrialists.[97] His mission, though unsuccessful,
had won him the gratitude and confidence of the Russian émigrés in
Bavaria and between 1921 and 1923 he organised *'Aufbau'*,a society
promoting economic, cultural and political understanding between
Germans and Russians. Scheubner-Richter managed to ectract
considerable financial support from one of the claiments to the Czarist
throne, Prince Cyril of Coburg.[98] Such financial assistance would
obviously be conditional upon Nazi adherence to plans for economic
reconstruction in Russia and Russo-German cooperation, which
Scheubner-Richter pioneered. It is significant that the latter spoke at
the Bad Reichenhall congress of Russian monarchists of sending
German technical experts to Russia to facilitate her recovery.[99] If the
Nazi party was not to lose an indispensable source of funds in 1922-23,
there could be no open advocacy of a policy of territorial annexations
in Russia. In addition, in 1924 during his imprisonment, Hitler was
more concerned than ever before to avoid committing himself publicly
to one line in foreign policy; his desire to maintain the leadership of the
Nazi party by avoiding any choice between competing factions may
have been more important than the possibility of forfeiting Russian
patronage.

By 1925 the Russians had directed their money and energies
elsewhere because of the collapse of both the Nazi party and the
'Aufbau' organisation following Scheubner-Richter's death in the
Munich putsch.[100] Hitler was now free to make a clear statement of his
views in *Mein Kampf.* The ultimate incompatibility of the Nazi party
programme and the schemes of the Russian exiles was highlighted by

Rosenberg in 1927. Rosenberg appears to have taken up Scheubner-Richter's mantle and re-opened negotiations with the Russians in Bavaria. No corroborative evidence for this has emerged but in his fundamental statement on foreign affairs in 1927,[101] Rosenberg criticised Prince Cyril of Coburg for expecting the help of German technicians in the reconstruction of Russia without making any concessions to Germany's spatial requirements in return. 'This kind of Russian brotherhood', Rosenberg concluded, 'is to be rejected.'[102] Whether or not negotiations actually took place, Rosenberg's conclusion shows clearly that the aims of the Russian émigrés and the Nazis were completely at variance and that Hitler had been right to avoid revealing his hand before 1925.

A final possible reason for Hitler's caution in 1924 was the growing division of opinion within the Nazi party on the Russian question. The traditional anti-Bolshevism of the Russian émigrés and the Baltic Germans was not shared by all the Nazi party. After 1924, Rosenberg's anti-Bolshevik attitude was increasingly challenged by a pseudo-socialist anti-western group under the leadership of Gregor Strasser.[103] With his election to the Reichstag in 1924 Strasser became an important figure in the Nazi hierarchy and it is possible that Hitler, who was apparently aware of Strasser's political views, [104] hoped to avoid alienating him by publishing a non-committal analysis of foreign policy in the 1924 article. It is unlikely that Strasser's opposing views were as important a restriction on Hitler's freedom of activity as the need to keep the support of Ludendorff and the financial backing of the Russian émigrés. Only when the Strasser group produced their own draft party programme at the end of 1925 did Hitler intervene actively, reiterating his own views and preventing any discussion of them at a meeting in Bamberg in February 1926.[105] The foreign policy sections of the second volume of *Mein Kampf* (especially Chapter 14) can only be seen as a deliberate attempt to discredit the ideas of the pro-Strasser elements of the party,[106] and it was at this point that Haushofer's geopolitical arguments about territorial expansion proved so useful.

However, the main lines of Hitler's foreign policy programme — the English alliance, the wars of vengeance against France and of expansion against Russia, the latter spiced with virulent anti-Bolshevism — were already finalised long before Hitler wrote *Mein Kampf.* In the period 1919-23, behind the facade of conventional Pan-German and revisionist propaganda, Hitler and Rosenberg were formulating many of the aggressive plans which were to characterise Nazi policy for the next twenty years. Not that there was much novelty in them; most of what passed for 'Nazi' ideas on foreign policy were in reality a re-hash of policies pursued by Germany between 1917 and 1918 cloaked in Hitler's stridently anti-semitic world-view.

Notes

1. cf. E. Jäckel, *Hitlers Weltanschauung. Entwurf einer Herrschaft* (Tübingen, 1969).
2. K. Hildebrand, *Vom Reich zum Weltreich. Hitler, NSDAP und koloniale Frage 1919-1945* (Munich, 1969).
3. J. Dülffer, *Weimar, Hitler und die Marine. Reichspolitik und Flottenbau, 1920-1939* (Düsseldorf, 1973).
4. J. Thiess, *Architekt der Weltherrschaft. Die 'Endziele' Hitlers* (Düsseldorf, 1976).
5. A. Kuhn, *Hitlers aussenpolitisches Programm. Entstehung und Entwicklung* (Stuttgart, 1970).
6. This is particularly true of the work of Axel Kuhn.
7. ibid., pp. 84-91; cf. also Hildebrand, op. cit., pp. 84-5.
8. cf. in this connection B.M. Lane, 'Nazi Ideology: Some Unfinished Business', *Central European History* 7 (1974).
9. G. Schubert, *Anfänge nationalsozialistischer Aussenpolitik* (Cologne, 1963).
10. K. Hildebrand, *The Foreign Policy of the Third Reich* (London, 1973), pp. 19-20.
11. R.H. Phelps, 'Hitler als Parteiredner', *Vierteljahrshefte fuer Zeitgeschichte* 11 (1963), p. 290. An account of a speech by Hitler on 12 December 1919.
12. A second account of the same speech in E. Deuerlein, 'Hitlers Eintritt in die Politik und die Reichswehr', *Vierteljahrshefte fuer Zeitgeschichte* 7 (1959), p. 209.
13. Phelps, op. cit., p. 290.
14. A speech on 17 April 1920, an account in R.H. Phelps, op. cit., p. 297.
15. G. Schubert, op. cit., p. 27. It has been pointed out that the German Workers' Party had used the *'Protocols'* as propaganda material in January 1919, cf. N. Cohn, *Warrant for Genocide. The Myth of the Jewish World Conspiracy and the Protocols of the Elders of Zion* (London, 1967), p. 140; whilst Hitler probably knew of the *'Protocols'* before April 1920, there are no indications that he recognised its relevance to foreign affairs before this date.
16. A. Rosenberg, *Die Spur des Juden im Wandel der Zeiten* (Munich, 1920), pp. 79-84.
17. R.H. Phelps, op. cit., p. 308. Report on a speech by Hitler on 27 July 1920.
18. ibid., p. 306, from a speech on 6 July 1920.
19. ibid., p. 308.
20. A. Kuhn, op. cit., p. 55.
21. A. Rosenberg's 1918 article, 'Der Jude' in *Schriften und Reden* (Munich, 1943), pp. 107-8.
22. A. Rosenberg, *Die Spur des Juden,* pp. 151-8.
23. ibid., pp. 84-5.
24. ibid., pp. 105-7.
25. In a speech on 10 December 1919, R.H. Phelps, op. cit., p. 290.
26. In a speech on 19 November 1920, ibid., pp. 328-9.
27. *Die Spur des Juden,* p. 112. A reference to the possibility of an 'Anglo-Jewish world-rule' was significantly omitted from later editions.
28. A. Rosenberg, 'Borsenjuden und Revolution', *Völkischer Beobachter*

(henceforth VB), 22 February 1921. The article is unsigned but Rosenberg later referred to it as his own work; cf. 'Schicksalswende in London', *VB*, 6 March 1921.

29. A. Rosenberg, 'Der Schurkenstreich des "Obersten Rates"', *VB*, 18 August 1921; cf. Hitler, 'Der ewige Gimpel', *VB*, 22 May 1921.
30. 'Der Schurkenstreich' *VB*, 18 August 1921.
31. A. Hitler, 'Oberschlesiens Schicksal', *VB*, 29 May 1921.
32. See *VB*, 15 March, 28 April, 15 May 1921 for Hitler's hostile references to England.
33. A. Hitler, *Mein Kampf* (London, 1969), p. 617.
34. For details W. Horn,'Ein unbekannter Aufsatz Hitlers aus dem Frühjahr 1924', *Vierteljahrshefte fuer Zeitgeschichte* 16 (1968), p. 291; and A. Kuhn, op. cit., pp. 88-9.
35. A. Rosenberg, 'Lloyd Georges Rücktritt', *VB*, 21 October 1922.
36. ibid.
37. ibid.
38. A. Kuhn, op. cit., p. 91.
39. A. Rosenberg, 'Der neue Gimpelfang', *VB*, 14 July 1923.
40. A. Rosenberg, 'England, Frankreich und Alljudaan', *VB*, 5 July 1923.
41. A speech by Hitler reported in *VB*, 22 March 1923.
42. A speech by Hitler reported in *VB*, 7 September 1923.
43. A. Kuhn, op. cit., p. 91.
44. 'England, Frankreich und Alljudaan', *VB*, 5 July 1923.
45. A. Rosenberg, *Die Zukunftsweg einer deutschen Aussenpolitik* (Munich, 1927), p. 69.
46. Hitler saw 'everywhere' – in Russia, Italy, France and England – 'a relentless struggle between the ideals of nationally-minded elements and the intangible suprastate International'. The English were, he believed, ruled by the Jews without their knowledge – report on speech by Hitler in *VB*, 16 August 1922. An unsigned article, 'Jüdische Weltpolitik', *VB*, 4 October 1922 purporting to give the National Socialist view, claimed that 'if England had been ruled by the British, the anti-German stance would have had to end after Versailles.'
47. A. Hitler, 'Deutschlands letzte Hoffnung', *VB*, 6 March 1921 and 'Staatsmänner und Nationalverbrecher', *VB*, 15 March 1921.
48. Report on a speech by Hitler in *VB*, 26 April 1922.
49. A. Kuhn, op.cit., p. 69.
50. Foreword to second edition (1924) of his *Pest in Russland* (originally Munich, 1922). Rosenberg criticised those who viewed Soviet Russia as an 'unchangeable fact'.
51. *Pest in Russland,* p. 12.
52. ibid., p. 14, cf. pp. 79-81.
53. Report on a speech by Hitler on 19 November 1920 in R.H. Phelps, op. cit., p. 328.
54. Report of a speech by Hitler in *VB*, 26 April 1922. Earlier he had suggested that it was not possible to help the Russian people as yet because all the assistance went to Russia's exploiters, the 'Jewish' commissars, report on a speech by Hitler in *VB*, 11 August 1921.
55. E. Ludendorff, *My War Memories* (London, n.d.), pp. 534-61.
56. ibid., p. 561.
57. 'He (Scheubner) was in close contact with me and kept me fully in the picture about the intentions of the Kampfverbände.' Ludendorff, *Vom Feldherrn zum Weltrevolutionär und Wegbereiter deutscher Volkschöpfung* (Munich, 1940),p. 242.
58. Report on a speech by Hitler, *VB*, 13 January 1921.

59. A. Kuhn, op. cit., pp. 102-4; E. Jäckel, op. cit., pp. 38-9.
60. Hitler pointed out in a speech in August 1920 that his main aim was to get rid of the Versailles treaty and 'to this end, we must use all means at our disposal, chiefly the tensions between France and Italy so that we can win Italy to our side,' Heinz Preiss (ed),*Adolf Hitler in Franken. Reden aus der Kampfzeit* (Nuremberg, 1939), p.11.
61. Ernst Boepple, *Adolf Hitlers Reden* (Munich, 1923),pp. 28-32.
62. *Bundesarchiv Koblenz,* Reichskanzlei R 43 I / 2681. Scharrer seems to have acted as a political agent for Cuno, though he was favourably disposed towards the Nazi party having apparently supported it financially. cf. K.H. Harbeck (ed.),*Akten der Reichskanzlei. Das Kabinett Cunos* (Boppard, 1968), p. 360.
63. ibid, report headed 'Bericht nach Hitlers persönlichen Ausfuhrungen'.
64. ibid.
65. ibid.
66. ibid.
67. ibid.
68. Scharrer had several meetings with Hitler about possible financial support and he may have requested a confidential statement of Hitler's views as a condition of his support; on an other occasion he had asked for an assurance that Hitler would take no moves to jeopardize the present Bavarian government. Cf. G. Franz-Willing *Krisenjahr der Hitlerbewegung 1923* (Munich, 1975), p. 24.
69. 'Der Schurkenstreich', *VB,* 18 August 1921.
70. *Pest in Russland,* p. 63.
71. 'Lloyd Georges Rücktritt', *VB,* 21 October 1922.
72. K. Hildebrand, op. cit., p. 75.
73. A letter from Haushofer to an unnamed friend, 8 May 1934, quoted in D.H. Norton, 'Karl Haushofer and his influence on Nazi Ideology and German Foreign Policy 1919-1945', unpublished Clark University PhD, 1965, p. 83.
74. Haushofer's introduction to F. Ratzel, *Erdenmacht und Völkerschicksal* (Stuttgart, 1940), p. xxvi.
75. Text in W. Hofer *Nationalsozialismus. Dokumente 1933-45* (Frankfurt, 1957), p. 28.
76. For details, R. Pechel,*Deutscher Widerstand* (Zurich,1947), pp. 277-80.
77. Report on a speech by Hitler in *VB,* 5 June 1921.
78. ibid.
79. Hitler was preoccupied with the treaty of Brest-Litovsk from the beginning of his career. Cf. *Mein Kampf,* pp. 425-6 for his own explanation.
80. August Winnig, *Heimkehr* (Hamburg, 1935), p. 60.
81. Information from Scheubner-Richter's report to the German Foreign Office on his activities: Public Record Office (PRO). German Foreign Ministry GFM 21/432 vol. 42, 'Übersicht über die Tätigkeit des wirtschaftspolitischen Aufklärungsdienst fuer den Osten'.
82. Hauptarchiv der NSDAP, folder 1263 cutting from *Der Kampf* of 7 June 1921.
83. Bundesarchiv.Reichskanzlei R 43 I/268/Scharrer document.
84. K. Hildebrand, op. cit., p. 75 and E. Jäckel, op. cit., p. 157.
85. *Mein Kampf,* p. 598.
86. ibid., p. 125.
87. Most recently A. Dorpalen commenting on an article by R. Binion in *History of Childhood Quarterly. The Journal of Psychohistory* 1 (1973), p. 243 has suggested that 'Hitler's implementation of his call for more space through eastern expansion should be traced back to the geopolitical doctrines of the geographer Friedrich Ratzel and the latter's disciple,

General Karl Haushofer.'

88. K. Haushofer, 'Geographische Grundlage auswärtige Politik', *Süddeutscher Monatsheft* (1927), p. 260.

89. K. Haushofer, 'Die geopolitische Betrachtung grenzdeutscher Probleme' in K. von Loesch and Ziegfeld, Volk unter Völkern (Breslau, 1925), pp. 188-9.

90. K. Haushofer, 'The defence of German Geopolitics' in E.A. Walsh, *Total Power, A Footnote to History* (New York, 1948), p. 348.

91. T. Taylor, *Hitler's Secret Book* (New York, 1961), p. 45.

92. Whilst geopolitics contributed little more than attractive terminology and pseudo-scientific justification for Hitler's preconceived ideas on the first stage of his programme – the acquisition of *Lebensraum* in Russia with English assistance, it may have been instrumental in inspiring Hitler's vaguer notions of a future global confrontation between Germany and the USA (the second phase).

93. A. Hitler, 'Warum musste ein 9 November kommen?', *Deutschlands Erneuerung* (1924), p. 199.

94. A. Kuhn, op. cit., pp. 102-3; E. Jäckel, op. cit., pp. 38-9.

95. *VB,* 5 July 1923, cf. note 40.

96. E. Ludendorff, op. cit., p. 562.

97. P. Leverkuehn, *Posten auf ewiger Wache. Aus den abenteuerlichen Leben des Max von Scheubner-Richter* (Essen, 1938), pp. 174-84.

98. W. Laqueur, *Russia and Germany. A Century of Conflict* (London, 1965), p. 62.

99. See page 38.

100. Aufbau soon disintegrated into squabbling factions, cf. R. Williams, *Culture in Exile. Russian Emigrés in Germany, 1881-1941* (London, 1972), p. 220.

101. *Die Zukunftsweg einer deutschen Aussenpolitik,* pp. 90-92.

102. ibid.

103. For Strasser's views on Foreign affairs see 'Russland und wir', *VB,* 22 October 1925 and 'Abrechnung', *VB,* 23 May 1925.

104. Otto Strasser, admittedly an unreliable witness, maintains that he and his brother Gregor quarrelled with Hitler over socialism as early as 1920 (rather too early?): *Hitler and I* (London 1940) pp. 19-21.

105. For a good summary of the issues involved see J. Noakes, *The Nazi Party in Lower Saxony 1921-33* (Oxford, 1971).

106. In *Mein Kampf,* p. 570, Hitler admitted that 'even for us, of course, it is hard to represent England as a possible future ally in the ranks of our movement.' There will be a fuller discussion of Hitler's defence against Strasser's ideas in my thesis, 'The Evolution of Hitler's ideas on foreign policy, 1919-28'.

2 GOTTFRIED FEDER AND THE NSDAP

Albrecht Tyrell

Every great idea requires two things: the will to power and
clear objectives. The will to power, for liberation burns
fiercely in our hearts; our aims have been described by
Gottfried Feder in his book *The German State on a National
and Social Basis* clearly and comprehensibly. It has given both
form and vigorous expression to the hopes and longings of
millions. It has provided our movement with its catechism.

Adolf Hitler[1]

In the studies which deal with the political development, ideology,
propaganda and organisation of the NSDAP in the period up to 1933,
and in the first two years after the seizure of power, the figure of
Gottfried Feder remains peculiarly blurred. General accounts mostly
content themselves with the statement that the propagandist of the
'breaking of the slavery of interest' and author or co-author of the
Party programme of 1920 had been Hitler's and the Party's main economic
and financial expert until he lost influence after Hitler turned towards
big business at the end of the 1920s. For a time, he had been employed
in rather unimportant posts in the headquarters of the NSDAP and,
during 1933-4, in the government apparatus before he finally
disappeared from sight.[2]   Even specialist studies, which deal with
aspects of internal Party development or the relations between Hitler
and business circles, do not really succeed in clearly defining Feder's
relationship with Hitler and his role in the growth of the Party.[3]   The
casual treatment which he generally receives has had the result of
leaving unsolved a number of obvious contradictions.[4]

This article does not presume to provide a substitute for a full-scale
biography of Feder for which there is certainly a need.[5] Its intention is
rather, first, to define Feder's precise position at the time when he
established his initial links with the NSDAP, and then to elucidate his
role within the Party. This essay argues that, even between 1923 and
1929-30, he was in fact unsuccessful in removing the obstacles to his
ambition to become *the* official economic and financial expert of the
NSDAP. And if one assesses his actual role during these years, the thesis
that his influence was drastically reduced at the beginning of the 1930s
appears dubious since in fact his position within the Party remained

virtually unchanged throughout the whole period up until the 'seizure of power'. The analysis of Feder's objectives and of his attempts to secure acceptance for his particular programme within the Party may perhaps also facilitate a more precise definition of the limits within which the Nazi ideologists operated.

During the first thirty years of Gottfried Feder's life there is hardly anything to indicate the future political and ideological activities of this 'world reformer'.[6] Feder was born in Würzburg on 27 January 1883. He studied civil engineering at the *Technische Hochschulen* of Munich, (Berlin−) Charlottenburg and Zurich and specialised in the technique of reinforced concrete which was to have such importance in the future.

In 1908 Feder joined the construction firm of Ackermann & Co. as a partner and manager of their Munich branch. During the following years he built warehouses, bridges and other large-scale buildings in Germany, Italy and Bulgaria. After the beginning of the war, he extended his range to munitions factories and aircraft hangars. Since Feder and his firm had only limited capital they required considerable credits for the execution of these building projects. In Feder's later descriptions we hear of the 'demoralising' experience the young engineer and entrepreneur had in trying to finance ambitious projects through outside credits. One is led to suspect that these experiences were caused in part by his own arrogance and naivety. He took some time, however, to draw from his personal experiences with big banks general conclusions about the 'iron and heartless grip of the impersonal financial power which at first offers and grants the required "credit" but then in an economic crisis acts only according to selfish capitalist interests'.[7]

During the first years of the war he had to carry out large state projects. Since Feder was not called up, however, he had sufficient time to give some thought to the problem of Germany's post-war development. Feder also took up questions of financial theory. His resentment at what he saw as the dangers of interest was now strengthened by his concern about the effects of the increasing indebtedness of the state as a result of war loans. But for a long time he obviously shared the general hope of a victorious peace settlement which would enable these debts to be transferred to the losers. It was only when this self-delusion broke down with the defeat that Feder appears to have realised in a 'flash of inspiration' how Germany could be saved; he 'suddenly clearly recognised' that the damaging effects of interest were the root of all the evils that bedevilled Germany.[8]

In the introduction to the 'Manifesto for the Breaking of Interest Slavery' (*Manifest zur Brechung der Zinsknechtschaft des Geldes*), written in the days following the capitulation and printed as a brochure in 1919, Feder wrote, 'The concept of interest is the devilish invention of big capital which alone facilitates the indolent, drone-like existence of a minority of plutocrats at the cost of the productive nations and their labour; it has led to the deep, unbridgeable conflicts, to the class hatred from which civil and fratricidal war is born.'[9]

Feder's accusation makes it clear that he was not merely concerned with the solution of a technical problem of finance. Like most members of the bourgeoisie in Germany he had not seriously doubted the stability of the Reich during the war. With the military defeat and the revolutionary events of the first months after the war, this apparently stable, familiar order collapsed. A deep sense of uncertainty emerged. It stimulated a search for explanations and scapegoats for what had happened; but also for spiritual certainties, for signposts in a political and social landscape which had suddenly become completely obscured.

Feder found his personal conviction in an economic theory, the essence of which was the demand for the 'breaking of interest slavery' through the abolition of all interest payments and through the nationalisation of banks and the stock exchange. If this idea now seems naive, one should not overlook the fact that it had a certain attraction during and after that period of upheaval and Feder was not alone in being fascinated by what appeared to be a brilliantly simple and radical solution. At a time when the waves of nationalism which had already been whipped up before and during the war and now continued to foam, it was tempting to interpret the international character of capital within the capitalist economic system as the greatest threat to the future political independence of Germany. Moreover, Feder's approach, though derived at least in part from economic theories of the *völkisch* movement and by no means original,[10] must be seen in the context of the broad stream of anti-liberal attitudes, which were directed at high finance, but at the same time hostile to Marxism, and were very influential among Germany's confused and bewildered bourgeoisie in 1918/19.

Not only the workers but also the middle classes were badly hit by the serious economic consequences of the war, by the shortage of goods, price increases and unemployment. Yet these groups were prevented by their nationalist convictions and their non-proletarian consciousness from seeking their salvation in the political and social revolution preached by the Socialist parties. The 'breaking of interest slavery' here offered itself as a good campaign slogan for a middle way to a 'German Socialism' between capitalism and Marxism. It did in fact quickly gain a degree of popularity in *völkisch*-nationalist circles outside Feder's immediate sphere of influence.[11]

Feder did not oppose capital and private ownership as such but wanted to tie both to individual achievement and social obligation and give priority to the state where the public interest required it. Feder made a rather artificial distinction between rapacious (*raffendes*) and productive (*schaffendes*) capital — terms which had been coined several decades previously in *völkisch*, anti-semitic circles.[12] By rapacious capital he understood commercial and finance capital, which was in the hands of a few 'big power-hungry capitalists' all over the world (e.g. the Rothschilds) and which subjugated more and more nations by means of loans of all kinds. By contrast, Feder wished to transform money from being an end in itself to being once more an instrument of the economy.

Feder's attack was directed against a modern phenomenon which he did not fully comprehend and whose effects appeared to him as the operation of an 'uncanny, invisible, mysterious power'.[13] His suspicion of a conspiracy was combined with disgust at the apparent increase of a materialistic 'view of life purely concerned with the things of this world' which strove for an 'income without labour and effort' derived from interest and annuities. Both of these views probably stemmed in part from Feder's own business setbacks referred to earlier. In the concrete post-war situation, however, both these complaints had a representative character beyond their purely personal significance; they were symptomatic of the outlook of wider circles of the bourgeoisie.

Feder, then, distinguished 'productive capital' required for national industrial production from this international commercial and finance capital which in his view grew 'endlessly' by means of interest alone and without work. Finance for industry was in future to be distributed and controlled by the state alone. In order to make Germany independent of the 'international money powers' Feder demanded an absolute ban on all international loans.

According to Feder, the beneficial effect of the struggle for the 'breaking of interest slavery' would emerge not simply in a growing international independence but also in the removal of the internal divisions within the nation. Feder, in agreement with many people striving for a reduction of class differences through a 'German Socialism', countered by proclaiming: 'Workers and employers belong together.' Their mutual interest in the productivity of the national economy was, he argued, greater than the differences between them which would be solved 'to their mutual satisfaction by means of wage agreements and plant organisation'.[14]   Feder supplemented his main demand during the following years with additional demands for economic and financial measures to benefit low-income groups; he also commented on constitutional, social and cultural questions.

Feder was aware of the fact that in practice the abolition of interest would adversely affect many ordinary people who were dependent on their savings and pensions. He forestalled these objections, which could weaken the effectiveness of his programme with the public, by advocating 'welfare benefits' for those who could no longer work for their living.[15] Later on, it became clear that this was the first of the critical points which forced Feder to modify his original radical programme and restrict himself to the demand for a 'just interest rate'.

Feder, however, stuck to his idea that 'the breaking of interest slavery' was 'the core of our policy.'[16] Even in his first publication he had made it clear that he did not regard himself merely as a financial reformer but as the founder of a new political dogma claiming universal validity. The fact that he called his pamphlet a manifesto and, even more, the similarity of its concluding sentence with that of Marx and Engel's *Communist Manifesto* —'Join hands with me, workers (*Werktätige*) of the world, unite!' — illustrate his self-confident claim to rival Marxism.[17]

Feder's rejection of the Marxist form of anti-capitalism was unmistakable. His attitude to anti-semitism on the other hand was more ambiguous. At a time when people were frantically searching for political and ideological certainties and when crude anti-semitic agitation was rampant, it was tempting to depict 'the calculated co-operation of the power-hungry big capitalists of all nations' as the work of a Jewish world conspiracy. This was the line being taken by the anti-semitic economic propaganda of the *Deutschvölkischer Schutz- und Trutzbund* which had considerable success with it.[18] Nor did Feder resist this temptation, if only because it gave his demands a greater chance of success. As far as Feder was concerned, however, the economic and financial aspects of his doctrine always took priority over

the anti-semitic aspects. In his interpretation of the NSDAP programme
which had an enormous circulation after 1926, he described anti-
semitism as 'the emotional foundation of our movement as it were'
(*'gewissermassen der gefühlsmässige Unterbau unserer Bewegung'*).[19]
Feder saw Jews as agents of the evil and considered that their
elimination would not bring about a fundamental change in the
situation.

His revelation had the impact of a political conversion for Feder and
at once he took steps to implement it. Immediately after drafting his
basic principles and demands, he forwarded them, on 20 November
1918, to the new Bavarian government under its Independent socialist
Prime Minister, Kurt Eisner. The fact that he met 'with little
understanding from the Marxist ministry' caused him almost more
annoyance than the fact that 'the capitalist-orientated press reacted at
first with an icy silence'.[20]

At first sight this reaction appears astonishing. Yet it is explicable in
terms of the extremely narrow standpoint from which the autodidact
Feder regarded economic problems. In his list of priorities the question
of interest stood in lonely isolation at the top; only after it had been
solved could all the other economic problems be tackled really
effectively. Since he was not committed to any more general political or
economic programme, Feder could feel fairly unrestricted in his
freedom of manoeuvre and thus even approach a Socialist government.
For it seemed to him of decisive political importance that his plan
should be adopted at once. But he was also encouraged to make a direct
appeal to the existing government by the fact that, despite his hostility
to Marxism, he believed that it shared in common with his own theory
a rejection of big capital.

After the destruction of this illusion he soon discovered that his
public activities met with a better response from the political right.
Following his vain attempt to win acceptance for his theory by
appealing directly to the authorities, Feder at first continued the
struggle on his own – and with a personal commitment that was total.
In the course of 1919 he gave up his business. This was not exactly a
normal step for a father of three children to take, particularly in view
of the economic uncertainty, even allowing for the fact that his
business prospects must have appeared rather gloomy at this time of
economic crisis and without foreign and armament contracts. However,
from 1919 onwards, Feder's campaign slogan aroused considerable
interest. His attempt to reach the public took two main forms: active
journalism and public speaking whenever the opportunity offered

itself — even small audiences were not turned down. The *völkisch* movement with its various groups — in 1919/20 there were over twenty in Munich alone[21] — offered a rich field for both activities. As mentioned above, the fight against interest had already played a role in the *völkisch* amalgam of ideas, consisting of nationalism, anti-liberalism, anti-semitism, and bourgeois anti-Marxism, even before Feder's appearance on the scene. Susceptibility to an attractive economic slogan such as that offered by Feder was heightened by the social problems which were pushed into the foreground by defeat.

Even before he had published his 'Manifesto' and 'State Bankruptcy — the Salvation' (*Der Staatsbankerott — Die Rettung*) as separate pamphlets, a number of Munich papers of the right had opened their columns to him. The first occasion on which Feder made his attack on loan capital and put forward his radical and 'at first sight apparently fantastic' antidote before a wider public was in the February 1919 edition of the influential nationalist *Süddeutsche Monatshefte* to which Feder's brother-in-law, the historian Karl Alexander von Müller, was a contributor.[22] This in turn led to further contacts. The conservative Munich publicist Karl Graf von Bothmer quoted a longish excerpt from Feder's essay in his contribution 'The Great Public Swindle' (*Der grosse Volksbetrug*) in the extreme anti-semitic paper *Auf gut deutsch*, which had been edited by Dietrich Eckart since 1918 and which bore the characteristic subheading 'Weekly Paper for Order and Justice'.[23] Bothmer may have introduced Feder to Eckart; on the other hand, they may have become acquainted through the Thule Society, a Munich Club organised in the form of a Freemasons' lodge, which carried on pre-war anti-semitic traditions. Allegedly, Feder had given his first talks to them as early as December 1918.[24]

In Feder and Eckart there was a meeting of minds similar in their rigid fixation on a monocausal explanation of the German catastrophe. Their relationship quickly bore fruit. A pamphlet, edited and signed by Eckart, of which 100,000 copies were distributed in the streets of Munich on 5 April — two days before the proclamation of the Bavarian Soviet Republic — repeated Feder's demands in detail.[25] On 22 August 1919 Eckart and Feder both spoke in the Nuremberg *Herkules-Saalbau* on 'Loan capital, its international power and how to combat it'.[26]

In the summer of 1919, Feder found a further field of employment, together with K.A. von Müller and also von Bothmer. Immediately after the setting up in May of the information, press and propaganda department of the Bavarian *Reichswehr Gruppenkommando 4* — at that time the highest military authority in Bavaria — it had begun to prepare 'information courses' under Captain Karl Mayr. The purpose of these courses was to put members of the *Reichswehr*, seconded from their units, through courses in history and politics lasting several days, so that they could counteract socialist influences in the army.[27] In addition to other teachers from the upper middle classes, v. Bothmer, v. Müller (a school friend of Mayr's) and Feder acted as lecturers and course tutors of the seminars which were held in Munich University from June onwards with separate courses for officers and men.

The thesis developed by Feder in these courses impressed Captain Mayr. It also deeply impressed two other participants — Lance Corporal Adolf Hitler and the nineteen-year-old Hermann Esser, who was employed in Mayr's propaganda section.[28] The influence of Feder's ideas — though characteristically transmuted into overt anti-semitic agitation — can be clearly detected in their first written statements, even before they had both settled in their future political sphere, the German Workers' Party (DAP)/NSDAP.

In his statement on the Jewish question which, at Mayr's request, he wrote on 16 September 1919, Hitler directly identified loan capital with the Jews whereas Feder had merely hinted at it: 'His [the Jew's] power is the power of money which in the form of interest effortlessly and interminably multiplies itself in his hands and forces upon nations that most dangerous of yokes, the sad consequences of which are so difficult to perceive because of the initial gleam of gold'.[29]

Only a short time afterwards, Feder's and Hitler's paths crossed again. The DAP, led by Anton Drexler and Karl Harrer, planned to make another feeble attempt to widen their membership of three or four dozen by holding a semi-public meeting with Dietrich Eckart as the main speaker. He had already spoken on 14 August before an audience of thirty-eight people. Since Eckart was prevented by illness, Feder stood in for him and spoke on 'The breaking of the slavery of interest'. Hitler was among the audience of a little over forty people. He had been sent as an observer by Mayr's Information Section which wanted to maintain a tighter control over political developments, particularly at the grass roots, after the unpleasant political surprises of the past year.[30]

Shortly afterwards both Hitler and Feder joined the DAP,[31] but with that the similarity ended. Feder remained an outsider while Hitler found his political home in the DAP, which had been renamed the NSDAP at the end of February 1920, and became its driving force and propaganda attraction.[32] In the following period Feder's main interest in the DAP/NSDAP was as a suitable platform from which to spread his

theories. On 26 November 1919 and on 23 January 1920 he gave
further talks on his special subject to the DAP, on 9 April his disciple
Bernhard Köhler spoke on 'Working people as interest-slaves of loan
capital'.[33]

By this time the twenty-five point programme of the NSDAP had
already been made public. In paragraphs 10 and 11 it demanded:

> 10. It must be the first duty of every citizen to perform mental or
> physical work. The activities of the individual must not clash with
> the general interest but must proceed within the framework of the
> community and be for the general good. We demand therefore:

> 11. The abolition of incomes unearned by work. The breaking of
> the slavery of interest..

It is mainly on account of these demands and the fact that several
other economic points coincide with Feder's ideas that until recently
Feder has been seen as 'presumably the real author of the Party
programme of 1920'[34] or at least as a co-author together with the
founder of the Party and its chairman, Anton Drexler, and Hitler.[35] Yet
the evidence supporting this view is sparse and does not outweigh that
which contradicts Feder's direct participation.

The NSDAP party programme represented an incomplete cross
section of the anti-capitalist aspect of *völkisch* ideology. This element,
as has been previously suggested, stemmed from earlier theorising which
had found fertile soil among the middle-class sections of the population
after the war. A number of Drexler's rough drafts, which have survived,
show that by intensive reading and through personal contacts with
völkisch circles in Munich, he had drawn his concepts arbitrarily from
the complex amalgam of ideas which composed the *völkisch* ideology.
During 1919 Feder had spread his slogan 'The breaking of the slavery
of interest' within Munich, and also among the DAP, to such an extent
that its incorporation into the programme does not necessarily prove
Feder's personal involvement. In November 1919, mention was made
within the Party leadership of a plan to form a programme committee
consisting of five people of which Feder was to be one, but this plan
was not implemented.[36] In a comment which he made in 1923 on 'The
origin of the programme' Feder himself stated that a detailed
elucidation of the eleventh point of the programme had been
superfluous because his publications had been 'well-known and familiar
to the founders and the early supporters of the movement'.[37] Neither

on this occasion nor in any other of his numerous publications did Feder ever claim to have been directly involved in the composition of the party programme – with one possible exception.

This is the minute by Otto Engelbrecht, the district and local branch leader of the NSDAP in Murnau, Feder's home town, of a conversation between himself and Feder on 30 December 1932, three weeks after Gregor Strasser had resigned all his Party offices.* According to Engelbrecht, Feder had concluded a letter to Hitler in which he expressed regret at Strasser's step with the phrase: 'In unshakeable loyalty to the programme sanctioned by you (Hitler) and formulated by me'.[38]

This appears to be an unequivocal statement yet, apart from the Drexler drafts mentioned above, it is also contradicted by Drexler's repeated assertion that he had composed the Party programme with Hitler alone. Drexler had already maintained this in 1925 in meetings of his *Nationalsozialer Volksbund* after his reluctant separation from Hitler and the NSDAP. His remark was even printed by the *Völkischer Beobachter*, without arousing any protest. Drexler repeatedly gave the same assurance to the *Hauptarchiv* of the NSDAP which after 1933 collected material on the early period of the Party, and Rudolf Schüssler, who was the first secretary of the NSDAP from January 1920 until July 1921, made the same point.[39]

The fact of Hitler's participation is not contested by anybody although its extent cannot be accurately assessed. The single exception appears to be implied in the closing sentence of Feder's letter to Hitler referred to above. Yet it is by no means clear that this sentence refers to the twenty-five point programme; indeed it is inconceivable that Feder should claim sole authorship for it in view of the general acceptance of Hitler's participation. Feder's comment of 1932 has survived only in an indirect form, recorded by somebody who was not conversant with the discussions about the Party programme within the NSDAP leadership which had taken place since 1919/20. As long as the exact expression used by Feder is unknown, it seems at any rate plausible to associate the phrase 'the programme sanctioned by you and formulated by me' with the commentaries on the Party programme published by Feder in 1923 and 1927. As we shall see, they both received Hitler's specific approval. In addition, one cannot overlook the context in which, according to Engelbrecht, Feder's comment occurred: for in that

* See essay by Stachura in this volume – Editor.

conversation Feder criticised the fact that, as a result of Hitler's refusal to enter the Government except as Reich Chancellor, the economic measures which in his view were so urgently needed (i.e. *his* 'programme') could not be implemented.

As Reginald Phelps has already maintained, the final version of the twenty-five point programme of the NSDAP of 24 February 1920 must be regarded both in its structure and wording as the joint work of Drexler and Hitler. Moreover, the fact that Feder's further contacts with the NSDAP during the years 1920 to 1921 were restricted to occasional speeches in Munich NSDAP meetings does not indicate a particularly close relationship to the Party.[40] Indeed, it can be proved that significant differences emerged between the two sides.

While the NSDAP, stimulated above all by Hitler's energy, developed its propaganda activities in Munich and, from the autumn of 1920, increasingly also in the surrounding area, Feder continued to pursue his own narrow goal. In January 1920, the response from the public encouraged him to found the 'German Combat League for the Breaking of the Slavery of Interest' (*Deutscher Kampfbund zur Brechung der Zinsknechtschaft*).[41] Until then Feder had found his public in groups with varied political, social and cultural aims. In theory, therefore, the restriction of the *Kampfbund* to a single purpose and the intention 'of excluding party and particular political aims from the fundamental demand' appeared sensible.[42] His theory would then penetrate, via the membership, the political organisations and professional and economic associations to which they belonged in addition to the *Kampfbund*.

In practice, however, it became clear that the attraction of the slogan 'The breaking of the slavery of interest' was not sufficient to turn the *Kampfbund* into an independent and effective organisation. When in July 1921 the *Kampfbund*'s first newsletter reported on its development to date the body of Feder's supporters consisted of only seven small local groups. The *Kampfbund* was also severely hampered from the start by lack of funds. Under these circumstances it arranged relatively few public meetings, most of them in Munich. The majority of the thirty public speeches given by speakers of the *Kampfbund* — mostly by Feder — in 1920 were at the invitation of other associations.

Through correspondence and travelling, Feder continued to look for opportunities to establish 'valuable contacts with leading and influential personalities' in the *völkisch* movement,[43] and he used every possible means of canvassing for 'The breaking of the slavery of interest' such as through articles in newspapers and magazines. He wrote several times for the Nuremberg *Deutscher Sozialist*, the organ of the

Deutsch-Sozialistische Partei, the NSDAP's main rival.[44] Feder did not
shrink from violent, even slanderous polemics if rivals with differing
views — such as for example Silvio Gesell with his 'free money'
doctrine — found a response from groups which he himself was
courting.[45] There were frequent occasions for this. For, whereas Feder
had no doubts about the validity of his doctrine, the numerous *völkisch*
groups were still seeking the truth in the economic field. Feder aroused
great interest, for example, among the DSP-leaders Alfred Brunner
(Düsseldorf), Fritz Wriedt (Kiel), and Julius Streicher (Nuremberg) and
among the Austrian and Sudeten German National Socialists. They used
and recommended his publications[46] but hesitated to join him without
reservations in such a complicated and controversial matter. Nor did his
direct request to Streicher to join the *Kampfbund* on the grounds that
the DSP advocated 'The breaking of the slavery of interest' bear fruit.[47]
The DSP party conferences in Leipzig (30 July — 2 August 1920) and
Zeitz (26 — 28 March 1921) found fault with all of the systems of
financial reform under discussion, faults 'which could only be
recognised and corrected through practical experience'.[48] At Zeitz, the
Kiel local branch, which Feder had addressed in October, proposed that
the DSP should expressly acknowledge Feder's doctrine. But the final
resolutions of the party conference only made a general demand for
the nationalisation of the *Reichsbank* and the abolition of interest
payments on state debts.[49]

As early as March 1920 Feder had taken a further step to extend his
influence within the *völkisch* movement. He acquired one twelfth of the
shares of the *Völkischer Beobachter* publishing firm and was now one of
eight shareholders of the publishing firm *Franz Eher Nachf*. At the
beginning of November 1920 he succeeded in making the *Kampfbund*
secretary Bernhard Köhler editor of the paper and manager of the
publishing firm.[50] His ambitions, however, went even further. Since the
other shareholders gradually lost interest in the VB, which was in
permanent and considerable financial difficulties, Feder obviously saw
an opportunity to take over the paper together with Karl v. Bothmer
and make it his own mouthpiece. This plan failed, however, for the
NSDAP leadership, who were also keen on the VB, were quicker off
the mark and with the help of sponsors acquired the paper on
17 December 1920 under fairly dramatic circumstances.[51]

This event and the discussion which it subsequently provoked in
correspondence between Feder and Drexler illustrates clearly the gap
which existed between Feder as a formal member of the Party and
the NSDAP itself during 1920 and 1921. The letter with which Drexler

replied to one by Feder two months after the take-over shows that
there was no contact between the two men 'at the time of the struggle
for the *Beo[bachter]*' and that Feder was observing the development
of the NSDAP and Hitler's activities from the position of an outsider.[52]
The NSDAP had been engaged in the 'struggle' for the VB since the
summer of 1920. The news of Feder's and Bothmer's intention to buy
the VB, with which Hitler, Esser, and Party committee member Oskar
Körner alerted Drexler on 17 December, may even have been
incorrect. But characteristically the NSDAP leadership took it so
seriously that, despite their previous doubts regarding the financial
aspect, they acted at once.[53]

Nor did the National Socialists intend to let Feder keep his share in
the VB. But since the debts of the publishing firm were greater than
had been assumed at the time of its precipitate purchase, Drexler
had to ask Feder for a postponement of the repayment of his share of
RM 10,000. The paper was to be completely reorganised along the
lines of the 'revolutionary' mass agitation characteristic of Hitler's
style which Feder had deplored in his letter as superficial and biased.
Drexler in turn defended it in his reply by pointing to the steady
growth in the Party's membership.[54] In doing so he made a revealing
distinction between the aims of the NSDAP and Feder's narrowly
conceived programme: 'your goal too, Herr Feder, can only be achieved
by way of revolution'. And the conciliatory final remark with which
Drexler wished to bridge the gap to Feder — he too hoped, he wrote,
'that *your* idea will become *ours* and *our* ideas will become *yours* so
that *our combined* efforts can help our poor people out of their
misery' — demonstrated once again that the NSDAP leadership
regarded Feder's separate goal as merely one political task among
others.[55]

During the following period the gap between the NSDAP and Feder
still found expression in other forms. In 1920 Feder's demands had
received the unequivocal support of the Party and of its main speaker,
Hitler.[56] After the take-over of the VB by the NSDAP, the activities of
the *Kampfbund* continued to be reported and Feder and Köhler made
occasional contributions to the paper. Yet national socialist authors
now cautiously but unmistakably disengaged themselves from Feder,
who was, in their eyes, only combatting a symptom instead of removing
the causes of the evil. How this was to be achieved they too could not
say precisely. In any case they advocated that 'particularly in the
question of the "breaking of the slavery of interest" the baby should
not be thrown out with the water.' Later Rudolf Hess, who had

belonged to the Party since July 1920 and was gradually moving towards a close personal relationship with Hitler, once more made rather warmer references to Feder's theory and called on his critics to make better proposals themselves if they could.[57]

Feder too, however, continued to go his own way. During the crisis within the NSDAP in July 1921, which led to Hitler's take-over of the leadership, he did not make any obvious intervention, despite the doubts about Hitler which he had previously mentioned to Drexler. The crisis had been provoked by the attempts of Drexler and other party comrades to bring about a fusion between the NSDAP and the rather more cautious DSP, which was more concerned with a refinement of the points of its programme than with mass agitation. Hitler had strongly rejected these attempts.[58] After he had with some difficulty averted this threat to the activist style of the Party, Hitler refused to allow the participation of the NSDAP at the second international congress of representatives of the greater German National Socialist movement on 13 and 14 August 1921 in Linz.[59] Feder, however, paid no attention to this ban and attended the meeting. Together with other speakers, he spoke in the discussions on currency questions and, to his delight, secured from the conference a condemnation of Silvio Gesell's 'heresy' and the inclusion of the main principles of the *Kampfbund* in the official programme.[60]

Yet this triumph represented the apex of Feder's attempt to secure support for his theory on his own. For all the organisational props which he had hitherto used for his propaganda very soon proved to be brittle — with one exception. The greater German National Socialist movement did not expand beyond its impotent central office in Vienna, and the DSP waned during 1921. The *Deutschvölkischer Schutz—und Trutzbund,* which had provided Feder with a number of platforms, had already passed its peak when it was banned in 1922, following the murder of the Foreign Minister, Rathenau. Feder's *Kampfbund* remained as weak as before and the state authorities continued to ignore his proposals.[61]

Yet the idea of giving up the struggle was inconceivable to Feder. Thus during 1922, he had little alternative but to activate his connection with the NSDAP which had hitherto been loose, but had never been completely broken off. The NSDAP offered a not unfavourable basis from which to propagate his theory. It was above all Hitler's mass meetings which ensured the emergence of the Party as a factor which the main actors on the political stage in Bavaria saw, alongside the other *völkisch*-nationalist groups and paramilitary leagues, as a useful member of the nationalist opposition and hence worthy of support.[62] Yet the NSDAP's political programme did not go much further than vicious agitation against existing conditions in the Republic. The vague ideas about what kind of a national-socialist state they would create in the future, which the Nazi propagandists expressed on the platform and in print, added up to little more than that everything would improve and be different under a 'national dictatorship'. Apart from the attacks of the bi-weekly *Völkischer Beobachter* which also printed Hitler's speeches, and apart from a few pamphlets and giant posters, the Party's publications comprised little more than the brief interpretation of the twenty-five point programme, which Alfred Rosenberg had published in 1922.[63] Thus the NSDAP welcomed Feder as someone who would help fill the gaps in their programme.

He made his first important appearance during a Party conference which the NSDAP held in Munich at the end of January 1923 under somewhat turbulent circumstances.[64] To start with, Hitler addressed the assembly of Party members from outside Munich – according to the VB, 300 local branch leaders had turned up. He spoke on the three basic ideas of the future Germany: socialism, nationalism and anti-semitism. Then Feder spoke 'on the financial policy of national socialism and explained in detail the nature and aims of the struggle to break the slavery of interest'.[65] That is an apposite description of Feder's future role. He acted as if he was the NSDAP's spokesman on financial and economic policy and used this opportunity to advocate his old programme with great self-confidence. At least 'as far as financial and economic policy was concerned', he regarded himself and his work as 'the forerunner of national socialism'.[66]

Feder's ineffably high estimation of his own importance in the national socialist struggle for Germany's revival derived from various sources. He saw himself as the pioneer of the national socialist movement because he had appeared in public before Drexler and Hitler who had then adopted his demand – in a way he had even given Hitler his first basic understanding of politics as he was later never tired of stressing.[67] Moreover, Feder could claim that his writings had added some substance to the NSDAP's programme. This was even more true after Feder was able to tell Hitler in August 1923 that 'after months of work I now have finished my new book . . . , a book which undertakes to outline the whole structure of the future national-socialist state'.[68] Feder had no doubt about the fact that this book, entitled 'The German State on a National and Social Basis' with a subtitle which summed up its main topics, 'New Paths for State, Finance and Economy', would be regarded as the 'official publication of the whole party' which the national-socialist propagandists were already impatiently awaiting.[69]

His letter to Hitler of 10 August 1923, which illustrates the strange contrast between Hitler's bohemian private life and the revolutionary image of his political appearances, as well as the rather chaotic structure of NSDAP leadership,[70] also gives a good impression of how Feder saw his relationship with Hitler. The latter had by this time established himself as the unchallenged leader of the NSDAP mainly through the success of his mass meetings. Toying with the idea of a coup d'état, the dominant military and political forces in Bavaria regarded the 'drummer' as a useful tool for the 'national revolution' and were already letting him take part in their plans for a putsch. Feder, however, considered that he and the other men who were striving to give national socialist propaganda a more concrete political and economic programme were Hitler's equals.[71] He did acknowledge that the previous success of the NSDAP was mainly due to Hitler, but he was convinced that 'the ideologists' (*die Programmatiker*) would come into their own at the latest when the NSDAP gained political power. His complaints, which he had already made verbally, that Hitler was evading invitations to discuss the manuscript of his (Feder's) book, that he was failing to coordinate the advice of 'the groups who run along side by side knowing nothing about each other', and that he was not even appearing at their discussions finally led Feder to make an emphatic proposal. He suggested that Hitler should surround himself with an 'intellectual general staff' composed of his most important associates and pay more attention to their views. 'Although we gladly grant you the honour of being the first, you are only the first among equals and free men, as was the old and best Germanic custom'.[72]

Hitler was furious about this attempt to dictate to him. His response, however, followed the usual pattern when he was pressed by people whom he did not wish to antagonise because they were useful to the Party: he evaded an unequivocal statement and to begin with did nothing. In his letter Feder had adopted a suggestion by Max Amann, the manager of the Party publishing house and Hitler's former regimental sergeant-major, that Hitler should underline the official character of Feder's publication by writing a foreword for it. Hitler promised to do so but Feder waited in vain for it and finally, disgruntled, sent his manuscript to the printers in September.[73] It was only when the book was published that Feder received a short

introduction from Hitler on 8 November. This testimonial from
Hitler — 'it has provided our movement with its catechism' — does at
first sight appear an unequivocal commitment to Feder.[74]

Feder was unaware that, on the very evening of that day, Hitler
would endeavour to push the dominant political and military forces in
Bavaria, who were still hesitant but in principle ready for a putsch, into
taking an irrevocable step. The proclamation of the provisional national
government amidst the tumult of the *Bürgerbräukeller* was to be the
spark for the 'revolution'. He and others had propagated it for years
and many of the enemies of the Republic, both within and outside the
state apparatus, would have participated. Spreading outwards from
Munich, it was intended to set in motion all the anti-republican forces
in Bavaria and the *Reich* against the *Reich* government in Berlin which
Hitler declared deposed.[75] The course of events has been reconstructed
in great detail by various authors. In this context, the most significant
fact is that Hitler, presumably when still in the *Bürgerbräukeller*, put
Feder in charge of the Finance Ministry in the provisional government.

In order to ascertain Hitler's real relationship with Feder we must
at this point look back on the development since their first meeting. As
already mentioned above, Feder's basic idea had played a key role in
the formation of Hitler's political ideology. Hitler admitted this himself
in his account of the beginnings of his political career in *Mein Kampf* in
1925.[76] Its importance, however, lay not in the *contents* of Feder's
financial programme, but in the fact that it provided Hitler, right at
the beginning of his political activity, with 'scholarly' confirmation as
it were for his already existing resentments; perhaps it even gave them
a focus round which they could develop. For Hitler, who was already
infected with anti-semitic ideas[77] but had not yet systematised them,
Feder's ideas offered themselves as a convenient theory, though with
Hitler's own sharp anti-semitic bias characteristically imposed upon it.
The popular slogan of 'the breaking of the slavery of interest' of
international Jewish loan capital played a considerable part in Hitler's
speeches in 1919 and 1920, but soon he avoided being pinned down as
to the details of its implementation.[78] For Hitler's attitude towards
statements about the programme underwent a general change in 1920.
As he saw it, Germany's renewal could not be brought about by the
proclamation of a detailed programme, but only by the success of
counter-revolutionary action which would then make such measures
possible. For, in the meantime, Hitler had recognised that the fanatical
will to extinguish the 'November revolution' and those responsible for
it existed in many quarters and demanded both less and at the same

time more than concrete proposals for change, namely, a focal point for counter-attack.

Hitler's attitude towards those who wished to concentrate on concrete proposals was from now on determined by considerations of expediency. He allowed them to operate because they attracted followers to the movement and fulfilled other useful functions, mostly of a propaganda nature. He gave them a free hand as long as they did not harm the propaganda effect of the Party by dogmatic quarrels or jeopardise his position as a leader vis-à-vis the public.[79] This was an attitude that affected Feder as well; positively through the freedom to proclaim his financial programme as that of the NSDAP, but also negatively inasmuch as it lacked validity without Hitler's express support.[80] Hitler stubbornly gave priority to political action over a concrete programme; and he did this also in his relations with the Bavarian authorities, on whom his hopes for a putsch rested, because in his way he had just as narrow a view of politics as Feder, namely, the view of a mere propagandist. Even immediately before the putsch he maintained in discussions with Lieutenant-General von Lossow, the Chief of the *Reichswehr* troops in Bavaria, that 'the programme should be worked out later on, one could not wait for it now. One could quite easily start to govern now [!], the programme would then follow'.[81]

The situation in which Hitler wrote his introduction on 8 November, however, was different from that which prevailed during these discussions with, for example, von Lossow. Hitler now found himself compelled to make the first move on his own and in this he was evidently reassured by the fact that he had the backing of a few theorists to act as experts. Without wishing to identify himself with Feder and the contents of the book, Hitler used self-confident but vague phrases in his introduction in order to prove to himself that, in this connection too, he was prepared for the great undertaking.

Feder's appointment as 'Minister of Finance' did not reduce the gap between Hitler and himself. Since the economic experts in Berlin, who had been in contact with the Bavarian rebels,[82] had to be pushed into action, Hitler in the meantime turned to the man who had been offering his services for some time. Moreover, Feder had a certain amount of support in Bavarian right-wing circles and, last but not least, was acceptable to General Ludendorff,[83] whom Hitler himself regarded as the symbol and the key military figure of the coup.

When Feder later proudly mentioned the favourable references which Hitler had made to him in *Mein Kampf*,[84] he deliberately overlooked the unequivocal reservation which immediately followed it

and which was directed at all theorists in the NSDAP who
narrow-mindedly claimed priority for their particular theory: 'Every
idea, even the best one, becomes dangerous when it claims to be an end
in itself but is in reality only a means to an end – for me and for all
true National Socialists, however, there is only one doctrine: nation
and fatherland . . . Everything else must be examined in this light and
either be used or rejected *according to its expediency*. In this way no
theory can become ossified into lethal dogma since everything must
serve life'.[85]

The gap between Hitler and Feder, based on their different political
perspectives, remained the decisive element in their relationship. If
under these circumstances Feder wished his economic programme to
achieve lasting success in the Party, it was imperative for him to secure
a position within the Party that would induce Hitler to adopt the
programme. If this could not be achieved through direct influence on
Hitler, Feder could try to spread his doctrine within the Party and
among its political sympathisers to such an extent that the general
desire to implement it became strong enough to win Hitler over.[86]
But this second possibility required that Feder not only was active and
successful with his propaganda but also that he made himself
indispensable by acquiring a fairly stable base within the Party and
thereby achieve a degree of independence. We will now turn to the
attempts which he made in these two directions.

On 9 November 1923 Feder only just had time to publish an
announcement in the *Völkischer Beobachter* of the temporary
suspension of all cash and credit transactions by the banks before the
collapse of the coup.[87]   Feder took part in the march through Munich,
which ended in police gunfire in front of the Feldherrnhalle, and
together with other theorists such as Rosenberg, he marched in the
front ranks behind Hitler, Ludendorff and other leaders of the
paramilitary leagues. Unhurt, he fled abroad like Göring, Esser and
others. By a lucky coincidence he already possessed a visa for a
planned visit to the Sudeten German National Socialists in
Czechoslovakia. A few months later, things had cooled down
sufficiently as a result of the farcical trial of Hitler and Ludendorff in
Munich for Feder to be able to return safely.

The mood of excitement provoked by the attempted coup, and by
the flagrant agitation which the accused had been permitted to indulge
in during the court proceedings, led to the electoral success of the
völkisch candidates in the *Reichstag* elections of 4 May 1924. Feder
was among the 32 (of 472) *Reichstag* deputies elected on the *völkisch*

ticket and remained in the *Reichstag* until 1936. Feder had pleaded for
parliamentary seats as propaganda platforms as early as 1923 when
Hitler was still opposed to this idea.[88] Now he began to use the
Reichstag and the parliaments of the states, which were also being
penetrated by National Socialists, as a base from which to advance his
programme. The main proposal was the establishment of a national
construction bank (*Staatliche Bau-und Wirtschaftsbank*) to cope with
the housing shortage, a proposal which he had already put forward in
1921.[89] The motions were unsuccessful, however, because everywhere
the *völkisch* or national socialist parliamentary groups represented an
uninfluential minority.

In the bitter struggles over positions of leadership, parliamentary
seats and the whole question of participation in Parliament, which
preoccupied the various *volkisch* groups during 1924, Feder sought
unity in the interests of efficiency and, after Hitler's imprisonment in
Landsberg, he supported the *völkisch* 'Reich leadership' of
Ludendorff – von Graefe – Strasser.[90] In the conflict between the
former NSDAP members in Bavaria he was on the side of Rosenberg,
Gregor Strasser and the *Völkisch-Sozialer Block,* who were being
viciously attacked by Esser, Streicher, and the *Grossdeutsche
Volksgemeinschaft*, on the grounds that they had led the 'Hitler
movement' on to the pernicious path of parliamentarism.[91]

The refounding of the NSDAP by Hitler on 26-27 February 1925
did not apparently involve Feder in any great conflict of loyalty.
Together with his *Reichstag* colleagues Strasser, Dr Frick, and Hans
Dietrich of Coburg, he decided in favour of the NSDAP against its
rival, the *Deutschvölkische Freiheitspartei* (DVFP), which in the six
years of its existence (1922 to 1928) could never overcome its
deficiencies as a former parliamentary splinter group of the
Deutschnationale Volkspartei.[92] Hitler's intention of reconciling the
Bavarian National Socialists, who had been at loggerheads during his
imprisonment, was realised in the first big meeting in the
Bürgerbräukeller on 27 February. Feder himself took part in the
theatrical scene of reconciliation which took place between some of
the main rivals. It was also reflected in the carefully handled
distribution of the new membership numbers: after Hitler as No. 1,
Esser was demonstratively given No. 2, his main opponent, the Bavarian
Landtag deputy Buttmann, the No. 4, the Reichstag members Strasser,
Frick and Feder the numbers 9-11, Streicher No. 17 and Rosenberg
No. 18.[93]

Their free railway passes and allowances greatly facilitated the

propaganda activities of the new *Reichstag* deputies and Feder made
great use of them. In 1926, for example, he held 107 meetings.
Although Feder's economic programme had not convinced the sceptics
in the DVFP, such doubts were not obvious in the NSDAP – at any
rate in the Party press Feder was represented as possessing 'one of the
clearest and most comprehensive minds in our movement'.[94] He himself
gave instructions to the local branches which invited him to speak to
give due emphasis to his 'position within the national socialist
movement', by referring to the passages in Hitler's recently published
Mein Kampf quoted above at the beginning of the meeting.[95]

Feder evidently now had more frequent contact with Hitler. Yet
Feder did not possess any clearly defined office with executive
functions in the NSDAP, whose organisation in 1925 was at an
embryonic stage, though as the 'expert of the Party HQ for theoretical
questions of financial policy', he was at the Party's disposal to answer
queries on economic and financial questions.[96]

This basis within the Party organisation was not sufficiently stable
to provide effective backing for Feder's claims, but it could be
extended. The opportunity for a major step forward arrived
unexpectedly at the turn of the year 1925-6. While in Bavaria the
NSDAP stagnated, and Hermann Esser's demagogy dominated the
campaign in Munich against the renegades round Drexler who had
formed a splinter group, the NS-*Volksbund*, in West, North and central
Germany a number of vigorous groups emerged, some of whom had
only established contact with Munich during 1924-5. Already in March
1925, Hitler had instructed Gregor Strasser, who had been elected to
the *Reichstag* in December 1924 in the electoral district of Westphalia-
North, to undertake a provisional division of these regions into *Gaue*.
The contacts between these groups, which had preferred the NSDAP to
the DVFP precisely because of its activism, and the indefatigable Gregor
Strasser led in September 1925 to the setting up of the 'Working Group
of the North and West German Gaue' (AG).[97] While it was not an
opposition movement aimed directly against Munich the AG was
concerned to establish a clear party line vis-à-vis day-to-day political
questions. Their annoyance at the 'bragging' of Esser & Co. made the
need for effective work in the interests of the Party as a whole appear
particularly urgent. Already in June, Gregor Strasser had approached
the philosopher Oswald Spengler expressing the wish 'to discuss the
problems of National Socialist foreign, domestic, and economic policy
independently of any official pressure'.[98] The Working Group
seemed to provide the appropriate framework for this plan as well.

Hitler, who was informed by Strasser of their intentions – including the aim of dealing with 'basic problems' in their organ, the *Nationalsozialistische Briefe* – at that stage saw no grounds for suspicion.[99]

It soon became apparent from the initial discussion within the AG that many and very varied opinions were marching under the banner of 'National Socialism', despite the vague unanimity within the north and west German Gaue about the inadequacy of the twenty-five point programme and about the necessity of giving more emphasis to the 'socialist' components. Gregor Strasser's draft programme, which he himself regarded as an unofficial basis for discussion but for the time being kept from Hitler, in fact provoked much opposition.[100] While the initial discussion had caused no problems, the production of further draft programmes and commentaries and their debate in the AG created a rather ambiguous situation vis-à-vis Party headquarters. Strasser was fully conscious of this, although he quite openly proclaimed the necessity for a debate about the programme in the *Völkischer Beobachter* and had involved its chief editor, Rosenberg, in the discussion.[101] For they had very soon abandoned the original idea of keeping the discussion about the programme confidential within a close circle of friends in favour of a broad debate, in order that, in view of the unedifying situation in Munich, the AG might 'set the trend' within the Party.[102]

Feder first learnt of the discussion of the programme at Christmas through a letter from Dr Alfred Freyberg, an acquaintance from central Germany, who did not play any particular role in the AG, but in 1932 was to become the NSDAP's Prime Minister of Anhalt. Feder was absolutely furious that he had been completely ignored and at the fact that, by raising the question of the core of the National Socialist concept, they threatened to undermine the basis of the programme which, along with Hitler, he had laid with his book. He also sharply rejected particular aspects of the Strasser programme.[103] Gregor Strasser failed in his attempt to keep him out of the discussion even after Feder's complaint over his exclusion. Feder took the opportunity of scheduled speeches in north Germany to make an unexpected appearance at the meeting which the AG held in Hanover on 24 January 1926. Here he was confirmed in his suspicion that efforts were being made which threatened to undermine 'the internal stability of the movement in the most dangerous way'.[104] On the basis of notes which he had made in Hanover, he quickly succeeded in 'rousing Hitler'.[105] On Feder's initiative, the Party leader summoned

the conference at Bamberg for 14 February, to which some sixty
Gauleiter, parliamentary deputies, and editors of Party newspapers were
invited. On the car journey to the meeting Feder had the opportunity of
once again pointing out to Hitler the threat to his leadership and to
reinforce his determination to nip the potential opposition in the bud.
Feder also spoke at the meeting and did not spare Strasser, who gave
in.[106]

In view of the outcome of the Bamberg conference, the very
heterogeneous Working Group was virtually finished before it had had
time to establish itself properly. Feder, on the other hand, had
consolidated his position. During the Bamberg conference and, as a
reward for his vigilance as it were, Hitler put him in charge of the
'maintenance of the bases of the programme' (*Wahrung der
programmatischen Grundlagen*) of the NSDAP. [107]

What this appointment meant in practice was never clearly specified.
It was obviously one of those spontaneous, ad hoc appointments which
Hitler was in the habit of making when he had to give in to pressure
from representatives of particular interests without at the same time
wishing to tie his hands. Feder's alertness had — in this particular
context — proved useful to Hitler. By now giving him such a broadly
defined appointment, he had, on the one hand, temporarily satisfied
Feder, who was longing for such an official acknowledgement by the
Party, and also encouraged him to further vigilance. On the other hand,
the vague terms and the informal character of the appointment ensured
that his own position as supreme leader was not restricted to such an
extent that he could be pushed in any particular direction or be forced
to take any particular action against his will. For Feder could not
seriously assume that Hitler was intending to subject himself to his
judgement when he delegated to him 'the final decision . . . on all
matters relating to the programme'.[108] Hitler did however share Feder's
concern to prevent all unauthorised attempts at improving the Party's
programme and to protect it from the 'continual "suggestions for
improvement" made by unauthorised critics, grumblers and know-alls'
which would have the effect both of absorbing energy and producing
conflict.[109] Apart from this, the importance of such an appointment
depended entirely on what the person appointed managed to make
of it.

From now onwards Feder called himself 'The Ideologist
(*Programmatiker*) of the Movement' and was described as such by the
Party press.[110] In his new function Feder exploited the fact that the
slightly modified statutes of the NSDAP, which were adopted at the

annual General Meeting on 22 May 1926, still contained the clause
stating that the twenty-five point programme was immutable.[111] On the
basis of this clause and of his Bamberg appointment, he conceived his
position in the Party as follows: he acknowledged Hitler as the supreme
leader, but saw himself as equal in rank as far as questions relating to the
programme were concerned,[112] and deduced from that a dual task for
himself – that of guardian of the interpretation of the existing NSDAP
publications concerned with the programme, and that of guarantor of the
uniformity of future statements.

Despite his unshakeable conviction of his own importance, Feder must
have been aware of the fact that his claim to equality of rank was not
supported by equality of power within the Party. He could not win in a
conflict if Hitler considered statements or actions, of which Feder did
not approve, to be necessary in pursuit of his main political aim: the
achievement of an official or unofficial political position which would
enable him to guide Germany's domestic and international fortunes in
what seemed to him the right direction. For that reason, during the
months following Bamberg Feder endeavoured to initiate the 'urgently
necessary definition of the particular posts' within the leadership
apparatus of the NSDAP and thereby to gain a firm foothold for
himself.[113] At the Party Rally in Weimar on 3 and 4 July 1926 he put
forward several motions which complemented one another. One of them
demanded categorically: 'An intellectual general staff is to be created',
and thus took up his old demand of 1923. The second motion repeated
the suggestion contained in his letter to Hitler of 2 and 3 May 1926 of
holding regular conferences for the most important Party functionaries
(*Gauleiter*, deputies, editors) to be chaired by Hitler four times or at
least twice a year. Feder's reasons – the clarification of topical
political questions and the exchange of views – were plausible in the
light of recent events. These motions barely disguised the fact, however,
that they would establish a certain degree of participation and control
through the Party functionaries and also institutionalise and consolidate
Feder's position in the ideological sphere.[114] The Party functionaries,
who discussed this under Strasser's chairmanship in the special session of
the Party Rally devoted to organisational questions, welcomed both
proposals 'most warmly' and recommended them to Hitler 'most
urgently'. Hitler, however, was not impressed and ignored both
proposals and recommendation. He was empowered to do this by the
directives for the special sessions which he had previously issued.[115]

Feder was more successful with his motion for the publication of a
series in which, under the supervision of the Party leadership, 'all

important fundamental political, economic, social, and cultural questions' were to be discussed. Hitler entrusted Feder with the selection of authors and subjects for this 'national socialist library'. On 17 November 1926, 'the ideologist of our movement' was able to make the following announcement to his Party comrades in the *Völkischer Beobachter*:

> After its publication the series will represent the official literature of the movement to supplement the 25 point programme and the two basic works by Adolf Hitler, *Mein Kampf*, Vol. I, and Vol.II: 'The National Socialist Movement', and Gottfried Feder's work, *The German State on a National and Social Basis*.[116]

On the whole, the years from 1926 to 1928 must have been the most pleasant ones in Feder's Party career. The gradual consolidation of the Party promised for the first time hope of realising his economic aims. He was fully occupied as a speaker; his interpretation of the Party programme, which appeared as the first volume of the NS-Library before the Nuremberg Party Rally in 1927, reached its fifth edition in February 1929; by the end of 1928 'The German State' had had a sale of 20,000 copies.[117]

There were, however, disagreements about the meaning and content of particular points in the Nazi programme. For example, Rosenberg challenged Feder's assertion that 'the breaking of interest slavery is the heart of National Socialism' with the argument that 'even the most radical financial and economic programmes' only acquired significance through the creation of the 'germanic man'. Thus the protection of the race was 'the heart of our theory'.[118] For the time being this conflict remained as sterile as did the disagreements with Otto Strasser and Dietrich Klagges about the interpretation of the demand in the Party programme for 'participation in the profits of big firms'. Feder sharply rejected the interpretation that this implied participation in the ownership and direction of a business in addition to a participation in the proceeds of one's own labour which, in his view, should take the form of a general reduction in prices combined with stable wages and salaries.[119]

This disagreement also demonstrates that one cannot simply categorise Feder as a member of the so-called 'left' or 'socialist' wing of the NSDAP as often occurs.[120] This faction was, both in terms of its ideology and in terms of its organisation, a very loose group whose size is difficult to determine. Not even its supposed exponents,

the brothers Gregor and Otto Strasser, had uniform ideas.[121]
The ideological influence of Gregor derived from the sympathy felt by
many members for his emotional, petty bourgeois form of Socialism
which was directed primarily towards the interests of the middle classes
and above all the self-employed.[122] This was also the basis for the
agreement on a number of concrete issues which emerged between Feder
and Gregor Strasser during the years 1930 to 1932.

Yet, from the point of view of the future, Feder's position was by no
means secure. He was presumably aware that he had benefitted from the
fact that, during its years as a fringe group in the political wilderness
between 1926 and 1929, the NSDAP had not been forced to make
binding commitments. Within the framework of the Party organisation
he had still not found a position round which his close friends could
coalesce and establish a power base. And his office as watchdog
certainly did not carry with it any executive functions. He, therefore,
seized the opportunity which presented itself at the end of 1928, of
securing a foothold in the Party's press by acquiring the *Fränkischer
Volksverlag* publishing house which produced — rather inefficiently —
a number of south German *Gau* newspapers, including the
Hessenhammer, the official newspaper for *Gau* Hesse-Darmstadt.

In the following three years, however, the newspaper business proved
a fiasco, and finally, at the beginning of 1932, Feder pulled out having
made substantial losses and antagonised several *Gauleiter*.[123] In the
meantime, Feder's contacts with Hesse had nourished in him the hope
of becoming *Gauleiter* of the rather unstable *Gau* Hesse-Darmstadt. This
failed to materialise, however, as did his hopes of a ministerial post in
the state of Hesse in which, after the state elections of 1931, the
NSDAP had become the largest party but did not succeed in entering
the government.[124]

Feder's drive to acquire these posts, which would have offered him
more opportunity for practical political activity, is all the more
remarkable in view of the fact that, meanwhile, things in Munich seemed
to be developing along the lines which he had advocated since 1923.
With the setting up of the Organisation Department II (0 II) under
K. Hierl in June 1929, the Party leadership had taken account of the
fact that up until then very little had been achieved in 'theoretical
planning for the construction of the future national socialist state'.[125]
Within the framework of 0 II the discussions about economic questions
played an important role. Already in August 1929, Hierl contemplated
initial plans for the composition of a simple 'catechism' of national
socialist economic principles to be set against the liberal-capitalist and

Marxist economic theories'.[126]   In December, a commission was set
up to prepare a 'Handbook of national socialist economic theory'. Its
membership under Feder's direction initially consisted of long-standing
Party functionaries, who had been involved to a greater or lesser
extent with economic questions – people such as G. Strasser, F. Stöhr,
F. Reinhardt, R. Hess, H. Himmler. It was then extended to include
further members. The meetings, or a number of them at any rate,
were attended by Hitler and evidently lasted into 1931. Apparently,
there were considerable differences of opinion; in any case, the
discussions did not produce any concrete results.[127]

In the meantime, the situation of the NSDAP had undergone a
significant change. After the September 1930 election when it became
the second strongest parliamentary group after the Social Democrats,
the Party was not only nearer its goal of the take-over of political
power, but there was a corresponding growth in the practical demands
made upon it. In the middle of the world economic crisis it was – if
only for reasons of propaganda – compelled to a greater extent than
hitherto to make clear its views on economic questions which were
being debated in parliament and to make practical proposals for the
relief of the economic crisis. The kind of continuous activity required
in this sphere could not be provided by such a loosely organised body
as Feder's commission. After an agricultural department had been
set up within the framework of the O II in August 1930 under a recent
Party member, R.W. Darré,[128]   an Economic Policy Department (WPA)
was established in December of that year under the chairmanship of
Dr Otto Wagener. In October 1929, Hitler had appointed Wagener Chief
of Staff to the Supreme SA leader, v. Pfeffer, though Wagener was
really more interested in economic questions. In his new post Wagener
pressed far more vigorously than either Feder or Strasser had done for a
corporate system and worked out a detailed plan for a national socialist
corporate state. According to Wagener's later statements, the setting up
of the WPA was prompted by his suggestion.[129]

Feder's attitude to his appointment can be surmised. In August,
Hierl had still made the appointment of an economic expert to O II
dependent on Feder's agreement. He had, however, pointed out that
Hitler's decision would be final in the event of Feder failing to agree.[130]
In the light of Wagener's statement that in the disagreements referred to
above he had Hitler on his side, and in view of the fact that the
relationship between Feder and Wagener remained very tense, one can
deduce that Feder had to give way to the new man. This would also
explain his efforts to acquire other posts at this particular time.

Gottfried Feder and the NSDAP

Feder, however, succeeded in winning back the lost ground. For, on 2 November 1931, Hitler transferred to him the responsibility for establishing and directing the Economic Council, which Feder in his vanity renamed the Reich Economic Council (RWR).[131]   Hitler, however, characteristically did not define the respective competencies of the RWR and WPA. He himself had virtually no expertise in this field.[132] But he was aware of the fact that the maintenance and expansion of his mass following required relatively uniform statements on economic policy, which in their general line would correspond with previous propaganda. Yet, he had a strong interest in ensuring that the anti-liberal petty bourgeois ideologists — a category which covers both Feder and Wagener despite their differences — however useful they might be in propaganda terms, should not commit him to one-sided concrete programmes. For, and that was clearly the most important reason for Feder's appointment, Hitler needed a free hand in his wooing of industry, business, and bankers, without at the same time alienating the existing Party supporters. Hitler acted on the principle that, without the support of these established groups let alone against them, it would be impossible to restore Germany to political power.[133]

In this situation it seemed appropriate to let Feder and Wagener keep each other in check. This would satisfy both the needs of propaganda and of the internal Party situation as well as the broader political requirements. Hitler's regulation defining the relationship between the Economic Council and the WPA was designed to ensure that neither Wagener nor Feder should feel slighted. Without making any further reference to Feder's task as guardian of the programme, it laid down that the WPA should consult the Economic Council 'concerning the preparation of all official Party declarations, all official instruction pamphlets, the preparation of economic legislation, as well as all economic matters of fundamental importance'. As a result, each felt that he was the superior of the other.[134]

In 1932, Feder had a considerable advantage over Wagener in that his views accorded far more with those of Gregor Strasser than did Wagener's[135] and Gregor Strasser was regarded as the most important national socialist public spokesman in the economic field. Feder found his views reflected to a considerable extent in Strasser's big *Reichstag* speech of 10 May 1932 and in the 'Emergency Economic Programme', published before the *Reichstag* election of July 1932. This programme demanded among other things: the reorientation of the German economy towards the domestic market, state measures to reduce unemployment (e.g. the construction of private housing estates for workers), foreign exchange controls, state control of the banks, a reduction in interest rates and price controls.[136]

Walther Funk, the long-established business correspondent of the *Berliner Börsenzeitung*, who had acted for Hitler as a contact man to industry and business circles since the end of 1930, was also a member of Feder's Reich Economic Council.[137]   But there can be no question of Hitler having replaced Feder by Funk in 1931.[138] It is highly probable of course that Hitler believed that Funk would act as a moderating influence on Feder's 'struggle against high finance'. But it became clear during 1932 that Feder and Funk got on quite well together. Feder's demands for the 'nationalisation of the whole money and credit system', a general reduction in interest rates, debt conversion etc. were very prominent in the official Party 'Programme of Economic Reconstruction' drawn up by Funk with Feder's cooperation in the autumn of 1932.[139]

The view that Feder's influence had virtually disappeared by 1932 is based on erroneous assumptions.[140]   It presupposes that he had held before a position of considerable influence which he in fact never possessed, although it must be said that his own interpretation of the role of the 'ideologist of the movement' helped to produce this erroneous impression.We have, however, seen that Feder had been neither Hitler's adviser on economic and financial questions, nor had he exercised influence on his political attitude in these matters. He had also been unable effectively to assert his claim to act in Hitler's name, or at any rate with Hitler's approval, as the official interpreter of the economic concepts of the NSDAP. Compared with the actual role which Feder had played in the Party since 1926, however, he was relatively successful in 1932. He secured a position within the Party leadership which in terms of formal status almost accorded with his old ambition.

In June 1932, the Organisation Departments I and II were amalgamated under Strasser as Reich Head of the Party Organisation (ROL) and in the reorganisation of the apparatus of the ROL the overlapping of functions within the economic sector was removed.[141] The *Reich* Economic Council was now directly subordinated to Hitler and was to serve as 'the supreme organ of the Party headquarters for all fundamental questions of national socialist economic policy'. Feder remained chairman and Funk became deputy chairman. After Wagener left the ROL in September, the Economic Policy Department was reorganised into a Main Department IV A (State Economy) under

Feder, and a Main Department IV B (Private Economy) under Funk.[142] These two departments were now left only the task of 'the implementation of the directives given by the *Reich* Economic Council '. The heads of main departments IV A and B, V (Agriculture), and VI (Factory Cells) were to be ex officio members of the *Reich* Economic Council which was to be expanded by the appointment of individuals from the business world. The 'Programme of Economic Reconstruction' was the first result of this reorganisation.

At the end of the year, however, it became only too apparent that, even with this promotion, Feder was only successful within the limits which had defined his role within the Party already in 1923 and then again since 1925. He had remained a propagandist and theorist, who had failed to commit the NSDAP definitely to his financial and economic programme. It was significant that since 1926-7 Hitler had not cared to consult Feder on his contacts with representatives of big business, one of the politically influential groups with whose help he hoped to smooth his path to the Chancellorship.

The activities of Feder and the petty bourgeois, anti-capitalist propagandists of the NSDAP were not, as a result, simply of no importance whatever. Their work not only reassured the membership and supporters about the paths which Hitler was following. It is often overlooked that Hitler aimed at his goal along several different lines. One of these consisted of retaining the Party as an independent political instrument. One of the basic political lessons which the mistrustful Hitler had learnt in the course of his career was that he should avoid becoming directly dependent on political and social forces which had their own particular goals. This was also valid for his contacts with people from industry, commerce and banking. For it was by no means yet certain whether their assistance would bring about success. At any rate until August 1932, it looked as if the impetus of the electorate mobilised by the Party could bring the NSDAP to power. It was, therefore, in any event expedient to have the loyal personnel of the Party at his disposal. Moreover, it must be remembered that it was not just Hitler who was interested in the support of business, for they also courted him. For this reason too it was advisable for him to demonstrate his independence when they, for example, complained about the Party's economic proposals. Thus, during 1931-2, Hitler manoeuvred between big business and the economic apparatus of the Party.

From November 1932, however, the situation developed in such a way that the Party's dynamic was considerably reduced, as the loss of

votes in the *Reichstag* election of 6 November indicated. At the same
time, the mediation of business circles with the *Reich* President
and the former Chancellor von Papen offered prospects of real
success and that had an effect on the situation. Hitler's intention of
dissolving the new unified economic apparatus of the Party
Headquarters must be seen in this context. The former President
of the *Reichsbank*, Schacht, played a leading role in the attempts to
make Hitler *Reich* Chancellor. It can surely be assumed that the
demands of the 'Programme of Economic Reconstruction' for the
nationalisation of the whole money and credit system and a general
reduction in interest rates, whose official character had just been confirmed
were more than 'the small irregularities which are liable to occur in
propaganda' which Schacht was prepared to tolerate.[143] After all, he
had repeatedly advised Hitler against publishing further statements
like the July Emergency Programme.

Feder learnt of Hitler's intention through Gregor Strasser just
before Strasser resigned from all his Party offices on 8 December.[144]
He now found himself in a particularly unfavourable position. He had
not even succeeded in securing through his own efforts 'the position
within the *Reich* leadership which in a way is historically due to
me'.[145]   He owed it to Strasser. The latter's resignation plunged Feder
into confusion. He had shared Strasser's view that, for the sake of its
political survival and of its supporters, the NSDAP should take over
political responsibility 'on cheaper terms'[146]   than Hitler was prepared
to demand. Loyalty to Strasser but above all annoyance at the
dissolution of his office prompted him to write an agitated letter of
protest to Hitler at the end of which he requested 'several weeks
leave'.[147]   On 9 December, however, he withdrew from this step
with a humble declaration of loyalty to Hitler who honoured Feder's
act of submission by appointing him to a less high ranking position.
Feder was appointed head of the Sub-Commission for Work Creation
and Economic Technology within the new Political Central
Commission headed by Hess, while Funk, who in view of his contacts
was far more useful, received the Sub-Commission for Economic Policy.

This development did not yet imply that Feder was definitely
excluded from access to leading positions in the Third Reich. The
opportunities open to top functionaries of the NSDAP to climb to high-
ranking posts in the government, in business and professional
organisations were also open to Feder. One cannot even say that
his behaviour in December had particularly reduced his chances. For,
in view of the limited use which he had previously possessed for

Hitler, he could hardly have climbed higher than he actually did. There were basically two possibilities open to Feder: first, the takeover of one or other of the government posts which had to be filled with National Socialists in order to satisfy, or at any rate give the appearance of satisfying, the expectations of Party members for a new social order; or, second, the conquest of professional organisations. Feder had both chances open to him. On 1 July 1933 he became State Secretary in the Ministry of Economics, and in March 1934, *Reich* Commissioner for Settlement Policy as well. In April 1933, Feder, who had been head of the Engineering Technology department of the ROL since October 1931 as well as Chairman of the Combat League of German Architects and Engineers, also took over the chairmanship of the *Reich* Association of German Technology. He could utilise these positions to secure acceptance for his economic policies in the sphere of technological organisations.

Feder's activities in these offices require further investigation.[148] Light also needs to be thrown on the events which, in the aftermath of the Röhm *putsch* and following Schacht's appointment as *Reich* Minister of Economics in August 1934, led to his losing these offices one by one and spending the period between November 1934 and his death in 1941 in a mood of resignation far from the political stage as a Professor for Settlement, Area Planning and Urban Development. This much seems clear however: this development was essentially the result of the barriers which had restricted his influence in the NSDAP ever since his first attempts to obtain a foothold in it. Feder had never given up the practice of regarding the Party as an instrument for the dissemination of his programme instead of regarding himself as an instrument of Hitler's Party. His dogmatic rigidity had prevented him from adapting his ideological demands to Hitler's domestic and foreign policy goals — the take-over of power and the restoration of Germany to world power status — in a flexible way. Feder did not possess the combination of sharp elbows, opportunism, and resignation which would have been required to make himself indispensable within the Party apparatus. Moreover, what tentative attempts he made in this direction were ruined by the way in which this dogmatic loner kept getting involved in disputes. Thus, before 1933, it was only as a propagandist that Feder had been of some use to the Party. In view of these limitations, his failure under the concrete conditions in which economic policy was made in the Third Reich appears more or less inevitable.

Notes

1. Hitler's foreword in G. Feder, *Der deutsche Staat auf nationaler und sozialer Grundlage* (Munich,1924, 3rd edn.) and all later editions.
2. See for example L.L. Snyder, *Encyclopedia of the Third Reich* (New York, 1976), pp. 90f.; M. Broszat, *Der Staat Hitlers* (Munich, 1969), p.77; U.D. Adam, *Judenpolitik im Dritten Reich* (Düsseldorf, 1972), pp.19, 85; R. Hambrecht, *Der Aufstieg der NSDAP in Mittel-und Oberfranken 1925-1933* (Nuremberg, 1976), p.155.
3. See for example J. Nyomarkay, *Charisma and Factionalism in the Nazi Party* (Minneapolis, 1967); D. Orlow, *The History of the Nazi Party: 1919-1933 (Pittsburgh, 1969);* W. Horn, *Führerideologie und Partei-organisation in der NSDAP 1919-1933* (Düsseldorf, 1972) ; K.H. Ludwig, *Technik und Ingenieure im Dritten Reich* (Düsseldorf, 1974); G. Schulz, *Aufstieg des Nationalsozialismus* (Frankfurt/M, 1975); D. Stegmann, 'Kapitalismus und Faschismus in Deutschland 1929-1934', in *Gesellschaft, Beiträge zur Marxschen Theorie* 6, (Frankfurt/M, 1976), pp. 44, 49, passim.
4. See, for example, K.D. Bracher, *Die Auflösung der Weimarer Republik* (Villingen, 1964,4th Edn), pp. 113, 681.
5. Such a study is in the course of preparation by Manfred Riebe (Nuremberg), who is also using Feder's private papers.
6. There are details on Feder in A.R. Herrmann, *Gottfried Feder. Der Mann und sein Werk* (Leipzig, 1933), and in the *Reichstags-Handbücher* 1924-1933. See also B. v. Schirach (ed.), *Die Pioniere des Dritten Reiches* (Essen, undated [1933]), pp. 62ff; E. Seidl, (ed.), *Kampfgenossen des Führers: Hitler und die Männer seiner Bewegung* (Linz, 1933), p.13; S. Noller, 'Gottfried Feder', in *Neue Deutsche Biographie* Bd. V, (Berlin, 1961), p.42; H.H. Hofmann, 'Gottfried Feder', in *Biographisches Wörterbuch zur Deutschen Geschichte*, vol.I, 2nd revised edn (Munich, undated [1974]) pp.67lf. See also the description of Feder's character by his brother-in-law, the Munich historian K.A. v. Müller, *Mars und Venus: Erinnerungen 1914-1919* (Stuttgart, 1954), p.114, and by the NSDAP Gauleiter of Hamburg (1928), A. Krebs, in W.S. Allen (ed.), *The Infancy of Nazism: The Memoirs of ex-Gauleiter Albert Krebs 1923-1933*, (New York, 1976), pp.257ff.
7. G. Feder, 'Innere Geschichte der Brechung der Zinsknechtschaft', in Völkischer Beobachter (VB), 72, 12 August 1920.
8. ibid.
9. Diessen vor München, 1919, p.5 (reprinted in an abbreviated version in G. Feder, *Kampf gegen die Hochfinanz*, Munich, 1933, pp.51ff).
10. It would be the task of a Feder biography to unravel the links between Feder and his predecessors and contemporaries. This would also involve clarifying the authorship of the slogan 'the breaking of the slavery of interest' which may have come from Silvio Gesell (1862-1930), the money reformer and Finance Minister of the Munich Soviet Republic of 1919. See A. Barkai, 'Die Wirtschaftsauffassung der NSDAP', in *Aus Politik und Zeitgeschichte*, Nr. 9/1975, p.6; c.f. S. Gesell, *Die neue Lehre vom Geld und Zins* (Berlin-Grosslichterfelde, 1911; S. Gesell, *Die natürliche Wirtschaftsordnung durch Freiland und Freigeld* (Leipzig, 1916; Berlin, 1920, 4th edn). The reduction in interest and the elimination of the 'slavery of interest which derives from the Orient' was demanded for example, by the basic principles of the German Socialist Party (DSP), drawn up in 1918 by a Düsseldorf engineer, Alfred Brunner, i.e. at a time when Feder had not yet published anything on this topic. See A. Tyrell,

Vom 'Trommler' zum 'Führer': Der Wandel von Hitlers Selbstverständnis zwischen 1919 und 1924 und die Entwicklung der NSDAP (Munich, 1975), pp.78, 240.

11. U. Lohalm, *Völkischer Radikalismus: Die Geschichte des Deutschvölkischen Schutz-und Trutzbundes 1919-1923* (Hamburg, 1970), pp.140f; on the attempts to propagate a 'German Socialism' see also Tyrell, *Trommler*, pp. 18ff.
12. Cf. Schulz (f.n. 3) p.126.
13. Feder, *Manifest*, p.11. For an early and detailed critique of Feder's economic ideas see Th. Heuss, *Hitlers Weg* (Stuttgart, 1932; 2nd edn, Tübingen, 1968).
14. Feder, *Manifest*, p.55.
15. ibid., pp. 30f.
16. E.g. Feder in his Reichstag speech of 4 December 1930 (Feder, *Kampf*, pp. 279f.). See also G. Feder, *Das Programm der NSDAP und seine weltanschaulichen Grundlagen* (Munich, 1927), 184/185 edn, 916.-924. thousand,(Munich, undated) p.19.
17. Feder, *Manifest*, p.62.
18. ibid., p.12; on the DVSTB see Lohalm (f.n. 11), pp.139ff.
19. Feder, *Das Programm*, p.26; see also already in Feder, *Manifest*, p.62; and further in G. Feder, *Die Juden* (Munich, 1933), pp.8f.
20. Feder, *'Innere Geschichte'*, (note 7).
21. Tyrell, *Trommler*, p.191; in general see H. Fenske, *Konservativismus und Rechtsradikalismus in Bayern nach 1918* (Bad Homburg, etc. 1969); also now the survey by H. Auerbach, 'Hitlers politische Lehrjahre und die Münchener Gesellschaft 1919-1923' in *Vierteljahrshefte für Zeitgeschichte*, (VfZG), 25 (1977), pp. 1ff.
22. 'Das Radikalmittel', in *Süddeutsche Monatshefte* 16 (1918/19), pp.307ff.; on the importance of the SM see Fenske, pp.292ff.
23. *Auf gut deutsch*, vol. I, pt. 9/10, 28 March 1919. On Eckart (1868-1923), his role as an anti-semitic propagandist, and his importance for Hitler's development (which the author sometimes, however, exaggerates) see M. Plewnia, *Auf dem Weg zu Hitler: Der 'völkische' Publizist Dietrich Eckart* (Bremen, 1970).
24. R. von Sebottendorff, *Bevor Hitler kam: Urkundliches aus der Frühzeit der nationalsozialistischen Bewegung* (Munich,1933), pp. 62, 73.
25. Facsimile in A. Reich and O. R. Achenbach, *Vom 9. November 1919 zum 9. November 1923: Die Entstehung der deutschen Freiheitsbewegung* (Munich, 1933), pp. 14f. (the text also in Feder, *Kampf*, pp. 97ff.).
26. 'Mittendurch', in *Auf gut deutsch*, vol. 1, pt. 25, 29 August 1919.
27. For this and the following see the documentation by E. Deuerlein, 'Hitlers Eintritt in die Politik und die Reichswehr', in VfZG 7 (1959), pp. 177ff.
28. ibid, p. 202 (Mayr), p. 196f. (Esser); on Mayr see also Auerbach (fn.21), pp. 17f.
29. Hitler to A. Gemlich, 16 September 1919,in Deuerlein, p. 204; translation in J. Noakes & G. Pridham, *Documents on Nazism 1919-1945* (London, 1974), pp. 36-37. Esser too referred Feder's thesis about the 'exploiting high finance' to 'international jewry' (Deuerlein, pp. 196f.).
30. Tyrell, *Trommler*, p. 23; VB 45, 19 September 1919.
31. In the first membership list of the DAP, which was started on 2 February 1920 and which distributed the membership numbers to the 190 members in alphabetical order, Feder received the number 531, Hitler No. 555, Alfred Rosenberg No. 625. Esser became No. 881 on 8 March 1920. Cf. the first membership lists in the Bundesarchiv Koblenz (BA), NS 26-111,

171, 215, 230.
32. On Hitler's development in the NSDAP in detail, see Tyrell, *Trommler*, passim.
33. Deuerlein, 'Hitlers Eintritt', p. 207; VB 6, 21 January 1920.
34. e.g. Barkai (note 10), p. 5.
35. e.g. Broszat (note 2), pp. 37ff; H. J. Gordon jr., *Hitler and the Beer Hall Putsch* (Princeton, 1972); B. M. Lane, 'Nazi Ideology: Some Unfinished Business', in *Central European History* 7 (1974), p. 11.
36. 'Hitler and the Deutsche Arbeiter-Partei', in *American Historical Review*, 68 (1962/63), pp. 980f.; Tyrell, *Trommler*, pp. 29, 200.
37. G. Feder, *Der deutsche Staat auf nationaler und sozialer Grundlage*, (Munich, 1923, 2nd edn), p. 43.
38. Aufzeichnung O. Engelbrecht, 5 January 1933, printed in A. Tyrell (ed.), *Führer befiehl . . .* , (Düsseldorf, 1969), p. 351.
39. Excerpt from the Police report W[ürttemberg] Nr.27, 5 August 1925 (Bayerisches Hauptstaatsarchiv: Allgemeines Staatsarchiv (Bay. HSA:ASA), Sonderabgabe 1738); VB 177, 25/26 October 1925; Drexler to Hauptarchiv der NSDAP, 24 February 1941; Schüssler to Hauptarchiv der NSDAP, 11 March 1941 (BA, NS 26-110).
40. Phelps (note 36), p. 982. Apart from the meetings mentioned already, Feder also spoke to the NSDAP on 18 June and 20 August 1920. See VB 58 and 76, 24 June and 26 August 1920.
41. VB 6, 21 January 1920.
42. Mitteilungen des Deutschen Kampfbundes zur Brechung der Zinsknechtschaft, 1. Ausgabe, 1 July 1921, p.6: 'Bericht aus dem Kampfbund' – also for the following.
43. Report by Feder on his journey to Kiel, Magdeburg, and Leipzig, see VB 99, 14 November 1920.
44. On the DSP see Tyrell, *Trommler*, pp. 65f., 72ff.
45. e.g. Feder, 'Die Irrlehre des Freigeldes', in *Hammer* (Leipzig) 441, 1 November 1920, pp. 405ff; also H. Dolle, 'Zum Streit um Gesells Geld–Theorie', ibid., 444, 15 December 1920, pp.478f. See also S. Noller, *Die Geschichte des 'Völkischen Beobachters' von 1920-1923* (Diss. Munich, 1956), pp. 94ff. 118 with fn. 74.
46. See A. Brunner to J. Streicher, 6 July 1920; Feder to Streicher 26 May, 8 October, and 28 December 1920 (BA, Nachlass Streicher 72); A. Brunner *Deutsche Not und Rettung* (Duisburg, 1921); R. Jung, *Der nationale Sozialismus: Seine Grundlagen, sein Werdegang, seine Ziele* (Munich, 1922), pp.149ff. See also Feder's bibliographical references in *Der deutsche Staat* (note 37), pp. 192f.
47. Feder to Streicher, 26 May 1920.
48. Report on the DSP Party Congress's economic session on 30 July 1920 (BA, NS 26-109).
49. 3. *Reichsparteitag der DSP . . . Ausführlicher Bericht.* Hrsg. Ortsgruppe Zeitz der DSP (Zeitz, 1921), pp.25f, 29f.(BA, NS 26-109).
50. VB 97, 7 November 1920.
51. VB 109, 19 December 1920. On the background to the acquisition of the VB by the NSDAP, see Tyrell, *Trommler*, pp. 175ff.
52. Draft letter from Drexler to Feder, 13 February 1921, sent off on 9 March 1921 (printed in W. Maser, *Die Frühgeschichte der NSDAP*, Frankfurt/M, 1965, p.484ff.).
53. Drexler himself speaks of 'rumours' about Feder. See also the minute on Drexler's comments at the Hauptarchiv on 23 January 1936 (BA, NS 26-27).
54. In June 1920, the Party had 1100 members; in December 1920, 2000; in

August 1921, 3300. See Tyrell, *Trommler,* p.33; on the expansion of the NSDAP outside Munich see ibid. pp. 66ff., 227ff.

55. Author's italics. The statement that the interest issue could only be solved in the context of a national revolution was also issued by the NSDAP headquarters in March 1921 to the *Deutschvölkische Arbeitsgemeinschaft* in reply to their query. See Brieftagebuch der NSDAP, Nr. 878, 25 March 1921 (BA, NS 26-222).

56. VB 76 and 77, 26 and 29 August 1920. In addition, see the first pamphlet of the NSDAP 'Warum musste die Deutsche Arbeiterpartei kommen? Was will sie?' of the Spring of 1920, printed in E. F. Berendt, *Soldaten der Freiheit* (Berlin, 1938,2nd edn), pp.192ff.

57. See Tyrell, *Trommler,* p.89.

58. On the background and course of the leadership crisis and Hitler's role see ibid. pp.95ff., 116ff.

59. On 7 and 8 August 1920, the representatives of the national socialist and German socialist groups from Austria, Czechoslovakia, Poland, and the Reich had established a coordinating office in the presence of Drexler and Hitler.

60. Feder, *Der deutsche Staat,* p.193; Berendt (note 56), p.171.

61. See e.g. Feder's letter to the Bavarian Prime Minister v. Kahr of 26 December 1920 (also published as a pamphlet by the *Kampfbund* under the title 'Billiges Brot oder neue Steuern?', printed in Feder, *Kampf,* pp.104ff.); a joint petition of the *Kampfbund* and the *Bund Bayerischer Kapitalkleinrentner* in support of the small savers sent to the governments and parliaments in Munich and Berlin (*Der Nationalsozialist* (Munich) 6, 14 July 1921); see also A. Buckeley and G. Feder, *Die soziale Bau-und Wirtschaftsbank* (Weimar, 1924), pp.4f.

62. On the preconditions for Hitler's activities and his impact in Munich, see the comprehensive survey by Auerbach (note 21).

63. A. Rosenberg, *Wesen, Grundsätze und Ziele der NSDAP* (Munich, 1922).

64. See Gordon (note 35).

65. VB 9, 31 January 1923.

66. Feder, *Der deutsche Staat,* p.192.

67. e.g. Feder, *Kampf,* p.8. See below p.65, note 84.

68. O. J. Hale, 'Gottfried Feder Calls Hitler to Order: An Unpublished Letter on Nazi Party Affairs', in *Journal of Modern History* 30 (1958), p.362.

69. 1st and 2nd edition, Munich 1923; 14-15. edition, 71-80 thousand, Munich 1933.

70. See also Tyrell, *Führer* (note 38) pp.58ff.

71. Feder was the co-author of proclamations of the *Deutscher Kampfbund* composed of the *SA, Bund Oberland* and *Bund Reichskriegsflagge* (E. Röhm, *Die Geschichte eines Hochverräters,* Munich, 1933 (3rd edn, p.210) and, together with others, had prepared a 'draft constitution' (Hale, p.361). See also Tyrell, *Trommler,* p.362.

72. Hale, pp.361-2.

73. Feder, *Staat,* foreword to the 3rd edition (Munich 1933, 14/15, p.7); see also the well-informed report on Feder's letter and its consequences in: *Fränkische Tagespost* (Nuremberg) 66, 8 March 1925 (printed in Tyrell, *Führer* (note 38), pp.59f.).

74. See p.48.

75. On the Hitler-Ludendorff putsch see above all the documentation by E. Deuerlein, *Der Hitler-Putsch,* (Stuttgart, 1962), and the accounts by H. H. Hofmann, *Der Hitlerputsch* (Munich, 1961), and Gordon (note 35).

76. A. Hitler, *Mein Kampf* (Munich, 1940), 504-508, pp.228f.; see also below note 84.

77. See now R. Binion, *Hitler Among the Germans* (New York, 1976) pp.2ff.

78. 'Is the breaking of the slavery of interest not a socialist demand?', Hitler asked in a meeting on 9 May 1920 (Police report, BA, NS 26-81); see also R. H. Phelps, 'Hitlers "grundlegende" Rede über den Antisemitismus' [13 August 1920], in VfZG 16 (1968), pp.410f. Hitler continued to agitate against the 'international Jewish loan capital'. In particular see his speech on the political situation given at the Annual General Meeting in Munich on 30 July 1927, particularly pages 31ff. of the direct transcription (BA, NS 26-81/82).

79. It was the breaking of this barrier which brought down the former *Gauleiter* of Thuringia, Artur Dinter (see Tyrell, *Führer* (note 38), pp. 149f.), and, in 1930, Otto Strasser. On this whole question see also Nyomarkay (note 3).

80. In 1923 the same was true of Max Sesselmann who dealt with food questions. See Tyrell, *Trommler,* pp. 160f.

81. Statement by v. Lossow in *Der Hitler-Prozess vor dem Volksgerichtshof in München* (Munich, 1924), Part I, p.164.

82. See Deuerlein, *Hitler-Putsch* (note 75), pp.301ff.

83. Feder had introduced Mathilde von Kemnitz, a doctor, who was destined to become Ludendorff's second wife, to the General. He too sympathised with Feder's economic plans. See E. Ludendorff, *Vom Feldherrn zum Weltrevolutionär und Wegbereiter deutscher Volksschöpfung: Meine Lebenserinnerungen von 1919 bis 1925* (Munich, 1941), p.252.

84. Hitler, *Mein Kampf* (note 76), pp.232f. 'When listening to Gottfried Feder's first lecture on 'The Breaking of the Slavery of Interest', I knew at once, that what was involved was a *theoretical* truth, which must achieve enormous importance for the future of the German people. The sharp separation of the stock exchange capital from the national economy offered the possibility of fighting the internationalisation of German economic life without this struggle against capital in general also threatening the bases of our independence and *völkisch* survival . . . In Feder's lecture I sensed a powerful *slogan* for this coming struggle'. (Author's italics).

85. ibid., p.234 (author's italics).

86. See Nyomarkay (note 3), pp.39f.: but see also A. Tyrell, 'Führergedanke und Gauleiterwechsel', in VfZG 23 (1975), pp.346ff.

87. VB 230, 9 November 1923 (printed in Feder, *Kampf,* p.150).

88. Hale, p.362.

89. See A. Buckeley and G. Feder, *Die Soziale Bau- und Wirtschaftsbank: Die Retterin aus Wohnungsnot, Wirtschaftskrise, Erwerbslosenelend* (Weimar, 1924), pp.5, 11, 12f.

90. W. Jochmann, *Nationalsozialismus und Revolution* (Frankfurt/M, 1963), pp.113, 118f.; Ludendorff (note 83) p.349; 'Die Tagung der national-sozialistischen Freiheitsbewegung Grossdeutschlands in Weimar (15-17 August 1924)' in *Völkischer Kurier* (Munich) 165, 19 August 1924, 2. Beilage. On A. von Graefe, Reichstag deputy 1912-1928, see W. Liebe, *Die Deutschnationale Volkspartei 1918-1924* (Düsseldorf, 1956), and R. Wulff, *Die Deutschvölkische Freiheitspartei 1922-1928* (Diss. Marburg 1968).

91. See G. Schildt, *Die Arbeitsgemeinschaft Nord-West. Untersuchungen zur Geschichte der NSDAP 1925/26* (Diss. Freiburg, *1964*) *pp.18ff.;* A. Werner, *SA und NSDAP,* (Diss. Erlangen-Nuremberg) 1964, pp.232ff.

92. On the DVFP see Liebe and Wulff (note 90).

93. On the refounding of the Party see *Völkischer Kurier* 58/59, 1/2 March 1925; VB 2, 7 March 1925. The membership numbers are based on documents in the Berlin Document Center (BDC).

94. VB 175, 23 October 1925; *Der Nationale Sozialist für Sachsen* (Berlin) 43,

26 December 1926; see also 'Am Scheideweg', in VB 6, 28 March 1925.

95. 'Merkblatt zu den Feder-Versammlungen' sent by Feder to *Gauleitung* Rhineland-South in December 1925 (BA, NS 1/341).

96. *Politischer Almanach, Jg. 3.,*(Leipzig 1926) p.234 – see the correspondence between the publisher of the PA and the Reich headquarters of the NSDAP 1925-26 (BA, Sammlung Schumacher 374); on the structure of the Party headquarters from 1925 see Tyrell, *Führer*, pp. 355ff., and the *National-sozialistisches Jahrbuch 1927* (Munich, 1926).

97. On the AG North-West see above all Schildt (note 91); Wörtz, *Programmatik und Führerprinzip. Das Problem des Strasser-Kreises in der NSDAP,*(Diss. Erlangen)1966; J. Noakes, *The Nazi Party in Lower Saxony* (London, 1971); most recently, Schulz (note 3), pp.386ff.

98. Strasser to Spengler, 2 June 1925, in A. M. Koktanek (ed.), *Oswald Spengler, Briefe 1913-1936* (Munich,1963), p.392.

99. Rundschreiben der Kanzlei Hitler sgd. R. Hess, 11 December 1925 (Tyrell, Führer, p.117); see also the directive of the AG in *Nationalsozialistische Briefe* (Elberfeld) 5, 1 December 1925.

100. On Strasser's programme and the discussion about it see Schildt (note 91), pp.72ff., 125ff. R. Kühnl, *Die nationalsozialistische Linke 1925-1930* (Meisenheim, 1966); R. Kühnl, 'Das Strasser-Programm von 1925/26',in VfZG 14 (1966), pp.316ff.

101. VB 3, 5 January 1926.
Strasser to Goebbels, 11 November 1925 (Tyrell, *Führer*,pp.115f.).

103. Feder's reaction is summed up in his letter to Hitler and to the chairman of
102. Uschla,Lieut. General Heinemann of 2/3 May 1926 (ibid., pp.124ff.).

104. ibid., p.125. See also O. Strasser to Goebbels, 26 January 1926 (Jochmann (note 90), p.222).

105. G. Strasser to Goebbels, 8 January 1926 (ibid., p.220). It is often overlooked that it was Feder who took the initiative in Munich, e.g. Horn (note3), p. 237.

106. On the Bamberg conference see Schildt, pp. 154ff.; VB 46, 25 February 1926; H. Heiber (ed.), *The Early Goebbels Diaries 1925-26* (London,1962); Bericht Stadtkommandant Bamberg zu Regierungspraesidium Oberfranken, Bayreuth, 17 February 1926 (Bay. HSA:ASA: Sonderabgabe 1739).

107. Thus Feder to Goebbels 26 February 1926 (BA, NS 1/338, f. 60).

108. Feder, *Programm,* p.19.

109. ibid.

110. See, for example, *Illustrierter Beobachter* (München) 2, 28 January 1928, p.28; see also 'Kämpfer für Deutschlands Wiederauferstehung' in *Der Angriff* (Berlin) 66, 17 August 1930, Beilage.

111. The thesis suggested by Feder *(Programm,* p.18) and still current among scholars (e.g. Barkai (note10), p.5; H. A. Turner, 'Hitlers Einstellung zu Wirtschaft und Gesellschaft vor 1933',in *Geschichte und Gesellschaft* 2 (1976), p.103) that the 25-Point Programme was only declared immutable in the Party statutes of 1926 is wrong. Hitler had already introduced this clause into the statutes in 1921, when he took over the Party leadership. See Tyrell, *Trommler*, p.135; the statutes of 1921 and 1926 in Tyrell, *Führer*, pp.32,137.

112. See his announcement of the series below p.72.

113. Feder to Hitler/Heinemann, 2/3 May 1926 (note 103).

114. Motions Nos. 7 and 11 on questions of organisation (BA, NS 26-389). Goebbels had also proposed the idea of an 'intellectual general staff' in an open letter to Hitler in May 1926. See *NS Briefe* 16, 15 May 1926.

115. See the text of the directives in Tyrell, *Führer*, p.153ff.

116. VB 266, 17 November 1926.

117. VB 289, 12 December 1928.
118. Feder, *Programm*, p.19; Feder, 'Das Herzstück unseres Programms', in *Nat. soz. Jahrbuch* 1927 (Munich, 1926), pp.111ff.; A. Rosenberg, 'Nürnberg 1927', in Rosenberg und W. Weiss (eds.), *Der Reichsparteitag der NSDAP. Nürnberg 19/21 August 1927* (Munich, 1927), p.3; Speech by Rosenberg in Munich on 24 February 1928 (VB 48, 26/27 February 1928).
119. Feder, *Programm*, pp.54ff.; O. Strasser, 'Gewinnbeteiligung!', in *NS Briefe*, Jg. 4, 15 January 1929, pp.223ff.; see also Feder's letter of 26 July 1930 which was published and commented on in O. Strasser's *Berliner Arbeiterzeitung* 36, 7 September 1930.
120. See for example, K. D. Bracher/W. Sauer/G. Schulz, *Die Nationalsozialistische Machtergreifung* (Cologne, 1962, 2nd edn), p.176; Stegmann (note 3) p.44 and passim.
121. See Wörtz (note 97) particularly pp.141ff.; Tyrell, *Führer*, p. 312f.; M. H. Kele, *Nazis and Workers* (Chapel Hill, 1972), pp.159f. See also Stachura's discussion of this point in this volume.
122. Kühnl, *Programm* (note 100), p.322.
123. On Feder's newspaper publishing activities see the documents in the BDC, Personal and Party Court files of Feder; BA, Slg. Schumacher 319 (including letters to Strasser of 26 December 1931 and 12 February and 1 August 1932); also P. Hüttenberger, *Die Gauleiter* (Stuttgart, 1969), p.63; Hambrecht (note 2) pp.181f.
124. Feder to Strasser, 26 December 1931 (note 123); in general E. Schon, *Die Entstehung des Nationalsozialismus in Hessen* (Meisenheim, 1972), pp.182ff.
125. A memo by Hierl of 22 October 1929 (Tyrell, *Führer*, p.327, see also p. 310).
126. Hierl note of August 1929 (ibid., p.296).
127. Rundschreiben O II, 23 December 1929 (BA, Slg. Schumacher 373); Hierl to Bouhler, 26 February 1930; Rundschreiben Hierl, 3 July 1920; Restprogramm für die wirtschaftspolitische Besprechung; sgd. Dr. Wagener, 10 February 1931 (Slg. Schumacher. 212): O. Wagener, Erganzende Aufzeichnungen (Institut für Zeitgeschichte, Archiv, ED 60, p.12).
128. See H. Gies, 'R. Walther Darré und die nationalsozialistische Bauernpolitik in der Jahren 1930 bis 1933', Diss.(Frankfurt/M.)1966.
129. See Strasser to Gauleiter W. F. Loeper, 17 November 1930 (BA, Slg. Schumacher 204); Rundschreiben Oberste SA-Führung, Stabschef II A, 17 December 1930 (Slg. Sch. 212); Wagener, Aufzeichnungen (note 127), f. 11f. On Wagener see also H. A. Winkler, 'Unternehmerverbände zwischen Ständeideologie und Nationalsozialismus', in VfZG 17 (1969), pp.357ff.; Barkai (note 10), pp.8ff.
130. Darré to A. von Renteln, Berlin 16 August 1930 (BDC, Personal files v. Renteln).
131. Verordnungsblatt der Reichsleitung der NSDAP, Jg. 1, 16 November 1931, p.26 (BA, NSD 7).
132. See Turner, Hitlers Einstellung (note 111), pp.89ff.
133. On Hitler's contacts to big business and on the contact men such as W. Funk, W. Keppler, H. Schacht etc. see the contradictory researches of H. A. Turner, 'Grossunternehmertum und Nationalsozialismus 1930-1933', in *Historische Zeitschrift* 221 (1975), pp.18ff., and Stegmann (note 3).
134. On the dispute over the publication of Wagener's pamphlet, *Das Wirtschaftsprogramm der NSDAP* (Munich, 1932), which had displeased Feder, see the documents on the session of the RWR on 27 April 1932 (BA, NS 22/11). The relationship between the WPA and the RWR is

erroneously described by Schulz (note 3) pp.623, 630.

135. See Feder to Strasser, 28 September 1931 (BA, NS 22/348). According to this letter Strasser had asked Feder 'to keep a sharp eye . . . on Dr Wagener and his new course'. But see Stachura's different interpretation of the Strasser-Wagener relationship in 'Der Fall Strasser' (this volume).

136. Printed in H. A. Jacobsen and W. Jochmann (eds.) *Ausgewählte Dokumente zur Geschichte des Nationalsozialismus 1933-1945* (Bielefeld, undated). Excerpts from Strasser's speech in G. Strasser, *Kampf um Deutschland* (Munich, 1932), pp.345ff. See also Feder's manuscript of June 1932 'Arbeitsbeschaffung'. BA, NS Mischbestand 1122.

137. On Funk see P. Oestreich, *Walther Funk* (Munich, 1940), pp.80ff.; H. A. Turner, *Faschismus und Kapitalismus in Deutschland* (Göttingen, 1972), pp.23, 141.

138. Thus Bracher (note 4) p.113; E. Czichon, *Wer verhalf Hitler zur Macht?* (Cologne, 1967), p.20.

139. Printed in Feder, *Kampf,* pp.371ff.

140. Thus Schulz (note 3), p.630.

141. Bekanntmachung Strasser, 29 July 1932; Verfügung Hitler, 22 September 1932 (Verordnungsblatt (note 131), Jg. 2, pp.63, 72).

142. On the reasons which probably played a part in Wagener's resignation, see Winkler (note 129), pp. 361f.

143 Schacht to Hitler, 12 November 1932 (Czichon, note 138), p.64. The reconstruction programme had been publicly announced by Strasser on 20 October 1932 in the Berlin Sportpalast. Those business circles which were interested in the *NSDAP* had already had the impression in October 1931 that Funk, the co-author of the reconstruction programme, had little understanding of financial questions, see Czichon, p.61; see also Turner, *Faschismus* (note 137), p.141.

144. A report in *Vorwärts* (Berlin) 580, 9 December 1932 contains a summary of Feder's letter to Hitler.

145. Thus Feder to Strasser, 28 September 1931 (BA, NS 22/348), with the request to secure him this position which he had long promised him!

146. Strasser to E. Graf Reventlow, Berlin, 23 March 1932;(BDC. Personal files of Reventlow.)

147. See note 144.

148. On economic policy see A. Schweitzer, *Big Business in the Third Reich* (Bloomington, Ind., 1964); W. Birkenfeld, *Der synthetische Treibstoff 1933-1945* (Göttingen etc. 1964), pp.24f., 29. On technology see Ludwig (note 3).

I would like to sincerely thank my friends Ingrid and Jeremy Noakes for having translated this article so quickly and precisely into English.

3 'DER FALL STRASSER': GREGOR STRASSER, HITLER AND NATIONAL SOCIALISM 1930-1932

Peter D. Stachura*

The resignation of Gregor Strasser from his Party offices on
8 December 1932 caused a major sensation in Weimar political circles,[1]
and at the same time threw the NSDAP into one of the most serious
crises of its early history. Strasser, elder brother of Otto Strasser who
had already broken with Hitler in July 1930, was widely regarded as the
Führer's right-hand man,[2] and his reputation as a brilliant organiser,
polemical public speaker, and forceful personality extended far beyond
the National Socialist movement. As organisation leader of the Party
(*Reichsorganisationsleiter*) since January 1928, Strasser had been
primarily responsible for building up the NSDAP's organisational and
administrative structure into perhaps the most efficient of all German
political parties, and thus providing an indispensable ingredient
of the Party's dramatic ascent during the early 1930s. Indeed, Strasser's
overall contribution to the successful development of National
Socialism before 1933 was overshadowed only by that of Hitler
himself. The astonishment and general furore which greeted his
resignation decision bore unequivocal testimony to Strasser's
substantial political standing.

The Strasser affair, one of the numerous institutional and personal
conflicts which characterised the history of the NSDAP, has
nonetheless received comparatively perfunctory treatment in scholarly
studies of the period. Accounts of his resignation have usually been
slotted in as a tailpiece in most works, with little attempt to situate the
episode in a necessary broader historical perspective.[3] They invariably
centre on events immediately preceding Strasser's action, emphasising the
abortive endeavours of General Kurt von Schleicher to split the NSDAP
with the aid of Strasser and a putative leftist element in the Party. This

* I would like to acknowledge my gratitude to the British Academy for helping to
provide the financial support which made possible archival research in Germany
on Gregor Strasser.

approach provides only a partial and even misleading explanation. While it is undeniable that during the last six months of 1932 the NSDAP was confronted by a major dilemma over political tactics, which became crystallised in what is commonly referred to as the uncompromising 'all or nothing' school around Hitler and the much more flexible 'pro-coalition' outlook associated with Strasser, the crisis of December 1932 can be properly assessed only if we probe much deeper into the longer term development of the conflict. Equally necessary, and again something which previous studies have ignored, is a thorough investigation of Strasser himself as man and politician, and of his wider role in the National Socialist movement from at least 1930 onwards.[4] The task of penetrating beyond the rather superficial chronicles of the affair is complicated by the considerable amount of conflicting evidence on the theme, and more importantly, by the contradictions and complexities apparent in Strasser's political and ideological development between 1930 and 1932. The motives of this somewhat strange and enigmatic personality are often difficult to ascertain with precision, and this is certainly one of the principal reasons why the resignation issue has hitherto been shrouded in an unacceptably high degree of nebulosity, distortion and myth.

By adopting a wide framework of reference, this paper is concerned with elucidating the fundamental reasons for Strasser's resignation, and also with throwing some additional light on the nature of NSDAP development in late Weimar politics. In particular, it is hoped to demonstrate that Strasser was not the leader of a 'left-wing' faction in the Party as was believed at that time and as has been constantly alleged since,[5]   that in fact it may be erroneous to argue that the NSDAP possessed a recognisable left-wing or 'socialist' entity in any case by 1932. Whatever the complexion of the crisis, it is not to be understood in terms of a last stand of the 'Nazi Left' against the increasingly conservative and pro-industrialist orientation adopted by Hitler. Many socialistically inclined members naturally viewed NSDAP connections to big business with profound suspicion (though a good many of them were prepared to rationalise it on the grounds of political and tactical expediency), but if Strasser did offer an alternative to Hitler's brand of National Socialism in 1932, it was something much different from some kind of 'socialism'.[6]   This paper's final hypothesis is that Strasser must be regarded after 1930 not so much as a typical National Socialist party leader, but rather as a developing Weimar politician (*Volkspolitiker*) of progressively widening horizons and correspondingly narrowing party loyalties.

I

Gregor Strasser had quickly built up a solid image during the mid-1920s as the NSDAP's most outspoken socialist. He had been the principal organiser of the National Socialist revival in northern Germany following the unsuccessful 1923 *Putsch*, concentrating his efforts on establishing a foothold among the industrial proletariat. In contrast, the southern branch of the movement under Rosenberg, Streicher, Amann and Esser continued to stress 'bourgeois' themes including, of course, a virulent anti-semitism. The events leading to the formation of the *Arbeitsgemeinschaft* in 1925,[7] the drafting of an alternative party programme[8] and the subsequent meeting at Bamberg, all served to strengthen Strasser's leftist reputation. This was underlined during 1926-8 when he supplied the main impetus behind the Party's major appeal to the industrial working classes.

Strasser's socialism was vague, populistic, eclectic, pseudo-medievalist, and devoid of substantive content, as the emotional and demagogic flavour of his early speeches and writings seem to show.[9] He never systematically developed his concept of 'national Socialism' (*nationale Sozialismus*),[10] yet there is no denying the fervour and sincerity of his anti-capitalist and anti-bourgeois sentiments. Essentially, his socialist perceptions had more to do with the peculiarly introverted resentments of Weimar's white collar and petty bourgeois classes than with the mainstream of orthodox European and German socialist thought.[11] Nor were his ideas in any sense original. They were collated from a wide variety of diverse sources, including Spengler,[12] Rudolf Jung (the Sudeten German NS leader),[13] Gottfried Feder[14] and his brother Otto, underpinned by the early influence of his parents and his experiences as a front-line soldier in the First World War.[15] Nonetheless, at least until the 1928 *Reichstag* election Strasser was a fully committed adherent and propagator of a distinctly nationalist socialism.

The election, however, unmistakably demonstrated that the NSDAP could never hope to base its political future on the working classes and consequently the Party almost immediately afterwards underwent a fundamental reorientation in respect of propaganda, tactics, and organisation which prepared the way for its emergence as a movement supported in the main by the Protestant *Mittelstand* and peasantry.[16] Strasser could perceive the implications of the Party's lack of success in 1928. His ideological outlook was never so rigid as to be incapable of modification, or even of sweeping reassessment if necessary. Recognising that the Party's position also demanded a re-think of his own situation, Strasser could admit, albeit reluctantly, that for the NSDAP to survive politically a decisive shift in emphasis regarding ideology and propaganda would have to take place.[17] Henceforth, themes attractive to the middle classes had to be adopted. The basic transformation in character which overcame the NSDAP after 1928 was therefore paralleled by gradual but significant changes in Strasser's personal *Weltanschauung*. He could still appear on many occasions to be as much of a radical as ever, as in his widely distributed article on the politics of catastrophe in June 1929[18] or in his infamous Stuttgart speech in December 1931;[19] his numerous brushes with the legal authorities for slandering the Republic and some of its most prominent representatives conveyed a similar impression,[20] and it was the vehemence of his outbursts which earned him the description, 'Terror of the Reichstag' (*Schrecken des Reichstages*).[21] Yet after 1928 there was an insidious but nonetheless definite trend towards more and more moderation in Strasser's whole approach which came strikingly into public view in his 'New Tone' declaration in early 1929 when he called on the Party to show a more responsible and constructive attitude in dealings with political opponents.[22] A generally more measured tone is evident in a number of his other speeches and writings after 1928.[23] In this respect, the resultant ambivalence in Strasser's make-up corresponds to the uncertainty felt by many contemporary observers even until 1933 about the exact nature of the NSDAP. As he became immersed in the onerous duties of the Party organisation leader, assuming the role of an administrator therefore rather than of a rabble rouser, Strasser's 'socialism' was blunted.[24] The fact that he was physically removed from the radical-minded group at the *Kampfverlag* after 1928 when he took up residence in Munich, where he inevitably came into closer contact with Hitler and his much more conservative acolytes,[25] also helps explain Strasser's changing priorities. One practical illustration of this came in late 1929 when he agreed to act as the NSDAP's coordinator with the other right-wing organisations involved in the campaign against the Young Plan,[26] but the first really telling incident which underlined Strasser's development was Otto Strasser's secession from the Party in summer 1930.

Strasser went out of his way to disassociate himself entirely from his brother's action. Declarations of loyalty to Hitler, which he had been making at frequent intervals since 1928,[27] were forthcoming in a series of meetings and newspaper articles throughout the spring and early summer,[28] culminating in his resignation from the *Kampfverlag*[29] and his active cooperation in purging suspect elements from the Party.[30] His

genuine embarrassment and disapproval of Otto was clearly expressed
in private correspondence to a number of close friends, including
Rudolf Jung,[31]   Dr Curt Korn[32]   and Alois Bayer.[33] The reasons why
Strasser remained with Hitler are the subject of considerable
disagreement. To argue that he believed his chances of persuading Hitler
to adopt a 'socialist' course would be improved by staying in the
Party,[34]   rests on the erroneous supposition that it was Strasser's aim to
continue promoting 'socialism'. Nor is it valid to assert he had serious
misgivings about not joining Otto in opposition,[35]   while Otto's cynical
remark that Gregor was financially dependent on Hitler and hence
unable to secede cannot be taken seriously.[36]   There is also sufficient
evidence to refute the theory that the whole episode was a smokescreen
to cover a carefully planned operation by the two brothers acting
together to undermine Hitler's standing in the Party and to prepare for
the advent of a Strasserite movement at some future date.[37]   More to the
point was Gregor's alienation from Otto's ideological outlook after
1928 which indeed caused their personal relationship to deteriorate
markedly even before Otto's final confrontation with Hitler.[38]   Indeed,
during the remainder of the Weimar period, the brothers had no
personal or political contact.[39]   Gregor had become progressively
disinterested in the affairs of the *Kampfverlag* in 1929 as in the
aftermath of the 1928 election he abandoned his former objective of
constructing the NSDAP on a socialist and working-class basis.[40]   He still
believed in 1930 that Hitler was essentially genuine and open to
persuasion,[41]   so that any ideas he conceived for the Party's future could
be put across to him with a reasonable possibility of success. Believing,
perhaps too optimistically, that his standing with Hitler had not been
shaken by the affair,[42]   he was content, for the time being at least, to
remain in a party where after all he already enjoyed important status
and influence. Although he was now deprived of an effective personal
press platform, Gregor had too much to lose in 1930 by going into
opposition. The oblivion into which Otto and his 'Black Front' quickly
sank completely vindicated his judgement.

   The Otto Strasser episode revealed the severe limitations already
impinging on Gregor's socialist perspectives in 1930. Kühnl's assertion
that after this date there was no longer an effective left-wing element in
the NSDAP since the really convinced socialists withdrew either to the
Black Front or to other leftist groups, is generally valid.[43]   Some other
members, especially in northern Germany, may have remained in the
Party because Gregor did so.[44]   They could not see that his continuing
image as the spiritual leader of the NSDAP's socialists was becoming

increasingly unwarranted. But Gregor's political activity in the years following could leave no one in doubt, not even his most devoted followers, that his 'socialism', if not wholly a thing of the past, was now of a much more temperate kind and was in any case being rapidly superceded by other political considerations.

II

The most salient and intriguing feature of Strasser's political interests between 1930 and 1932 is their diversity and increasingly extra-National Socialist dimension. During this period, he constructed a veritable network of important contacts and relationships with a broad range of personalities and organisations drawn from different sections of the Weimar political spectrum. Strasser was thus able to develop, while retaining a position of authority within the Party, a growing body of opinion and support sympathetic to his ideas outside the NSDAP. By the end of 1932 this following constituted a vital calculation in Schleicher's attempt to split the NSDAP and bring Strasser and his supporters into a new government administration. The cultivation of these non-National Socialist links had simultaneously a profound effect on Strasser's political style and disposition. He abandoned the role of polemical revolutionary to become a much more moderate and cautious politician whose ultimate loyalties lay beyond the NSDAP. An anxious concern for what the political and economic crises of the early 1930s meant for Germany rather than the NSDAP in particular motivated him. Consequently, Strasser emerged for many contemporary observers as the only statesmanlike personality in the National Socialist movement.[45]

The metamorphosis in Strasser's politics, already in evidence in the Otto Strasser crisis, was significantly encouraged by his association the same year with *Oberleutnant* a.D. (retired) Paul Schulz[46] who, from the moment of joining the NSDAP in October 1930 as Strasser's deputy and Chief of Staff[47] until the crisis of December 1932, exercised a decisive and eventually tragic influence on his ideas and activities.[48] This former principal organiser of the Black *Reichswehr* and notorious *Feme* murderer had established informal links with certain high ranking National Socialists, including Strasser, during his term in prison,[49] and on his release as a result of a political amnesty in October 1930 joined the party which had been vigorously campaigning for him to be pardoned since 1928.[50] Schulz was attracted to the NSDAP on account of its ultra-nationalism and apparent preparedness to defend conservative middle-class values.[51] He had no toleration of socialism and set out with the backing of his numerous contacts with the army, civil service, and industry[52] to promote a more decidedly anti-socialist direction in the Party, and at the same time to eliminate or neutralise the influence of radical figures, among whom he counted Goebbels, Himmler and Röhm. Schulz saw his role as strengthening those within the NSDAP who favoured a moderate conservative-nationalist course, and after 1930 Strasser came very much into the reckoning as the most important anti-radical voice in the Party, his demagogic style notwithstanding. Highly capable in his own right, as shown by his successful clean-up operation in the Berlin party organisation following the Stennes revolt in spring 1931,[53] and by his instrumental role in setting up the Party's early labour service system in 1931/2,[54] Schulz very soon established a warm personal friendship and sound political understanding with Strasser, and became his indispensable intermediary to influential people outside the NSDAP. The nature of Schulz's impact, facilitated as it was by inherent changes already taking place in his chief's political conceptions since 1928, was poignantly revealed in early 1931 when what was tantamount to a volte-face in Strasser's relations with big business took place.

When the NSDAP began to attract the serious interest of some parts of industry after the September 1930 elections, it might have been expected that this growing but still limited rapprochement[55] would have caused vehement opposition from the allegedly anti-capitalist Strasser. On the contrary, he now displayed a striking propensity to cooperation which completely belied his 'socialist' reputation — a reputation which for the post-1930 period rests on a serious misinterpretation of his major pronouncements and speeches, particularly his 'anti-capitalist yearning' address in the *Reichstag* in May 1932. After 1930, in line with his mellowing ideological attitudes, Strasser was prepared to initiate a serious dialogue with industrialists, especially with regards to the mining and chemical industries in the Ruhr where Schulz had important contacts.[56] Sympathetic industrialists wanted to be certain that their donations to the NSDAP would be controlled by responsible hands[57] and August Heinrichsbauer, chief editor of the *Rhenisch-Westfälischen Wirtschaftsdienst* in Essen[58] and principal link man of Ruhr industry to the political right (as well as a friend of Schulz), states that some businessmen saw their 'responsible' man in Strasser.[59] As a result, he received from spring 1931 a monthly subvention of RM10,000 from the mining industry with the specific objective of strengthening both

himself and his 'moderate' associates in the Party, and of helping them
to advance cooperation with other acceptable right-wing circles.[60]
Strasser's 'socialism' was obviously not taken too seriously by these hard-
headed businessmen.[61]

One fairly immediate outcome of Strasser's cooperation with
industry was the appointment largely at his instigation of Walther Funk,
editor of the conservative and pro-business *Berliner Börsenzeitung*, to
the NSDAP economic department in late 1931.[62] Strasser wanted him to
act as a counterweight to the radical economic theories being propagated
by the likes of Gottfried Feder which alarmed industrialists.[63] Shortly
afterwards, Funk began to receive funds from the same industrial
sources as Strasser who incorporated many of the latter's ideas into his
major economic policy statements in 1932, and in the summer of the
same year appointed Funk his chief economic advisor.[64] At the same
time, Strasser's close friendship with Otto Wagener underlined this
increasingly cautious approach.[65] Wagener's ideas, far from being
radical as many industrialists believed, were essentially based on notions
of a corporative *Volksgemeinschaft*[66] which were similar to Strasser's
views in 1931/2.[67] Moreover, Wagener's keen interest in bringing the
trade unions into governmental responsibility coincided with Strasser's
own collaborationist attitude,[68] as will be seen later. In short,
Wagener's somewhat idiosyncratic brand of neo-conservatism fitted
well into Strasser's evolving political scenario in the early 1930s.[69]

During 1932 Strasser and the mining magnates shared a deep unease
at the growing totalitarian and inflexible character of Hitler's
policies, and funds continued to be allotted with the aim of resisting
this development. Strasser's prestige in Ruhr industrial circles resulted
in he, not Hitler, being the original choice to address the Düsseldorf
Industrieklub in January 1932,[70] and throughout 1932 Strasser
enjoyed good relations and backing from many leading industrialists
including Otto Wolff,[71] Paul Silverberg,[72] Hugo Stinnes, Dr Erich
Lübbert, Paul Reusch, Albert Vögler and Fritz Springorum.[73] At the
end of 1932 many of these industrialists actively favoured a
Schleicher-Strasser alliance,[74] in stark contrast to the efforts of
extreme right-wing circles of big business, of whom Hjalmar Schacht,
Wilhelm Keppler and Fritz Thyssen were the most prominent, to
bolster Hitler against what they persisted in regarding as the radical
Strasser wing of the NSDAP. More to the point, however, is that
his links with industry illustrate how far Strasser had travelled from

his early socialist days. He was in no way a willing tool of industry but he was clearly enlarging his political perspectives into areas where before 1930 he would never have dreamed of treading. Indeed, it is not without ironic significance that following his rift with Hitler at the end of 1932, Strasser took up a top managerial position in the large industrial chemical combine Schering-Kahlbaum of Berlin, a subsidiary of I.G. Farben.[75]

Strasser's dealings with industry have to be understood as a part of the larger field of activity within which he promoted increasing opposition to Hitler's doctrinaire course in the Party. From at least the autumn of 1931 Strasser was privately encouraging the idea of a broad government front comprising moderate conservative and patriotic elements from the whole spectrum of politics, and including the trade unions, as the best way of tackling Germany's political and economic crisis.[76] By early 1932, he was advocating the need for the NSDAP to cooperate more constructively with other parties in the *Reichstag*, adding that the party 'had to be prepared under reasonable circumstances to enter coalitions'.[77] This in fact was established as the rationale behind Strasser's politics as 1932 unfolded and involved him in negotiations, often without Hitler's knowledge,[78] with a variegated assortment of groups and personalities. Much to the fore, and providing in many respects the essential foundation for his open-ended approach, were neo-conservative elements, particularly the *Tatkreis*.

The neo-conservative élitist conceptions of Hans Zehrer's *Tatkreis* exerted a powerful influence on many middle-class intellectuals during the early 1930s,[79] but while it emerged on the one hand as a kind of high-powered debating club, it also became an energetic promoter of ostensibly unlikely political contacts, beginning shortly after the presidential elections in April 1932. Zehrer, concluding that Hitler's failure to win the Reich Presidency had dealt a shattering blow to his prospects of gaining power,[80] began to propagate vigorously the idea of a 'revolution from above' which he hoped would clear the way for the emergence of a new ruling authoritarian élite. Zehrer's revolution was to be carried through by a so-called 'Third Front' headed by the army under Schleicher, with the cooperation of Strasser who, in a much noticed article in the *Tat* journal in April 1932, fully endorsed the notion of a broad political front, the central objective of the *Tatkreis*. From this point on, Zehrer's connections with Strasser intensified.[81] Strasser's gravitation into the neo-conservative orbit reflected a point of view which was intrinsically concerned with the interests of the bourgeoisie,[82] and flowed consistently from the changing nature of his outlook after 1930. His

friendship with personalities of a broadly neo-conservative orientation
helped accelerate this development. For instance, he had a long-standing
admiration for Oswald Spengler and his ideas,[83] and for his part,
Spengler regarded Strasser as the most capable NSDAP leader of all,
and the person who offered the most promising opportunity for a
responsible brand of National Socialism. He even went so far as to
describe him, after Hugo Stinnes, as 'the cleverest fellow that I have
ever met in my life'.[84] August Winnig (1878-1956) whom Strasser
had unsuccessfully tried to bring into the NSDAP in the mid-1920s,[85]
was another acquaintance. His concept during the late Weimar era of a
corporativist Christian *Volksgemeinschaft* brought Winnig into closer
personal and ideological rapport with Strasser.[86] Within the *Tatkreis*
itself, the role of Dr Hellmuth Elbrechter in winning Strasser for the
idea of broad political collaboration was of crucial importance in 1932,
complementing as it did the endeavours of Paul Schulz in the same
direction. A former *Bezirksführer* of the NSDAP in the Ruhr during
the mid-1920s, and a dentist in Berlin by profession, Elbrechter was a
persuasive and eloquent advocate of Zehrer's ideas, as shown by his
articles in the *Tat* journal and later the *Tägliche Rundschau*,[87] and
through his close personal friendship with Strasser was able to impress
the NSDAP leader with his ideas. Even Schulz saw him as a decisive
influence on Strasser.[88] Furthermore, Elbrechter became next to
Friedrich Wilhelm von Oertzen the *Tatkreis*'s most useful contact man
to the army[89] and it was he who brought Schleicher and Strasser
together for the first time at Zehrer's Berlin home in summer 1932.[90]
At the same time, he was an important promotor of a Strasser-Brüning
liaison[91] (see later).

   Hitler's unsuccessful interview with Hindenburg on 13 August gave a
new impetus to Zehrer's efforts, and he immediately let it be known
that his primary objective was to bring about not only a Schleicher-
Strasser understanding, but more dramatically perhaps, a Strasser-trade
union alignment.[92] Both courses of action had Schleicher's approval
since the General was now convinced that Hitler's chances of the
chancellorship were negligible and that his best strategy was to win
Strasser for his plans.[93] Strasser's interest in the trade union movement
was already well-known within the NSDAP, particularly with regards to
the Factory Cell Organisation (NSBO),[94] and the *Deutschnationaler
Handlungsgehilfen-Verband* (DHV), Germany's largest right-wing
white collar association, which had had informal ideological and
personnel ties with the Party during the 1920s.[95] The connection
had been broken off by 1930/31, however, because of the DHV's

rejection of Hitler's radicalism and its subsequent involvement with moderate conservative organisations like the *Volkskonservative Vereinigung* (VKV) and the *Konservative Volkspartei* (KVP).[96] After the failure of both the latter, the DHV in search of a new political home was drawn heavily into the network of developments emanating from the *Tatkreis*, and Elbrechter, helped by Albert Krebs and Franz Stöhr, made it his business in early 1932 to bring Strasser into a serious relationship with the organisation.[97] Their efforts were reciprocated most notably from the DHV side by Max Habermann (1885-1944), a leading member of the organisation's directorate who soon became a close associate of Strasser (and Brüning).

Habermann firmly believed that Strasser represented the most constructive and amenable part of National Socialism, and it was his aim to contribute to the forging of a working relationship between Strasser and moderate, conservative christian-social groups, including the DHV, the christian trade unions and, most notably, the Centre Party. He was prompted to make his first move in that direction by the formation of the Harzburg Front in autumn 1931 which Habermann feared would result in a permanent coalition between the NSDAP and the forces of political reaction.[98] On 25 October 1931 he published a leading article in the *Deutsche Handels-Wacht* entitled, 'Brüning and Hitler', in which he argued for the establishment of a government embracing all socially progressive forces from the NSDAP to the Centre Party.[99] Strasser wrote a positive reply in an article of the same title in the *Völkischer Beobachter* on 31 October, suggesting that the NSDAP would negotiate even with the devil if it would help the German people. Habermann declared his readiness to open contacts and a meeting was held in Munich on 6 November involving Habermann and Hans Bechly of the DHV and Hitler, Hess and Strasser. The meeting amounted to little more than a tentative exchange of views which was as far as Hitler wanted to take matters anyway, but Strasser was eager to have further exchanges,[100] and in a subsequent article entitled 'Sozialreaktion? ' in the *Völkischer Beobachter* on 15/16 November, he stressed the NSDAP's attachment to socially progressive ideas. The article curiously met with Hitler's warm approval[101] because it was specifically designed as a sop to Habermann, who was now encouraged to pursue his plans openly, at least until the presidential election in spring 1932 when the DHV's support for Hindenburg inevitably led to official connections with the NSDAP being severed.[102] Links were maintained on a private and personal level between Strasser and Habermann, however, especially

after the Schleicher initiative got under way in the early autumn of
1932. Habermann played a useful supportive role in the discussions
between the General and Strasser,[103] who was keen to include the DHV
in any broadly based government that might evolve.[104]

Against the background of Strasser's increasingly complex links with
neo-conservative circles and Schleicher, one vital calculation emerged
which was a major key to making the concept of a wide government
front a feasible proposition: the blue collar trade unions had to be
involved. By the early summer of 1932 it had become Strasser's
overriding aim to reach an understanding with the unions. His
relationship with them formed in many respects the most significant
and vexatious component of his whole 'coalition' strategy of 1931-2,
while providing the critical basis for his negotiations with Schleicher.
The fact that at the same time Strasser had contact with certain
industrial parties, as we have noted, did not involve a contradiction in
relation to his own terms of reference, for it was his concern to attract
the support of all 'moderates', whatever their genesis and regardless of
their narrow spheres of professional or occupational interest, so long
as they were prepared to work for the national good. It is from this
perspective that his relationship with the trade union movement in 1931-2
is to be seen.

In his 'Sozialreaktion? ' article in November 1931 Strasser had taken
care to indicate his interest in the possibility of NSDAP cooperation with
the unions. Shortly afterwards, informal and secret talks took place on
this subject between Strasser and representatives of the Christian trade
union newspaper *Der Deutsche* which continued intermittently over
the next six months. At the end of this period both sides had indicated
willingness to establish a basis for cooperation.[105] It was also known
that Theodor Leipart (1867-1947), President of the General German
Trade Union Federation (ADGB), was alarmed by the danger posed by
extremism on the far right and left to the Republic and was prepared
therefore to talk to people like Strasser who by early 1932 could be
seen to be pursuing a cooperative course within the NSDAP.[106] The
critical breakthrough came with Strasser's 'Arbeit und Brot' speech to the
Reichstag on 10 May 1932[107] in which, much to Hitler's annoyance,[108]
he clearly held out the hand of reconciliation to the trade union
movement which, in turn, responded positively. The essential point of
contact was the agreement of both sides that urgent measures were
mandatory to deal with the twin problems of unemployment and work
creation which by this date had understandably become among the most
important political issues in Germany.[109] In his speech,[110] Strasser

endorsed the general principles of the trade union's previously
announced work creation (*Arbeitsbeschaffung*) programme,[111] put
forward a few additional points, and followed up in July by putting his
full authority behind the NSDAP's realistic emergency economic
programme (*Wirtschaftliches Sofortprogramm der NSDAP*).[112] With
the exception of how this scheme should be financed, the unions gave
their approval to it.[113] From this time onwards, contact between
Strasser and the unions increased significantly and soon involved a
host of intermediaries, including Schulz, Elbrechter, industrialists
Otto Wolff[114] and Dr Erich Lübbert, Reinhold Cordemann[115] and
conservative reformist-minded economic theorists like Heinrich
Dräger, Werner Daitz, and Dr Günther Gereke,[116] whose common aim
was to promote a Schleicher-Strasser-trade union alliance on the
principles of a moderate social conservatism. Strasser's subsequent
attitudes heavily underlined his desire to bring the unions into
governmental partnership. In a speech in Dresden on 4 September
he called for the formation of a 'Front of Arbeitsbeschaffung',[117] while
on 9 September he joined with Otto Wagener, Schleicher, and trade
union leaders Peter Grassmann and Wilhelm Eggert (the ADGB's work
creation expert) in detailed discussion about what form a broad
coalition government should take.[118] Strasser and Wagener, well
aware of the growing estrangement at this time between the ADGB
and Social Democratic Party (SPD) over a number of issues, including
work creation and contacts with the Strasserites in the NSDAP,[119]
urged the union leaders to assume their share of responsibility in
government. Strasser in particular stressed the urgent necessity of
former political enemies coming into a working partnership. The unions
had to move cautiously for obvious political reasons, of course, but
Strasser intensified his efforts to win them over. In a major speech to
the NSBO at Berlin's *Sportpalast* on 20 October he made further
conciliatory remarks about the unions and praised the sound common
sense of their work creation ideas.[120] In addition, he extended his
call for cooperation beyond the unions to groups as far to the right
as the DNVP, an appeal not lost on moderate industrial circles.[121]
'Our line is clear', said Strasser, 'National freedom and social
justice . . . Whoever wants to go along with us is welcome', and pledged
'to work together with anyone who believes in Germany, and who
wants to save Germany'. Anyone who believed after this speech that
Strasser was not working directly against the uncompromising
Machtpolitik of Hitler was guilty of a fundamental misreading of how
Weimar politics were developing in late 1932. Strasser clearly wanted

participation in government by conservative-minded but socially responsible elements drawn from a wide range of political organisations apart from the NSDAP.

Strasser's political development was naturally viewed with bitter distrust by Hitler and the extremist wing of the Party, above all, Goebbels.[122] The NSDAP could ill-afford a public disagreement, however, because of the delicate political situation it was in during the summer of 1932.[123] Although the Party had made substantial gains at the July *Reichstag* elections, a parliamentary majority still eluded it and there was a growing feeling that National Socialism had exhausted its electoral potential.[124] When Hindenburg rejected Hitler's demands for the chancellorship on 13 August a hint of desperation crept into the NSDAP ranks, and part of the immediate response, especially from those around Strasser who favoured a more flexible approach to the task of coming to power, was to press ahead in August and September for an accommodation with the Centre Party. These negotiations, which Strasser pursued more enthusiastically of course than any other NSDAP leader, constituted a further dimension of his alignment strategy, and were helped also by his personal friendship with Heinrich Brüning.[125]

The starting point of this relationship was Habermann's article in October 1931 calling on the Brüning government and NSDAP to work together and, helped considerably by Schulz who 'had the closest connections' with the chancellor,[126] the DHV leader arranged a meeting between Strasser and Brüning on 1 and 2 December 1931 at the Freiburg home of Centre Party *Reichstag* deputy, Dr Föhr – thus at approximately the same time, as we have seen, that Strasser was urging collaboration with non-NSDAP political interests. At this meeting, agreement was reached on the basis of a Centre-NSDAP government coalition, but Hitler vetoed the arrangement.[127] Political and personal links were maintained between Brüning and Strasser nonetheless, and significantly, Strasser was strongly advocating NSDAP toleration of the Brüning government as early as January 1932.[128] For his part, the chancellor expressed strong reservations about imposing a ban on the SA in spring 1932 for fear that there would be unfavourable repercussions on Strasser's standing in the Party at a time when both men were conducting secret talks on the question of forming a coalition in Prussia.[129] The relationship was further strengthened by Brüning's warm approval of Strasser's 10 May speech in the *Reichstag*, particularly those sections dealing with work creation, and his conciliatory remarks about Brüning's leadership of government.[130]

Speaking in the *Reichstag* the following day, Brüning expressed his government's 'extraordinary interest' in Strasser's speech,[131] but his dismissal from office at the end of that month thwarted this phase of his coalition discussions with Strasser until these were revived following the débâcle of 13 August.

III

Strasser was now being urged by supporters to assert his opinions more decisively within the Party, even if it meant confrontation with Hitler.[132] It was argued that after all his position in the NSDAP hierarchy had been considerably boosted by important organisational changes that summer, particularly the implementation of a reinvigorated Inspectorate system. Accordingly, Strasser arranged further meetings with Brüning during August at the last of which (30 August) other top NSDAP leaders (but not Hitler) were present.[133] The *Führer*, it soon became apparent, was not seriously interested in these talks because he felt that any kind of coalition would bring unbearable constraints on his aims, and by early September the whole scheme had floundered on his intransigence.[134] But the estrangement between Hitler and Strasser continued more markedly than ever before as the latter grew in conviction that the Party should play a constructive rather than a negatively oppositional role in Weimar politics as soon as possible.[135] Hitler sought to counter Strasser's threat by making it appear that his activities and ideas were untypical of general sentiment in the movement. Hence, in September he dissolved the Party's Economic Department which had been closely associated with Strasser, forbade further distribution of the *Sofortprogramm* (partly in response to pressure from industrial circles headed by Schacht), and in October refused to endorse Strasser's *Sportpalast* speech to the NSBO.[136] The critical showdown between Hitler and Strasser, however, came immediately after the November *Reichstag* election.

The considerable setback sustained by the NSDAP at the election came as no surprise to Strasser who had in early October predicted a loss of at least forty seats.[137] The result set the seal on his conviction that Hitler's inflexible tactics were leading the Party into a political cul-de-sac from which extrication would be virtually impossible. While Hitler deluded himself into believing that Strasser's alleged 'socialist' views had alienated middle-class voters at the election,[138] Strasser was more disposed than ever to falling in with the coalition plans being promoted by Schleicher and other interested parties. He resolved to throw his considerable organisational and political ability behind the idea of a broadly-based coalition front involving what support he could muster within the NSDAP.[139] Strasser was simply not prepared to have all his sacrifices and work for National Socialism destroyed by what he regarded as Hitler's unjustifiable political recalcitrance; he sincerely believed that he had as much right as anyone to determine the Party's future. His course of action between September and December 1932, including the act of resignation, followed on logically from the policies and attitudes which had determined his political behaviour from 1930 onwards. Strasser was offering, though not publicly, nor even explicitly, an alternative strategy for the NSDAP, and also in a qualified sense, a different brand of National Socialism than that presented by Hitler. Though accepting the main constituents of the Hitlerian *Weltanschauung*, including racism and anti-semitism,[140] the Strasserite conception of National Socialism was altogether more pliable and moderate. It was not without good reason, therefore, that the Gereke-Circle could inform Colonel von Bredow, Chief of the *Ministeramt* at the *Reichwehr* Ministry on 23 November (the same day as Hitler once again unsuccessfully demanded the chancellorship) that Strasser 'was ready to throw himself personally into the breach . . .'. Cordemann also informed Schleicher at the same time that in the Party 'an extraordinarily powerful element was on hand which would "regret" if the party once again lapsed into "fruitless opposition"', adding that 'a considerable part' of the NSDAP would be prepared to secede if this happened.[141] Subsequent political developments in November and December clearly seemed to vindicate Strasser's assessment of the NSDAP's situation, and to reassure him that if he failed to bring Hitler round to his way of thinking, he would be faced with two alternatives: to cease playing a major political role in the NSDAP, or to try to seize the initiative by leading a revolt of his followers.

The November election had produced a drastic decline in morale and cohesion in the NSDAP,[142] leading Strasser to believe in the possibility of the Party disintegrating.[143] As *Reichsorganisationsleiter* he was daily in touch with grassroots opinion and could readily perceive the widespread disenchantment with Hitler's negative opposition to the government. In industrial areas, a worrying percentage of members were resigning and going over to the KPD,[144] subscriptions to Party newspapers dropped off, secessions occurred at a local level,[145] serious rumblings of discontent surfaced in the SA,[146] and most of all, the financial position of the Party was hopeless, with debts totalling RM twelve million.[147]

Uschla was progressively tightened in an attempt to stifle frustration and tension in the movement but to little avail.[148] Political opponents freely predicted the rapid decline of National Socialism, especially in view of shattering losses sustained by the Party in a series of local elections during November in Saxony, Lübeck and Bremen-Land.[149] Accordingly, Strasser had every reason to believe that if another general election were called in the immediate future, which was not unlikely, the Party would be irrevocably destroyed. In a major speech entitled *Das Gebot der Stunde* on 14 November he reiterated his policy of doing everything possible 'to introduce the extraordinary strong, constructive, sacrificial and energetic powers of National Socialism into government', even if it meant cooperating with the DNVP.[150] Strasser by this time was in despair over what he thought had become of the NSDAP under Hitler. Not only the sterile oppositional tactics, but the increasing violence of the SA which Hitler encouraged (the notorious Potempa incident was only one example) repelled him,[151] as did the widely publicised exploits of the homosexual circle around Röhm. An important part of Strasser's anti-Hitler psychosis in November/December 1932 was his genuine fear of the calamitous implications for the future of Germany which National Socialism under the *Führer* signified.[152]

At the same time in November, Strasser felt his position directly vis-à-vis Hitler was becoming distinctly less favourable. Since the election he had been excluded more and more from Hitler's inner circle of advisers while the influence of rivals (and enemies) such as Goebbels and Göring was increasing, and although he continued to issue public declarations of loyalty to the Führer,[153] he often expressed quite the opposite in private. From the beginning of his political career, Strasser had insisted on being regarded as a colleague (*Mitarbeiter*) and not a subordinate follower (*Gefolgsmann*) of Hitler.[154] He never unconditionally identified Hitler with National Socialism, stressing that the leader and idea of the movement were separate and distinct, and if necessary the latter should have preeminence.[155] He never employed the greeting, *Heil Hitler*, which to his horror his close friend Konstantin Hierl had introduced into the Party at the time of the Stennes Revolt, nor did he use the form *Mein Führer*, preferring *Der Chef*.[156] Hence, Strasser never openly acknowledged the pseudo-religious Führer Myth, and his independence of mind had always set him apart from the vast majority of sycophantic NSDAP leaders. When he had misgivings about Hitler's policies he was not afraid of voicing them, though by being a continuous thorn in Hitler's side, their personal relationship always had an essential element of instability and tension which was exacerbated by Hitler's apparent jealousy of the highly capable Bavarian.[157] By December 1932, Strasser's alienation from Hitler had reached a critical juncture and was accentuated during the first week of that month when Göring replaced him as Hitler's nominee for the post of Prussian Minister of the Interior.[158] By then, Strasser had no further illusions concerning his standing with Hitler, as he revealingly confided to Party lawyer Hans Frank.[159]

Not to be dismissed in this situation is the question of Strasser's personal ambition, an indefinable and elusive factor which perhaps has been too readily discounted by most historians. Only a handful of contemporary observers like Goebbels,[160] Hans Frank,[161] Konrad Heiden,[162] and Kurt Ludecke[163] noted the ambitious streak in Strasser's political make-up. He had been to the fore so frequently and over so many important issues during his Party career, and taken so many fundamental initiatives that it seems only reasonable to pinpoint ambition — an ambition which stretched to the highest level of the Party — as a primary motive force behind his rise to the political limelight. Coupled with his vital disagreements with Hitler by the end of 1932, it would appear more likely than not that he would not have been averse to taking over the leadership of the NSDAP. After all, Strasser had always been a natural leader of men, as shown by his distinguished army record in 1914-18,[164] his prominence in the Bavarian paramilitary and SA organisations in 1920-23,[165] his contribution to the reconstruction of the NSDAP in northern Germany 1924-6, and his subsequent role as Party organiser, ideologue and propagandist. In any case, by December 1932, convinced as he was of the NSDAP's imminent decline, Strasser took seriously Schleicher's offer of governmental participation in the form of the vice-chancellorship and the Minister-Presidency of Prussia. The prospect of cabinet office appealed not only to his political wisdom, but also to his personal ambition.

The so-called Strasser wing of the NSDAP was the key to the success of Schleicher's plans to construct an administration composed of disparate 'socially progressive' elements, and Strasser had informed the General of his willingness to act independently if Hitler continued to refuse cooperation.[166] At a top level Party meeting in Weimar on 30 November Hitler did reaffirm his negative attitude to the idea of a Schleicher cabinet. On hearing of this, Schleicher despatched *Oberstleutnant* Ott to Hitler on 1 December ostensibly to make the *Führer* a final offer of cabinet posts [167] but in fact to use his intransigence, which Schleicher could have no reason to believe would be modified at this late hour, as final and conclusive evidence to convince Strasser and Hindenburg that the only way out of the political crisis was to entrust him with the chancellorship from where he could implement his 'split the NSDAP' strategy. This hypothesis is supported by the fact that on the very same day as Ott's visit to Hitler, Schleicher was doing his utmost to convince Hindenburg and Papen of the soundness of the plan, and he finally succeeded. Hindenburg agreed to appoint Schleicher chancellor largely on the understanding that Strasser could be brought into the cabinet as a stabilising factor. Despite warnings from Papen, Schacht and Otto Braun that his quest to split the NSDAP had no hope of success,[168] Schleicher approached Strasser with a formal offer of the vice-chancellorship and the Minister-Presidency of Prussia at a secret meeting in Berlin on 3 December. Strasser's eagerness to accept could only have been sharpened when on the following day in local elections (*Gemeindewahlen*) in Thuringia, long regarded as a leading bastion of the NSDAP, the Party suffered a shattering reverse.[169] Strasser's pessimism about the Party's future once again appeared fully justified. More importantly, at this point in time Schleicher's aims coincided exactly with Strasser's. There can be no question of the General deviously using Strasser for his own selfish ends, or using him specifically as an indirect threat to bring Hitler round to a compromise position.[170] Both men realised the decisive moment for governmental cooperation had arrived. For Strasser, this was the logical climax to all he had been striving for during the last few years. He and Schleicher knew what they wanted from each other, both were aware what was involved, and both were equally sensitive to the consequences of failure.

At a specially convened meeting of Party leaders in Berlin's Kaiserhof hotel on 5 December, Hitler, who probably did not know yet of Schleicher's specific offer to Strasser, brusquely reaffirmed his all-or-nothing policy and forbade Strasser from having any further talks with the General on behalf of the NSDAP.[171] The meeting therefore brought into unequivocal perspective the nature of the Hitler-Strasser conflict and the contrasting alternatives over policy and tactics being pursued by both. Strasser now had to decide what his future course of action should be. There were a number of possibilities. Firstly, he could accept Hitler's policy, sever his connections with Schleicher and other pro-coalitionist elements outside the NSDAP, and repudiate therefore all that he had been working for since about 1930/31; secondly, he could publicly demonstrate his disapproval of Hitler by leading a Party revolt against him; lastly, he could adhere to his principles but avoid an open confrontation with Hitler by withdrawing from the NSDAP hierarchy and from active politics altogether.

The first course was inconceivable. Strasser had gone too far in his opposition to attempt a humiliating volte-face against his better judgement. The second alternative was much more problematical. Strasser would have to decide whether he had the necessary support in the movement to lead a successful palace revolution. This raises an important question: was there a 'Strasser faction' or a 'Strasser wing' in the NSDAP, as numerous historians have suggested? Was Strasser the leader of a 'socialist' or 'left-wing' stream in the NSDAP which would form the basis of any projected revolt?

There can be little doubt that by 1932 Strasser had made such a favourable impression on a relatively significant number of Party members that they might legitimately be regarded as Strasser sympathisers. But apart from his closest advisers such as Schulz and Alexander Glaser, his Chief of Staff (*Hauptstabsleiter der Reichsorganisationsleitung*),[172] Strasser faced the difficulty of not knowing with absolute certainty how far this sympathy stretched, whether in fact his supporters would be prepared to follow actively him against Hitler − if that had been his intention. In December 1932, Strasser was still widely but unjustifiably regarded as the leader of that nebulous entity, the 'Nazi Left'.[173] His 'socialism' of the 1920s gave him a reputation as a revolutionary which was hard to lose in the popular mind. Prominent among his supporters in this category were those who had joined the NSDAP from the *Deutschvölkischer Freiheitspartei* (DVFP) in 1927 because they were attracted by the Strasserite concept of a nationalist socialism:[174] Franz Stöhr, Wilhelm Kube [175] and Count Ernst zu Reventlow.[176] At least until 1933 there existed a basic mutual distrust, even antipathy, between these three and Hitler, particularly Reventlow and Hitler.[177] The former's radical *Reichswart* publication was a constant irritation to the *Führer* as he sought right-wing support in 1930-32.[178]

The general public and most Party members could hardly have perceived how fundamentally Strasser's ideological attitudes had been changing as he became less and less a 'socialist' and more of what might be termed a social conservative. For this reason, his stock in 1932 remained high among both working class NSDAP voters[179] and largely working class sections of the National Socialist movement, particularly in the Hitler Youth and NSBO.[180] Leading NSBO officials like Reinhold Muchow, Walter Schuhmann, Ludwig Brückner and Otto Krüger were

Strasser men,[181] and by December 1932 their support could have been especially valuable in view of the organisation's substantial increase in size, and its strengthened position within the movement's organisational structure following Strasser's spate of reforms in mid-1932.[182] The NSBO was allowed direct access to Party funds for the first time, and its new status was reflected in the presence of eleven of its officials in the 230-strong NSDAP *Reichstag* faction after the July 1932 election.[183] Robert Ley later exaggerated when he said that Strasser had specifically built up the NSBO as his personal army (*Hausmacht*), but it is clear in which direction the organisation's propensities lay.[184]

Although the 'proletarian' SA was showing unmistakable signs of deep unrest at the end of 1932,[185] including outright revolt in some areas,[186] the main cause was traditional SA-NSDAP antagonism and local personal rivalries. Hence, any serious SA support for Strasser is extremely doubtful, even in industrial areas such as the Ruhr.[187] After all, the SA had always been loath to become involved in intra-party disputes, and moreover, there was a long standing personal and political enmity between Strasser and Röhm which in 1931/32 reached the point where Strasser was trying hard to have the SA Chief of Staff dismissed from the movement altogether.[188] In December 1932, therefore, the SA remained a factor of support for Hitler.[189]

Within the NSDAP itself, pockets of at least potential support for Strasser are identifiable. His position as *Reichsorganisationsleiter* enabled him to build up an organisation and leadership much to his own liking, especially in northern Germany. Strasser took on personnel whom he believed could be trusted and a large number of organisational leaders identified with him.[190] Into this category came Otto Wagener, Walther Funk and Konstantin Hierl,[191] and a number of *Gauleiter*, many of whom had been associated with Strasser in the north during the mid-1920s. These included Karl Kaufmann, Josef Terboven, Josef Wagner (Westphalia), Bernhard Rust, Karl Röver, Erich Koch, Hinrich Lohse, Helmut Brückner (Silesia), Wilhelm Murr, Josef Bürckel, Rudolf Jordan, Friedrich Hildebrandt and Dr Erich Schlange (Brandenburg).[192] Strasser was on friendly (and often *Du*) terms with all of them. Also to be regarded as pro-Strasser are most of the team of *Landesinspekteure* appointed by him in 1932 as a kind of high-powered watchdog of the Party organisation.[193] Some other *Gauleiter,* such as Otto Erbersdobler of Lower Bavaria, resented not being included in the scheme and in consequence were probably alienated from Strasser.[194]

Strasser's principal source of support lay, however, in the NSDAP

Reichstag faction where as many as one third of the deputies inclined to his position.[195]   At a specially convened meeting on 7 December, these deputies agreed to follow Strasser if he gave the signal.[196]   This may also have applied to a certain number of top Party leaders who had individually declared support for Strasser's pro-coalition policy: Wilhelm Frick, who had been closely involved in Strasser's discussions with non-NSDAP groups during 1931-2;[197] Gottfried Feder, who endorsed Strasser's view of the Party's gloomy future,[198] as did, more surprisingly, Alfred Rosenberg[199] and Walter Buch, head of *Uschla* (*Oberster Parteirichter*).[200]

It would be quite wrong to contend that the aforementioned sources constituted a Strasserite faction within the NSDAP. These elements were too variegated and diverse, ranging from 'socialists' to conservative economists, to be described as anything other than a loose assortment of support. Furthermore, they can in no way be seen as being the 'Nazi Left' in either an organisational or ideological sense. Consequently, although the extremely serious position of the NSDAP in December 1932 is not to be underestimated, the unorganised and incohesive nature of Strasser's support removed any real possibility of his being able to split the Party had he so desired.[201] The threat to the NSDAP at this time was admittedly more concrete and of a different kind than in 1924, 1926 or 1930, but it could be ultimately contained within the structure of a totalitarian party based on the *Führerprinzip* and Hitler's charismatic leadership. On the mundane practical level, the *Führer*'s control of the Party's press and propaganda network, the SA and SS, and the solid support of leading figures such as Goebbels, Göring and Röhm, militated decisively against a successful Strasser initiative. It still remained to be seen, however, what action, if any, Strasser would take following his final and acrimonious confrontation with Hitler in the Kaiserhof hotel on 7 December.[202] Hitler, who by this date had got to know of Schleicher's formal offer to Strasser on 3 December, remained totally unshaken in his determination to pursue his quest for the chancellorship and nothing less. A break of some kind between the two men became unavoidable. But would Strasser on a point of principle take his long-standing opposition to Hitler to its logical conclusion by calling on his supporters to leave the NSDAP with him?

IV

Based on a careful scrutiny of what lay before him, especially the power situation in the Party, Strasser was constrained to sacrifice principle and defy the logic of the political crisis his activities since 1930 had

produced. He made no declaration to his followers,[203] no dramatic
statement to the press, and no appeal to Hitler. Emphasising the
personal nature of his decision, he simply withdrew to his room at
the Hotel Exzelsior in Berlin where he wrote out his letter of
resignation which was delivered to Hitler at noon on 8 December.[204]

This famous letter, which is now published for the first time,[205]
tells only in part and then only in bare outline why Strasser was
resigning his Party posts. The letter does not even refer to his extensive
dealings with other non-NSDAP political elements in 1930-32 which
lay at the heart of his disillusionment with Hitler, nor does he indicate
the rather different interpretation of National Socialism he offered.
Instead, Strasser indicates in a tone of hurt pride and self-justification
his inability to accept an intolerable degree of organisational disarray
in the movement, particularly regarding the attitude of Hitler himself
to his organisational methods. More importantly, Strasser criticises
the Party's selfish approach to winning power which is 'not in the
interests of Germany', and reiterates his basic theme of bringing
together creative and constructive people in one large, broad front
for the purpose of governing the country. Strasser's protestation that
he remained and would always remain a National Socialist is ironical
in view of his emphatic rejection of Hitlerian National Socialism,
while his allusion to Hitler's present advisers underlines his feeling of
alienation in the top ranks of the Party.

Strasser added to his explanation in later correspondence with his
friend Dr Curt Korn of Hamburg:[206]

> You can be assured that I took my decision only after mature
> deliberation and with a full sense of responsibility once my
> endeavours to carry through a necessary clearing operation
> (*Reinigungsaktion*) in the Party had failed, and also once my view
> that we had to participate in the running of the state and to appeal
> to the people with deeds rather than words had been utterly
> rejected ... I want to promote the coming together of all
> constructive-minded people, no matter where they come from, on the
> basis of new ideas in government, the economy and the cultural
> sphere. I am convinced that the time of agitation and of parties is
> fast disappearing and that the immediate future calls for men who are
> prepared to come into government with courage and a sense of
> responsibility, who amidst the most difficult personal and objective
> circumstances attempt to finally draw conclusions from an
> understanding of the present time, and achieve results.

Strasser obviously had himself in mind here and his steadfastness in the belief that his decision was correct is rather striking. Having made that decision in December 1932, Strasser left Berlin for Munich and then to Italy on holiday, thus effectively withdrawing from politics for good and leaving behind a Party which frantically tried to grasp the implications of his action.[207]

Strasser's insistence on making hsi resignation a purely personal matter followed on, as we have seen, from his realistic appraisal of the power situation in the NSDAP. But it is also possible to supplement this fundamental explanation with reference to a number of political and character weaknesses which at the critical moment let him down. It was not that he was too idealistic, honest or good-natured;[208] he had plenty of determination, independence of mind, energy and even ruthlessness. Nor is it fair to suggest Strasser was a poor politician[209] because his whole understanding of Weimar politics during the early 1930s was founded on a considerable and sensitive skill. But unlike Hitler, essentially a politician of instinct and intuition who was not afraid of a gamble, Strasser was to his own detriment too much of a *Realpolitiker* who could not move very far without knowing exactly what lay ahead. In addition, and very necessary to an understanding of Strasser the man in December 1932, was his complex and tortuous relationship with Hitler. Despite the differences in their respective political outlooks by 1932, Strasser continued to harbour a perverse personal loyalty of sorts to Hitler which may only be intrinsically explicable by what Karl Paetel has called Strasser's 'curious Paladin-complex' (*merkwürdigen Paladin-Komplex*).[210] It froze Strasser against his better judgement into meek submission at Bamberg in 1926, and contributed psychologically to his inability to make the final challenge in December 1932. The irony is that while Strasser had consistently and overtly repudiated the quasi-mystical leader-cult around Hitler, it would appear that for all his assertiveness and bluffness the innately sensitive Strasser really was captivated by Hitler's charismatic personality. He thus became the most unsuspecting victim of the *Führer Myth*.

The manner in which Strasser made his resignation meant that the crisis in the NSDAP effectively ended almost as soon as it had come publicly to a head. An editorial by Hans Zehrer in the *Tägliche Rundschau* on 11 December tried to project Strasser as about to take over the Party but this was clearly a rather clumsy piece of speculative optimism.[211] Equally clumsy, and quite unappreciated by Strasser, were Otto Strasser's efforts to use the affair for his own political ends.

For his pains, he received a sharply worded letter from Gregor on
31 December 1932 in which he disparaged the Black Front and
exhorted Otto to 'leave me out of your game in 1933!'[212] More
relevant, was that with Strasser out of the way and his followers
without guidance, it was relatively easy for Hitler to regain his
composure and to turn the situation to his advantage by rallying
support from all sections of the movement. He did so with that
consummate blend of pathos, cunning and unscrupulousness which had
served him so admirably in previous times of Party crisis. Emotional
meetings during the following weeks with Party officials all over
Germany, especially in areas where Strasser's influence was thought
to have been important, brought forth a stream of declarations of
unconditional loyalty to Hitler.[213] Many of Strasser's 'friends' were
among those joining the ritual.[214] His major creation, the organisational
apparatus, was thoroughly remodelled[215] and purged of suspected
Strasserites, including personnel regarded as being 'left wing'.[216] Close
advisers to Strasser, such as Schulz, Glaser, and his private secretary
(and brother-in-law) Rudolf Vollmuth, were the first to go.[217] At the
same time, the numbers seceding or resigning from the movement in
sympathy with Strasser were insignificant.[218] Consequently, his enemies
had no difficulty in denouncing him as a traitor to the Party,[219] a
stigma which made Strasser a compromising figure in NSDAP circles
until his murder in 1934.[220] More immediately, he became the popular
scapegoat for all the failures sustained by the Party during the preceding
months.[221]

Strasser's departure from the scene dealt Schleicher's political plans a
mortal blow despite the General's belief, which persisted until mid-
January 1933, that Strasser could still be brought into government. At a
cabinet meeting on 16 January 1933 he talked of constructing an
administration comprising Strasser, Hugenberg, Seldte (*Stahlhelm*) and
Stegerwald (christian trade unions).[222] It was also rumoured that he was
to promote a Strasser-led *Soziale Nationalpartei* to contest the next
general election,[223] and only when Schleicher had failed to realise any
of these plans by the time the *Reichstag* reassembled on 24 January did
he realise that Strasser, in the words of Goebbels, was politically 'a dead
man'.[224] The flurry of activity throughout January, involving meetings
and interviews between a tired and disillusioned Strasser and Schleicher,
and Strasser and Hindenburg, had an air of unreality about them, and
must be seen as little more than a tawdry epilogue to the
December 1932 crisis in the NSDAP. The expanding vacuum in
government which ensued allowed Papen to seize the political

initiative from Schleicher and bring Hitler into contact with big business interests. Industrialists who had watched the Schleicher-Strasser dialogue with deep alarm[225] were finally convinced by the latter's resignation that 'socialism' in the NSDAP had been eliminated, and thus felt more confident about lending support to a conservative NSDAP-Nationalist coalition government.[226] Simultaneously, the failure of the trade unions to commit themselves positively to Schleicher's overtures — largely through their innate distrust of him and also through pressure from the SPD[227] — and the NSDAP resurgence that was evident at the Lippe-Detmold state election on 15 January 1933,[228] put the final nails in the General's attempt to keep Hitler from power. At a meeting of *Gauleiters* in Weimar on 16 January, Hitler demonstrated that his old confidence had returned and that the Strasser crisis had been fully overcome.[229]

The undisputed beneficiary of the Strasser crisis was, of course, Adolf Hitler. Not only had he rid himself at long last of his most capable and dangerous rival in the Party (*der gross Gegenspieler*),[230] but also paradoxically, it was Strasser who, having set out to prevent Hitler and his brand of National Socialism from coming to power, merely succeeded in accelerating the chain of events that led to the Führer's appointment as Reich Chancellor. The major losers were naturally Strasser himself, but more importantly, Germany.

Appendix: Gregor Strasser's Letter of Resignation, 8 December 1932.*

Gregor Strasser   den 8. Dezember 1932

Herrn
Adolf Hitler
z.Zt. Berlin
Hotel Kaiserhof.

Sehr geehrter Herr Hitler!

Mit diesem Schreiben bitte ich Sie zur Kenntnis zu nehmen, dass ich mein Amt als Reichsorganisationsleiter der Partei niederlegt und gleichzeitig meinen Verzicht auf mein Reichstagsmandat aussprechen werde.
Zur Begründung dieses von mir nach schweren inneren Kämpfen unternommenen Schrittes führe ich folgendes an:

Es ist mir unmöglich, in einer Zeit, die infolge der politischen
Verhältnisse und des inneren Zustandes der Bewegung straffste
autoritative Führung zur allergrössten Notwendigkeit macht, die
Organisationsarbeiten durchzuführen, wenn der Führer der Bewegung die
von ihm unterzeichneten Anordnungen den wenigen die erhöhte
Kontrolle mit Recht führenden Gauleitern gegenüber heruntersetzt und
sabotiert und dadurch diese Gauleiter, die durchweg zu den schlechtesten
Verwaltern ihres Amtes gehören, zur offenen Meuterei auffordert. Das
ist für mein soldatisches Denken unerträglich. Nachdem Sie auch dritten
gegenüber die von mir durchgeführte Neu-Organisation der Partei als
prinzipiell falsch bezeichnen, ist meine organisatorische Aufgabe
unlösbar geworden und ich ziehe daraus die Konsequenzen.
Ich glaube, dass kein Redner der Partei ausser Ihnen so stark die
weltanschaulichen Fragen des Nationalsozialismus in den Vordergrund
gerückt hat wie ich.
Darum habe ich das Recht zu sagen, dass die NSDAP nach meiner
Auffassung nicht nur eine zur Religion werdende Weltanschauungs-
bewegung ist, sondern eine Kampfbewegung, die die Macht im Staate in
jeder Möglichkeit anstreben muss, um den Staat zur Erfüllung seiner
nationalsozialistischen Aufgaben und zur Durchführung des deutschen
Sozialismus in allen seinen Konsequenzen fähig zu machen.
    Die brachiale Auseinandersetzung mit dem Marxismus kann und
darf nicht – dem Einzelnen überlassen – in dem Mittelpunkt der
innerpolitischen Aufgabe stehen, sondern ich sehe es als das grosse
Problem dieser Zeit an, eine grosse breite Front der schaffenden
Menschen zu bilden und sie an den neugeformten Staat heranzubringen.
Die alleinige Hoffnung auf das Chaos als das Schicksals-stunde der
Partei halte ich für falsch, gefährlich und nicht im gesamtdeutschen
Interesseliegend. In allen diesen Fragen ist ihre entscheidende
Meinung eine andere und damit ist meine politische Aufgabe als
Abgeordneter und Redner der Partei unlösbar geworden und ich ziehe
daraus die Konsequenzen.
Ich war in meinem Leben nichts anderes als Nationalsozialist und werde
es nie anders sein; darum trete ich – ohne Rücksicht auf meine Person
und ohne persönlichen Groll – in die Reihe der einfachen Parteigenossen

* Printed in Paul Schulz: Rettungen und Hilfeleistungen an Verfolgten
1933-1945 durch Oberleutnant a.D. Paul Schulz, pp. 9-11. Available in
Bundesarchiv Library, reference BIP Paul Schulz, Nr.2.

zurück und mache den Platz frei für die Ratgeber, welche Sie zur Zeit
mit Erfolg zu beraten in der Lage sind.

Dieser mein Entschluss ist der schwerste meines Lebens; denn ich habe
der Bewegung und Ihnen 11 Jahre lang treu gedient.

Da ich unter allen Umständen ablehne, irgendwie der Mittelpunkt von
Oppositions-bestrebungen oder auch nur Erörterungen solcher Art zu
werden, verlasse ich heute noch Berlin und anschliessend für längere
Zeit Deutschland.

Als meinen Nachfolger schlage ich pflichtgemäss den früheren Leiter
der Organisationsabteilung II Herrn Oberst Hierl vor.

Von diesem Brief erhalten nur Sie Kenntnis. An die Presse werde ich
keine irgendwie gearteten Erklärungen meines Schrittes geben.

    Mit deutschem Gruss

                                    stets Ihr ergebener,
                                    gez: Gregor Strasser

Gregor Strasser   8 December 1932

Mr Adolf Hitler,
at present, Berlin,
Hotel Kaiserhof

Dear Mr Hitler,

I would ask you to take note with this letter that I am resigning my
post as Reich Organisation Leader of the Party, and at the same time
declaring my resignation of my parliamentary seat.

As for the reasons behind this step, which I have taken only after
painful inner conflict, I would state as follows:

In a period when, as a result of the political situation and the internal
condition of the Movement, the strictest authoritative leadership is
absolutely necessary, it is impossible for me to carry out organisational
work when the Leader of the Movement curtails and sabotages
regulations, which he himself has signed, concerning those few
Gauleiters who are empowered to undertake additional supervisory
responsibilities. These belong in any event to the worst administrators
of their office and are thereby provoked into outright mutiny.

According to my soldiery way of thinking, that is insupportable. Since
you have also described the reorganisation of the Party carried out by
me as mistaken in principle to third parties, my organisational task has

become unresolvable, and I am drawing the necessary conclusions from
this.

I believe that no other Party spokesman, except yourself, has pressed
the ideological questions of National Socialism into the foreground as
strongly as I have.

I have therefore the right to say that, in my opinion, the NSDAP is not
only an ideological movement which is developing into a religion, but
also a fighting movement which must strive for power in the state at
every opportunity so as to enable the state to fulfil its National
Socialist tasks and to realise German Socialism in all its facets.

The brutal confrontation with Marxism can and may not — left
to individuals — stand at the centre of the internal political task; rather,
I see the great problem of this age as the creation of a great, broad front
of constructive people and their integration into the new-styled state.
The single-minded hope that chaos will produce the Party's hour of
destiny is, I believe, erroneous, dangerous, and not in the interests of
Germany as a whole. In all of these matters your fundamental view is
different from mine, and hence my political task as a member of
parliament and Party spokesman is rendered untenable, and I am
drawing the necessary conclusions from this.

During my life I have been nothing other than a National Socialist and
will never be anything else; I am therefore returning — without regard
for my personal interests and without personal rancour — to the ranks
of ordinary Party members, thus making room for the advisers who are
at present in a position of being able to advise you.

This decision of mine is the most difficult of my life; after all, I have
loyally served the Movement and yourself for eleven years.

As I refuse under all circumstances to become the focal point of
oppositional endeavours or conflicts of such kind, I am leaving Berlin
today and subsequently leaving Germany for a considerable period.

In accordance with my duty, I nominate the former Head of
Organisation Department II, Colonel Hierl, as my successor.

Only you are receiving a copy of this letter. I shall make no statement
of any kind to the press about my decision.

With German Greeting,

Constantly yours truly,
Gregor Strasser

Notes

1.   See the extensive collection of press comments and reports in
      Bundesarchiv (BA), Nachlass Gottfried Zarnow, Nr.44.
2.   Institut fürZeitgeschichte (IfZ): Zeugenschrift (ZS) 265, Hinrich
      Lohse, *Der Fall Strasser* , p.26.
3.   Among the works which have to a limited extent broken away from
      this general rule and which allude to earlier phases of Strasser's career
      are: K.D. Bracher, *Die Auflösung der Weimarer Republik. Eine Studie
      zum Problem des Machtverfalls in der Demokratie* (Stuttgart, 1957),
      pp. 108-16, 362 ff, 376-7, 507-8, 663-705; H. Bruening, *Memoiren
      1918-1934* (Stuttgart, 1972 edn), pp. 488-9, 600-3, 657-9, 675-9;
      A. Bullock, *Hitler. A Study in Tyranny* (rev. edn. London, 1965),
      pp. 135-7, 171-3, 235-40, 245-6; H. Frank, *Im Angesicht des Galgens.
      Deutung Hitlers und seiner Zeit auf Grund eigener Erlebnisse und
      Erkenntnisse* (Munich, Gräfelfing, 1953), pp. 107-9; W. Horn,
      Führerideologie und Parteiorganisation in der NSDAP (1919-1933),
      (Düsseldorf 1972), pp. 358-60, 367-74; R. Jordan, *Erlebt und Erlitten.
      Weg eines Gauleiters von München bis Moskau* (Leoni am Starnberger
      See, 1971), pp. 66-83, 89-96; M.H. Kele, *Nazis And Workers. National
      Socialist Appeals to German Labor, 1919-1933* (Chapel Hill, 1972),
      pp. 169-76, 192-5; A. Krebs, *Tendenzen und Gestalten der NSDAP.
      Erinnerungen an die Frühzeit der Partei* (Stuttgart, 1959), pp. 32-7,
      72-3, 182-93; S. Lang & E. von Schenck, *Portrait eines
      Menschheitsverbrechers. Nach den hinterlassenen Memoiren des
      ehemaligen Reichsministers, Alfred Rosenberg* (St. Gallen, 1947),
      pp. 158-63; H.O. Meissner & H. Wilde, *Die Machtergreifung. Ein Bericht
      über die Technik des Nationalsozialistischen Staatsstreichs* (Stuttgart,
      1958), pp. 94-8, 135-45, 149-52; O. Meissner, *Staatssekretär Unter
      Ebert-Hindenburg-Hitler. Der Schicksalsweg des deutschen Volkes von
      1918-1945 wie ich ihn erlebte* (Hamburg, 1950), pp. 251-3, 360-6;
      J. Nyomarkay, *Charisma and Factionalism in the Nazi Party*
      (Minneapolis, 1967), pp. 102-9; D. Orlow, *The History of the Nazi
      Party: 1919-1933* (Pittsburgh, 1969), pp. 254-60, 268-75, 278-98;
      G. Schulz, *Aufstieg des Nationalsozialismus. Krise und Revolution in
      Deutschland* (Berlin, 1975), pp. 387-9; see last chapter, 'Strasser oder
      Hitler?'; A. Tyrell: *Führer befiehl . . . Selbstzeugnisse aus der
      'Kampfzeit' der NSDAP* (Düsseldorf, 1969), pp. 312-17, 323-6,
      329-33, 342-9; T. Vogelsang, *Reichswehr, Staat und NSDAP. Beiträge
      zur deutschen Geschichte 1930-1932* (Stuttgart 1962) pp. 269-76,
      340-2. In a different category are to be placed the often tendentious
      and unreliable accounts provided by Otto Strasser, such as *Hitler and I*
      (London, 1940), pp. 131-3, 149 ff; *Mein Kampf. Eine politische
      Autobiographie* (Frankfurt, 1969), pp. 38-9, 75-82, 90-2; *History in
      My Time* (London, 1941), pp. 239-43; *Exil* (Munich, 1958), pp. 63-6,
      72-4; and *30. Juni, Vorgeschichte, Verlauf, Folgen* (Prague, n.d.),
      p. 4 ff. Another brother, Bernhard, has written a brief account (heavily
      influenced by Otto's writings) entitled: *Gregor und Otto Strasser.
      Kurze Darstellung ihrer Persönlichkeit und ihres Wollens* (Külheim,
      1954), pp. 4-12.
4.   The following doctoral dissertations have been completed: J.M. Dixon,
      Gregor Strasser and the Organisation of the Nazi Party, 1925-32
      (Stanford, 1966). This is based on extremely limited primary sources
      and offers at best rather pedestrian interpretations of Strasser's activity;

U. Kissenkötter, *Gregor Strasser in der Spätphase der Weimarer Republik* (Cologne, 1974). Based on massive but largely undigested documentation: U. Wörtz, *Programmatik und Führerprinzip. Das Problem des Strasser-Kreises in der NSDAP* (Erlangen, 1966). More useful than Dixon's work, it is based on wider research and has more challenging viewpoints, but succeeds in only partly explaining Strasser. Additionally, there are two unimportant biographies written before his death in 1934: H. Diebow, *Gregor Strasser und Der Nationalsozialismus* (Berlin,1932/33) – a 65 page simplistic panegyric designed for popular consumption; and M. Geismaier (alias Otto Strasser!), *Gregor Strasser* (Leipzig, 1933), 95 pages of uncritical narrative.

5. The Berlin police were convinced in a report of 22 July 1932 that he was indeed the 'leader of the socialist wing in the NSDAP' (BA, NS26: Hauptarchiv der NSDAP:/1370). Konrad Heiden, *Geburt des dritten Reiches. Geschichte des Nationalsozialismus bis Herbst 1933* (Zurich, 1934), p. 88 calls him 'the intellectual High Priest of the social wing of the NSDAP', while in *Entstehung und Geschichte der Weimarer Republik* (Frankfurt, 1955), A. Rosenberg saw the Strassers together as constituting a 'determinate socialist left-wing' of the Party (p. 476). Kele, op.cit. pp. 173-6, argues that Goebbels was the leading socialist in the Party 1928-33.

6. O.E. Schüddekopf, *Linke Leute von Rechts. Die nationalrevolutionären Minderheiten und der Kommunismus in der Weimarer Republik* (Stuttgart, 1960), p. 380, depicts December 1932 as representing the final victory of the anti-semitic 'Munich' wing over the 'socialist' concept. For a counter-argument see B. Millar Lane, 'Nazi Ideology: Some Unfinished Business', *Central European History*, VII, 1974, p.19.

7. See G. Schildt, *Die Arbeitsgemeinschaft Nordwest* (Dissertation, Freiburg, 1964); Wörtz, op. cit. p. 80 ff.

8. cf. R. Kühnl, 'Zur Programmatik der Nationalsozialistischen Linken: Das Strasser-Programm von 1925/26', in *Vierteljahrshefte für Zeitgeschichte*, 14 (1966), 317-33.

9. Many are collected in G. Strasser, *Kampf um Deutschland. Reden und Aufsätze eines Nationalsozialisten* (Munich, 1932), esp. p. 130 144 ff; G. Strasser, *Freiheit und Brot* (Berlin, 1928), 2 vols.; G. Strasser, *Hammer und Schwert* (Berlin, 1929). Reference should also be made to *NS-Briefe, Berliner Arbeiterzeitung* and *Der Nationale Sozialist*.

10. As illustrated, for example, by his discussion with Rosenberg in February 1927 on the meaning of 'National Socialism' (BA, NS8, Kanzlei Rosenberg, 143); in his article 'Nationaler Sozialismus' in *NS-Briefe*, Nr.34, 15 February 1927; and his article 'Wie wird man Nationalsozialist?' in *Völkischer Beobachter*, 21 December 1927.

11. cf. A. Leppert-Fögen, 'Der Mittelstandssozialismus der NSDAP', *Frankfurter Hefte*, 29 (1974), p. 656 ff. See also by the same author *Die deklassierte Klasse. Studien zur Geschichte und Ideologie des Kleinbürgertums* (Frankfurt, 1974); and H.A. Turner, 'Fascism and Modernization', *World Politics*, 24 (1971/72), p. 547 ff.

12. Principally, 'Preussentum und Sozialismus' (1919). See A. Koktanek (ed.), *Oswald Spengler. Briefe 1913-36* (Munich, 1963), pp. 391 ff.

13. R. Jung, *Der nationale Sozialismus, seine Grundlagen, sein Werdegang, seine Ziele* (Munich, 1919). Otto Strasser has confirmed Jung's influence on Gregor (IfZ, ED-118, Otto-Strasser-Sammlung, Bd. 25).

14. Millar Lane, op.cit. p. 21.

15.   BA, NS 22, Der Reichsorganisationsleiter der NSDAP, 1.
16.   This theme is the subject of my forthcoming article, 'Die NSDAP und die Reichstagswahlen vom 20. Mai 1928 – der entscheidende Wendepunkt?' in *Vierteljahrshefte für Zeitgeschichte* (1977). For further analysis of the electoral implications see J. Holzer, *Parteien und Massen. Die Politische Krise in Deutschland 1928-1930* (Wiesbaden, 1975), pp. 44-6, 93-8; and T. Childers, 'The Social Bases of the National Socialist Vote', *Journal of Contemporary History*, 11, 1976, p. 28 ff. For recent discussion of the NSDAP-middle class relationship cf. H.A. Winkler, 'Vom Protest zur Panik: Der gewerbliche Mittelstand in der Weimarer Republik', in H. Mommsen u.al (eds.), *Industrielles System und politische Entwicklung in der Weimarer Republik* (Düsseldorf, 1974); A. Leppert-Fögen, *Die deklassierte Klasse*, op.cit.; R. Saage, 'Anti-sozialismus, Mittelstand und NSDAP in der Weimarer Republik', *Internationale Wiss. Korrespondenz zur Geschichte der Deutschen Arbeiterbewegung*, 11, 1975, pp. 146-77. See also for the peasantry, J.E. Farquharson, *The Plough and the Swastika: The NSDAP and Agriculture in Germany 1928-1945* (London, 1976), Ch.1.
17.   In a memorandum of 22 June 1928 he states that the election must be seen as signifying the closing of an era, and he refers to the 'new tasks and situations' in the future (BA, NS22/348).
18.   *NS-Briefe*, June 1929: 'Everything which is damaging to the existing order of things will have our support . . . because we want catastrophe . . . in a word: we are pursuing a policy of catastrophe . . .!'
19.   The text in BA, NS26/1370, part of the speech ran: 'If we come to power there will no longer be any more marxists or democratic republicans. Those who owe allegiance to any international, or who perhaps shout 'Hail Moscow', will be strung up . . . if we have to wade up to the knees in blood for Germany's sake, so be it'.
20.   Details in BA, NS26/1370; BA, Zeitgeschichtliche Sammlung (ZS)g 103; Zeitungsausschnittssammlung Lauterbach, 781.
21.   BA, ZSg 2, Allgemeine Drucksachen, 196.
22.   BA, ZSg 103/782. For the reaction of opponents see Bayerisches Hauptstaatsarchiv (Bay.HSA), Staatsarchiv München (SAM), Polizeidirektion München, 6772.
23.   BA, ZSg 103/789. Kele, op.cit. p.135 notes a similar tendency.
24.   BA, NS22/1065 & /1069; BA, NS1 (Reichsschatzmeister der NSDAP), 7.
25.   BA, Sammlung Schumacher, 373.
26.   BA, NS26/203.
27.   See his panegyric of Hitler entitled *Das Hitlerbüchlein. Ein Abriss vom Leben und Wirken des Führers der nationalsozialistischen Freiheitsbewegung Adolf Hitler* (Berlin, 1928), pp. 13-16.
28.   At a meeting in Stuttgart on 11 April 1930 he said: 'Hitler is really the kind of man one dreams about' for whom, he continued, 'I have increasing respect . . . ' Bay. HSA, Allgemeines Staatsarchiv (ASA), Sonderabgabe I, 1740, Details of other meetings in Bay. HSA, SAM, Polizeidirektion 6791; and BA, NS26/190.
29.   BA, NS26/1176.
30.   BA, Sammlung Schumacher, 313.
31.   Letter of 22 July 1930 (BA, Sammlung Schumacher, 313) in which he describes Otto's action as 'pure madness' (*heller Wahnsinn*).
32.   Letter of 25 July 1930 (IfZ, F28, Private Dokumente Dr Korn).
33.   Letter of 17 September 1930 (BA, NS22/1062).
34.   W. Schäfer, *NSDAP. Entwicklung und Struktur der Staatspartei des Dritten Reiches* (Hannover, 1957), p.5. See also D. Reed, *Nemesis?*

(London, 1940), pp. 92, 115; K.O. Paetel, *Versuchung oder Chance?* *Zur Geschichte des deutschen Nationalbolschewismus* (Göttingen, 1965), pp. 29-32, 208-17; P. Gottfried, 'Otto Strasser and National Socialism', *Modern Age*, 13, 1969, p. 150, note 3.

35.   C. Bloch, *Die SA und die Krise des NS-Regimes 1934* (Edition Suhrkamp, 1970), p. 16; E. Niekisch, *Gewagtes Leben. Begegnungen und Begebnisse* (Cologne, 1958), p. 179.

36.   O. Strasser, *Aufbau des deutschen Sozialismus* (2nd edn) (Vienna, 1936), p. 120. Underlying this point was Otto's insistence that Gregor had made a loss of RM25,000 when selling his pharmacy in 1925 (BA, NS26/1370).

37.   In this connection see a most interesting letter from Gregor to Otto of 31 December 1932 (BA, R43, Reichskanzlei, II/1194).

38.   Otto himself admits this in *Hitler and I*, op.cit., p. 103, while Gregor confirmed it in letters to Dr Korn (see note 32), and to Wilhelm Loeper (1 October 1930) (BA, Sammlung Schumacher, 204); also see K. Ludecke, *I Knew Hitler. The Story of a Nazi Who Escaped the Blood Purge* (London, 1938), p. 374.

39.   O. Strasser, *Exil,* op.cit., p. 72, says they did not meet again until May 1933, adding that Hitler had forbidden Gregor from having anything further to do with his brother. A Gestapo report of 10 January 1934 (BA, R43II/1196a) corroborates Otto's assertion. See also letter from Gregor to a Herr Erckmann of 7 August 1930 in which he speaks most disparagingly of his brother (IfZ, Z18, Deutsche Nationale-Zeitung, 1969).

40.   BA, Sammlung Schumacher, 278.

41.   O. Strasser, *Mein Kampf*, op.cit., p. 38.

42.   Krebs, op.cit., p. 188, argues his position was considerably weakened.

43.   R. Kühnl 1, *Die Nationalsozialistische Linke 1925-1930* (Meisenheim, 1966), pp. 1, 89, 260. K.D. Bracher et al, *Die Nationalsozialistische Machtergreifung. Studien zur Errichtung des totalitären Herrschaftssystems in Deutschland 1933/34* (Cologne, 1960), p. 360 agrees the affair was the beginning of the end for NS socialism which was henceforward 'buried piece by peice'.

44.   O. Strasser, op. cit., p. 9; R. Schapke, *Die Schwarze Front. Von den Zielen und Aufgaben und vom Kämpfe der Deutschen Revolution* (Leipzig, 1932), p. 58.

45.   This was especially the case following Strasser's speech on radio in June 1932. The speech, the first to be given on the air by a NSDAP member, was entitled: *Die Staatsidee des Nationalsozialismus,* and drew favourable comment from many quarters (text in BA, NS 26/1370). For reactions to the speech, BA, NS22/3. See also B. Granzow, *A Mirror of Nazism. British Opinion and the Emergence of Hitler 1929-1933* (London, 1964), pp. 167, 201.

46.   Schulz's thin account of his relationship with Strasser is contained in a 71-page booklet entitled, *Rettungen und Hilfeleistungen an Verfolgten 1933-1945 durch Oberleutnant a.D. Paul Schulz*, available in Bundesarchiv library (BA, Bibliothek, BIP Paul Schulz, Nr.2). On his own background and career see P. Schulz, *Meine Erschiessung am 30. Juni 1934*, available also in the Bundesarchiv library (BA, Bibliothek, BIP Paul Schulz, Nr.1).

47.   BA, NS22/348.

48.   There is a wide range of important documentary evidence on this theme. See BA, Nachlass Zarnow, Nr.1 (Fall Schulz), esp. letter of 16 August 1934 from Zarnow to Hans Werner (Magdeburg), and letter

of 7 August 1934 from Zarnow to Schulz himself; BA, Nachlass
Friedrich Grimm, Bd.6, p. 6 ff; BA, NS26/1375 for correspondence
between J. Lehmann, the Munich racist publisher, and Walter Buch on
10 July 1934, and between Schulz and Lehmann on 12 June 1934.
Refer also to J. Goebbels, *Vom Kaiserhof zur Reichskanzlei. Eine
historische Darstellung in Tagebuchblättern (Vom 1 Januar 1932 bis
zum 1. Mai 1933)* (24th edn Munich, 1938), pp. 150, 219, 225.

49.   BA, NS26/1374. For Schulz on his Black Reichswehr activities, see his
correspondence in BA, Nachlass Zarnow, Nr.1; BA, Nachlass F. Grimm,
Nr.5; and F. Grimm, *Politische Justiz. Die Krankheit unserer Zeit*
(Bonn, 1953), p. 63 ff.

50.   BA, NS26/1374. At the first meeting of the newly elected 12-man
NSDAP Reichstag faction in May 1928 it was agreed to make the
campaign for Schulz' release its primary concern. (Bay HSA, SAM:
Polizeidirektion 6779). In June 1929 an NSDAP motion for all *Feme*
prisoners to be amnestised was rejected by the *Reichstag* (BA,
Sammlung Schumacher, 381).

51.   Schulz, op.cit., Nr.2. p. 7 ff, 20 ff.

52.   BA, Nachlass Grimm, Nr.5. See also A. Rosenberg in H. Härtle (ed.),
*Letzte Aufzeichnungen. Ideale und Idole der nationalsozialistischen
Revolution* (Göttingen, 1955), p. 113.

53.   He was appointed temporary *SA Grüppenführer* East in April 1931
(BA, NS22/5006); W. Hoegener, *Die Verratene Republik. Geschichte
der deutschen Gegenrevolution* (Munich, 1958), p. 233.

54.   W. Benz, 'Vom Freiwilligen Arbeitsdienst zur Arbeitsdienstpflicht',
Vierteljahrshefte für Zeitgeschichte, 16, 1968, p. 330.

55.   For a recent appraisal of this ongoing historical controversy see
R. Saage, 'Zum Verhältnis von Nationalsozialismus und Industrie',
Das Parlament: Aus Politik und Zeitgeschichte, 25, 1975, pt. 9,
pp. 17-20, 24-7, 30-5; H. A. Turner, 'Big Business and the Rise of
Hitler', *American Historical Review*, 75, 1969/70, pp. 56-70;
D. Stegmann, 'Zum Verhältnis von Grossindustrie und
Nationalsozialismus 1930-1933. Ein Beitrag zur Geschichte der sog.
Machtergreifung', *Archiv für Sozialgeschichte*, XIII, 1973, 399-483;
H.A. Turner's scathing criticism of the latter in 'Grossunternehmertum
und Nationalsozialismus 1930-1933', *Historische Zeitschrift*, 221,
1975, p. 1 ff; and H.A. Turner: 'Hitlers Einstellung zu Wirtschaft und
Gesellschaft vor 1933', *Geschichte und Gesellschaft*, 2, 1976, p. 89 ff.

56.   BA, Nachlass Grimm, Bd. 6, p5.

57.   H.A. Turner, *Faschismus und Kapitalismus in Deutschland* (Cologne,
1972), p. 19 ff. For Fritz Thyssen's support for Göring see IfZ, Otto
Wagener, ED-60/5.

58.   BA, Nachlass Zarnow, Nr.1; Schulz, op. cit., Nr.2, p. 20 dates his
association with Heinrichsbauer from 1930.

59.   A. Heinrichsbauer, *Schwerindustrie und Politik* (Essen-Kettwig, 1948),
p. 40. See also BA, NS26/87. Heinrichsbauer's interest in the NSDAP
dates from December 1926 when he heard Hitler address industrialists
in Essen (Hauptstaatsarchiv Düsseldorf, RW23, NS-Stellen/NSDAP,
Gauleitung Ruhr).

60.   Heinrichsbauer, op.cit. pp. 40-41.

61.   Ibid., p. 65; Stegmann, op.cit., p. 418.

62.   *The Trial of German Major War Criminals. Proceedings of The
International Military Tribunal* (London, HMSO), 1946-51), Part 13,
p.100.

63.   A. Barkai, 'Die Wirtschaftsauffassung der NSDAP', *Das Parlament: Aus*

122 *'Der Fall Strasser': G. Strasser, Hitler and Nat. Socialism 1930-2*

Politik und Zeitgeschichte, 25, 1975, Pt. 9, pp. 5-7.
64. Orlow, *Nazi Party*, op. cit., p.263.
65. For Wagener's positive assessment of Strasser, cf. IfZ: Otto Wagener, ED-60/1 & /2. For a discussion of Wagener's work as Leader of the *Wirtschaftspolitische Abteilung (WPA)* in the *NSDAP Reichsleitung* from his appointment in January 1931, cf. Barkai, op.cit., pp. 8-9. In 1931-32, the WPA was the hub of NSDAP economic thinking.
66. H.A. Winkler, 'Unternehmerverbände zwischen Ständeideologie und Nationalsozialismus', *Vierteljahrshefte für Zeitgeschichte*, 17, 1969, pp. 356-7.
67. R. Vogelsang, *Der Freundeskreis Himmler* (Göttingen, 1972), p. 17.
68. BA, NS22/9 & /10.
69. Wagener's influence in the Party was severely curtailed following Hitler's reorganisation of the NS economic department in autumn 1932 – see H.A. Winkler, 'German Society, Hitler and the Illusion of Restoration 1930-33', *Journal of Contemporary History*, 11, 1976, p.6.
70. F. Thyssen, *I Paid Hitler* (London, 1941), pp. 132-3.
71. BA, Nachlass Zarnow: Nr. 44.
72. W. Maser (ed.), *Mein Schüler Hitler. Das Tagebuch seines Lehrers Paul Devrient* (Pfaffenhofen, 1975), p. 200, note 3.
73. Heinrichsbauer, op.cit., p. 49.
74. For Silverberg's support in this regard see P. Silverberg, *Reden und Schriften* (Cologne, 1951), p. 82, and the account given by his former private secretary Otto Meynen in *Der Volkswirt*, No. 18, 4 May 1951.
75. BA, Nachlass Grimm, Bd. 6, pp. 129-30. Kurt Gossweiler goes so far as to label Strasser an agent of I.G. Farben! (Gossweiler, *Die Rolle des Monopolskapitals bei der Herbeiführung der Röhm – Affäre* (Berlin-East, 1963), p. 287 ff.
76. Writing to Erich Koch on 1 September 1931, Strasser affirmed his belief in a broad right-wing coalition as the way forward for both the NSDAP and the country (BA, NS22/1065). See also letter to Dr Schlange, *Gauleiter* of Brandenburg, on 12 September 1931 (BA, NS22/1046) in which Strasser states that the best way for National Socialism to attain power was 'through the expedient of a so-called right-wing cabinet'.
77. Letter to Reventlow of 23 March 1932 (Berlin Document Center (BDC), Personal File Ernst Graf zu Reventlow).
78. Krebs, op.cit., p. 182; Lang & Schenk, op.cit., p.161.
79. For discussion of the group's ideas cf. K. Sontheimer: 'Der Tatkreis', *Vierteljahrshefte für Zeitgeschichte*, 7, 1959, 229-60; W. Struve, 'Hans Zehrer as a Neoconservative Elite Theorist', *American Historical Review*, 70, 1964/5, p. 1055 ff.; and W.E. Braatz, 'Two Neo-Conservative Myths in Germany 1919-32: The "Third Reich" and the "New State"', *Journal of The History of Ideas*, 32, 1971, pp. 577-80.
80. IfZ, Zeugenschrift 1723, Hans Zehrer.
81. ibid.
82. W. Struve, *Elites Against Democracy. Leadership Ideals in Bourgeois Political Thought in Germany, 1890-1933* (Princeton, 1973), p. 374.
83. See interesting exchange of letters between the two men in A. Koktanek (ed.), *Oswald Spengler*, op.cit., pp. 391-3, 397-401.
84. A. Koktanek, 'Spenglers Verhältnis Zum Nationalsozialismus in Geschichtlicher Entwicklung', *Zeitschrift für Politik*, 13, 1966, p. 49.
85. A. Winnig, *Aus Zwanzig Jahren, 1925 bis 1945* (Hamburg, 1951), pp. 14-19. An account of Winnig's colourful political career is provided in W. Ribhegge, *August Winnig. Eine historische Persönlichkeitsanalyse* (Bonn-Bad Godesberg, 1973).

86.   See their exchange of correspondence in November/December 1931
       (BA, NS22/348).
87.   A good example is, 'Wider den Sozialismus in jeder Form?', *Tat*, XXIV,
       July 1932, pp. 310-17. Zehrer took over the *Tägliche Rundschau* in
       May 1932 with largely army financial backing (Meissner & Wilde,
       op.cit., p. 74).
88.   BA, NS26/1375. Letter of 12 June 1933 from Schulz to Lehmann.
89.   E. Demant, *Von Schleicher zu Springer. Hans Zehrer als Politischer
       Publizist* (Mainz, 1971), p. 69.
90.   ibid. For conflicting reports on the date of this meeting, cf. F.G. von
       Tschirschky, *Erinnerungen eines Hochverräters* (Stuttgart, 1972),
       p. 88; Meissner & Wilde, op.cit. p. 98.
91.   Elbrechter was dentist to both Strasser and Brüning, G.R. Treviranus,
       Das Ende von Weimar. Heinrich Brüning und seine Zeit (Düsseldorf,
       1968), p. 345. See postwar correspondence Brüning-Elbrechter in
       H. Brüning, *Briefe 1946-1960* (Stuttgart, 1974), pp. 310, 424, 429.
92.   *Tat*, 24, August 1932, Heft. 5. A detailed examination of Zehrer's
       approach to the unions is given in U. Hüllbüsch, *Gewerkschaften und
       Staat. Ein Beitrag zur Geschichte der Gewerkschaften zu Anfang und
       zu Ende der Weimarer Republik* (Dissertation, University of Heidelberg,
       1961), p. 160 ff.
93.   Demant, op.cit, p. 99.
94.   BA, NS1/258. Strasser letter to Schulz of 27 March 1931; BA,
       Sammlung Schumacher, 374. Strasser letter of 21 March 1931 to all
       Gauleiters.
95.   BA, Nachlass Albert Krebs, Nr. 7. Strasser correspondence with Krebs
       of 28 January 1929. For Strasser on other DHV problems, cf. BA,
       NS22/1049. *Gauleiters* Albert Krebs, Wilhelm Murr, and Albert Forster,
       as well as Reinhold Muchow and Franz Stöhr were former DHV
       officials.
96.   L.E. Jones, 'Between the Fronts: The German National Union of
       Commercial Employees from 1928 to 1933', *Journal of Modern
       History*, 48, 1976, pp. 471-2.
97.   BA, NS26/1369.
98.   I. Hamel, *Völkischer Verband und nationale Gewerkschaft* (Frankfurt,
       1967), pp. 248-9.
99.   The article is reprinted in W. Jochmann, *Nationalsozialismus und
       Revolution. Ursprung und Geschichte der NSDAP in Hamburg
       1922-1933. Dokumente* (Frankfurt, 1963). Document 104, pp. 351-6.
100.   Hamel, op.cit., p. 249 ff.; Krebs, op.cit., p.33.
101.   BA, Sammlung Schumacher, 319. Letter from Strasser to Stöhr of
       20 November 1931.
102.   Jones, *Between the Fronts*, op.cit., p. 478.
103.   T. Vogelsang, *Reichswehr*, op.cit., p. 276.
104.   BA, NS26/1370.
105.   H. Heer, *Burgfrieden oder Klassenkampf? Zur Politik der
       sozialdemokratischen Gewerkschaften 1930-1933* (Neuwied, 1971),
       p.50.
106.   ibid., pp. 50-51.
107.   The full text is available in BA, NSD 12, Reichspropagandaleiter der
       NSDAP, 16 (Strasser-Rede 'Arbeit und Brot').
108.   Concretely expressed when he ordered the *Völkischer Beobachter*'s
       report of the speech to omit all references to the unions and social
       ideas. (A. Grosser, *Hitler, la Presse et la naissance d'une dictature*,
       Paris, 1959, p. 26).

109.   Ref. D. Petzina, 'Hauptprobleme der deutschen Wirtschaftspolitik 1932/33', *Vierteljahrshefte für Zeitgeschichte*, 15, 1967, 18-55.
110.   Heer, op.cit., p. 58 states that Elbrechter wrote the speech, while M. Schneider, *Das Arbeitsbeschaffungsprogramm des ADGB. Zur gewerkschaftlichen Politik in der Endphase der Weimarer Republik* (Bonn-Bad Godesberg, 1975), p. 153 argues that Bernhard Köhler, a former chief editor of the *Völkischer Beobachter* and later editor of the NSDAP economic department's publication, *Wirtschaftspolitischen Pressedienst*, was the author.
111.   The programme is given in full in W. Grotkopp, *Die Grosse Krise Lehren aus der Uberwindung der Wirtschaftskrise 1929/32* (Düsseldorf, 1954), p. 352 ff., and discussed in detail by Schneider, op.cit., p.140 ff.
112.   Barkai, op.cit., pp. 14-15 discusses in detail the genesis of the ideas behind the *Sofortprogramm*, and shows how it merely represented a synthesis of previously conceived notions from a wide variety of reformist economists and theorists.
113.   Schneider, op.cit., p. 153.
114.   At Schleicher's behest, Wolff's main contribution to the broad front strategy was to supply Strasser with fairly generous funds (E. Czichon, *Wer Verhalf Hitler zur Macht? Zum Anteil der deutschen Industrie an der Zerstörung der Weimarer Republik*, (3rd edn. Cologne, 1972), p. 54, note 210.
115.   A former employee of the *Allgemeine Elektrizitäts-Gesellschaft* (AEG) who had joined the NSDAP at the express wish of his friend Schleicher, Cordemann played a useful role not only in promoting the Schleicher-Strasser dialogue, but also in strengthening links between Strasser and both the *Tatkreis* and the Gereke-Circle of which he was a member. See IfZ, Zeugenschrift, 1862, R.H. Cordemann.
116.   The work creation plans of Gereke-Circle approximated very closely to Strasser's programme and moreover were fully supported by Schleicher (Czichon, op.cit., p.34).
117.   BA, Z Sg 103/776.
118.   Minutes of the meeting in BA, R43II/1309.
119.   For a bitterly critical assessment of the Strasser-union relationship from a Social Democratic standpoint, see F. Stampfer, *Die ersten Vierzehn Jahre der Deutschen Republik* (Hamburg 1947) p. 656 ff.
120.   The full text of the speech entitled *Das Wirtschaftliche Aufbauprogramm der NSDAP* is given in BA, Nachlass Zarnow, Nr.44.
121.   W. Müller & J. Stockfisch, 'Die "Veltenbriefe". Eine neue Quelle über die Rolle des Monopolkapitals bei der Zerstörung der Weimarer Republik', *Zeitschrift für Geschichtswissenschaft*, 17, 1969, p. 1588.
122.   cf. Goebbels, Kaiserhof, op.cit., entries for 6 January (p. 19); 20 January (p. 27); 14 March (p. 63); 18 March (p. 67); 19 March (p. 68); 10 May (p. 94); 19 May (p. 99).
123.   Serious disagreements about Party policy and tactics between Strasser and Hitler had already come to light in spring 1932 over the presidential elections (BA, NS26/1169).
124.   See letter from Gauleiter Josef Wagner to Strasser on 4 August lamenting the absence of the former élan in the Party (BA, NS22/382). See also a NSDAP *Reichspropagandaleitung* report of August which officially records gloomy feelings about the Party's future prospects (BA, Sammlung Schumacher, 382).
125.   Brüning, *Memoiren*, op.cit., p. 488 refers to 'my lasting secret association with the Strasser wing of the NSDAP'.
126.   Brüning, *Briefe und Gespräche 1934-1945* (Stuttgart, 1974), p. 319 −

letter from Brüning to G.L. Warren of 18 September 1940. See also
Schulz, Nr. 2, op.cit., p. 7.

127. Treviranus, op.cit., p. 164.
128. Bracher, *Auflösung*, op.cit., p. 448.
129. Brüning, *Memoiren*, op.cit., p. 600.
130. Brüning, *Reden und Aufsätze eines deutschen Staatsmanns* (Münster,
1968), p. 151 ff; H. Marcon, *Arbeitsbeschaffungspolitik der
Regierungen Papen und Schleicher* (Frankfurt, 1974), p. 83.
131. Brüning, *Reden*, op.cit., p. 150.
132. See revealing letter of 15 August 1932 from Reventlow to Strasser
(BDC, Personal File Ernst Graf zu Reventlow).
133. D. Junker, *Die Deutsche Zentrumspartei und Hitler 1932/33. Ein
Beitrag zur Problematik des politischen Katholizismus in Deutschland*
(Stuttgart, 1969), p. 97.
134. The talks had been bitterly denounced by many Protestant NSDAP
circles in northern Germany (Bay HSA, Geheimes Staatsarchiv (GSA),
MA/101235/3). The only positive result was the agreement of the
NSDAP and Centre to support (with the DNVP) Göring's election as
Reichstag President on 30 August.
135. Brüning continued to regard Strasser, even after his final break with
Hitler, as the only person who could bring the NSDAP into responsible
government. (IfZ, Otto-Strasser-Sammlung, ED – 118. Bd.2). Refer
also to Brüning, *Memoiren*, op.cit., 675-9.
136. On big business fears of a Strasser-trade union rapprochement, see
M. Schneider, *Unternehmer und Demokratie. Die freien Gewerkschaften
in der unternehmerischen Ideologie der Jahre 1918 bis 1933*
(Bonn-Bad Godesberg, 1975), pp. 111-12; H. Müller, *Die Zentralbank –
eine Nebenregierung. Reichsbankpräsident Hjalmar Schacht als
Politiker der Weimarer Republik* (Opladen, 1973), p. 110. See also
interesting letter of 20 September 1932 from Heinrichsbauer to
Strasser in which he complains among other things about recent
'Marxist-type' agitational methods and accompanying 'socialistic'
demands in the Party – evidence that Heinrichsbauer misunderstood
Strasser's strategy at this time (BA, NS20: Kleine Erwerbungen, 122).
137. At a *Reichspropagandatagung* of the Party in Munich on 5-7 October
1932 (Bay.HSA, GSA, MA 101235/3).
138. See Munich Police Report of 30 December 1932 (Bay. HSA, SAM,
Polizeidirektion 6781). See also Goebbels, *Kaiserhof , op.cit.*, entry
8 November 1932 (p. 198) on Strasser's 'sabotage work'.
139. IfZ, Zeugenschriften, 1926, Walter von Etzdorf.
140. It has been remarked however, that his anti-semitism was much more
temperate than Hitler's; cf. G.L. Mosse, *Germans and Jews. The Right,
the Left, and the Search for a 'Third Force' in pre-Nazi Germany* (New
York, 1970), p. 103. In a *Reichstag* speech on 17 October 1930 he
denied the Party wanted to persecute Jews, only to exclude them from
their alleged dominant position in German economic life (BA, ZSg 103/
795). A Berlin Police Report of 27 March 1931 describes him as being
'in no way a rowdy anti-semite' (BA, NS26/1370).
141. IfZ, F41. Bd.4, Kurzorientierung des Ministeramtes vom 23. November
1932.
142. BA, NS22, 1 (Verschiedene Angelegenheiten der NS-Propaganda) –
Stimmungsberichte 6-15 November 1932.
143. BA, NS26/1511. See also *Gauleiter* reports in BA, NS22/347.
144. BA, NS26/1508. See also IfZ: MA/1300/2, Niederschrift Otto Meissner.
145. J. Noakes, *The Nazi Party in Lower Saxony 1921-1933* (Oxford, 1971),

p. 242 for details of the 'German Socialist Workers' Party'. For developments in Dresden, cf. Staatsarchiv Koblenz (SAK), 403, Oberpräsident der Rheinprovinz, 16764.

146.   BA, NS26/1759.

147.   H.R. Berndorff, *General zwischen Ost und West. Aus den Geheimnissen der Deutschen Republik* (Hamburg, 1951), p. 212 states Schleicher let it be known that these debts would be paid from secret army funds if Hitler agreed to Strasser becoming vice-chancellor in a cabinet led by himself.

148.   D.M. McKale, *The Nazi Party Courts. Hitler's Management of Conflict in His Movement, 1921-1945* (Lawrence, Kansas, 1974), pp. 102-5.

149.   M. Ekstein, *The Limits of Reason. The German Democratic Press and The Collapse of Weimar Democracy* (Oxford, 1975), p. 256 remarks, 'The entire democratic press took every conceivable opportunity to trumpet the decline of National Socialism'. From the SPD, cf, W. Hoegener, *Der Schwierige Aussenseiter. Erinnerungen eines Abgeordneten, Emigranten und Ministerpräsidenten* (Munich, 1959), p. 71.

150.   Text of speech in BA, NSD13 (Reichspressechef der NSDAP), 11.

151.   Paul Schulz, BA, Bibliothek, BIP, P. Schulz, Nr. 1. p.5; and Schulz, op.cit. Nr.2, pp. 9, 22, 43 emphasizes the SA terror campaign as a critical turning point in Strasser's relations with Hitler. For general background, cf. P. Kluke, 'Der Fall Potempa. Dokumentation', *Vierteljahrshefte für Zeitgeschichte*, 5 (1957), pp. 279-97.

152.   cf. Krebs, op.cit., p. 182; Heinrichsbauer, op.cit., p. 48 puts it rather well: 'The fundamental difference between Hitler and him [Strasser]was that although Hitler talked a great deal about Germany, he in fact only thought of the Party and himself, while Strasser placed the welfare of his Fatherland above everything else, including the interests of the Party. Hitler was a party man, Strasser a patriot'.

153.   eg. in *Völkischer Beobachter*, 25 November 1932. Many writers have taken such statements at face value; hence Dixon, op.cit., p. 3 says Strasser had 'an excellent relationship' with Hitler.

154.   K. Heiden, *Geschichte des Nationalsozialismus. Die Karriere Einer Idee* (Berlin, 1932), pp. 195-6.

155.   IfZ, Zeugenschrift 177, Franz von Pfeffer.

156.   BA, NS22/1045.

157.   E. Hanfstaengl, *Hitler. The Missing Years* (London, 1957), pp. 130, 182.

158.   Bracher, *Auflösung*, op.cit., p. 672.

159.   Frank, op.cit., p. 108. Schulz, op.cit., Nr.2, p.9 writes that by December 1932 the conflict had become 'Unbridgeable'.

160.   H. Heiber (ed.), *Das Tagebuch Joseph Goebbels 1925/26* (Stuttgart, 1961) entry for 2 October 1925: 'He [Strasser]has certainly no small ambition, even if he always likes to say the opposite'.

161.   Frank, op.cit., p. 108 goes so far as to state that he was a 'victim of his own ambition'.

162.   K. Heiden, *Der Führer. Hitler's Rise to Power* (London, 1967), pp. 227-9.

163.   Ludecke, op.cit., pp. 392-3.

164.   See the glowing report on his military career, dated 10 January 1919 in Bay. HSA, Kriegsarchiv, Akten des König. Kriegsministeriums, OP 49979.

165.   BA, NS26/1370.

166.   T. Vogelsang, 'Zur Politik Schleichers gegenüber der NSDAP, 1932',

Vierteljahrshefte für Zeitgeschichte, 6 (1958), p. 105, note 44.
167. The version adduced by Vogelsang, *Reichswehr,* op.cit., pp. 340-1. See also IfZ, Zeugenschrift, 279, Eugen Ott.
168. F. Papen, *Vom Scheitern enier Demokratie* (Mainz, 1968), p. 362; H. Schacht, *76 Jahre meines Lebens,* (Bad Wörishofen, 1953), p. 375; O. Braun, *Von Weimar zu Hitler* (Hamburg, 1949), p. 274.
169. Losses of up to 40% on the November *Reichstag* election figures were recorded. The consequent atmosphere of profound depression in the movement is amply conveyed by A. Schröder, *Mit der Partei vorwärts! Zehn Jahre Gau Westfalen-Nord* (Detmold, 1940), p. 24.
170. As suggested (unconvincingly) by General Hans-Henning von Holzendorf (BA, NS20/242-2. Niederschrift vom 22 June 1946).
171. Full description of the meeting in Goebbels, *Kaiserhof,* op.cit., entry 5 December 1932, p. 216 ff.
172. BA, NS1/258.
173. See letter of 7 May 1932 to Strasser from Wilhelm Zimmermann, a Karlsruhe publisher, who says: ' . . .you are . . . also still today the honest German socialist . . . an idea which many old former Party comrades continue to share . . . ' (BA, NS22/1044).
174. BA, NS26/1103.
175. See letter of 28 December 1931 from Kube to Strasser (BA, NS22/1064).
176. See Reventlow-Strasser correspondence during last six months of 1932 (BDC, Personal File Ernst Graf zu Reventlow). Also see an unconfirmed report in Otto Strasser's newspaper, *Die Schwarze Front* of 8 January 1933 that an exchange of letters between Reventlow and Hitler on Gregor Strasser played an important part in the political developments which led to the latter's resignation. (BA, ZSg 1, Partei-und Verbandsdrucksachen/240).
177. BA, NS26/1363.
178. The situation changed, however, in 1933 when, with the NSDAP. in power, Reventlow attempted a reconciliation. See his praise for Hitler in his book, *Der Weg zum neuen Deutschland. Der Wiederaufstieg des deutschen Volkes* (3rd edn Essen,1933), p. 344.
179. Frank, *Angesicht des Galgens,* op.cit. p. 107.
180. P.D. Stachura, *Nazi Youth in the Weimar Republic* (Santa Barbara & Oxford,1975), p. 83.
181. M. Broszat, *German National Socialism 1919-1945* (Santa Barbara, 1966), p. 198; H. G. Schumann,*Nationalsozialismus und Gewerkschaftsbewegung* (Hannover, 1958), p. 39.
182. T.W. Mason, *Arbeiterklasse und Volksgemeinschaft. Dokumente und Materialien zur deutschen Arbeiterpolitik 1936-1939* (Cologne-Opladen, 1975), p. 30.
183. BA, NS1/258.
184. P. Meier-Benneckenstein, *Dokumente der deutschen Politik* (Berlin, 1938), Bd.V, p. 367; see also Goebbels, *Kaiserhof,* op.cit., entries of 9 June 1932 (p. 109) and 27 June 1932 (p. 119).
185. BA, NS26/1759; National Archives Microfilm Collection, FA 49, Bd.3, NSDAP, T81, 159 (Oberste SA-Führung), Roll 91.
186. For example of Nuremberg/Franconia, see E.G. Reiche, *The Development of the SA in Nuremberg 1922-1934* (Dissertation, University of Delaware, 1972); R. Hambrecht, *Der Aufstieg der NSDAP in Mittel-und Oberfranken 1925-1933* (Nuremberg, 1976).
187. IfZ, Aufzeichnung Otto Erbersdobler, Juli 1968.
188. BA, R22, Reichsjustizministerium, 5006. Both Hierl and Epp were

being tipped in April 1932 as possible successors: see letter of 24 March 1932 from Hierl to Strasser demanding Röhm's expulsion (reprinted in H-A. Jacobsen & W. Jochmann (eds.), *Ausgewählte Dokumente zur Geschichte des Nationalsozialismus* (Bielefeld, 1961).

189. H. Bennecke, *Hitler und die SA* (Munich, 1962), p. 212; for the opposite view, cf. Wörtz, op.cit. p. 228.

190. Orlow, op.cit. p. 258 states that the mid-1932 organisational reforms were partly designed by Strasser to further his coalition strategy. But Pfeffer rejects this view (IfZ, Zeugenschrift, 177, Franz von Pfeffer).

191. BDC, Personal File Konstantin Hierl.

192. See Correspondence between Strasser and many of these *Gauleiters* in NS26/1068-1076. According to *Vorwärts* of 13 December 1932 Brückner came out openly in support of Strasser, and the *Münchener Post* of 17/18 December 1932 reported Schlange as having done the same. Also see an interesting memorandum written by *SS Brigadeführer* Berger on 3 December 1940 about Murr's reaction to the Strasser crisis (IfZ, MA-329).

193. These were: Lohse, Rust, Heinrich Haake, Jacob Sprenger, Wilhelm Loeper, Martin Mutschmann, Brückner, Theo Habicht (Austria) – all of whom were sympathetic towards Strasser – and Goebbels, who was not. Schulz was *Reichsinspekteur I*, and Robert Ley *Reichsinspekteur II*. Contrary to Nyomarkay, op.cit., p. 45, Ley was not pro-Strasser (BA, NS22, 348).

194. P. Diehl-Thiele, *Partei und Staat im Dritten Reich, Untersuchungen zum Verhältnis von NSDAP und allgemeiner innerer Staatsverwaltung 1933-1945* (Munich, 1969), p. 204; cf. IfZ, Aufzeichnung Erbersdobler.

195. F. Papen, *Memoirs* (London, 1952), p. 217; O. Strasser, *History in My Time*, op.cit., p. 80.

196. O. Strasser, *Exil* , op.cit., p. 65 writes 'They waited on Gregor. He had their trust. He had never let them down. They had decided to follow him . . .'

197. Strasser had a very high opinion of Frick (BA, NS26/1403).

198. Bay, HSA, SAM, Polizeidirektion 6791. For Feder's ideological reservations about Hitler's course, cf. Broszat, *German National Socialism*, op.cit., p. 23, A. Tyrell, *Vom 'Trommler' Zum 'Führer'. Der Wandel von Hitlers Selbstverständnis zwischen 1919 und 1924 und die Entwicklung der NSDAP* (Munich,1975), p. 192. See also report by Otto Engelbrecht of his meeting with Feder on 30 December 1932 in BA,NS20/22.

199. R. Cecil, *The Myth of the Master Race. Alfred Rosenberg and Nazi Ideology* (New York, 1972), p. 108.

200. Krebs, op.cit., p. 199.

201. Scholarly opinion is sharply divided on how seriously the crisis threatened the unity of the NSDAP. Among those who believe Strasser could have split the Party are Horn, op.cit., p. 373; Wörtz, op.cit., p. 4; Bullock, op.cit., p. 239. See also a Württemberg Police report of 23 December 1932 which did not rule out 'a catastrophic collapse' of the Party as a result of the crisis (BA, NS26/1405).

202. A full description of the immediate prelude to and events of 8 December is provided by Lohse, *Fall Strasser*, op.cit., p. 23 ff.

203. Strasser, *Exil*, op.cit., p. 74 says Gregor felt let down by his friends and supporters in December 1932; but in O. Strasser, *30 Juni*, op.cit., p. 36 it is claimed that Gregor deeply regretted his decision to resign.

204. A few hours before Hitler received the letter, Strasser called a brief meeting of the *Landesinspekteure* (except Goebbels) to his *Reichstag*

office at which he intimated his decision. He referred to there being
'reasons of an objective as well as a personnel and personal nature . . . '
behind his resignation and went on to outline the substance of his
disagreement with Hitler's policies and methods which, he believed,
were confusing and incapable of bringing the Party to power on the
Führer's terms. Indeed, he stated that Hitler's inflexible attitude was
imposing a severe strain on the unity of the movement whose ideals and
aims no longer complemented one another. Finally, he criticised the
'game of intrigue' in Hitler's entourage (an oblique reference to
Goebbels, Göring, etc.) which Strasser complained shut him out from
important decision-making. (Lohse, op.cit., pp. 23-6).

205. See Appendix.
206. IfZ, F28, Dokumente Dr Korn, letter of 21 February 1933.
207. cf. Goebbels, *Kaiserhof,* op.cit., entry 8 December 1932, pp. 218-20.
      Goebbels wanted to have Strasser expelled from the Party altogether,
      but Hitler refused. (IfZ, MA 1300/1). See also Meissner, *Staatssekretär,*
      op.cit., p. 252.
208. As suggested, for example, by Bullock, op.cit., p. 171; and Ludecke,
      op.cit., pp. 226, 550.
209. cf. O. Strasser, *History in My Time,* op.cit., p. 242; Also see IfZ,
      Zeugenschrift Cordemann, op.cit.; Strasser 'at the decisive moment
      reacted not politically, but personally . . . '.
210. Paetel, *Versuchung oder Chance,* op.cit., pp. 209-10.
211. BA, NS20/102, writing in *Die Tat,* 24 (January 1933), Rolf Boelke
      praised Strasser as the representative of 'true' National Socialism.
212. BA, R43II/1194.
213. cf. Lohse, op.cit., p. 27 ff.
214. Included were Frick (though he continued to be on friendly terms
      with Strasser – See O. Strasser, *Exil,* op.cit. p. 72), and Feder – see
      Frankfurter Zeitung, 10 December 1932.
215. Details in Orlow, *Nazi Party,* op.cit., pp. 293-6.
216. cf. IfZ, ED-118 Bd. 25.
217. Glaser was subsequently employed in the NSBO (BA, Sammlung
      Schumacher, 375). He was shot along with Strasser and Schulz in June
      1934, though the latter miraculously survived (BA NS23, SA/475).
      For Vollmuth information see BA, NS22/317. Strasser's lawyer,
      Dr Voss, who had been given Strasser's private documents relating to
      the December crisis, was also murdered in June 1934. The papers have
      never been recovered. (See IfZ, MA/1300/1; BDC, Ordner 402)
218. For details of HJ secessions cf. Stachura, *Nazi Youth,* op.cit., p. 83
      See also Hoegener, *Verratene Republik,* op.cit., p. 333. The authorities
      exaggerated in their reports: cf. Bay HSA, GSA, MA 1943, 102157,
      Halbmonatsbericht vom 19 December 1932. For a description of the
      situation in Württemberg see Berger's memorandum of 3 December
      1940 in IfZ, MA/329.
219. Goebbels, *Kaiserhof,* op.cit., entry 8 December 1932 (p. 220);
      H.G. Seraphim (ed.), *Das politische Tagebuch Alfred Rosenbergs,
      1934/35 und 1939/40* (Munich, 1964), p. 48. See also a revealing
      speech by Himmler on 21 July 1944 in which he compares Strasser's
      'Verrat' (treachery) with the July 1944 Plot (IfZ, MA/315).
220. In this connection the case of Strasser's erstwhile close friend, NSDAP
      Reichstag Deputy Fritz Kiehn of Trossingen (Württemberg) is
      instructive. In 1933 and subsequently, Kiehn went to considerable
      lengths with the authorities to disclaim persistent rumours that he had
      been a Strasser sympathiser in 1932. See Kiehn-Frick, and Kiehn-Hess

correspondence October/November 1933 (BA, R18, Reichsministeriums des Innern, 5035).

221. Bay. HSA, SAM, Polizeidirektion 6781.
222. BA, R43 I/678. See also G. Gereke, *Ich war Königlich Preussischer Landrat* (East Berlin, 1972).
223. IfZ, MA/1300/2.
224. *Kaiserhof*, entry 9 December 1932 (p. 223).
225. H.A. Winkler, 'German Society, Hitler and the Illusion of Restoration 1930-33', op.cit. p. 7.
226. This link-up has been the subject of recent scholarly debate. The classic Marxist statement was originally given by F. Klein, 'Zur Vorbereitung der faschistischen Diktatur durch die deutsche Grossbourgeoisie (1929-1932)', *Zeitschrift für Geschichtswissenschaft*, 1 (1953), pp. 872-904. Recently, E. Czichon, *Wer Verhalf Hitler zur Macht*, op.cit., p. 20 ff., and D. Stegmann, *Verhältnis von Grossindustrie und NS*, op.cit., pp.437-8 have basically endorsed this view. H.A. Turner, *Grossunternehmertum und Nationalsozialismus*, op.cit., p. 60 ff, criticises this whole hypothesis.
227. G. Braunthal, 'The German Free Trade Unions During the Rise of Nazism', *Journal of Central European Affairs*, XV (1956), p. 345.
228. On 21 May 1942 Hitler remarked that the result was 'a success whose importance it is not possible to over-estimate . . . ' H.R. Trevor-Roper (ed.): *Hitler's Table Talk 1941-44. His Private Conversations* (London, 1973, edn), p. 196. A detailed examination of the election is provided by J. Ciolek-Kümper, *Wahlkampf in Lippe. Die Wahlkampfpropaganda der NSDAP zur Landtagswahl am 15. Januar 1933* (Munich, 1976).
229. Bay. HSA, SAM, Polizeidirektion 6735.
230. H. Rauschning, *Gespräche mit Hitler* (Vienna, 1973 edn), p. 153; cf. Schäfer, NSDAP, op.cit. p.10.

4 THE OCCUPATIONAL BACKGROUND OF THE SA's RANK AND FILE MEMBERSHIP DURING THE DEPRESSION YEARS, 1929 TO MID-1934

Conan Fischer

National Socialism can be described as a movement which had penetrated most spheres of German political, social and economic activity by 1930. Its political wing, the NSDAP, was managed by the Political Organisation (PO). The party was increasingly successful in local, state and national elections between 1929 and mid-1932, winning many seats in the name of the National Socialist movement. The movement created other formations to perform other, less purely political functions. The SS acted as the movement's internal police force until January 1933 and with the Nazi assumption of power extended its activities to cover state police forces, before indulging in less auspicious affairs. The Hitler Youth attracted male teenagers to the movement while the German Girls' League sought their female counterparts. The Factory Cell Organisation (NSBO) recruited white and blue collar employees, principally from within larger firms.

However, the activist, paramilitary Storm Division (SA) was the only National Socialist body to rival the party in terms of mass following in the period 1929 to 1934. It was linked to the movement, and more specifically the party, through Hitler. Despite this personal link the two bodies coexisted uneasily in the period 1929 to 1934 and at times there were open disputes between them.

The SA man was virtually an everyday sight in Germany by 1930. His existence pervaded most spheres of life during the closing years of the Weimar Republic and the early months of Nazi rule. Official papers demonstrate that the authorities of the day were deeply concerned about the growing strength of the SA.[1] Contemporary (non-Nazi) newspapers reported SA affairs in alarmist tones whilst few political and historical analysts of the time ignored the SA.[2] By 1933, the SA man had become as much a part of the German scene as the dole queues of that Depression afflicted era.

Few historical works on the period have subsequently ignored the SA man, or more precisely, the SA. Much has been written of SA leaders; in particular Röhm who expanded the SA into a mass movement in its own right during the early 1930s and thereby

131

greatly assisted the Nazi drive to, and consolidation of power.[3]   The
indispensability of the SA as an instrument of propaganda on the one
hand and terror and coercion on the other is in little doubt.[4]

However, whilst it does not escape mention, the number of works
specifically concerning the SA is limited.[5] This is not only surprising
because of the SA's role in the National Socialist drive to power, but
because of its sheer numerical strength. To quote a few figures:
60,000 in November 1930, 77,000 in January 1931, 290,941 in January
1932 and 700,000 in January 1933.[6] In the seventeen months between
the Nazi accession to power and the political emasculation of the SA in
the Röhm purge, growth was still more rapid. The picture is
complicated by the forcible amalgamation of some paramilitary
organisations into the Nazi movement as auxiliary SA formations,
notably the Stahlhelm. However, the strength of the SA itself,
excluding these auxiliary groups who did not, in any case, regard
themselves as SA men, was around two million by May 1933,[7]
2.5 million by September[8] and near three million in the spring of
1934.[9]

Relations between the party management (*politische Organisation*)
and the SA have been described and analysed in a number of works.[10]
These ambivalent and often acrimonious relations, both on an official
and a personal level, were certainly one factor leading to the purge of
the SA leadership on 30 June 1934 and during the following week.
Equal, if not greater attention has been paid to SA – army relations.[11]
The SA was a paramilitary body in its conception and organisation and
its leadership entertained hopes of replacing the *Reichswehr*[12] with a
national, popular militia under their command. This too has been
shown to have influenced events in mid-1934 when the army command
pressurised Hitler to remove the SA leadership and the threat they
posed to the army.

Other issues, which concern the vast rank and file membership of
the SA, have not escaped attention. Their use as a propaganda
instrument has been mentioned, whilst more recent works have
considered the social and economic significance of the SA to a certain
extent.[13] However, although most facets of the SA's history are, in
themselves, uncontroversial, its social and economic history has led to
considerable disagreement. On the one hand, Röhm has been described
'with reservations' as the representative of serious, social revolutionary
forces on German soil by 1934, and the enemy of the middle classes.[14]
On the other hand, the Nazi 'second revolution' of which the SA was
the leading proponent and motive force, has been described as an anti-

capitalist movement of those lower-middle-class groups which yearned for a return to a pre-capitalist order.[15] The former interpretation, in contrast, described an alliance of sorts between the SA and the most advanced sectors of industry (chemicals, electrics) against traditional heavy industry.[16] For his part, Röhm believed that by expanding the SA during a time of acute economic crisis, he had deprived the KPD of most of its potential membership.[17]

There is evidence to support both historical interpretations, as well as Röhm's more political observation, albeit with definite socio-economic undertones. Certain assumptions concerning the SA's social background are explicitly or implicitly built into each interpretation. Those mentioned above are not the only such in existence. Another historian describes the SA as an instrument for the oppression of the working classes;[18] others point out that cooperation between the SA and KPD in Berlin during the autumn of 1932 in strike actions lost the NSDAP middle-class support in the November election of that year.[19]

There is ample evidence for both these interpretations, as well as the three preceding viewpoints. However, the assumptions concerning the social background of the SA inherent in the above instances cannot tally. A single example must suffice here; if a key function of the SA was to preempt KPD recruitment of certain groups, and if it succeeded in this, the picture of the SA as a lower-middle-class, pre-capitalist corporatist-oriented organisation is extraordinary. The word 'assumption' has been used advisedly, for none of the interpretations mentioned presents primary (or even much secondary) evidence to support their description of the SA's social background.[20] Röhm is clearly an exception, at least with regard to access to relevant information, but a knowledge of the SA's social background would be useful to test the reliability of his assertions! In other cases descriptions of the SA's social background vary considerably, and, it would not be wholly unfair to say, vary according to the argument being advanced.

Many sources note that the SA's rank and file was largely unemployed; indeed no disagreement arises over this. However, the occupational or class background of the SA leads to considerable disagreement. Some historians refrain from a precise description: Allen writes, 'many Stormtroopers were rough types, and at least some were former Communists',[21] whilst Heiden describes the SA as 'the Uprooted and Disinherited',[22] an assessment not devoid of certain connotations. Others consider the SA as a basically lower-middle-class body. Schweitzer lists the 'second revolution's adherents as 'salaried white collar workers, marginal independents, peasants, traders and artisans'.[23] Fetscher writes: 'In the SA, the diehard mercenary, the failed student and the proletarianised semi-intellectual dominated above all.'[24] Sohn-Rethel remarks that the SA attracted its unemployed membership 'not from the proletariat, but indeed dominantly from those of petty-bourgeois origin'.[25] Kater, who uses some primary evidence in his work regards the SA as largely lower-middle class,[26] but with a high proportion of unskilled or skilled workers.[27] On the other hand Bloch regards the SA as lumpenproletarian: 'Lumpenproletarians from a working-class background . . . . under the leadership of lumpenproletarians from a better background'.[28] The East German handbook, *Die Bürgerlichen Parteien* , comments on the SA's success in 1930 and 1931 in attracting 'sections of the working class' and also 'sections of the unemployed and declassé proletarians' and notes a resulting rivalry between the SA and KPD.[29] Diels, writing of the Berlin SA of 1933 believed that the 'proletarian element by far outweighed the middle class',[30] whilst Kele writes of a largely working-class SA in Germany as a whole throughout the period.[31]

The above variations and outright contradictions invite investigation of primary sources. In 1929 the NSDAP in Elbing, East Prussia, wrote: 'Our SA numbers over seventy men. We are winning recruits daily, above all from the working class'.[32] In 1930 the SA command in Petersdorf, eastern Brandenburg, reported:

> The SA's membership is absolutely first rate. It not only consists of younger people, there are older, front-line soldiers in its ranks. Its composition is eighty per cent manual workers.[33]

The Berlin SA wrote in the same year of 'the pleasingly large number of proletarians in our ranks.'[34] In 1932 the commander of the sub-Group (*Untergruppe*) of Upper Silesia found that his proletarian following was becoming restless:

> The attitude of the present government to the Movement, especially here in Upper Silesia where the SA recruits from the working class and the poorest sections of the population, has aroused a bitterness which requires my every effort to prevent violence on a grand scale.[35]

The Nazi party history of Widminnen in East Prussia drew a social distinction between the Nazi electorate and the SA. 'While the NSDAP voters were in the main from the middle classes, the SA were mainly the sons of workers, or their fathers were petty officials.'[36] In late 1934, the SA commander in Rheinhessen (Mainz, Worms and their hinterland) wrote that 'the SA is largely composed of manual workers', a group which he distinguished from farm workers, who also formed part of the SA's membership.[37]

The Nazi movement did not abandon attempts to win a greater degree of working-class support after 1930, although the party itself succeeded to a limited degree with its main effort aimed at the lower-middle classes. It was still two-thirds middle class in January 1933 and the SA's claims might therefore appear exaggerated, or perhaps wishful thinking. However, the vigorous propaganda campaign waged by the KPD within the SA indicates that at least some SA units contained large numbers of workers. This propaganda was sometimes threatening: 'Attention! Proletarians of the SA and SS, listen! . . . We warn you [*Euch*]! Our patience has now run out!'[38] On other occasions it appealed for class solidarity:

> Proletarians of the SA and SS Companies. . . . Break with Hitler! Come to us! . . . We'll win anyway, with or against you [*Euch*]! Proletarians, consider where you belong! Workers as poor as yourselves are speaking to you. . . . Proletarians to us and with us. Red Front![39]

Propaganda written after the Nazi takeover reminded the SA of unfulfilled Nazi pledges: 'Nazi proletarians! The factories and banks belong to the working people. Only the Communists are fighting for this!'[40]

The evidence is still inconclusive. Such appeals do not quantify the proportion of workers within the SA, and say nothing of the background of remaining SA members. This need not trouble us, for extensive membership lists and files of SA members are available from all parts of Germany: from East Prussia to Baden and from Holstein to Upper Bavaria. The complex conclusions to be drawn from these sources and their further historical implications form the basis of a more extensive work. However, their presentation here in summarised form provides an insight into the social background of the SA's rank and file.

The intricate maze of terminology surrounding the occupational structure of the Weimar era might be the despair of the non-German reader. For instance, many relatively humble occupations within the state sector of the economy were elevated to salaried status. The term 'artisan' (*Handwerker*) could apply to both a traditional, independent, rural craftsman and a skilled wage-earner in a modern, industrial undertaking such as I.G. Farben in Frankfurt-am-Main. Descriptive, rather than interpretative classification of occupations partly resolves the problem. Nonetheless, in Figures 1a and 1b, it was found necessary to use collective, interpretative concepts such as 'unskilled workers' or 'salaried white collar', partly for brevity's sake, but also to assess the significance of the results obtained.

It can be seen in Figures 2a and 2b that the largest single social group, both within the male working population and the SA, is termed 'workers'. The remaining terms are more precisely descriptive, although 'independents' is also very much a collective one. By virtue of the other terms used, that of 'workers' is not entirely ambiguous, but a more precise definition is helpful. A striking and frequently cited division within society is that between manual and non-manual employees.[41] The different nature of work in the respective groups as well as their differing pay structure, promotion prospects and pension schemes make this an important split which is often equated with that between the working and middle classes. However, increasing technical sophistication within advanced industrial societies has led to the development of a salaried manual group whose overall conditions of employment resemble those of other salaried employees rather than those of manual wage-earners. This group may, therefore, be included within the middle classes. Indeed this overall interpretation accords basically with the German census of 1925 or that of 1933, which in essence defined a worker as a manual, wage-earning employee[42] and it is against the official figures that the significance of any findings must be assessed.

A number of alternative definitions have been proposed in recent works. Firstly, it has been argued that blue and white collar employees were of a kind.[43] The preceding arguments make this appear an inadvisable definition. At the other extreme, it has been argued that by the Weimar era, skilled workers cannot be regarded as working class by virtue of their rising earnings and changing social attitudes.[44] The theory of embourgeoisement has been frequently and forcefully argued throughout the century, but if unskilled workers alone are considered as working class, one is left with a mere 6.5 per cent of the SPD being working class![45] Moreover, unskilled workers were very much a minority group within the male working population, their overall representation being somewhere around fifteen per cent at most.[46] It has also been suggested that one works with the *Klasse für sich* *notion of the working class to the exclusion of the *Klasse an sich**.[47] This once again raises problems of definition. The author concerned argues that public identification with the working-class movement's traditional organisations is the necessary prerequisite for inclusion within the working class of any individual.[48] Since this definition, a priori, excludes all Nazi bodies, its usefulness is severely limited here. Finally, the vague concept of the German working class being, in essence, city dwellers employed in large industrial concerns has gained some currency. In fact less than a third of the German working class were city-dwellers at this time; thus the proletarian of Berlin, Hamburg, Essen or Frankfurt-am-Main was more the exception than the rule.[49] Moreover, well under half the working class were employed in industrial undertakings with a pay-roll of over fifty employees, irrespective of whether these were urban, small town or rural.[50]

A sample of SA men from the late Weimar period (1929 to January 1933) is presented in Figure 1a. Almost half the sample is derived from small lists; largely of complete urban, smaller town and rural units. The remainder comprise a proportion of the Munich SA in the autumn of 1931. Since all available compatible material is presented (to the exclusion of other, non-compatible material), certain potential distortions are present. The predominance of urban samples exaggerates the potential number of salaried employees (a decidedly urban group),[51] while the potential number of independents is somewhat, and that of assisting family members considerably, diminished.[52] A further distortion is introduced by the 1931 Munich list. Many of the Companies (*Stürme*) listed were from the northern-central part of the city, including the university quarter of Schwabing, and consequently contained an extremely high proportion of students.[53] Only twelve students in Figure 1a were not from the Munich SA.

If this final distortion is taken into account, the results are remarkably consistent. The small sample element is 64.6 per cent working class and the 1931 Munich sample, with the exclusion of the students, 59.3 per cent working class. Differences exist: the small samples contain a high proportion of unskilled labour (22.6 per cent) and the 1931 Munich sample contains a high proportion of skilled labour (45.1 per cent), salaried employees (25.9 per cent), students (12.0 per cent) and members of the professions (4.3 per cent). The final group basically contains junior university staff and junior doctors and

---

*   *Klasse für sich* = 'class for itself'. A social class aware of, and acting in its
        common interests.
    Klasse an sich = 'class in itself'. The objectively defined notion of class,
        whether or not the class is conscious of its common interests.

Fig. 1a: Occupational Background of SA Rank and File Members
1929 to 30 January 1933[54]

Occupational Groups		Frequencies	Percentages
1.	Unskilled workers	176	13.4
2.	(Semi-) skilled workers	575	43.8
3.	Salaried manual	71	5.4
4.	Salaried white collar	219	16.7
5.	Civil servants	20	1.5
6.	Master craftsmen	9	0.7
7.	Independent traders, salesmen.		
	Small businessmen	31	2.4
8.	Farmers, peasants	45	3.4
9.	Assisting family members	1	0.1
11.	Professions, independents	37	2.8
12.	Schoolboys	8	0.6
13.	Students	105	8.0
14.	Former soldiers	10	0.8
16.	Retired	5	0.4
Totals		1,312	100.0

Notes: *Civil servants* — Lower and middle grades here.
Assisting family members (mithelfende Familienangehörige) —
Essentially family members helping on farms and in small firms.
Professions, independents — Members of the professions, senior civil
servants, large property owners, industrialists etc.

lawyers, not long out of university.

Taking Figure 1a as a whole, it is clear that the SA was not a predominantly lower-middle-class body. Only the salaried employees form a coherent lower-middle-class element. Nonetheless, the manual workers are not entirely dominant although in a clear majority. The use of the term lumpenproletarian to describe the SA's membership appears misleading in the light of the high ratio of trained SA members, both working and middle class.[55]

The SA kept more extensive, detailed and systematic records of its membership after the Nazi takeover. Figure 1b is therefore derived from a larger and more balanced sample and fewer reservations need be made about its representativeness. Non-compatible sources excluded from this table are in broad agreement with the result obtained here. The increase in the proportion of workers is notable, but, because of the student factor in the previous sample, should not be overstated. Nonetheless, the slight decline in middle-class strength (including salaried groups) is unmistakable. Thus in this latter period, social polarisation between a largely working-class SA and a lower-middle-class Nazi Party increased.

The official statistics include working members of the population only, when analysing the occupational background of the population.[56] Groups such as schoolboys and students are regarded as family dependents (*Berufszugehörige*) within the various occupational groups. Therefore, in order to compare results with the official statistics, schoolboys etc. must be excluded and slightly smaller, nominal samples used. In their simplified form the official statistics divide the working population into five groups.[60] The concept of 'worker' has been discussed. The independents are an especially disparate group, as the

Fig. 1b: Occupational Background of SA Rank and File Members 31 January 1933 to 30 June 1934[57]

Occupational Group		Frequencies	Percentages
1.	Unskilled workers	658	16.7
2.	(Semi-) skilled workers	2006	50.8
3.	Salaried manual	171	4.3
4.	Salaried white collar	581	14.7
5.	Civil servants	110	2.8
6.	Master craftsmen	46	1.2
7.	Independent traders, salesmen.		
	Small businessmen	39	1.0
8.	Farmers, peasants	80	2.0
9.	Assisting family members	18	0.5
10.	SA administration	1	0.0
11.	Professions, independents	102	2.6
12.	Schoolboys	21	0.5
13.	Students	97	2.5
14.	Former Soldiers	14	0.4
15.	Invalids	2	0.1
16.	Retired	1	0.0
Totals		3,947	100.1

Notes: As for Figure 1a.

Fig. 2a: Social Background of SA Rank and File Members
1929 to 30 January 1933 [58]

| Social Groups | Sample Results | | German Census |
	Frequencies	Percentages	Percentages
1. Workers	751	63.4	53.2
2. Salaried employees and civil servants	310	26.2	18.7
3. Independents	122	10.3	21.7
4. Assisting family members	1	0.1	6.3
5. Salaried domestic servants	—	—	0.1
Totals	1,184	100.0	100.0

Fig. 2b: Social Background of SA Rank and File Members
31 January 1933 to 30 June 1934 [59]

| Social Groups | Sample Results | | German Census |
	Frequencies	Percentages	Percentages
1. Workers	2,664	69.9	53.2
2. Salaried employees and civil servants	863	22.6	18.7
3. Independents	267	7.0	21.7
4. Assisting family members	18	0.5	6.3
5. Salaried domestic servants	—	—	0.1
Totals	3,812	100.0	100.0

official sources admit. Here are found peasant and great landowner,
small shopkeeper and surgeon, senior civil servant and master craftsman.
However, all independents are either self-employed or undertake
decisions at an executive level, thus distinguishing themselves from the
wage-earner, or middle and lower grade salaried employee and civil
servant. The remaining groups are comparable with the relevant
categories in Figures 1a and 1b.[61]

The workers are over-represented in the SA, particularly so in

Figure 2b. Figures 1a and 1b indicate that few SA men were civil servants, and therefore the over-representation of salaried employees is greater than that of the workers.[62] However, the relative drop in the former's strength between Figures 2a and 2b should be noted; particularly because the proportion of civil servants in the SA increased somewhat – perhaps for political reasons. In fact, what little direct evidence there is suggests that the proportion of workers within the SA after the takeover was indeed rising due to a very high proportion of workers among recruits.[63] A far lower proportion of these recruits were salaried employees and thus the observed trend is plausible.

In this descriptive work, historical reasons for the above results cannot, unfortunately, be discussed, given the limited space available, but the occupational structure of the SA will appear less surprising in due course for more functional reasons.

Further information concerning the occupational structure of the SA is presented in Figures 3a and 3b. The economic sector in which SA men worked or had worked immediately before becoming unemployed was established for a largely south German, rural sample (Berlin Document Center) and a north German, largely urban sample (North Rhineland). The original samples were larger (BDC 854, North Rhineland 223), but necessary information was often unavailable. The name or nature of the workplace was sometimes mentioned in the individual case files, but in other instances its nature was gathered from a declared occupation: factory worker, farm labourer, coal miner, railway clerk, shop assistant etc.

In Figure 3a, many of the unskilled workers were employed in agriculture, although three of these were in forestry rather than farming. Of unskilled, industrial employees, one worked for a master craftsman, two in quarries and twenty-five in factories. A further thirteen worked in workshops or factories of indeterminate size and nature. Nine unskilled workers in communications and commerce worked for the railways – eight of these in workshops or in track work. The (semi-) skilled workers are found predominantly in industry. Four were miners, twelve employed by master craftsmen and the remainder working in firms of varying size. The names Bosch, I.G. Farben and Siemens do arise however. Of those (semi-) skilled workers in communications and commerce, eight were railwaymen – six working in workshops or on track work. From the nature of their occupations, it may be assumed that many of the 259 (semi-) skilled workers from the original BDC sample who are excluded here worked in industry, or communications: bricklayers, mounters, fitters, machinists, lathe

Fig. 3a:Distribution of SA Rank and File Members within the Economy. Berlin Document Center, 1934 [64]

Occupational Group		Economic Group				Totals
		a	b	c	d	
1.	Unskilled workers	56	41	17	3	117
2.	(Semi-) skilled workers	5	56	13	1	75
3.	Salaried manual	1	5	1	6	13
4.	Salaried white collar	1	4	19	3	27
5.	Civil servants	—	—	3	21	24
6.	Master craftsmen	—	4	—	—	4
7.	Independent traders, salesmen	1	1	2	—	4
8.	Farmers, peasants	59	—	—	—	59
11.	Professions, independents	1	4	5	20	30
Totals		124	114	61	54	353

Fig. 3b: North Rhineland, 1933/4 [65]

Occupational Group		Economic Group				Totals
		a	b	c	d	
1.	Unskilled workers	—	16	—	—	16
2.	(Semi-) skilled workers	2	37	4	—	43
3.	Salaried manual	—	3	—	1	4
4.	Salaried white collar	1	3	1	2	7
5.	Civil servants	—	—	1	7	8
7.	Independent traders, salesmen	—	—	2	—	2
9.	Assisting family members	—	—	2	—	2
11.	Professions, independents	—	2	1	5	8
Totals		3	61	11	15	90

Notes: Economic Groups — a, agriculture, b, industry, crafts;
c, communications, commerce; d, health, administration, professions.

operatives, drivers and so on. The high proportion of salaried employees who could be classified within commerce largely results from occupational terminology. Four white collar employees worked in

industry and two in commerce in the six cases where an actual workplace was given. Of the civil servants, eight were teachers. The farmers
and peasants appear to have been small landowners in many cases and
some probably spent part of their working week in another employer's
pay.

The stark contrast between Figures 3a and 3b indicates that the
occupational structure of the SA depended largely on the nature of the
local economy rather than its appeal to a particular economic sector.[66]
Heavy industry, manufacturing and mining were the predominant
employers in the latter sample. Thirteen unskilled workers were
employed in factories and three in the building trade. Workplaces
included Krupp of Essen,[67] Besselmann und Hermes of Essen,[68] Bauer
und Schamte of Neuss where an SA man belonged to the Bauer
und Schamte 'Works Company' of the SA,[69] Ruhrchemie,[70] and an
unnamed steelworks in Duisburg.[71] Seventeen (semi-) skilled workers
were coal miners. One worked at the Katherina pit in Essen and in
September 1933 his 'strenuous job' compelled him to leave the SA.[72]
Three (semi-) skilled workers were employed by master craftsmen,
another in a small workshop and another in the building trade. Fifteen
certainly worked in factories and heavy industry, and many more
probably did. These latter are excluded for want of positive
identification, but their professions often sound remarkably apt for the
steelworks of the Ruhr: smelter, furnaceman, stoker, metal caster. Six
of the fifteen identified workers were employed by Krupp,[73] the
remaining nine by various firms: Rostek und Pesch of Krefeld,[74]
Hertmanni und Pongs of Mönchengladbach,[75] Kabelwerk A.G. of
Rheydt,[76] Köhler-Bowenkamp of Wuppertal,[77] Phönix Werke of
Ruhrort,[78] Siemens Schuckert of Mülheim/Ruhr,[79] Härdrich of
Duisburg,[80] the abattoir in Essen[81] and the Internationale Harvestor-
Kompanie.[82]

In most cases, salaried employees also worked in industry. Of the
manual salaried, one worked in mining and two in the construction
sector. One white collar employee was employed by the Schinteln
Wäschefabrik of Gelsenkirchen,[83] another by Krupp[84] and a third by
Demag A.G. of Duisburg.[85] A factory owner and a manager comprise
the independents in the industrial sector.[86]

The samples from other economic sectors are small. Two civil
servants were railway officials,[87] two local government officers,[88] one
a teacher,[89] another a police official[90] and one a tax officer.[91] Among
the eleven SA members in communications and commerce are found
two railwaymen (workers), a barge hand, a shop assistant, postman

(in this case a civil servant!), tradesman, an innkeeper and the sons of two small businessmen (assisting family members).

The general applicability of these results seems in little doubt. The more extensive research forming the basis of this analysis indicates that many SA men in lists of rural units compiled in 1935 were, as in the BDC sample, farm workers. In Frankfurt-am-Main, Offenbach, Hanover and the southern Rhine basin, many SA men worked in industry; I.G. Farben employed considerable numbers of SA men in the Frankfurt-am-Main districts of Griesheim, Sindlingen and Hoechst as well as in Ludwigshafen. Alternately, it had employed them before they lost their jobs and joined the SA. The SA had members (workers) employed by Dyckerhoff Zement of Wiesbaden in 1932 in the Adlerwerke in Frankfurt throughout the period, as well as in numerous other firms.[92] Of course, most SA members were jobless, but internal SA correspondence indicates that many SA men were factory workers both before and after periods of unemployment. In August 1933, for instance, the authorities in Bobenheim near Ludwigshafen reported that 'in the past few days, some SA men have been re-employed in the factories',[93] while the attitude of industry throughout Germany was generally considered vital to the successful re-employment of SA men.[94]

The question of social mobility deserves some consideration. Before considering primary material, one observation may be made immediately. Most SA men had been trained — either in blue or white collar occupations. This usually involved three years of apprenticeship or training which could prove a considerable financial burden to the trainee's family. Indeed, some unskilled SA men were untrained because of their fathers' deaths during the First World War or because of family poverty. Thus one might say with confidence that most SA men were in that occupation (or a similar one) envisaged for them when they left school at fourteen. Any social trauma had therefore not in all likelihood resulted from their occupation, but from losing the job for which they had trained over years, and for which their families had made sacrifices. They were not an exceptional group in the Germany of their day, as will be shown, for the registered unemployed embraced close on a third of the male wage-earning and salaried population by early 1933.

Figure 4a combines a largely rural sample (BDC) with a largely urban sample (Frankfurt-am-Main).[95] The table simplifies the picture by showing the frequencies in any particular occupational group, but not the shifts from one group to another between the two generations. The most important should be mentioned, dealing with the rural and urban elements in Figure 4a in turn.

In the rural sample most workers' sons remained within the working class. Five out of sixty-three did obtain middle-class jobs, while most unskilled workers' sons did attain a skill. A third of (semi-) skilled workers' sons, conversely, did not. No clear pattern emerges in the salaried sector or among civil servants' sons. A quarter of farmers' sons became (semi-) skilled workers, a sixth unskilled, and over a third farmers in their turn. Almost half the twenty-six master craftsmen's sons attained a skill (twelve), but only three worked as regular, paid employees in their fathers' firms. A further five were assisting family members and three had obtained a master's certificate themselves.

In the urban sample, a high transfer rate between the wage-earning and salaried sectors is evident, in both directions. In a sample of 144 (semi-) skilled workers, seventeen workers were the sons of white collar employees, six of blue collar salaried employees. Ninety (semi-) skilled workers were of working-class parentage. Conversely, three salaried manual employees out of fifteen and fifteen salaried white collar employees out of fifty were the sons of skilled workers. Once again, most unskilled workers' sons had attained a skill. Of the twenty-five civil servants' sons, over half were in salaried occupations and only six in manual jobs (five skilled). Master craftsmen's sons tended to become skilled workers in factories, many of their fathers also being factory employees, or they became salaried employees.

The reasons for these shifts are intricate, usually owing a great deal to individual family circumstances. Limited space precludes a meaningful examination here. It is however important to establish how typical such shifts were in German society of the day. Figure 4b presents information which has hitherto not received the attention it deserves. When subdivided into age groups, the official figures reveal a marked upward social mobility with an increase in age. The lower age group selected here reflects the predominant age groups in the SA rank and file. It was assumed that fathers would be approximately twenty-five years older than their sons. It must be stressed that were the age discrepancy larger, the upward mobility would be more marked and vice versa.[98]

In fact, the occupational difference between SA men and their fathers differs little from the national picture. The reasons for the somewhat large number of SA men in independent occupations and the small number of assisting family members are not unconnected; a question to be considered when analysing the age structure of the SA. Allowing for the smallness of the sample, it can be asserted fairly that

Fig. 4a: SA Rank and File Members Parental Backgrounds, 1934[96]

Occupations		Frequencies		Percentages	
		SA Men	Parents	SA Men	Parents
1.	Unskilled workers	70	56	15.7	12.6
2.	(Semi-) skilled workers	217	140	48.8	31.5
3.	Salaried manual	18	21	4.0	4.7
4.	Salaried white collar	61	43	13.7	9.7
5.	Civil servants	11	40	2.5	9.0
6.	Master craftsmen	3	59	0.7	13.3
7.	Independent traders, salesmen, small businessmen	2	10	0.4	2.2
8.	Farmers, peasants	16	53	3.6	11.9
9.	Assisting family members	9	–	2.0	–
11.	Professions, independents	17	17	3.8	3.8
12.	Schoolboys	5	–	1.1	–
13.	Students	12	–	2.7	–
14.	Former soldiers	4	–	0.9	–
16.	Retired	–	6	–	1.3
Totals		445	445	99.9	100.0

Fig. 4b: SA Rank and File Members, Parental Backgrounds,1934, Comparison with national statistics [97]

Social Groups		Percentages			
		SA Men	Parents	Nation[a]— Aged:	
				20 to 30	40 to 60
1.	Workers	67.69	44.65	62.93	42.20
2.	Salaried employees and civil servants	21.23	23.69	20.09	19.96
3.	Independents	8.96	31.66	7.26	36.80
4.	Assisting family members	2.12	–	9.95	0.97
5.	Salaried domestic employees	–	–	0.07	0.07
Totals		100.00	100.00	100.00	100.00

[a]Male working population.

the preponderance of workers and salaried employees was greater in the SA than in the nation, as was the preponderance of SA men from such parental backgrounds. However, a case for upward or downward mobility cannot be made. The unemployment of the early 1930s affected father and son alike and does not, therefore, affect the *relative* picture being discussed at this point.

The German unemployment of the early 1930s was virtually unparalleled elsewhere in Europe in its severity. With seasonal fluctuations, the level rose from 3,258,000 in January 1930[99] to 6,013,612 registered unemployed in January 1933.[100] This category applied to wage earners and salaried employees alone; thus within these occupational groups the unemployment rate had peaked at above thirty-three per cent registered unemployed. The situation only improved slowly during 1933 and 1934, with over four million jobless in the New Year of 1934.[101]

Using the very small samples which are available, Kater assesses the SA's unemployment rate at between sixty and seventy per cent, with extremes on either side.[102] Other primary sources suggest that the rate was probably nearer the top of this scale. As early as 1929 most of the Wiesbaden SA was unemployed[103] and there is little doubt that the rate was high outside the cities. The SA in Widminnen, East Prussia 'was largely composed of unemployed, who could barely pay the membership dues'.[104] In January 1931 the National Socialist leadership in Tilsit, also East Prussia wrote: 'The difficulties confronting our unemployed party members and SA comrades ... are especially severe this winter. A large number receive no unemployment benefit whatsoever.'[105] Most of the Giessen SA, Hessen-Nassau, were jobless in 1931[106] while Eberstadt, also in Hessen-Nassau, had little better to report between 1929 and 1933.[107] In February 1931, the commander of the SA Group East, Captain Stennes, grew tired of Hitler's preoccupation with winning elections, since he felt this 'legality policy' neglected the material well-being (or survival) of his men. He wrote bitterly to Röhm in February 1931: 'In Berlin there are Regiments containing sixty-seven per cent unemployed. In Breslau a Company could not turn out for inspection — in frost and snow — because it completely lacked footwear.'[108]

There was no improvement during 1932. In January the police reported that Company 24 of Munich 'contained about eighty SA members; most unemployed'.[109] With the opening of an SA hostel in Eglharting, Upper Bavaria, in the same month it was taken for granted that the SA was largely unemployed.[110] In September, the SA commander in Breslau wrote to Munich headquarters that: 'Sixty per cent of the SA men are long-term (jahrelang) unemployed and it would not conform with the facts if I were to report that morale is especially good'.[111] A summary of conditions in Germany as a whole during 1932 was written by the *Gau* chronicler of Hessen-Nassau. He commented that the SA 'had Companies which were composed solely of unemployed. For these men in particular, the creation of SA hostels was especially fortuitous. For a large section . . . these hostels became their real home.'[112] The change in the NSDAP's political fortunes might have brought better employment opportunities for SA men, with the resources of the state, potentially, at their disposal. However, the general picture did not improve significantly and eventually, there were bitter recriminations.

The period began badly. On 1 February 1933 the Hamburg SA commented that 'seventy-five per cent of all SA and SS men are long-term unemployed (*seit langer Zeit arbeitslos*)'.[113] The Ludwigshafen area was one to show a slight improvement during the summer of 1933,[114] but by September the Munich-based SA High Command voiced concern about the general situation:

> The allocation of vacant jobs to our SA, SS, and Stahlhelm men is not occurring to the extent desired by the SA High Command.
> Although it must be considered a moral duty to provide the National Socialist Revolution's fighters with work and bread, there are very many employers – both in private and state-owned concerns – who still distance themselves somewhat from National Socialism. Instead of drawing on our fighters to fill vacancies, as should be their duty, they actually appoint members of disbanded parties and organisations on a preferential basis.[115]

Thus it is not surprising that the Hamburg SA was still hard-pressed at the year's end. On 22 December its commander, Böckenhauer, wrote to Group Headquarters in Hanover:

> . . . Because of the duration of severe unemployment, there is a growing need to accustom men to an ordered existence; i.e. a daily routine, food, clothing etc. through short-term attendance at a welfare camp. This applies especially to the urban SA whose sufferings are extreme.[116]

During the first half of 1934, local economic conditions may have caused some variation in conditions. Bavaria seems to have fared best. Battalion III/J3 of Bad Reichenhall contained a mere six unemployed 'veterans'[117] on 5 April. Seventy-three newer recruits were jobless on 1 April compared with 185 on 1 March.[118] Company 21/25 of Neuötting, Upper Bavaria, reported 41.2 per cent unemployed in January, but this rate had halved by the summer.[119] However, the SA in the Rhine-Main basin fared worse. Gross Gerau was an exception,[120] but in Buchschlag most 'veterans' were still jobless in June.[121] The commander of the Wiesbaden SA wrote in the same month that 'providing work is proving very difficult'.[122] In Offenbach too, the SA was scourged by unemployment or subsistence wages where members had found work.[123]

The situation in Germany as a whole was unfavourable. Indeed on 20 June 1934 the SA Central Office in Munich attacked employers in industry and agriculture for their reluctance to employ SA members.

> Recriminations concerning employers' egoistic and anti-social attitude. Veterans are complaining about bad pay and the employers' scanty awareness of National Socialism, which includes little inclination to employ SA veterans . . . Farmers prefer labourers who do not belong to the SA, because they do not have to attend musters and exercises.[124]

Thus unemployment typified the lot of the SA man throughout the period 1929 to mid-1934. Rates of around seventy per cent unemployed appear representative, this making the incidence of jobless within the SA slightly higher than that of any particular class. The continuation of these high rates well into 1934 should be noted, for there is no doubt that they led to extreme frustration among the SA's rank and file despite a wide range of efforts by the SA's leadership to remedy the situation at this politically sensitive juncture. This complex question would in itself be worthy of an extended analysis were sufficient space available here to do it justice.

Figures 5a and 5b analyse the SA's age structure, using all available information from the sources for Figures 1a and 1b. SA regulations set lower and upper age limits at eighteen and forty-five although some exceptions were made. The bunching of membership below the age of twenty-five is evident.

This result confirms the outcome of the occupational analysis (Figures 1 and 2) in essentials, while bringing some details into question. The high proportion of wage earners and salaried employees appears virtually unavoidable, particularly after January 1933 when the SA measured its membership in millions. Since around 75 per cent were younger than thirty, over two million SA men were of this age by spring 1934. Within the German economy as a whole, there were only 394,074 male independents (master craftsmen, traders, shopkeepers, merchants, farmers and peasants, outworkers, members of the professions, executives, senior civil servants, big property owners, etc.) aged under thirty.[127] Even if they had joined the SA to a man, (which

Fig. 5a: The Age Structure of SA Rank and File Members 1929 to 30 January 1933[125]

Age	Occupational Groups												Totals	
	1	2	3	4	5	6	7	8	9	10	11	12	Fre.	%
19 minus	10	29	3	11	–	–	–	–	3	1	–	–	57	17.3
20 - 24	15	82	7	14	2	–	–	–	4	2	9	1	136	41.2
25 - 29	6	39	2	9	–	–	1	–	4	–	1	1	63	19.1
30 - 34	6	16	–	1	1	–	–	4	2	–	–	2	32	9.7
35 - 39	3	5	–	1	3	–	1	–	1	–	–	–	14	4.2
40 - 44	2	4	–	1	–	–	2	–	–	–	–	–	9	2.7
45 - 49	1	5	2	2	2	1	–	–	–	–	–	1	14	4.2
50 plus	2	1	1	–	–	1	–	–	–	–	–	–	5	1.5
Totals	45	181	15	39	8	2	4	4	14	3	10	5	330	99.9

Fig. 5b: 31 January 1933 to 30 June 1934 [126]

Age	Occupational Groups														Totals	
	1	2	3	4	5	6	7	8	9	9a	10	11	12	13	Fre.	%
19 minus	43	135	7	28	–	—	–	–	11	6	11	10	–	–	251	8.7
20 -24	155	593	40	155	22	3	1	–	27	9	7	66	21	–	1099	38.2
25 - 29	102	401	31	146	24	7	3	–	11	–	–	18	39	–	782	27.2
30 -34	74	227	26	76	19	4	3	6	8	–	–	2	19	1	455	16.1
35 -39	18	60	10	39	9	4	2	–	5	1	–	–	11	–	159	5.5
40 -44	5	35	4	16	6	3	1	–	–	–	–	–	6	–	76	2.6
45 plus	6	18	3	8	5	2	–	–	1	–	–	–	4	1	48	1.7
Totals	403	1469	121	468	85	23	10	6	63	16	18	96	100	2	2880	100.

Key to occupations: 1 Unskilled workers, 2 (Semi-) skilled workers, 3 Salaried manual, 4 Salaried white collar, 5 Civil service, 6 Master craftsmen, 7 Independent traders, salesmen, small businessmen, 8 Former soldiers, 9 Farmers, peasants, 9a Assisting family members, 10 Schoolboys, 11 Students, 12 Professions, independents, 13 Invalids.

they did not) most SA members could not have been independents.

Assisting family members provide a further source of recruitment from a similar social background. Within the German economy as a whole, there were 657,415 such males aged between eighteen and thirty,[128] but 602,293 were engaged in agriculture.[129] Therefore one can reaffirm without further ado that the urban and small-town SA must have consisted largely of wage-earners and salaried employees *by virtue of their age alone.*

There are no grounds for concluding otherwise with respect to the rural SA. SA members who gave their occupation as 'farm worker' (Landarbeiter, Knecht) are must unlikely to have been over-modest farmers! Indeed, the rural samples may have contained fewer farmers and peasants than figures 1a and 1b suggest. They indicate that around 2.5 per cent of the SA's membership were farmers or peasants between 1929 and mid-1934, giving a total figure near 75,000 in early 1934. Since half the farmers in Figure 5a, and over half in Figure 5b were younger than twenty-five, around 32,500 farmers and peasants in the SA would have been younger than twenty-five in spring 1934. However, had every farmer, peasant and independent forester aged under twenty-five in Germany joined the SA, it would have won 21,395 recruits.[130] Where further information concerning 'farmers' within the SA came to light, it transpired that many were either assisting family members or farm-workers. These were classified accordingly. The discrepancy between the projected figure of 32,500 and the maximum possible figure of 21,395 can doubtless be explained by assisting family members anticipating their future occupation (farmer) or farm workers exaggerating their position. Therefore among the SA in Figure 4b, there were probably fewer independents and more assisting family members then appears the case. The proportion of workers was probably slightly higher.

Therefore, the SA rank and file were a young body of workers and salaried employees, most of whom had lost their jobs during the economic crisis of the early 1930s. This result provides a basic picture of the SA's rank and file's social background, but leaves some issues unexplored. By all appearances, SA men were unmarried (about eighty per cent in 1932 and sixty-five per cent in 1934). By virtue of their age most of them could not have fought in the Great War. Other traits such as denominational and political background exceed the purely descriptive brief of this analysis.

This investigation has dealt exclusively with the social backgrounds of the SA's rank and file. However, as Rohe reminds us in his work on the *Reichsbanner,* a largely working-class organisation is liable to take its lower and middle ranking leadership from the middle classes for functional reasons.[131] This also applies to the SA, whose leadership differed markedly from the rank and file. The former were 33.4 per cent workers, 38.3 per cent salaried employees and civil servants, 27.9 per cent independents and 0.4 per cent assisting family members.[132] A more detailed analysis reveals a trend towards the middle class with a rise in rank. Thus the commanders of the smallest SA unit (*the Scharführer*) were not especially distinguishable from the rank and file: workers 52.5 per cent, salaried employees and civil servants 32.8 per cent, independents 13.7 per cent and assisting family members 1.1 per cent.[133] The middle and higher leaders (*Sturmführer* and above) were much more middle class: workers 15.7 per cent, salaried employees and civil servants 40.4 per cent and independents 43.9 per cent.[134] Not surprisingly, age tended to rise with rank, although most middle ranking and senior leaders were younger than forty.[135] The contrasts in educational background are striking. More than three-quarters of SA men had left school (*Volksschule*) at fourteen.[136] The corresponding rates for leaders were *Scharführer* 64.9 per cent, *Truppführer* 42.2 per cent, *Sturmführer* and above 31.1 per cent.[137] The degree of war experience likewise rose with rank. In sharp contrast to their following, most middle and higher ranking SA leaders were war veterans.[138]

This study demonstrates that the National Socialist movement was more diverse socially than has hitherto been believed. Alongside a party which was over two-thirds middle class, there existed in the SA an activist movement which won sizeable numbers of workers for the National Socialist cause. Moreover, while the middle-class element in the party was disparate and certainly shared few common interests (Bracher),[139] it was dominated by the salaried employees within the SA. The 'pre-industrial' middle class, the old 'Mittelstand', is scarcely found here. The integrative capacities of the Nazi movement therefore extended throughout the population, with the SA serving among other things as an instrument for the penetration of the working classes.

The political developments which involved the SA cannot, consequently, be analysed in the same terms as those applied to other parts of the National Socialist movement. A revision of the historical interpretation of these events is clearly called for.

c **Notes**

1. For example, at national level; Bayerisches Hauptstaatsarchiv (Bay. HSA),

Allgemeines Staatsarchiv (ASA); Sonderabgabe I, 1774. Meeting in the Reich Ministry of the Interior on 5 April 1932 under the chairmanship of Reichsminister Groener; the same, on 13 April 1932. At local level, police forces kept a close watch on SA activities. In Bavaria, for instance, see Bay. HSA, ASA, Sonderbgabe I, 1554, PND Nr. 719 and for Prussia, Bay. HSA, ASA, Sonderabgabe I, 1871. Bericht des Preussischen Min. des Innern über die Entwicklung der NSDAP, pp. 132-85 for report on the development of the SA. Many Prussian police reports for the years 1930 and 1931 are contained in BA, NS 26/596.

2. Re. *Germania, Vorwärts, Berliner Tageblatt, Münchener Post* etc. on almost any day between New Year 1930 and January 1933. An especially striking example of a newspaper's alarm is found in Bay. HSA, ASA, Sonderabgabe I, 1774. *Regensburger Anzeiger,* No. 270, 30 September 1932, p.2. Among contemporary analyses, S. Neumann, *Die Parteien der Weimarer Republik,* republished (Stuttgart, 1965) provides a useful description of the political movements and parties of the early 1930s.

3. H. Bennecke, *Hitler und die SA* (Munich, 1962) passim; A. Werner, *SA und NSDAP: SA: 'Wehrverband', 'Parteitruppe', oder 'Revolutionsarmee',* Dissertation (Erlangen, 1964), Chapters 2-4; C. Bloch, *Die SA und die Krise des NS-Regimes 1934* (Frankfurt, 1970), p.33.

4. J. Noakes, *The Nazi Party in Lower Saxony, 1921-1933* (Oxford, 1971) p.185; J. Fest, *The Face of the Third Reich,* trans, M. Bullock (Pelican, 1972), pp 216, 219, 220; R. Diels, *Lucifer ante Portas, Zwischen Severing und Heydrich* (Zurich, 1949), pp.154, 155, 158, 164; P. Merkl, *Political Violence under the Swastika, 581 Early Nazis* (Princeton, 1975), pp.383-409.

5. See note 3. Also M. Gallo, *Der Schwarze Freitag der SA. Die Vernichtung des revolutionären Flügels der NSDAP durch Hitlers SS im Juni 1934,* (Cologne, Hamburg, 1972). E.G. Reiche, *The Development of the SA in Nuremberg 1922-1934* (Dissertation, University of Delaware, 1972).

6. Werner, *SA und NSDAP,* pp.544-52.

7. M. Broszat, *Der Staat Hitlers. Grundlegung und Entwicklung seiner inneren Verfassung* (Munich, 1969), p. 256.

8. Bloch, *Die SA,* p.45.

9. BA, NS23/127; OSAF F. Nr 4513, München, 27 März 1934. Membership 2,950,000 by 1 January 1934.

10. Bennecke, *Hitler und SA*; Werner, *SA und NSDAP*; Bloch, *Die SA.*

11. See note 10. Also R. O'Neill, *The German Army and the Nazi Party 1933-1939* (London, 1966). F. L. Carsten, *The Reichswehr and Politics, 1918 to 1933* (Oxford, 1966).

12. The *Reichswehr* was strongly monarchist in its sentiments, the manifestations of this ranging from political intrigue to persistent display of the old Imperial Colours, as against those of the new republic. The SA was highly contemptuous of this traditionalist mood.

13. Bloch, *Die SA;* Werner, *SA und NSDAP*; A. Schweitzer, *Big Business in the Third Reich* (London, 1964).

14. Bloch, *Die SA,* p.146.

15. Schweitzer, *Big Business,* pp.117-19.

16. Bloch, *Die SA,* p.146.

17. *Die Bürgerlichen Parteien in Deutschland. Handbuch der Geschichte der bürgerlichen Parteien und anderen bürgerlichen Interessenorganisationen vom Vormärz bis zum Jahre 1945* (Leipzig, 1970), Vol. II, p.403; BA, NS23/1; Der Oberste SA-Führer, Zentralamt; 'Kampf gegen die SA', pp.3-4

18. T. W. Mason, 'Labour in the Third Reich, 1933-1939', *Past and Present,*

1966, p.113.
19. A. Nicholls, *Weimar and the Rise of Hitler* (London, 1968), p.165.
20. Merkl, *Political Violence,* p.595. He presents a table which analyses the occupational background of a mixture of SA and SS leaders and rank and file from both organisations. Unfortunately this analysis does not distinguish between these different categories. He concludes that his mixed sample was 'far more heavily blue-collar and white collar workers and farmers than the non-stormtroopers'.
21. W. S. Allen, *The Nazi Seizure of Power. The experience of a single German Town, 1930-1935* (Chacago, 1965), p.74.
22. K. Heiden, *Der Fuehrer. Hitler's Rise to Power,* trans. R. Manheim (London, 1967), p.431.
23. Schweitzer, *Big Business,* pp.75-6, 113-19.
24. I. Fetscher, 'Zur Kritik des sowjetmarxistischen Faschismusbegriffs', in G. Jasper (ed.), *Von Weimar zu Hitler 1930-1933* (Cologne, Berlin, 1968) p.157.
25. A. Sohn-Rethel, *Ökonomie und Klassenstruktur des deutschen Faschismus. Aufzeichnungen und Analysen* (Frankfurt-am-Main, 1973), p.191.
26. M. Kater, 'Zum gegenseitigen Verhältnis von SA und SS in der Sozialgeschichte des Nationalsozialismus von 1925 bis 1939', *Vierteljahrschrift für Sozial- und Wirtschaftsgeschichte,* 62. Band, Heft 3, 1975, p. 370 : SA 'about 70 to 80 per cent lower middle class'.
27. Kater, *Verhältnis,* p.371. The majority of unemployed were 'unskilled workers or insufficiently trained skilled workers or artisans'.
28. Bloch, *Die SA,* pp.37-8.
29. *Bürgerlichen Parteien,* Vol. II, p.403.
30. Diels, *Lucifer,* p.157.
31. M. Kele, *Nazis and Workers. National Socialist Appeals to German Labor, 1919-1933* (University of North Carolina, 1972), p.148.
32. Staatliches Archivlager in Göttingen Staatsarchiv Königsberg (Archivbestände Preussicher Kulturbesitz) (SAG), Rep. 240 C 80a. Ortsgruppe Elbing, II 8. 19
33. BA, NS 26/214, Bericht über den SA-Aufmarsch am 5/6. IV. in Stentsch und Schwiebus. Petersdorf, den 7. April 1930. gez. Friedrich u. Lindemann.
34. BA, NS 26/133, Anonymous testimonial concerning Berlin SA (73 pp.), p. 63.
35. BA, NS 23/474, SA der NSDAP, Oppeln, den 22.September 1932. Bezug 2580/32. An Chef des Stabes, Ernst Röhm, München.
36. SAG, Rep 240 C 61b(1), Ortsgruppe Widminnen.
37. BA, NS 26/262, SA der NSDAP, Führer der Brigade 150, Rheinhessen. Lagebericht für das 4. Vierteljahr 1934. Mainz, den 19. Dezember 1934.
38. BA, Sammlung Schumacher, 330. Achtung! Proleten der SA und SS mal herhoren!
39. BA, Sammlung Schumacher, 330. Achtung! Lesen! Proleten der SA- und SS-Stürme. Die Kommune spricht zu Euch! (6 November 1932).
40. BA, Sammlung Schumacher, 331, 'Nazi-Prolet, Augen auf!' *Hamburger Volkszeitung,* den 26. März 1933.
41. Among the enormous range of literature on this subject, A. Giddens, *The Class Structure of the Advanced Societies* (London, 1973), pp.180-6 provides a useful summary of the problem.
42. *Statistik des Deutschen Reichs,* Band 453. *Volks- Berufs-und Betriebezählung vom 16. Juni 1933* (Berlin, 1936); Abschnitt 11/2/b, Abschnitt 11/2/c, Abschnitt V/3.
43. Kele, *Nazis and Workers,* pp.69-73.
44. M. H. Kater, 'Zur Soziographie der frühen NSDAP', *Vierteljahrshefte für Zeitgeschichte,* 19, 1971, pp.140-53.

45. R. N. Hunt, *German Social Democracy, 1918-1933* (Chicago, 1970), p.103.
    This includes the small proportion of farm workers within the SPD.
46. Their proportion was highest among the unemployed, this possibly
    accounting for the relatively high incidence of unskilled workers in some
    SA samples. 22.2 per cent of registered unemployed were unskilled
    workers. *Statistisches Jahrbuch für das deutsche Reich, 1934* (Berlin, 1934),
    p.307, table 11.
47. Anonymous, 'The Coming of the Nazis', *TLS*, 3,752, 1 February 1974.
    p.95.
48. ibid.
49. Statistisches Jahrbuch, 1, p.20, table 16c.
50. *Das Deutsche Reich von 1918 bis heute* (Berlin, 1930). Gliederung der
    Gewerbebetriebe, 1925.
51. As for note 49.
52. ibid.
53. Both the lists available and other information at hand left no doubt that
    the sample is only a partial one. It appears that around half the Munich SA
    is represented here, perhaps slightly less.
54. (a) Bay.HSA,ASA, Sonderabgabe 1, 1549, Companies from the Munich
    SA, 1931. 1870, Abschrift. Dienstelle:Trupp Weilheim Sturm 55. Stärke-
    bericht für den Monat Dezember 1930; 1549, Mannschaftsliste für Trupp
    Laim, Sturm 4 der NSDAP (1930); 1870, Verzeichnis der Mitglieder der
    SA des Sturmes 5 (Neuhausen); 1551, Auszug aus dem Bericht des
    Polizeipräsidenten in Berlin vom 19. September 1930, Tgb. 439 IA 7/1929
    Anlage 2. Verhaftete SA-Mitglieder; 1554, Namensverzeichnis der 23
    Berliner SA-Leute die sich vom 20. Mai bis 2. Juni in München aufhielten.
    (b) BA, NS 26/528-533, SA veterans (rank and file only included in article)
    from Hessen-Nassau, 1929; NS 26/522, Alfeld/Leine, Kriminalpolizei,
    Juli 1932; NS 26/523, 527, Miscellaneous police sources, 1930-32; NS
    26/596, Prussia, SA men arrested for possessing firearms, September 1930
    to August 1931; NS 26/513, Anklageschrift des Staatsanwaltes bei dem
    Landgericht München 1.
    (c) Hessisches Hauptstaatsarchiv Wiesbaden (HHW), Abteilung 483, 1053,
    Sturm 17/81 (Frankfurt-am-Main 1932) Namensverzeichnis; 6348,
    Sturmbann IV/115, Auerbach/Hessen 1931.
    (d) Institut für Zeitgeschichte (IFZ), MA 616/21, 474, 344, 45/46, Der
    Oberstaatsanwalt als Leiter der Anklagebehörde bei dem Sondergericht,
    Görlitz, 28 November 1932; MA 616/20, 2954, SA men Görlitz
    (Luetgebrune papers) September 1932; MA 616/21, 4353-4661, SA men,
    Luetgebrune papers, Nov./Dec. 1932.
    (e) Niedersächsisches Hauptstaatsarchiv (NHStA), Hann. 310 1 E1, SA in
    Anderten, 1930-1933; *Landratsamt Hameln-Pyrmont, Aktenstuck A4*[1], SA
    Gruppe in Halvestorf 1931.
    (f) SAG, Rep 240/C 39d, Ortsgruppe Allenstein (SA); Rep 240/C 40c,
    Geschichte Ortsgruppe Possessern; Rep 240/C 47e, SA Abteilung,
    Ortsgruppe Kiauten; Rep 240/C 61b(1), Ortsgruppe Widminnen,
    Geschichte, pp.20-21; Rep 37-5, SA involved in case Haffke u. Gen.
    Tannenwalde, August 1930-March 1931; Rep 37-5, SA men charged with
    arson, Königsberg, August 1932; Rep 37-14, SA men involved in fight with
    KPD, Königsberg, July 1932; Rep 37-15, Ortsgruppe Metgethen, attack on
    Reichsbanner, November 1930; Rep 18-14, Court proceedings, Lyck,
    15 March 1931; Rep 240/C 67b, Allenstein, 30 August 1932, der
    Oberstaatsanwalt als Leiter der Anklagebehörde beim Sondergericht.
    Anklageschrift; Rep 240/C 67b, Court proceedings, Ortelsburg, 21
    September 1931.

(g) Bay. HSA, Staatsarchiv München (SAM), NSDAP 803, SA
Sturmbann 11/4 Neuötting/Burghausen 1932.
(h) I am deeply grateful to Dr G. Stokes of Dalhousie University, Nova
Scotia (Canada), for allowing me to use a membership list for the SA in
Eutin, Holstein 1929, which he kindly provided. 231 SA men in the total
sample are from police and court sources; the rest from membership lists.

55. See page 134.
56. Statistisches Jahrbuch, p.19, table 14c.
57. Berlin Document Center (BDC), SA 774-878, HHW Abteilung 483 NSDAP,
Frankfurt am Main Standarte 25, 1381, 1382, 2522-2524; Standarte 81,
1346-1362, 2100-2213; Standarte 99, 1368-1379, 2214-2284. Results for
30 June 1934 achieved by combining results for 1 July 1935 and those for
men who left the SA in the intervening year (minimal new recruitment
during this year). Bay. HSA, SAM, NSDAP 833, Burghausen, Sturm 24/25,
1934; Bay. HSA, SAM, NSDAP 728, Sturm 1/10 Ingolstadt, Namenliste
1933-1934; BA, NS 23/8, 11, SA, Prussia, small, miscellaneous samples. BA,
NS 23/398, SA Hamburg, 1933-4 BA, ns 23/306, Sturmbann 11/2.
Pioniersturme 11/2, 12/2, 13/2, Standort Speyer, 26 June 1934; Standarte
31 Pioniersturm 14/31, Ludwigshafen, 19 June 1934; Standarte 22,
Pioniersturm 9/22, Zweibrücken, 21 June 1934; Standarte 8, Pioniersturm
16/8, Wolfstein, 22 June 1934; Pioniersturm 16/17, SA Gruppe Kurpfalz,
Maximiliansau, 21 June 1934; Haupstaatsarchiv Düsseldorf (HStAD) HStAD,
Gestapo(leit)stelle Düsseldorf, SA men in index file compiled by archive,
additional details from the relevant individual Gestapo case files; HStAD
RW 23, SA Standarte J8 Würselen, 1933/34; SA Standarte 25, Aachen
1 July 1934.
58. See notes 54 and 56.
59. See notes 57 and 56.
60. Statistisches Jahrbuch, p.19, Table 14c.
61. 'Workers' in Figures 2 = Groups 1 and 2 in Figures 1. 'Salaried employees
and civil servants' in Figures 2 = Groups 3, 4, and 5 in Figures 1.
62. Statistisches Jahrbuch, p.19, table 14c. Approximately seventy per cent
of this group are salaried employees and thirty per cent civil servants.
63. Bay. HSA, SAM, NSDAP 803, SA der NSDAP, Sturm 22/25. Probweise
Aufnahme von SA-Anwärtern vom 1. bis zum 5. 12. 1933 Altötting;
Generallendasarchiv Karlsruhe (GLAK): Abteilung 465d, 1307, SA der
NSDAP, Sturm 16/469 Eberbach, den 13. 12. 1933. Verzeichnis der in
der Zeit v. 1. – 5.November 1933 neu angemeldeten SA-Anwärter.
Verzeichnis der in der Zeit v. 1. – 5. November 1933 angemeldeten
und auswärts wohnenden SA-Anwärter.
64. BDC, SA 774-878, 63.6 per cent of sample from Bavaria, 8.3 per cent
from rural Hessen, 62.5 per cent of sample from communities with a
population of less than 10,000. This was a random sample of the material
available in the BDC. All names with initial letters FA to FL (the first half
of the letter F) were examined.
65. HStAD, Gestapo(leit)stelle Düsseldorf, SA men in index file compiled by
archive. Additional details from relevant individual Gestapo case files. The area
covered embraces the western Ruhr district and immediately
neighbouring areas.
66. Statistisches Jahrbuch, p.21, table 17. Proportions of population working
in different economic sectors. Bavaria: agriculture 43.8%, industry and

crafts 33.7%. Westphalia: agriculture 19.8%, industry and crafts 54.8%.
Rheinprovinz: agriculture 19.3%, industry and crafts 50.0%.
All file numbers quoted in reference numbers 67 to 91 derive from the Gestapo
files of the HStAD.

67. 31,064
68. 45,226
69. 31,652
70. 21,586
71. 21,601
72. 49,069
73. Es 28,261; D 29,429; 11,892; 43,718; 48,851; D 41,992; Es 60,916;49,130.
74. 19,368
75. 43,021
76. 25,197
77. D 38,771; Es 49,394
78. 10,469
79. 43,108
80. 44,961
81. 52,008
82. 8,676
83. 25,155
84. 16,279
85. 41,624
86. 30,828; 41,386
87. 13,626; 21,673; 52,257
88. 27,611; 1,495
89. 14,627S
90. 21,508
91. 45,661
92. Information from the files of HHW as quoted in note 57.
93. Landesarchiv Speyer (LAS): H33 1268II, Nr 1094, Gendarmerie-Station
     Bobenheim-am-Rhein, Betr. Halbmonatsbericht, II Sonstiges, den 17. August
     1933.
94. See pages 148-9.
95. BDC SA 774-878; HHW 483, 2100-2213.
96. ibid. The sample from Frankfurt is a small part of the Frankfurt sample
     included in Figure 1b, but representative of it in terms of SA men's
     occupational backgrounds.
97. As note 95. Also, Statistisches Jahrbuch, p.24, table 21.
98. Statistisches Jahrbuch, as above.
99. Statistisches Jahrbuch, p.307, Table II.
100. ibid.
101. Extrapolated from figure for 31 December 1933.
102. Kater, *Verhältnis,* pp. 361, 362.
103. BA, NS 26/530. Georg Weiss, Erinnerungen, den 19.Dez. 1936
104. SAG, Rep 240 C 61b(1), Ortsgruppe Widminnen, Party History.
105. SAG, Rep 240 C 33d2, Bezirk Tilsit der NSDAP, den 8.Jan. 1931.
106. BA, NS 26/528, Adolf Treser, Erinnerungen, Giessen, den 28. Dez.
     1936.
107. BA, NS 26/529, Adolf Weber, Erinnerungen, Eberstadt, den 5. Jan. 1937.
108. BA, NS 26/325, Abschrift, 1161/31 St/v.B., gez. Stennes.
109. Bay.HSA,ASA, Sonderabgabe 1, 1552, PND Nr. 764, Appell des SA Sturms
     24, . . . am 21. Jan. 1932 . . .
110. Bay.HSA,ASA, Sonderabgabe 1, 1870, 'Ein neues SA-Heim in Eglharting',

Die Front, den 8. Jan. 1932.

111. BA, NS 23/474, SA der NSDAP, Standarte 11, Breslau, den 22. September 1932. Stimmungsbericht.

112. A. Gimbel, So *kämpften wir,* (Frankfurt, 1941), p.175.

113. BA, NS 23/399, Gau Hamburg, den 1. Feb. 1933, gez. Wilhelm Grundlach.

114. LAS, H33 1268 II, as in note 93.

115. BA, NS 23/126, Der Oberste SA-Führer, München den 23. September 1933, Betr. Unterbringung von arbeitslosen SA, SS-und Sta. Angehörigen, p.1.

116. BA, NS 23/399, Untergruppe Hamburg, den 22. Dezember 1933; Der SA Gruppe Nordsee, Hannover, gez. Böckenhauer.

117. Those SA members who had joined before 30 January 1933 were regarded as 'veterans', cf. Party veterans who were required to have joined before 1930 to qualify for this status.

118. Bay.HSA,SAM, NSDAP 977, SA der NSDAP, Jägerstandarte 3, Sturmbann 111/J3, Versorgungsstelle, Reichenhall, den 5. April 1934.

119. Bay.HSA,SAM, NSDAP 678, SA der NSDAP, Der Führer des Sturmes 21/25. Geldverwaltung Neuötting, den 7. November 1934. This report only applied to non-party members who did form the majority of the unit.

120. BA, NS 23/266, SA der NSDAP, Standarte 13, Gross Gerau, den 14. Juli 1934, Vierteljahresbericht.

121   BA, NS 23/266, SA der NSDAP, Standarte 61, Buchschlag in Hessen, den 27. Juni 1934, Vierteljahresbericht.

122. BA, NS 23/266, SA der NSDAP, Standarte 80, Wiesbaden, den 26 Juni 1934, Vierteljahresbericht.

123. BA, NS 23/266, SA der NSDAP, Standarte 168, Offenbach/Main, den 27 Juni 1934, Vierteljahresbericht.

124. BA, NS 23/1, Der Oberste SA-Führer, Zentralamt, Bericht Nr. 4, Der SA-Mann und sein Arbeitsamt, München, den 20. Juni 1934.

125. Bay. HSA,ASA, Sonderabgabe I, 1549, SA Munich, Trupp M/IL, Stürme 2/L, 5/L, 7/L, 8/L; and Mannschaftsliste für Trupp Laim, Sturm 4 der NSDAP; NHStA, Landratsamt Hameln-Pyrmont, Aktenstück A4[1]. SA Gruppe in Halvestorf, 1931.

126. HHW Abt 483 NSDAP, Sources as in note 57. BDC; SA 774-878; HStAD, as in note 57; Bay.HSA,SAM, as in note 57; GLAK, as in note 63.

127. Statistisches Jahrbuch, p.24, table 21.

128. ibid.

129. ibid.

130. ibid.

131. K. Rohe, *Das Reichsbanner Schwarz Rot Gold. Ein Beitrag zur Geschichte und Struktur der politischen Kampfverbände zur Zeit der Weimarer Republik* (Düsseldorf, 1966), p.272; P. D. Stachura, *Nazi Youth in the Weimar Republic* (Santa Barbara, Oxford, 1975), p.58ff, shows that the Hitler Youth also conformed to this pattern.

132. BDC:SA 774-878; HStAD, Gestapo(leit)stelle Düsseldorf. Index file as compiled by archive. Additional details from individual Gestapo case files. Figures correct for 30 June 1934.

133. ibid.

134. ibid.

135. BDC: SA 774-878.

136. BDC:SA 774-878,HStAD RW 23, SA Standarte J8 Würselen, 1933-1934; SA Standarte 25 Aachen, den 1. Juli 1934; HStAD Gestapo. as in note 132.

137. BDC: SA 774-878.

138. BA, NS 23/125, OSAF II Nr 1290/33, München, den 19. März 1933.

139. K. D. Bracher, *The German Dictatorship,* trans. J. Steinberg (London, 1971), p.158.

5 THE RISE OF THE NATIONAL SOCIALIST STUDENTS' ASSOCIATION AND THE FAILURE OF POLITICAL EDUCATION IN THE THIRD REICH

Geoffrey J. Giles

The *Nationalsozialistischer Deutscher Studentenbund* (NSDStB) is often considered to have been one of the most successful branches of the Nazi Party. Many former students assert that it was impossible to escape its control (though this sometimes represents a veiled apology for collaboration). Even present-day scholars, failing to see through the image that the NSDStB itself tried to promote, claim that, despite initial teething troubles, it reached monolithic omnipotence by 1937 at the latest.[1] The purpose of this paper is to examine the rather limited ways in which the NSDStB did fulfil its aims and to suggest the causes of its failure.

One might wonder in the first place why such an overtly anti-intellectual party as the National Socialists should wish to found a special branch for university students. In fact, the initiative did not come from the Party, but from a couple of Munich law students. Hitler showed little interest but was persuaded by Hess, who had formed a special student company in the Munich SA in 1922, to give the scheme a trial run. The NSDStB was officially founded at the beginning of 1926, with one of the law students, Wilhelm Tempel, at its head. About twenty groups were established within a year, but at many universities membership barely reached double figures.[2] However, these small enclaves were nothing if not vociferous, and often created the impression that they were stronger than was actually the case. The eleven members of the Hamburg group scarcely met at all in the first half of 1928 — their leader claimed that he did not wish to destroy the widely-held view that the group was about forty strong by actually holding public meetings.[3] The NSDStB was greatly hampered at this early stage by an almost total neglect by Nazi Party headquarters, especially in the most urgently needed area of financial assistance. Tempel complained that he and his tiny staff frequently had to forego dinner in order to pay for postage of circulars and letters out of their own pockets.[4] The Party was waiting for the NSDStB to prove itself and show its worth, before

granting it any real support. There were in any case reservations
voiced from many quarters about the desirability of creating a
separate organisation for students as a social class, when the NSDAP
was supposed to unite all ranks and walks of life. To many Nazis, it
looked like yet another example of the snobbery of the intelligentsia,
a stigma which the NSDStB had both now and later to try and live
down by encouraging its members to participate in other branches of
the Party, such as the SA or the Hitler Youth.[5]

The charge was partly justified, since many NSDStB members did
feel that they had a special task within the Nazi movement, and one
on a somewhat higher plane than street-brawling. For a long time this
question remained in the air, and in the summer of 1929 there was
still bewilderment as to the true function of the *Studentenbund*:

Is the *Studentenbund* a corporative grouping of individual Party
members who happen to be studying, and should the work
therefore centre first and foremost on the local Party
organisation, and the advertising in the university of *its* meetings;
or is on the other hand that view correct which deduces special tasks
from the very existence of a separate national headquarters, namely
academic politics and an examination of National Socialist ideas
in a form corresponding to the education and mental ability of the
academic, *alongside* the work of the student in the Party? . . . We
don't want to be Party carthorses, delivering up our own political
will to the local Party leader, and timidly erring with the mass
rather than wanting, through productive self-criticism and the
struggle for our own judgements, to strive for the highest goal.[6]

Baldur von Schirach, Tempel's successor, responded to these and other
queries through the publication of a booklet on the tasks of the
NSDStB, which he defined in three categories as: scholarship (the
treatment of specialist questions of National Socialism), propaganda
(the spreading of Nazi ideology in the university), and training
(leader-training for the Party).[7] He thus pandered to the élitist
attitudes which were evident in many groups, by implying that
Studentenbund members would by rights become leaders, both in
terms of Party rank and as the arbiters of ideology. This élitism in
the NSDStB members was not really surprising, and represented a
widespread trait in the students at large. Student life still retained an
aura of gentility about it, even though the realities of the Weimar
Republic were far removed from this vision. In fact, it has been shown

that the students as a group suffered more greatly and consistently from socio-economic crises than anyone. These assertions of superiority were an attempt to shore up their collapsing status.[8]

In the event, almost nothing was done to meet the requests to wrestle with ideology, plan policy and rethink scholarship. Energies were directed instead towards other ambitions. Like many political student groups, the NSDStB dreamt of controlling the entire student body. The means of achieving this were seen to lie with the capture of the national students' union, the *Deutsche Studentenschaft* (DSt). This had been dominated from its very foundation in 1919 by the numerous and powerful, largely conservative student fraternities. It was they who had written the DSt constitution to include dubious and effective devices to protect the ruling party, which role they imagined they would always enjoy. Indeed, by the end of the twenties, some 60 per cent of all German students were members of a fraternity.[9]   Unlike his predecessor Tempel, who had railed against the monopoly of the fraternities and incurred their opposition, Baldur von Schirach surmised that the success of the NSDStB depended upon infiltration and persuasion rather than the rejection and destruction of the fraternities. The DSt was an attractive prize indeed as a vehicle for Nazi propaganda: every German student belonged automatically to it, and formal state recognition had brought with it the right to levy fees from the members. It was therefore important to keep the DSt intact, in order to facilitate the *Studentenbund's* quest for absolute power.

A seizure of the DSt was only possible if the NSDStB were to obtain a firm footing in the local students' representative councils, known as AStA (*Allgemeiner Studenten-Ausschuss*). It was these committees which appointed the voting delegates to the DSt Annual Conference, who then decided upon DSt policy and elected its executive officers. Almost from the beginning, NSDStB groups with only a handful of members had often managed to gain one or two seats on their local AStA, not always without some duplicity, such as campaigning under a false name like the '*Völkisch* Student Ring.'[10]   By the Winter Semester 1929/30, however, this was no longer necessary, as the NSDStB was becoming, if something of a nuisance, nevertheless an accepted part of the student scene. NSDStB groups everywhere entered the individual AStA elections with a vigour never before seen, beside which the campaigns of other groups were decidedly low-key. They alienated the university authorities by bringing politics onto the campus, they put up provocative and insulting notices, they held such heated meetings that the police often had to be summoned to restore the

peace, yet above all they began to make a deep impression. Fraternity
leadership of student politics did seem somewhat ossified by
comparison with the energy and eagerness with which the NSDStB
grasped firmly and openly the issues that appeared important. The
topics which it did take up were not new: *numerus clausus* to
alleviate the overcrowding of universities, the restoration of
military sovereignty for Germany, the dismissal of pacifist professors,
these were subjects which broad sections of the student body
espoused. In general, however, the fraternities trod somewhat gingerly
for fear of upsetting the authorities, whereas the NSDStB almost
enjoyed provoking the establishment, and emerged as the real
champion of all these causes. The *Studentenbund*'s campaigns were
conducted not only with an intensity, but with a seriousness
previously unknown in student politics. Nazi student leaders
actually went into debt, spending far beyond their means, in order
to have attractive posters and pamphlets printed. The campaigns
were also aided by the fact that the Nazi Party itself had earlier in
the year been accorded a certain stamp of respectability by the
German Nationalists' acceptance of it as an equal partner in the
fight against the Young Plan. The great effort expended by NSDStB
groups paid off during the Winter Semester 1929/30 with the first
significant electoral successes, which at two markedly right-wing
universities were little short of spectacular: 51 per cent of the
students voted for the Nazis at Erlangen, while at Greifswald the
NSDStB polled 53 per cent.[11]

The individual groups had reason to be pleased with their own
efforts but did not feel that they owed very much to their leader,
Baldur von Schirach, whose lack of specific guidance on policy
matters was resented. They were particularly displeased by his
handling of the *numerus clausus* question, which had from the start
been used to fan easily aroused anti-Jewish sentiment. Viennese
students had actually brought about a quota for Jewish students
there in 1922, and the issue was resurrected again in December 1928
at Berlin by the NSDStB, which pushed a motion through the AStA,
with the firm support of the fraternities, demanding a Jewish
numerus clausus from the rector. Similar motions were subsequently
passed elsewhere. The Prussian Education Ministry and most other
federal states withdrew official recognition in 1927 from the DSt
for its insistence on granting affiliation to the radically anti-semitic
Austrian students' unions, with their restricted 'aryan' membership
requirement.[12] It thus lost the right to levy fees, except in Bavaria.

From contacts in the Bavarian Education Ministry, it was clear that the DSt would now lose even this slender source of income, unless it quelled the anti-semitism emanating from the AStAs. The DSt chairman summoned Schirach for talks and persuaded him to support a temporary policy of moderation in order to placate the Bavarian authorities. Schirach, however, did not bother to inform his local groups of this, and the NSDStB delegates arrived at the DSt Annual Conference in 1930 eager for the fight for *numerus clausus*, in support of which they hoped for a motion from the national conference.[13] It was then, with great surprise that they listened to the speech of Schirach's deputy, pledging support for the moderate stance of the DSt executive, as had been privately pre-arranged. Most of the NSDStB leaders were outraged at being left out in the dark like this, and a large number sat down there and then to compose a letter of complaint to NSDAP headquarters. This letter was ignored, and was followed by lengthy memoranda on the state of the NSDStB, prepared independently by two leading members, Reinhard Sunkel and Ernst Anrich. Sunkel stressed that of the three tasks Schirach had defined for the NSDStB, he had only even touched upon one. He had indeed scored an impressive propaganda success in improving the NSDStB's image within the DSt, but he had failed utterly to institute anything in the way of leader-training or the nazification of scholarship.[14] Anrich, on the other hand, emphasised in his papers above all the necessity of promoting a definite class-consciousness among the NSDStB students and the furtherance of the special intellectual tasks, of which they alone could be capable.[15] In order to head off any threat to his position, Schirach showered special commissions upon the two dissidents, doubtless hoping to stifle opposition by overwork, yet himself did nothing to meet the criticisms levelled at him. Schirach's position eventually became extremely tenuous, with some thirty NSDStB groups backing a renewed attack against him by Anrich and Sunkel. However, as a favoured protégé, he was able to summon up the intervention of Hitler himself, who addressed all NSDStB group leaders on 2 May 1931. At this meeting, the opposition was utterly deflated by Hitler's unqualified praise for Schirach's leadership. And for the would-be intellectuals of the Movement Hitler had some surprising news: this was no time for contemplation, the NSDAP wanted people to march, not to sit and study. Theoreticians could come later, but only after the seizure of power. In a couple of sentences, Hitler had made nonsense of what most of the group leaders believed the central task of the NSDStB to be. Yet as his authority had never been called into doubt, so now the entire assembly adopted his standpoint as their own.[16]

There can be little doubt, however, that many group leaders, back at home and removed somewhat from the powerful magnetic field of Hitler's charisma, still harboured their dissatisfaction with Schirach's leadership. This may have led them to slacken their ties to the NSDStB headquarters, and build up their relationships with the local Party *Gauleitung*, for which there is some evidence.[17] The jubilation following the resounding success of the September 1930 *Reichstag* election was moreover reflected in greater benevolence on the part of the NSDAP towards its subsidiary organisations. In Hamburg, the *Gauleitung* showed for the first time an interest in the AStA election campaign, and even gave quite voluntarily some financial support.[18] On the *Gauleiter*'s instructions, the NSDStB stayed away from meetings of the Communist student group, in order to avoid charges of rowdy provocation.[19] They did attend meetings of the right-wing political groups, but now seemed anxious to use persuasive arguments more than facetious interjections and pointless interruptions. Their own meetings demonstrated this desire to win confidence as they took on a more serious air, and included lectures by well known right-wing public figures who were able to draw considerable audiences with topics of general concern, such as the question of rearmament and military sovereignty.

Yet all this would have come to little in the face of concerted opposition from the fraternities. The fact that there was none, but rather an attitude of benign tolerance, must be credited largely to the diplomacy of Schirach, particularly in bringing off the 'Erfurt Agreement' in January 1931. In this, the NSDStB and the fraternities mutually agreed not to force their members to vote for a particular list in the AStA elections.[20] In return, the NSDStB tried to alleviate the sticky problems of dual membership and allegiance by releasing its members from active service for fraternity activities when the occasion demanded (a promise which was not, however, kept, as NSDStB membership became more and more a full-time activity). And if there remained any doubt as to the 'social acceptability' of the NSDStB, a clause was inserted according all *Studentenbund* members the honour, rare indeed, of being allowed to duel with fraternity members. In a situation where it was widely felt that many issues of university politics needed to be solved by firm and insistent leadership, which the present (fraternity) DSt executive seemed incapable of providing, in its anxiety to placate the education ministries, there can be no doubt that fraternity students had few qualms after the Erfurt Agreement about voting for the active and dynamic candidates on the NSDStB lists.

By the end of the Winter Semester 1930/31, the NSDStB controlled the majority of AStA committees. It was apparent that they would be able to elect the DSt Chairman at the annual conference in July, for the ruling party in each AStA could appoint all the voting delegates from its own ranks alone (a highly undemocratic procedure which the fraternities had designed and hitherto used successfully each year to maintain their own sovereignty). This much was inevitable, but when it became known that Schirach intended to nominate the Deputy Chairman as well, the fraternities began to panic, as they saw themselves losing all grip on the reins of power. A representative was despatched to Hitler himself to beg for the deputy's post for the fraternities, but made no impression. In vain did they call for the mutual sharing of executive posts specified in the Erfurt Agreement: the Nazis were now showing their true face. Then on 13 July 1931, two days before the scheduled start of the DSt Annual Conference, the Danat Bank collapsed and all German banks closed in alarm. This gave the retiring DSt leaders the opportunity to cancel the conference. There were bound to be massive student demonstrations in the face of the economic crisis, they claimed, and the local student leaders had therefore better stay at home and keep order, rather than taking an expensive trip to distant Graz. Schirach, however, furious at the thought of being thwarted at the eleventh hour, was able to use a constitutional loophole to veto the cancellation. His appearance at the conference, flanked constantly by an SS guard of honour, was designed to impress, but only made the fraternities more determined than ever that the NSDStB should not have things all their own way. After Schirach had once more refused to allow them the post of deputy chairman, the fraternities announced that they would therefore withdraw altogether from the DSt. Since this near-decimation would ruin a glittering propaganda victory for the Nazis, and also rob the DSt of most of the funds which had kept it alive since its loss of state recognition, Schirach was forced to agree, with considerable loss of face, to a compromise: a deputy chairman who was a member both of a fraternity and of the *Studentenbund* would be nominated. As expected, the conference endorsed the nominations, and thus the national students' union fell under Nazi control, a full eighteen months before Hitler came to power as chancellor.

It was, then, a combination of unscrupulous yet clever politics on Schirach's part, and successes in the local AStA elections which made this

possible. Above all, it was accelerated by the tremendous activism of
the ordinary *Studentenbund* members which brought a new dimension
to student politics. What had previously been a more or less serious
game became for the Nazis a vital struggle. The NSDStB won before the
other contestants realised that they were playing by different rules. It
is their enormous dedication which marks out the NSDStB members in
this period. As students, of course, they were able to create much more
free time than the ordinary working citizen. It was not uncommon for
NSDStB members only to register for a single course per semester (which
even then they would not always attend), in order to fulfil the very
minimum requirement for university matriculation. Whilst other
students were at their books, the *Student enbund* was at the printing
press, preparing new posters and pamphlets for distribution. The
fraternities, with their vast resources of manpower, could have done
this, too, by a little simple organisation which would not have
demanded such sacrifice of time from the individual. Yet they failed
utterly to recognise the deadly earnestness of their rival until it was too
late. It was not that they were just gullible. They had accepted the
Nazis as co-equal partners, and expected gentlemen's agreements to be
honoured. Opposition from a declared ally was simply unthinkable. If
this had been merely suggested, they would have reacted like Nelson
lifting the telescope to his blind eye.

The following eighteen months till 1933 are marked not by the
consolidation of the NSDStB's victory, but by increasing alienation and
a steady decline in support for the Nazi leadership. The fraternities had
been calling since the early twenties for more authoritarian government,
but were upset when the NSDStB took positive steps to augment this
by introducing the *Führerprinzip* (leader-principle) at the 1932 DSt
Annual Conference. The Nazi delegates, who were in the majority,
passed a motion whereby the leaders of both the DSt and the local
students' union would appoint their own successors, disregarding any
electoral process. There now seemed no way of unseating the NSDStB.

A central concern of most of the student world at this time was the
question of Germany's military strength, starkly reduced by the
provisions of the Versailles Treaty. Despite the express ban on such
activities, several student groups were engaging more or less openly in
military training (under the rubric 'defence sports'), often with
professorial support. Indeed, various student groups vied with one
another to attract the students with their particular 'defence sports'
facilities. The *Stahlhelm* were the leaders here, but the fraternities, too,
possessed ample resources. The NSDStB, short of money as ever, trailed

far behind. Its members were required more and more for SA duties, largely drill, propaganda marches and streetfighting. This was simply not to the taste of many students, and a number of *Studentenbund* members preferred to return to their fraternities for less pugilistic martial training. Apart from supporting the SA, the NSDStB was doing very little as a separate body. Even a re-organisation, designed to relieve the members of the burden of constant SA duties, was ineffective.[21] Then all *Studentenbund* members were compelled to join the Party as well, thus adding even more to their duties. The leadership lamented once again that it had 'so far *never* been possible to carry out even approximately' the ideological training still considered by many to be the *raison d'être* of the NSDStB.[22] Although membership had risen at the universities from some 4,000 in mid-1931 to 6,300 in December 1932 (only about 8 per cent of the corresponding fraternity figures), new enrolments declined during 1932.[23] Throughout the Winter Semester 1932/33, electoral support in the AStA elections dropped almost everywhere, as indeed it did for the NSDAP itself, including those universities where the AStA elections took place after 30 January 1933.

Upon Hitler's accession to the chancellorship, the NSDStB was in a sorry state, but after the March *Reichstag* elections, it was deluged with new members, and no longer had to worry about ailing support. It seemed that everyone was jostling for position. This dramatic increase in numbers completely altered the character of the *Studentenbund*. Previously it had been for many a very attractive organisation, in that a proliferation of posts meant that almost everyone could be an office-holder with some area of responsibility.

Now, however, in 1933, the NSDStB ceased to be a small, tightly-knit revolutionary cadre, and became a mass organisation, rather puzzled as to its purpose now that the revolution had apparently been won. There was, and continued to be throughout the Third Reich, a romantic longing for the old dynamism of the Weimar period. These were the golden days, as the old guard saw it (and there were similar sentiments in other branches of the Party), when they had been welded together by the fervent struggle in dedicated and loyal fraternity. They imagined that this cameraderie could be maintained if only the NSDStB kept on the offensive. Initially this posed no problem, as there were plenty of old scores to settle with 'liberal' and Jewish professors. Demonstrations of such violence occurred that education ministries positively hurried to suspend or dismiss almost any professor in acquiescence to student demands.[24] But when this orgy of retribution had exhausted itself, there had to be found some other motive force for the Nazi student movement, for it still had no solid base on which to build. There was plenty of enthusiasm (and a good deal of opportunism) among students who joined the NSDStB, but nothing which might hold them lastingly. The student leaders turned once more to the area which had always been the object of their good intentions but perennial neglect, namely, ideology. As usual, destructive measures were easier to arrange than constructive ones, and purges of libraries were undertaken. These culminated in the students' bookburning demonstrations throughout Germany in May 1933.[25]

It was in connection with this that there arose one of the internecine feuds which were characteristic of the Third Reich. The trouble was that both the Nazi leader of the DSt, Gerhard Krüger, and the national leader of the NSDStB, Oskar Stäbel, considered themselves the supreme head of the student body. Each tried to wrest control of the major propaganda event that the bookburning promised to be, in order that their particular organisation might reap the glory from its success. The altercations continued even after the event, and by the summer of 1933 the two leaders had each engineered the other's arrest. Stäbel, however, proved to have the stronger backing, and emerged from the fray as the *joint* leader of both the NSDStB and the DSt. The marriage of the two organisations was largely reflected at the local level, too, and by the following Spring, Stäbel was so certain of the impossibility of a future conflict while a joint head remained that he took steps to split again the local leadership which had become overwhelmed with routine office work. He now proposed to make the *Studentenbund* a select, activist, leader-training corps for the whole student body, separated from the mushrooming bureaucracy of the DSt.[26]

He did not, however, have time to implement his plan, for immediately he encountered opposition in the newly-formed Reich Ministry of Education.[27] Bernhard Rust, the Minister, was anxious to establish as wide a power base as possible for the ministry, and took umbrage at the *de facto* Party suzerainty (through the NSDStB) over the state-controlled and subsidised DSt, which had now fallen under his own jurisdiction. Rust forced Stäbel to hand over the DSt leadership to a deputy and refused to have anything more to do with him. Shortly afterwards, it was discovered that Stäbel had been embezzling some 1,900 marks per month from DSt funds to maintain a somewhat lavish lifestyle, which served as a good enough excuse to engineer his fall from the NSDStB leadership as well.[28]

Although it was generally acknowledged that to continue the

temporarily split national leadership would prove disastrous to the progress of ideological training in the universities, this was just what occurred. Rudolf Hess, responsible at Party Headquarters for the NSDStB, could not agree with Minister Rust on a joint leader satisfactory to them both, and entirely separate appointments were made: Andreas Feickert gained the DSt leadership, while Albert Derichsweiler was to head the *Studentenbund.* An attempt was made to define areas of competence, in which Rust, weakly collapsing before Party opposition as usual, came out the loser. Hess proclaimed the ultimate leadership of the student body to be vested in the NSDStB, which was to become 'a sort of intellectual SS', a new elite order under his command which would provide the Party with the sound scientific background that Party doctrine lacked.[29] On 30 July 1934, he announced that 'in future the NSDStB alone is responsible for the entire ideological, political and physical training of the student body'.[30] It was difficult to think of any activity which might not come under this rubric. Yet Feickert, not wishing his eager DSt leaders to be consigned merely to the unrelieved drudgery of student registration and the issuing of certificates, took bold action.

The one concrete plan to come out of the NSDStB's vague deliberations on the ideological indoctrination of the student body was the setting-up of residential communities (to be known as *Kameradschaften*), similar to the fraternities' houses.[31] The fraternities still represented a powerful force in the universities, and had no feeling that they had become redundant. Many supported National Socialism, but were alienated by the high-handed behaviour of what they considered its aberrant offspring, the NSDStB, and saw a certain corrective role for themselves. The position of the NSDStB was double-edged: it upheld the continuation of the individual fraternities at the university, for it hoped to take them over lock, stock and barrel for an easy conversion into Nazi training cells. On the other hand, it feared the political power of the national unions, the 'fraternity associations' (*Verbände*), and wished nothing more earnestly than their disbandment or destruction.[32] This was no easy task, since the fraternity associations commanded great loyalty and active support from their alumni, who often held high and influential positions throughout society and state. Their most active lobbyist was State Secretary Hans Heinrich Lammers, a man who, as head of the Reich Chancellery, enjoyed Hitler's ear almost daily.[33] The various attempts in the year and a half following January 1933 to get the *Kameradschaft* scheme off the ground by commandeering fraternity houses were thus met with an opposition which could not be ignored. The fraternity associations considered that they were entirely capable of supervising training in National Socialism themselves and rejected the imposition of *Studentenbund* leaders upon their fraternity houses. So great had been the uproar caused by the fraternities that both Krüger and Stäbel had been forced to modify their respective plans and put them on an entirely voluntary footing.

Apparently learning nothing from this past experience, Feickert promulgated in September 1934 his own plan for political education: every freshman would be obliged to live in '*Kameradschaft* houses', wear a uniform and have his entire day regulated with study, sport and ideological training. As the DSt did not possess any houses, Feickert intended to use those of the fraternities, which would hence-forth fall under DSt supervision.[34] He had, of course, no business to announce this after the ruling on the supremacy of the NSDStB, and it was clearly an attempt at DSt re-assertion. He claimed that, as leader of all German students, only he was empowered to issue a general order to the whole student body, even on questions pertaining to 'political education'. A test of strength with the *Studentenbund* on almost any other issue would have been more circumspect, and to involve the fraternities as well was rash indeed. Education Minister Rust, after consulting with the fraternity leaders, backed down from his support of the 'Feickert Plan' and cabled all universities that the scheme would be voluntary, though he hoped that a large majority of students would nonetheless be able to live in *Kameradschaften*.[35] Meanwhile, State Secretary Lammers had already put the matter before Hitler himself for 'ultimate' arbitration.

Hitler's decision altered the whole course of the political education programme. He suddenly seized upon the idea that cohabitation would result in rampant homosexuality.[36] Such an absurd notion had previously occurred to no-one, and would be particularly difficult to explain to the fraternities, with their tradition of residential groups. Feickert had already caused enough embarrassment and was ordered by Rust to withdraw and leave the whole affair to Derichsweiler to explain. Yet this was an awkward situation for the NSDStB, too, for one of the few points on which both it and the fraternities agreed was that residential communities of students were the best path to successful ideological indoctrination (though the fraternities expressed this more in terms of 'character-building').[37] Students living under the same roof as their appointed leader represented a perfect captive audience. *Studentenbund* leaders felt that this base would make their didactic task much easier. Moreover, a number of fraternities had by now, following repeated demands since mid-1933, set about the costly

business of converting their houses into the large dormitories called for by
the student leadership. Could they simply be told at this stage that their
houses were no longer needed?

Derichsweiler tried to smooth over the problem with a compromise:
he announced that only one *Kameradschaft* house in each city would
be residential, namely that of the NSDStB leader corps, but that the
fraternity houses were nevertheless urgently desired as meeting-places
and clubrooms.[38] This did nothing to allay the fraternities' fears that
the NSDStB was ultimately out to destroy them, which increased with
every reversal or revision of NSDStB policy towards them. They banded
together for greater political weight, and by April 1935 seventeen
associations were joined under the leadership of State Secretary
Lammers, representing 180,000 fraternity students and alumni.[39] Their
position improved little, for despite apparent harmony and goodwill
between them and the NSDStB at the headquarters level, there
continued to be disturbances, even pitched battles, between local groups.
Lammers, tired of the constant charge of non-co-operation, wrote to
Derichsweiler,

> You have not yet, I am bound to say, done very much towards the
> ideological and political training of the students. The fraternity
> associations have waited eagerly for you to begin your work . . . It
> was *your* job to prepare this, instead of which your junior leaders
> incessantly accuse the fraternities of doing nothing towards
> ideological and political education.[40]

The last straw came when Derichsweiler announced his plan for
training camps in the summer. Each fraternity was to delegate three
members to the camps for training as political education instructors,
and they would automatically become *Studentenbund* members on
completion of the course. The fraternities quickly realised that this
would give the NSDStB a certain jurisdictional foothold and surmised
that 'the NSDStB leaders would be all too easily tempted to extend
their authority beyond the ideological and political to cover the whole
of fraternity life'.[41] Many baulked at the fifty marks registration fee
for the course, and once more it was felt that little would be gained in
the way of ideological insight. Lammers again arranged for the
fraternity question to be brought formally before Hitler himself in
order that the destructive hostility of the NSDStB might be curbed, so
that the fraternities could be allowed to continue in their own right,
conducting political education programmes on National Socialism, but

as they themselves saw fit. On 15 July 1935 Hitler held a secret conference in Berlin with Lammers and Derichsweiler, as well as a handful of top Nazi leaders, to debate the question. He surprised all present with a vehement two-and-a-half hour monologue deprecating the fraternities. He did not, he asserted, want them banned, just as the police did not close down bars frequented by criminals, for it was thus easier to locate certain types of people. Lammers was shocked to find that he had totally misunderstood Hitler's apparent support of the fraternities, which was in reality merely a device for more convenient scrutiny. Hitler forbade Lammers to reveal any details of this meeting to the fraternity associations, other than the fact that the fraternities would not be permitted to indulge in any kind of political activity in the future.[42] Derichsweiler confirmed this at the Nuremberg Rally in September 1935, adding that freshmen would henceforth have to choose between a fraternity and the NSDStB: dual membership would no longer be tolerated.[43] This was as far as he dared go towards a ban on fraternity membership, but after such an expression of official disfavour, many would think it expedient to stay away from the fraternities. As interest groups, the fraternity associations had failed to defend their position and status, and in October 1935 most of them decided to disband.

The result of this was rather disappointing for the NSDStB. It had been expected that, when the associations dissolved, the individual fraternities would break up, too, and turn their houses over to the *Studentenbund*. However, the fraternities themselves, though recruiting almost no freshmen, continued as before. A nationwide *Gestapo* enquiry in the Spring of 1936 concluded that 'not one fraternity has disbanded in the real meaning of the word' and that moreover 'the alumni section continues to flourish as ever'.[44] Thus what had appeared to be a decisive coup for Derichsweiler in fact did little to soften the tenacity of the fraternities, or indicate a clear victor in the struggle. The ingredients for potential strife remained virtually the same.

All the time the fraternity battle was being fought, a conflict of equally vigorous vituperation was being conducted with the DSt, as Derichsweiler assailed Feickert over the control of the student body. The DSt as the only organisation embracing every student, tried constantly to re-assert itself as the supreme authority for all students, but the aggressive and ambitious Derichsweiler kept up his offensive. Feickert was greatly hindered by the absence of support from Rust, who repeatedly refused to see the DSt leader, while exhorting him to carry on the good work, on the grounds that his thoughts were 'not yet sufficiently developed to allow the possibility of a fruitful discussion'.[45] He refused to accept Feickert's resignation on 11 March 1935, but was ready to let him go a few months later, by which time the discord was becoming a public embarrassment. At the local level, Feickert's and Derichsweiler's subordinates were often one and the same person. There was great discontent among these junior leaders, who were placed in an impossible position, as they received starkly contradictory orders from both DSt and NSDStB headquarters. Each of four likely candidates whom Feickert and the Ministry approached turned down the offer of the DSt leadership, seeing not the slightest hope of success with the continuation of the split with NSDStB headquarters.[46]

During 1934, a number of young university graduates, and some of their professors, enlisted in the Party's secret police force, the SD (*Sicherheitsdienst des Reichsführers-SS*). It was just acquiring a reputation particularly through the acerbity of its commentaries in the SS newspaper *Das Schwarze Korps,* as a kind of ideological watchdog, and these young men hoped to exercise a remedial influence on what they considered a disappointing outcome to the Nazi revolution, replacing opportunism and political insensitivity with idealism and intelligent leadership.[47] By the middle of 1936, it appeared likely that the student body, in the light of the endless bickering between the NSDStB and the DSt, would turn its back altogether on National Socialism. The SD (unlike Party circles in general) was convinced of the necessity for a loyal intelligentsia, and anxiously turned its attention to the impasse in the student leadership. The assistance of *Reichsführer-SS* Himmler was enlisted to intercede with Rust and Hess for the appointment of a joint leader once again.[48] In the absence of feasible counter-proposals, Himmler successfully proposed a man who had been extremely active in student politics since Weimar days, and who now happened to be a high-ranking officer in the SD: Gustav Adolf Scheel, who took office on 5 November 1936.[49]

Before accepting the appointment as head of the new *Reichsstudentenführung* (RSF), Scheel had extracted a promise from Minister Rust to revise a characteristic feature of German university study, the right of the student to move around the various universities at will, in order to hear the lectures of particular professors. Freshmen were now obliged to remain at their first university for at least three semesters. This, Scheel reasoned, would facilitate the completion of a coherent political education programme for every student.[50]

It was hoped that all freshmen would enrol in a *Kameradschaft* for this purpose, but membership was not made compulsory. Scheel was an idealist and believed that the ailing *Kameradschaften* could be enlivened so that they would attract students in the same way that the fraternities once had done. It gradually became apparent that, despite training courses for leaders, sadly few of them were capable of formulating imaginative activities for a *Kameradschaft* on their own initiative. The admission of a Hamburg student leader was typical:

> Apathy towards political training of any kind makes itself felt. Interest is still shown only in general topics, and it is sometimes rather difficult to give these subjects an ideological character: a task which relies utterly on the skill of the *Kameradschaft* leader. Unfortunately, only a few *Kameradschaft* leaders possess this adroitness. In general, it has to be said that the *Kameradschaft* situation remains mediocre.[51]

This lack of imagination had been part of the trouble in the past. The NSDStB had been unable to provide the students with any more stimulating fare than was served up to the rank and file of the SA. Himmler himself was struck by the inappropriate nature of most of the *Studentenbund's* activities to date:

> I regard it as a catastrophe when, as was the case in the last few years, the work of the *Studentenbund,* for example, . . . consisted in packing a fine rucksack and going on exercise. I don't need a *Studentenbund* for that. I spoke to the new *Studentenbund* Leader recently and I said to him: 'My dear Scheel, if I ever catch you drilling with your *Kameradschaften* you will have me as your absolute enemy. In student houses you're meant to work intellectually and lead intellectually and put society in order'.[52]

The call for intellectual leadership was not out of character for Himmler, would-be intellectual himself, and was reflected in his SD, but it was a far cry from the consensus in the Nazi movement as a whole. Indeed, there were occasions when the derisory remarks of Hitler about intellectuals as the 'eternal critics' who were 'useless as supporting elements of a society' caused grave upsets to the self-confidence of the academic world.[53]

For the Nazis, the *sine qua non* of intellectual leadership was political reliability. It was with this in mind that the RSF prepared a set of instructions for *Kameradschaft* leaders on the structure and content of their training programmes.[54] The core of this was the weekly meeting known as the 'political evening'. Yet the book of guidelines offered but little concrete help to the unimaginative leader. He was merely told that the themes covered should be linked to the special problems of the geographical area in which the university was situated, and that he should draw up in advance a curriculum for the whole semester. Apart from this, he was merely advised what not to do: not to treat topics such as the German Communist movement as isolated specialist questions but as a vital problem for the whole German nation; not to study subjects with no regional topicality; not to choose such a broad field that in-depth study became impossible. Thus the most central part of the training programme was passed over in this forty-page booklet in less than a single page, to be lost in a sea of trivia on the need for good Nazis to carry a clean handkerchief, eat without belching and surrender their seats to old ladies in trams! The absence of more specific information on the 'political evening' may be partly explained by Scheel's reluctance to allow the sessions to become stereotyped through the slavish following of model programmes. This, however, overlooked the crux of the matter: a model programme was better than no programme at all. If there were fears that leaders lacked the imagination to depart from the prescribed path, then they would *a fortiori* be surely incapable of laying down a path on their own.

Scheel. a fraternity alumnus himself, was conscious of the salutary effect that the involvement of alumni had on the vitality of a fraternity. They provided continuity to each group, they could be consulted for advice, they had experience of the relative success of various types of activity, they often helped with job placement for graduates, and not least it was largely they who financed the fraternity. An alumni association (*Altherrenverband*) was attached to each individual fraternity, and it was these which still kept the fraternity idea alive even now after several years of Nazi buffeting. Scheel hoped to harness their commitment to the student world for his own purposes, and tried to animate the dormant and thus far insignificant NSDStB alumni and supporters' association, the *NS-Studentenkampfhilfe.* Founded originally in 1931, it had already been revived in May 1936 by Hess, but a year later there were only 5,118 members.[55] By promising them an active role in shaping the activities of a *Kameradschaft*, Scheel believed he would be able to persuade many of the 240,000 fraternity alumni to grasp the opportunity of returning to the mainstream of student life. Although the membership of the *Studentenkampfhilfe* totalled 15,000 by the end of 1937, this still did little more than

scratch the surface.[56] Scheel grew impatient that his plan was not
proceeding at the desired pace, and began to show his petulance even in
public addresses:

> One day it will become clear whether the fraternity has pledged its
> members more to the fraternity itself or to *Volk* and fatherland.
> The healthy, active element among the alumni today is taking part
> in a revolution. Whoever tries any longer to condemn this work
> will merely condemn himself![57]

Even these threatening tones did little to goad fraternity alumni into
support, and so Scheel delivered an ultimatum at the beginning of
March 1938. Those alumni associations which did not make up their
minds by 15 May to give a 'binding written declaration' to support the
Studentenkampfhilfe would be excluded from any further active
participation in student life.[58] Many of the associations did now
disband and transfer their membership to the *Studentenkampfhilfe,*
though not so much because of the impression Scheel's threats made as
through the excited nationalistic fervour which swept over them with
the Austrian *Anschluss.* It became apparent, however, that the
numerous Catholic alumni associations had no intention of breaking up,
and so the RSF trumped up charges of treasonable activities by them,
leading Himmler, as Chief of the Gestapo, to ban them as 'politically
intolerable'.[59]

The stage now seemed set for the resolution of the *Kameradschaft*
problem. A putative opposition no longer formally existed. The RSF
controlled all branches of the student body, and could devote its entire
effort to making the *Kameradschaften* attractive. It must be stressed
that membership of the *Kameradschaften* and through them of the
NSDStB was and remained voluntary.[60] Inducement, persuasion, even
veiled threats occurred in greater or lesser measure at each university,
but students were never obliged to undergo political indoctrination as
members of NSDStB groups. The rationale behind this standpoint was
that it was useless preaching to deaf ears. Moreover, selection processes
would be made easier since those who turned their backs on the
Kameradschaften would never be allowed to rise to positions of
responsibility in the Nazi state (though chronic shortages of university-
trained personnel made it impossible to apply this). There is little
concrete evidence of how, if at all, the *Kameradschaften* did become
more attractive – the reason may be that students found it simply more
expedient to enrol in order to improve their prospects – but the year

1938/39 did show an increase in membership. The official RSF claim that there were 34,000 students in *Kameradschaften* by the summer of 1939 is heavily exaggerated.[61] The only plausible figures remaining refer to a single city, namely Hamburg, where one finds some two-thirds of the students (in their first three semesters) joining up, a higher proportion than at any other time.[62] However, this was still nowhere near the RSF's goal of having every single student pass through the *Kameradschaften* as a matter of course.

If the war had started three years later, wrote one NSDStB leader, the experience gained by then in administering the political education programme would have given it sufficient momentum to continue without difficulty.[63] But the war began in September 1939 and caught the RSF quite unprepared for the decimation of the student leadership which resulted as all the leaders clamoured to set a good example by enlisting in the armed forces, leaving almost no-one behind at the universities to carry on their work. Scheel not only lacked trained leaders but was faced with a student body which in his opinion needed more than ever the guiding hand of the NSDStB. He suspected that the universities were filled with 'draft-dodgers', the very last people to be likely to enthuse about the *Studentenbund.* In December 1939 Scheel reported his distress that students were quite openly refusing 'for ideological reasons' to join the NSDStB.[64] Fearing for his reputation as a political leader, he used a number of trivial incidents as an excuse to tighten substantially his control over the student body. He persuaded Rust to set up watchdog committees to investigate complaints 'from whatever quarter' about the behaviour and attitudes of students, 'even if the disciplinary code does not appear to provide grounds for action'.[65] For persistently recalcitrant individuals he considered the concentration camp an appropriate punishment.[66]

Yet punitive measures missed the heart of the problem once again, which was to provide convincing leaders, not to exclude uninterested followers. It was all but impossible to find permanent leaders during the war, as there was such a rapid turnover of students. Almost everyone at the university was there just for a few months and likely to be recalled to active service at a moment's notice, without regard to the university calendar but following the dictates of the military situation. The only students assured some measure of permanency were those physically unfit for military service, and it was to these youths, fresh from school, that the RSF had to turn for its leader corps, even though it was clear that they could rarely project themselves as convincing leaders in front of soldiers fresh from front-line battle:

'One really cannot expect a 28-year-old first lieutenant to submit to the authority of an 18-year-old *Kameradschaft* leader who has never even been in the ranks'.[67]

A major hindrance was the fact that the students on temporary study leave from the armed forces remained under military jurisdiction and were not obliged to follow the orders of the student leaders. Not surprisingly, they in fact displayed little interest in the NSDStB. As the SD reported:

> The students on leave from the *Wehrmacht* show in general the tendency to enjoy to the full the unfettered private life which study offers them in comparison with military service. It is difficult to involve them in rallies, Party work, political training, work in the NSDStB . . . After their long enlistment in the strictness of military life, they want to plan their own affairs again, to devote themselves to their studies and have the rest of the time to themselves.[68]

Yet here, the RSF decided, were the real leaders, among these soldiers who had been at the Front. All would be well again if only *their* support could be won. And so an all-out effort was made to woo the soldier-students into the ranks of the NSDStB. The campaign took on such proportions that almost everything else was neglected, including once again the ideological concerns that everyone agreed were central to the task of the NSDStB. Three complete revisions of the 1937 guidelines for *Kameradschaft* leaders were no more satisfactory than the original version.[69] What was really needed was a weekly or monthly package of notes and outlines of activities to fill the vacuum in the minds of the many leaders who had been hastily pushed into the leadership of a *Kameradschaft* without any preparation. There was even some recognition in the RSF that this was the only way to keep the *Kameradschaften* going and thus protect the very core of the NSDStB— but nothing was ever done. Too late did Scheel recall in April 1944 to his Director of Political Education:

> I already ordered the publication of a gazette of directives for the *Kameradschaft* leaders a long time ago. I expect this decision to be put into effect in the coming semester. Such a publication is utterly essential for the leadership of the *Kameradschaften* and for their uniform performance.[70]

In the worsening military situation, the universities themselves were struggling to remain open. At the start of the Winter Semester 1944/45, there occurred the most severe drain on the student body of the whole war, as 54 per cent of the students were recalled to active service at one time.[71] Almost all the student leaders disappeared once more from the scene. 'As so often, we are faced in the coming semester with yet another fresh start,' wrote one disheartened student leader who remained.[72] Yet not even this proved possible, for the students (and their professors) were now drafted into the local *Volkssturm* units to prepare for the final defence of their cities, and the NSDStB never recovered again.

It is worth repeating that there was little active opposition to National Socialism itself in the student body. The 'White Rose' resistance group during the war was an isolated instance which had little impact on the students in general.[73] The opposition of the fraternities had been directed more towards the NSDStB's style of command, the domineering nature of which was revealed as unjustified by the painfully apparent hollowness of the leadership. The real enemy of the NSDStB, and by far its most effective one, was apathy. This was an opponent who could not be thrown into a concentration camp. Yet the *Studentenbund* grew so used to facing problems with aggressive, destructive tactics that it was at an utter loss when constructive measures were called for. Instead, the NSDStB kept up a constant attack (to uphold its revolutionary ethic) against different groups of people: Communists, Jews, 'liberal' professors, DSt leaders, fraternity associations, fraternity alumni, theologians, 'draft-dodgers', foreign students – there was always someone upon whom the blame could be placed.

In part, the students' lack of interest derived from the wider structure of the Nazi state. Brought up from childhood in the Hitler Youth, and confined on top of two years' military service for a further six months in the strict discipline of the Labour Service camps, freshmen breathed a sigh of relief when they arrived in an atmosphere of relative freedom at the universities. Already full to the brim with Nazi indoctrination, they felt that there was little that the NSDStB could still tell them. In order to gain the ear of most, the NSDStB would have had to force them to join a *Kameradschaft*. On this question Scheel wavered. He looked forward to the time when every single student would pass through the *Kameradschaft* indoctrination mill. He wanted the non-members to 'get the feeling that they are nothing' , but in general he was opposed to force.[74] This derived partly from past experience, which indicated that attempts at coercion brought only resentment and created a hostile atmosphere. However, in moments of impatience, Scheel did try to introduce measures requiring all students to register with a *Kameradschaft.* Each time, however, he failed to gain the consent of either the Party or the Education Ministry. This might be ascribed to their belief in the concept of natural selection, whereby all worthwhile people would become ardent Nazis entirely voluntarily and without prompting. One should also bear in mind that, in the Party at least, there was often little realisation of the necessity to have a politically supportive intelligentsia, the feeling being rather that if the intellectuals chose to misbehave, all the more reason to deny them the leading role which they considered their due. In the Party itself there was sometimes a naive belief that 'intellectuals' (which term loosely covered *inter alia* all the professions requiring academic training) could be dispensed with altogether. As I have pointed out, this was never the view in the NSDStB, which considered itself responsible for ensuring that *every* graduate left the university as a sound supporter of National Socialism, even though he might not be a member of the elite corps of the *Studentenbund* itself. In this connection, the refusal of Party and Ministry to endorse Scheel's request for obligatory *Kameradschaft* membership stemmed very largely from his concealment of the actual grim state of the political education programme, in his fear that he and the RSF leadership might appear hopelessly incompetent. The Party and Ministry never saw a real need for drastic measures of compulsion, believing the work of the RSF to be showing the steady, if slow, improvement which its official reports for the most part indicated. In this situation, the RSF was condemned to permanent frustration, unless it devoted constant and close attention to the structure and content of its political education programme. Whether there was anyone in the RSF with the subtlety or agility of mind to overcome these difficulties is doubtful. What is certain, however, is that no-one did in fact step forward with sufficient insight to see that a concentrated effort had to be made in the first place.

Notes

1.   See for example Manfred Franze, *Die Erlanger Studentenschaft 1918-1945* (Würzburg, 1972), p. 377; or Anselm Faust, *Der Nationalsozialistische Deutsche Studentenbund, Studenten und Nationalsozialismus in der Weimarer Republik* (Düsseldorf, 1973), Vol. 2, p. 132.
2.   Tempel to Organisationsleitung NSDAP, 13 January 1927, Bundesarchiv Koblenz (BA), Sammlung Schumacher 279.

3. Auerswald to Reichsleitung NSDStB, 4 August 1928, Archiv der ehemaligen Reichsstudentenführung und des NSDStB, Würzburg (RSFWü) II*5 ∝461.

4. Tempel to Parteileitung NSDAP, 6 November 1927, BA Sammlung Schumacher 279.

5. Faust, op.cit., Vol.1, p. 60 f.

6. Meyer to Reichsleitung NSDStB, 11 June 1929, RSFWü II*5∝461.

7. Baldur von Schirach, *Wille und Weg des Nationalsozialistischen Deutschen Studentenbundes* (Munich, 1929), here p. 10.

8. Michael H. Kater, *Studentenschaft und Rechtsradikalismus in Deutschland 1918-1933, Eine sozialgeschichtliche Studie zur Bildungskrise in der Weimarer Republik* (Hamburg, 1975).

9. Hans Peter Bleuel & Ernst Klinnert, *Deutsche Studenten auf dem Weg ins Dritte Reich, Ideologien – Programme – Aktionen 1918-1935* (Gütersloh, 1967), p. 261 f.

10. Geoffrey J. Giles, 'The National Socialist Students' Association in Hamburg 1926-45', Ph. D. thesis, Cambridge University 1975, p. 34 f.

11. Karl-Dietrich Bracher, *Die Auflösung der Weimarer Republik* (Villingen, 1955), p. 147 f.

12. The Becker dispute is described in: Erich Wende, *C.H. Becker – Mensch und Politiker, Ein biographischer Beitrag zur Kulturgeschichte der Weimarer Republik* (Stuttgart, 1959), p. 257 ff.; cf. also Paul Ssymank, 'Organisation und Arbeitsfeld der Deutschen Studentenschaft,' in Michael Doeberl et al., *Das Akademische Deutschland* (Berlin, 1930/1), Vol.3, pp. 363-84

13. While actual voting was restricted to the AStA delegates (one per thousand students at each university), members of any student group were allowed to attend and address the DSt Conference.

14. Faust, op.cit., Vol 1, p. 154 ff.

15. Ernst Anrich, 'Skizzenhafte Denkschrift über Wesen und Gestaltung des NSDStB, der NS-Bewegung an der Universitat,' 9 August 1930, Library of Congress, Washington, DC, Manuscripts Division (LC) RSF 815. The paper is addressed, rather sarcastically, to 'Herrn *Baron* von Schirach' (my emphasis).

16. Faust, op.cit., Vol.1, p. 162 f.

17. Hans Ochsenius, 'Die Studentenschaft der Hansischen Universität zu Hamburg bis 1939 unter besonderer Berücksichtigung der gesamten studentischen Entwicklung im Altreich', Dissertation, Hamburg University, 1941, p. 130. The rapport even extended in Hamburg to unsolicited financial support from the Party. See Giles, National Socialist Students' Association, p. 61.

18. Von Allwörden to Schorer, 6 December 1930 & 12 January 1931, Staatsarchiv Hamburg NSDAP 35 Band 1.

19. Rundschreiben Nr. 20 NSDAP Gau Hamburg, 15 July 1930, ibid.

20. It had been common for pressure to be applied to fraternity students to vote for the fraternity list in an AStA election. *The Erfurter Abkommen* is reprinted in full in Faust, op.cit., Vol. 2, p. 155 ff.

21. Anordnung Roehm betr. Studentenstürme, 17 July 1931, BA Sammlung Schumacher, 279; Verfügung Roehm/Schirach/Rühle, 12 November 1932, RSFWü V * 2∝527.

22. Denkschrift Rühle, 'Die Neuorganisation des Nationalsozialistischen Deutschen Studentenbundes,' n.d. (October 1932) RSFWü V * 2 ∝ 527.

23. Faust, op.cit., Vol. 2, p. 91.

24. For a discussion of the weak resistance to these demands, see Geoffrey J. Giles, 'University Government in Nazi Germany: The Example of

Hamburg,' Yale Higher Education Program Working Paper Series, YHEP-15, December 1976.

25.   A somewhat superficial account of this is given by Hans Wolfgang Strätz, 'Die studentische "Aktion wider den undeutschen Geist" im Frühjahr 1933,' *Vierteljahrshefte fuer Zeitgeschichte*, 16, 1968, pp. 347-72.

26.   Rundschreiben Stäbel 16 April 1934, Microfilms of captured German documents filmed at Alexandria, Virginia (Mic. Alex.) T-81/236/ 5020683-87.

27.   Control over education had traditionally rested with the individual federal states, and there was no national education ministry. The *Reichsministerium fuer Wissenschaft, Erziehung und Volksbildung* was set up on 1 May 1934 to bring the education sector into line with the centralisation of other fields of government.

28.   Michael Steinberg, 'Sabres, Books,and Brownshirts. The Radicalisation of the German Student 1918-1935,' Dissertation, Johns Hopkins University, 1971, p. 745.

29.   Hess to Derichsweiler, 24 July 1934, RSFWü II * A17 ∝ 471.

30.   Erlass Hess, 'Aufgaben der neuen Studentenorganisation,' 30 July 1934, Hamburg University Archives (UniHH) 0.30.6.

31.   Giles, National Socialist Students' Association, pp. 122 and 128 ff.

32.   For an examination of relations with the fraternities, see my forthcoming essay, 'Die Verbändepolitik des Nationalsozialistischen Deutschen Studentenbundes 1933-1945', *Darstellungen und Quellen zur Geschichte der deutschen Einheitsbewegung im neunzehnten und zwanzigsten Jahrhundert*, Bd. XI, Heidelberg.

33.   Lammers was president of a small and exclusive fraternity, the *Miltenberger Ring*.

34.   'Die Kameradschaftserziehung der Deutschen Studentenschaft', *Völkischer Beobachter* 21 September 1934; 'Neugestaltung der studentischen Erziehung', *Völkischer Beobachter*, 22 September 1934.

35.   Aktennotiz Winter, 'Besprechung beim Reichsminister Rust am 25. Oktober 1934 über die Durchführung der Kameradschaftserziehung', BA R128/1008; Funkspruch Rust (durch Polizeibehörde Hamburg), 25 October 1934, UniHH O.1.4.

36.   Derichsweiler to Hess, 22 July 1936, Berlin Document Center (BDC) Oberstes Parteigericht file 'Derichsweiler contra Emil Hoffman'; Protokoll Reichstagung NSDStB in Frankfurt am Main, 11 May 1935, p. 22, RSFWü I * ∝ 319.

37.   For a discussion of the Studentenbund's indebtedness to fraternity traditions, see my paper, 'Der NSD-Studentenbund und der Geist der studentischen Korporationen', delivered to the Annual Conference of the *Deutsche Gesellschaft für Hochschulkunde*, Würzburg, 4 October 1975.

38.   Rundschreiben Sch/5/34 Derichsweiler, 'Richtlinien für die politische Erziehung (Kameradschaftshausfrage)', 26 November 1934, RSFWü I * ∝ 312.

39.   Some 40,000 fraternity students and alumni, largely of the Catholic fraternities, remained outside the so-called '*Gemeinschaft studentischer Verbände*'. Giles, National Socialist Students' Association, p. 163 ff.

40.   Lammers to Derichsweiler, 1 July 1935, BA R128/38.

41.   'Die Richtlinien des NSDStB vom 25. Juli 1935', *Deutsche Corpszeitung (Amtliches Mitteilungsblatt des Kösener SC-Verbandes)*, Vol. 52, Nr. 4, July 1935.

42.   My account of this secret meeting owes much to my interview with Albert Derichsweiler on 12 March 1973. Contemporary skeleton accounts

bear out the validity of it as far as they go, cf. Vorträge Derichsweiler & Ley, 16 & 17 July 1935, Mic. Alex. T-81/75/86582-91.

43. 'Rede des Reichsamtsleiters Derichsweiler auf der Sondertagung des NSDStB auf dem Reichsparteitag am 13.September 1935', BA NS38/1. On 6 December 1935, Derichsweiler extended the ban to all members of the NSDStB.

44. Bericht 'Entwicklung der Korporationsfrage', n.d. (May 1936?), Zentrales Staatsarchiv Potsdam (ZStA) REM 872.

45. Feickert to Rust, 11 March 1935, RSFWü II * A29 ∝ 477.

46. Vermerk Bachér, 14 August 1935, ZStA REM 868.

47. The substantial academic intake of the SD at this time is underlined by the fact that all but one of the department heads at SD headquarters were professors or holders of a doctorate. Heinz Höhne, *The Order of the Death's Head* (London,1969) p.211 ff.

48. Brandt to von Herff, 22 September 1944, BDC SS Officer's file Derichsweiler.

49. Scheel had already been a DSt Area Leader for the NSDStB in 1932. Whilst retaining this position until the Spring of 1936, he left Heidelberg in 1935 to become head of the SD School in Bernau. On his appointment as *Reichsstudentenführer*, he held the rank of *Obersturmbannführer* in the SS. BDC SS Officer's file Scheel.

50. Denkschrift Scheel, 'Die Neuordnung des deutschen Studententums', 2 November 1936, ZStA REM 894. The plan was designed to allow him a good deal of independence from both Party and Ministry.

51. Tätigkeitsbericht Killer, 28 May 1937, RSFWü V * 2∽ 539.

52. 'Rede Himmlers anlässlich der Gruppenführer-Besprechung in Tölz,' 18 February 1937, quoted in: Bradley F. Smith & Agnes Petersen, *Heinrich Himmler – Geheimreden 1933 bis 1945 und andere Ansprachen* (Frankfurt am Main, 1974), p. 99 f.

53. 'Adolf Hitlers Rede an Grossdeutschland', '*Völkischer Beobachter,* 10 November 1938; Giles, National Socialist Students' Association, p. 235 f.

54. Richtlinien für die Kameradschaftserziehung des NSD-Studentenbundes, RSFWü II * ﻉ 216.

55. Stand der NS-Studentenkampfhilfe am 15. Mai 1937, RSFWü II * 62 ∝ 16.

56. Stand der NS-Studentenkampfhilfe am 15. November 1937, ibid.

57. 'Studenten und Alt-Akademiker in einer Front – Reichsstudentenführer sprach zur Alt-Herrenschaft', *Hamburger Anzeiger*, 29/30 January 1938.

58. 'Hochschulnachrichten – Altherrenbund der deutschen Studenten', *Hamburger Nachrichten*, 3 March 1938.

59. 'Der NS-Altherrenbund – Seine erste Kundgebung – Verbot der Katholischen Verbände', *Frankfurter Zeitung*, 25 June 1938.

60. *Pace* Franze, op.cit., pp. 330 & 393, for example.

61. Draft of Scheel's speech for projected Reichsparteitag 1939, LC RSF 488. The increase in the Hamburg figures may well be the result of the rector's active encouragement of NSDStB membership in his address to freshmen at the matriculation ceremony, the first time a rector had ever done this. Giles, National Socialist Students' Association, p. 227.

62. Giles, National Socialist Students' Association, Appendix 5, p. 322.

63. Ochsenius to SD-Leitabschnitt Hamburg, 12 March 1943, RSFWü V * 2 ∾ 532.

64. Scheel to Hess, 16 December 1939, BA R43II/940b.

65. Geheimerlass Rust WA401/39gRV, 10 January 1940, RSFWü V * 2 ∝ 568.

66. K-Befehl Scheel RSF15/40, 1 February 1940, ibid.

67. Ochsenius to Thomas, 31 March 1943, RSFWü v * 2 ∝ 532.

68.   Meldungen aus dem Reich, 16 February 1942, Mic. Alex. T-175/262/ 2755905f.
69.   Dienstvorschrift für die Kameradschaften des NSD-Studentenbundes im Kriege, April 1940; Grundsätze für die Kameradschaftsarbeit des Nationalsozialistischen Deutschen Studentenbundes, October 1942; Dienstanweisung für die Kameradschaft vom 20.April 1943, Institut für Hochschulkunde, Würzburg F984-6;
70.   Scheel to Bässler, 5 April 1944, BDC Parteikorrespondenz Bässler.
71.   Rundschreiben Reichserziehungsministerium to rectors WA1960, 30 December 1944, UniHH N. 20.2.11. Of the 85,517 students of the Summer Semester 1944, 15,560 were recalled for active military service, while 26,403 girls and 4,393 male students were summoned for full-time civilian war duties, mainly in the armaments industry.
72.   Semesterbericht Formel, 7 September 1944, RSFWü V * 2 ∝ 532.
73   The best treatment of the activities of this group is by Christian Petry, *Studenten aufs Schafott, Die Weisse Rose und ihr Scheitern,* (Munich, 1968).
74.   Protokoll der Arbeitstagung der Reichsstudentenführung in Stuttgart vom 11. - 13. August 1937, RSFWü II * 83 ∝ 25.

6 THE NAZI ORGANISATION OF WOMEN 1933–1939

Jill Stephenson

While parties of the left, centre and even right admitted women to formal political activity, and sometimes to prominent positions within them, after 1918, the NSDAP's first general meeting in January 1921 unanimously resolved that 'Women cannot be admitted to the leadership or the executive committee of the Party'. Those women present apparently supported this decision enthusiastically.[1] Twenty-one years later, in the depths of the Second World War, Hitler was to boast that he had consistently adhered to this resolution: 'In no local section of the Party has a woman ever had the right to hold even the smallest post . . .'[2] At no time did the male leadership of the Nazi Party waver from its implacable opposition to feminism, although it insisted that this did not mean that it favoured the subordination of women to men; rather, in the Nazi view, there were men's affairs and women's affairs, and the latter did not include participation in politics. But, in reality, the result of this 'equivalent but different' theory was that while women might exercise some control over their own organisational activity, all that they did had to conform to specific policies dictated by the exclusively male leadership of the Party.

It would therefore be misleading to call any organisation of Nazi women a 'Nazi Women's Movement', since this would imply that the specifically female activity that there indeed was within the Party had feminist aims and enjoyed considerable independence from Nazi men. The latter was demonstrably not the case, and if there were manifestations of feminism among Hitler's early female supporters, they were quickly eradicated once he had established political control in Germany. Like the other ancillary groups of the Nazi Party, the women's organisation came into being only because it could serve certain needs of the male-dominated Party. It developed and became an integral part of the Nazi system, but always in order to perform a particular function in the interests of the Party itself; if any benefit accrued to individuals or to groups of women, this was only incidental to the benefit derived by the Party.

This, above all, conditioned the different functions assigned to the Nazi women's organisation in the three basic phases of the Party's history, that before the *Machtübernahme* (assumption of power), that

186

of the Third Reich at peace, and that of the Second World War. In the first period, the women's organisation developed from a loose association of *völkisch* (racist-nationalist) groups, which afforded material aid to Party members, into a highly centralised organisation of women Party members, the *NS-Frauenschaft* (Nazi Women's Group — NSF), which was integrated into the Party's organisational system and geared to its general political objectives.[3]   Chief among these, obviously, was the achievement of political power in Germany. Much later, during the Second World War, the *NS-Frauenschaft* had the tasks of maintaining morale and ideological conformity on the home front and of encouraging German women to undertake voluntary work to help the war effort.[4] In each of these periods the NSF had clearly identifiable functions. But in the intervening phase — the subject of this essay — when the NSF was the official German women's organisation in peacetime, its role was less immediately obvious, less clearly defined. Indeed its leadership developed a formidable administrative network during this time, but the constant propaganda — itself in aspect of this development — helped to disguise the fact that the intricate apparatus was to some extent a façade behind which there was a limited amount of activity. For the mass of German women did not want to be organised, and their passive resistance to attempts to involve the housebound housewife, above all, in the 'women's work of the nation' ensured that the Nazi women's organisation remained a minority concern.[5]

    With Hitler's appointment as Chancellor on 30 January 1933, the task of the NSF became, according to the official account, 'the construction of the work of women in the Third Reich and the education of the entire female population of Germany to think in the National Socialist way'.[6]   It was not to be as straightforward as that. The dissolution of non-Nazi women's groups was achieved easily enough,[7] but within the NSF the subordination of all else to working for the seizure of power had permitted the development of conflicts both of personality and of policy. This was the natural outcome of Gregor Strasser's creation of the NSF in autumn 1931 out of the various Nazi and pro-Nazi women's groups which had emerged during the 1920s, under the leadership of the founder of the largest of these groups, Elsbeth Zander. Women who had been leaders in other groups, or had been a *Gauleiter*'s choice for supervising women's affairs in a *Gau*, resented the creation of the centralised NSF and, above all, resented the new — if limited — authority delegated to Elsbeth Zander. But although she was unpopular with ambitious women in the Party

and was also severely criticised by Goebbels, for one, she retained her
position even after the fall of her protector, Gregor Strasser, until
spring 1933, doubtless to provide continuity over the *Machtübernahme*
period.[8]

Elsbeth Zander's dismissal led to almost a year of instability within
the NSF, with the failure to find a leader who would be obedient to the
Party leadership and also able to exert unchallenged authority in her
own organisation. In April 1933, Lydia Gottschewski, former leader
of the *Bund deutscher Mädel* (League of German Girls — BdM), was
chosen to succeed Elsbeth Zander, but she was found to be
unsatisfactory and soon replaced by a man, Dr Gottfried Adolf
Krummacher, in September 1933. To confuse the issue further,
Wilhelm Frick appointed Paula Siber, former NSF leader in *Gau*
Düsseldorf, 'adviser on women's affairs'in his Ministry of the Interior,
thus duplicating the Party's system in the State apparatus. Cutting
across the rivalries of the women leaders, then, was the complication
of Party-State conflict, with the Party's interests championed by
Rudolf Hess and Robert Ley and the State's by the ambitious Frick.
But the Party leaders were determined to control all aspects of
organisational life as a matter of principle and therefore, in order to
resolve the jealousies and recriminations which were turning the NSF
into a liability, they cast about for a suitable woman who would
provide the co-operation and authority they desired. In February 1934
they found their candidate in Gertrud Scholtz-Klink,[9] whose assiduity
in her duties as NSF leader in *Gau* Baden[10] had brought her leadership
of the new Women's Labour Service in the previous month.[11]   To
facilitate her appointment, the Party bosses manufactured charges of
mismanagement and corruption against her chief rival, Paula Siber,
which occupied her in a court case for months and stole a march on
Frick by removing his candidate from the contest. Gertrud Scholtz-
Klink was thus able to assume leadership of both the NSF and the new
combine of women's social and cultural groups, the *Deutsches
Frauenwerk* (DFW), which had been Paula Siber's creation,
unopposed.[12]   Her success in carrying out the will of the Party's male
leadership is evidenced by her retention of her position until the end
of the Third Reich.

From spring 1934, the Nazi women's organisation was a model of
harmony and a faithful agent of the Party's political and social policies,
in its local branches as well as in its national leadership. For this, the
Party owed a debt of gratitude to Gertrud Scholtz-Klink. She was to
provide the two things they sought in their women's leader, unreserved

co-operation and a firm hand to ensure uniformity within her
organisation, qualities which had been conspicuously absent in her
predecessors. Her reward was that she became the sole official
representative of German women, a position formalised when she was
accorded the title *Reichsfrauenführerin* (National Women's Leader) in
November 1934.[13] Her unchallenged dominance in the women's
organisation was underlined by her being invested as leader of every
group involving women. She retained the position of leader of the
Women's Labour Service when she became leader of the NSF and the
DFW in February 1934.[14] Then, in July 1934 she became leader of
the new Women's Office of the German Labour Front,[15] and in the
following month 'adviser for the protection of women at work' on a
committee of the NSBO.[16] Already Frau Scholtz-Klink had become
leader of the National Women's Association of the German Red Cross,
'by virtue of her appointment' as NSF leader, and in the years that
followed she continued to amass new titles.[17]

Frau Scholtz-Klink's appointments in organisations whose members
were overwhelmingly male gave women representation in these, and
thus at least gave the impression that women were fully involved in
most aspects of life in Nazi Germany — contrary to what were
characterised as the lies perpetrated abroad about women being
excluded from all activities outside the home.[18] But her role as the
'token woman' in the Nazi system was only confirmed by the doubts
that persisted about her status in the Party. For clarification, Bormann
eventually issued a statement in October 1937 to the effect that Frau
Scholtz-Klink held the rank of *Hauptamtsleiter* (leader of a main
department) in the Party's national leadership.[19] Nominally, this put a
woman in the top rank of the Party élite; but this was not a
contradiction of policy since she wielded no authority outside her own
organisations, and thus had no power within the Party itself, far less
in the Government. As late as January 1938 she had to admit that she
had never once had the chance to discuss the activities of the women's
organisations with Hitler,[20] while her contact with leading members
of the Party — apart from routine business with Rudolf Hess and
Robert Ley at Party headquarters — was chiefly confined to exchanging
birthday greetings and issuing invitations to speaking engagements.[21]

If Frau Scholtz-Klink was the show piece of German women, there
were others who achieved influential or prestigious positions — always,
however, either within the women's organisations or as a female
'adviser' on a committee otherwise composed entirely of men. For
example, Auguste Reber-Gruber, a married woman teacher who

joined the NSDAP in 1932, became 'adviser for girls' education' in the
Nazi Teachers' League in 1934, and in 1936 was, in addition, appointed
senior administrator in the Reich Ministry of Education.[22]   Again, there
was Dora Hein who, like Dr Reber-Gruber, was a prominent member of
the NSF; she joined the Party in 1925 and, as a career civil servant,
became 'expert on women's affairs' and leader of the women's section in
the civil servants' organisation, the *Reichsbund der Deutschen Beamten*,
in October 1934.[23]   Another Party veteran, Anne-Marie Koeppen,
whose membership dated from 1928, was a journalist who became
leader of a section in Walther Darré's office and editor of its women's
magazine.[24]   Both she and Dora Hein were awarded the Party's Gold
Badge,[25] with a select group of women on Frau Scholtz-Klink's staff,
in January 1939.[26] Gertrud Scholtz-Klink had received her Gold Badge
at the commemoration service for the 'martyrs' of 1923 on 9 November
1936.[27]

   Joining the Party after the *Machtübernahme* was not an obstacle to
the achievement of office in the women's organisation, as the example
of Dr Ilse Eben-Servaes shows. She joined only in April 1933, but went
on to become a member of the Party leadership in February 1935, and
leader of the section for women lawyers in the Nazi Lawyers'
Association. Dr Eben-Servaes had a successful legal practice, and her
professional experience was a valuable asset to Frau Scholtz-Klink's
office, where she became legal adviser in 1934 and, from the start of
1936, leader of the section for law and arbitration.[28]   Like Frau
Scholtz-Klink,[29] she was appointed a member of the Academy of
German Law in October 1936.[30] Although Else Paul was officially Frau
Scholtz-Klink's deputy in the National Women's Leadership,[31] she
remained in the background, and, in public at least, Dr Eben-Servaes
held a position among women second only to Gertrud Scholtz-Klink's
until 1942.[32] As such, she was similarly used as an example of what
women could achieve in the Third Reich.

   The organisation which these women and others built up, in the
NSF and, affiliated to it, the DFW, had begun to take shape during the
leadership struggle. After the *Machtübernahme*, the NSF's role changed
from that of a campaigning organisation into being the élite group
which, under Party control, was to direct the affairs of German women.
Here it benefited from the *Gleichschaltung* policy, by which the
women's groups of a political nature disappeared with their parties, and
organisations promoting aims opposed by the Nazis – particularly
pacifism and feminism – were banned.[33] Of the remainder, the
women's professional and vocational groups were absorbed, with the

men's, into the relevant Nazi organisation, and those found inoffensive
were allowed to continue in existence — for a time — if they became
corporate members of the DFW.[34]

The NSF continued to be essentially the collective body of women
Party members it had been from its creation, although during the 1930s
its composition was modified. Early in 1935, Ley altered Strasser's
original order that 'All women Party members are automatically
members of the *NS-Frauenschaft*' to read 'Only those women Party
members who are prepared to be active participants in the
NS-Frauenschaft automatically become members of it.'[35] Clearly,
there was no room for dead wood in the NSF. Even more, this
order was the start of a policy of controlling the size of the NSF,
which had grown from 109,320 members at the end of 1932 to
844,893 at the end of 1933 and to over two million at the end of
1935, in the rush to join the Party and its affiliates after the
Machtübernahme.[36] To retain its own élitist character, the Party had
placed a firm restriction on entry from 1 May 1933.[37] For
the same purpose, in January 1936 Gertrud Scholtz-Klink asked
Hess to call a moratorium on admission to the NSF as quickly as
possible. In response, the order went out that 'The *NS-Frauenschaft*
has now reached a membership which is fully sufficient for the
performance of its tasks . . . ', and that, therefore, there would be a
ban on admission for all except members of the BdM from
1 February 1936.[38] In fact, Hess intended that only members of the
BdM leadership should be admitted to the NSF, but as an interim
measure Gertrud Scholtz-Klink and the national BdM leader, Trude
Bürkner, agreed that, in 1936 only, BdM girls from other ranks would
be accepted to avoid disappointment among girls who would have
expected to be admitted automatically.[39] In subsequent years,
however, ordinary BdM girls would have to content themselves with
entering the new category of individual membership of the DFW.[40]

Three years later, Frau Scholtz-Klink issued new membership
regulations, 'since the *NS-Frauenschaft* should be consolidated more
strongly than hitherto as an élite organisation'. As a result, all women
who held office in the DFW or any organisation affiliated to the
NSDAP — for example, the Nazi welfare organisation (NSV), the Labour
Front, the Nazi Teachers' League — would be eligible for membership
of the NSF after eighteen months' 'faultless' tenure of office.
Members of the BdM leadership, officeholders and 'active comrades'
in the Group of Nazi Girl Students (ANSt), and leaders in the Women's
Labour Service would also be accepted.[41] By this time, in October

1939, with Germany at war, it was considered particularly vital that
anyone in a position of leadership should belong to the Party or to one
of its member-organisations, to secure the 'inner front' of ideological
conformity. For women in responsible positions, the NSF was the
relevant group, having been declared a member-organisation of the
NSDAP in March 1935.[42]   Thus, the needs of war – with NSF members
responsible for supervising women's war-work and for maintaining
morale among the female population[43] – led once again to an
expansion of the NSF's membership, beyond the two million reliable
women who belonged to it in 1938.[44]

The main function of the NSF was 'the cultural, spiritual and
political education of German women'.[45]   Thus, it was considered vital
that its members be thoroughly trained in Nazi ideas about racial
'science', militant nationalism, and enthusiasm for large families.
To this end, a special seminar was begun in January 1935, to provide
lectures and group discussion for NSF members. The topics were
either *weltanschaulich* (ideological), or else about German history and
culture, or about practical housekeeping. These were studied in an
intensive two-week course, which also included sight-seeing tours of
Berlin and visits to the city's museums as light relief.[46]   The literature
about the seminar explained that it was deliberate policy to lay strong
emphasis on 'political education' in the course, since most of the
participants were, by occupation, primarily involved in work of a
practical nature, and yet were now being put in the position of
providing spiritual leadership for the mass of German women.[47]
Certainly, of the 3,260 women who had attended the seminar by
autumn 1939, most were involved in practical occupations, the best
represented being that of clerical worker.[48]

The NSF, then, relied overwhelmingly on part-time, volunteer
officials: all of its 24,000 workers and leaders in the *Ortsgruppen*
(localities) served on this basis, while in the *Kreise* (districts) just
under 12 per cent of NSF officials were full-time salaried employees,
while a similar proportion, in addition, received an honorarium. Frau
Scholtz-Klink was pleased to boast, in April 1939, that only 1.5 per
cent of all NSF workers were full-time employees,[49] thus testifying
to the high degree of amateur enthusiasm which sustained NSF
activity and, it might be added, saved the Party Treasury from more
than a limited amount of expenditure on salaries. But at the national
and the *Gau* levels there was extensive use of full-time, professional
staff, in keeping with the centralised nature of the organisation. All
of the thirty-two – from 1938, forty – *Gau* NSF leaders and most of

their assistants were salaried, so that around 80 per cent of all NSF workers at the *Gau* level were professionals.[50]

The NSF's task was to give ideological leadership to the female population of Germany, and especially to ensure that the activities of the largest body of organised women, in the DFW, corresponded with the Nazi view of the nature and role of women. Thus, it was the task of the DFW to orientate its activities so that women were constantly reminded that child-bearing was not only the greatest joy they could experience but also a duty they owed to the nation. In addition, a large part of the DFW's work was to lie in encouraging women to keep physically healthy for this function, and in teaching them to bring up healthy children. Looking after children meant two more things: German women would have to learn proficiency in cookery, sewing, washing and ironing clothes, and general household management; and as the first educators of children, passing on their own views and standards to the young, they would have to be thoroughly inculcated with Nazi ideology. Finally, as recreation, women had a 'cultural' task in the promotion of interest in German literature, art and music, and the discouraging of foreign cultural influences.

In its first four months, when the DFW was run by Paula Siber, its work was concerned with co-ordinating agencies which already existed for promoting interest in German culture and advising women and girls on child-care and household management. It tends to be assumed that the Nazis initiated schemes of this nature, to foster German nationalism and force women to accept that their destiny lay in the home, with a family; certainly, these motives may reasonably be attributed to them, but the Nazis could claim no originality in devising organisations to promote them. Before 1933 there were large housewives' associations,[51] women's cultural groups, and organisations which gave instruction in infant and child-care.[52] The Nazis' aim was to nationalise existing activity, and to give it uniformity on the basis of Party ideology within the structure of the DFW, whose policy was determined by the NSF.[53]

The leadership struggle of 1933-4 had hindered the development, begun by Paula Siber, of a rationalised system of courses in child-care and domestic science within the DFW. For Gertrud Scholtz-Klink, this activity was a top priority — linked as it was to the Party's population policy — and within two months of her appointment in February 1934 she had drawn up regulations for a unified system, the *Reichsmütterdienst* (National Mothers' Service), which was to be

operated throughout Germany by the DFW. Its tasks fell into two main
categories, instruction for mothers and the provision of welfare for
mothers. The courses of instruction were to be supervised in each *Gau*
by a woman with a suitable professional qualification, while in the
welfare activities there was to be close cooperation with the NSV. The
groups which had formerly engaged in work of this kind were plainly
told that if they wished to continue their activity they would have to
work under the leadership of the DFW, or else be dissolved.[54]   This
ultimatum was considered necessary because the purpose of the
Reichsmütterdienst — which was inaugurated on Mother's Day in May
1934[55] — was

> not only to instruct women in domestic science within the context
> of national economic policy: the aim of the *Reichsmütterdienst* is
> political education [which is] the development of a particular
> attitude.[56]

The courses were well publicised in the Party's women's
magazines,[57] and meticulous records of attendance were kept in each
Gau.[58]   To try to accommodate employed women as well as
housewives, the courses were offered in mornings, afternoons and
evenings for three different groups in the cities, while in rural areas
travelling instructors were employed.[59]   The courses seem to have met
a real demand; if 100,000 participants was a modest beginning in their
first year,[60] the numbers soon rose sharply, so that in 1936 there were
452,000 participants in more than 22,000 courses.[61]   This was even
before an element of compulsion was introduced for certain categories
of women — for the fiancées of SS men from November 1936 [62] and
for the wives and fiancées of SA men in 1938.[63]   The wives of SS men
were also strongly encouraged to take part in a course.[64]   Altogether,
in 1944 it was estimated that in ten years about five million women and
girls had attended a *Reichsmütterdienst* course, at an average annual
rate of half a million women in thirty thousand courses.[65]   Large
numbers of staff were required to operate a scheme of this size, and
this created financial problems, although participants had to pay fees.
The situation was such that Frau Scholtz-Klink felt the need to express
regret at being unable to pay the various administrators and instructors
at a better rate, and as compensation she ensured that they had longer
holidays than other vocational workers.[66]   Meagre resources did not,
however, lead to a slowing down of the activity, since the courses were
felt to serve the interests of the Party's permanent preoccupation, the

raising of the birth rate.[67]

As part of the continuing expansion, residential courses were
provided in 1937, and there were special 'Brides' Schools' which were
run by the DFW for the wives and fiancées of SS and SA men and
members of the armed forces.[68] In these, an inexperienced young
woman was given the model of a home to manage for six weeks —
a home which included children, to emphasise that they were an
indispensable part of a complete household. The cost of this venture
was met by fees, which could be partly offset by the granting of a
marriage loan at a higher rate than usual, thus again encouraging
procreation, since the loan could be substantially redeemed by the birth
of children.[69]

While the *Reichsmütterdienst* was intended to be an exercise in
propaganda as well as one of practical value, the real work of 'political
education' was the responsibility of the DFW's section for
Kultur-Erziehung-Schulung (culture-education-training). By 1939 this
included, in addition to the provision of courses of instruction in
race, heredity and German history, divisions for 'academic work',
girls' education, literature, art and music, handicrafts and physical
training.[70] The content of the instruction given consisted mainly of
expositions of Nazi policy, of both a short and a long term nature,
and justification of this policy to encourage co-operation from as much
of the female population as possible.[71] In 1938, it was reported,
109,782 women attended 2,137 courses in general ideological
instruction, while, in addition, the *Gau* offices of the DFW's
Kultur-Erziehung-Schulung section mounted 293 special courses
on racial policy which were attended by 15,287 women.[72] These
figures are not particularly impressive given that the total individual
membership of the DFW for the Greater German Reich in 1938 was
1.6 million, of whom almost 470,000 were new recruits in Austria.[73]
In comparison with the figures for attendance at *Reichsmütterdienst*
courses, they are positively meagre.

The three other main sections of DFW activity were social
assistance, national economy/domestic economy and border and
foreign work. The last of these was designed to generate national
consciousness among Germans living abroad, particularly in
neighbouring countries such as Poland, Denmark and Czechoslovakia,
as well as in Austria before the *Anschluss*; this meant chiefly, once
again, the dissemination of pro-Nazi propaganda, especially among
visitors to Germany from these countries.[74] The work of the section
for national economy/domestic economy was particularly geared to

persuading German housewives to buy German goods and to learn thrifty ways with seasonal and substitute foodstuffs, to support the drive for autarky.[75] And the work of social assistance, too, increasingly betrayed Nazi policies which would run the risk of war, by encouraging German women to attend first aid courses, train as auxiliary nurses and social workers and undergo training in air-raid protection. It was no doubt a sign of the times that in 1938 the figure for attendance at the last of these was, at over 580,000, almost twice what it had been in 1937, while the other courses, although enjoying increases of a similar proportion, could barely muster 90,000 attendances between them.[76]

The task of ensuring that the DFW was kept under the leadership and control of the NSF was facilitated by the policy of *Personalunion*, the holding of analogous positions in both by reliable women. At the top, Frau Scholtz-Klink had been appointed leader of both groups at the same time, to provide uniformity at the national level; correspondingly, it had been policy from the founding of the DFW to continue this kind of arrangement in the *Gaue*, so that the woman responsible for the work of the DFW in the Party's largest administrative unit was normally the *Gau* NSF leader.[77] In 1934, this degree of personal union was declared compulsory.[78] But for the time being this was where the policy stopped; it was also decreed that no NSF official should preside over all the different groups of DFW activity in her area, because of the specialised nature of the work done in some of them.[79]

The DFW's structure and organisation were, however, felt by Hess and Ley to be unsatisfactory for the function the association was intended to perform, and after much discussion,[80] a new constitution was produced in April 1936 which described its aim as 'the organisational unification of women prepared to collaborate in the *Führer*'s work of construction, under the leadership of the NSF', and extended the policy of *Personalunion*. Now, the DFW was formally divided into the same geographical units as the NSF, and therefore as the NSDAP, and, as an innovation, the NSF leader in any area was designated the automatic choice for DFW leadership in the same area. This streamlining of the DFW, hitherto divided according to the interests of the constituent groups, was a natural result of its elevation to the status of an 'affiliated organisation' of the Party, to which the principles of the Party itself applied, whereas formerly its connection with the Party had been indirect, through its association with the NSF.[81] Thus, the Nazification of the women's organisation

followed upon the nationalisation of its work in the early
Gleichschaltung period; this further step involved a breach of the 1933
Concordat with the Vatican, as one of Frick's junior ministers,
Stuckart, pointed out to Hess,[82] but for the Party it was an
obvious step to take, to increase its control over the direction of
women's affairs.

It was not only the DFW which had to be kept in line with NSF,
and ultimately Party, policy; for there were other offices and
organisations which dealt with matters involving women. It was
to facilitate cooperation, and, it was to be hoped, uniformity, among
these that Frau Scholtz-Klink was given positions within the Labour
Front and the Red Cross, for example. Because she was thus expected
and enabled to provide 'unified leadership . . . for all areas of womanly
work in the community',[83] she built up a centralised bureau of
officials around herself as National Women's Leader, which was
formally accorded the title of *Reichsfrauenführung* (National
Women's Leadership) in June 1936. This, 'the only office responsible
for all matters of concern to the German woman', developed close
links with the other groups in which women were involved, but
which were outside Frau Scholtz-Klink's direct authority, by means
of agreements for cooperation, to avoid demarcation disputes and to
try to prevent duplication of functions. Such arrangements were made,
for example, with the NS-Cultural Community and with the ANS't in
January 1935, with the Nazi Teachers' League in June 1936, and in
the following month with the section for 'Mother and Child' in the
NSV.[84]

There were other groups, too, which were expected to co-operate
with Frau Scholtz-Klink's office; prominent among these was the Red
Cross and the *NS-Schwesternschaft*, the Party's own nursing corps,
which was under the jurisdiction of the NSV.[85] But Ley made it
clear in January 1934 that no agency of the Party nor any State
organisation was to try to establish its own women's groups which
would, in effect, be rivals to the NSF or the DFW. Ley emphasised
that these two were specifically intended to be monopoly
organisations, for women Party members and for other female
citizens respectively, to eliminate class or other divisions among
German women — chiefly, obviously, to avoid the kind of diversity
and conflict which the Party considered so harmful to national
harmony and uniformity. Ley pointed out that women might indeed
be members of an occupational or professional group, but such a
group would also have male members and would thus not aspire to

become a specifically women's interest group, taking a particular section of women out of the mainstream of female activity, which was to find its expression in the DFW.[86]   It was this attitude which underlay the Party's insistence on making women's sections of professional organisations, in particular, corporate members of the DFW, and, in the later 1930s, at least, involving their members as much as possible in the work of the DFW.[87]

Ley's edict did not prevent confusion from occurring subsequently. For example, Frau Scholtz-Klink found it necessary to resolve the 'considerable lack of clarity about the relationship of the housewife to the DFW and the Labour Front', in summer 1936. She had agreed with Hess and Ley that all employed housewives belonged, by virtue of their being employees, to the Labour Front, while all housewives who were not employed outside the home belonged — insofar as they wished to be organised, she was careful to add — to the NSF or the DFW, whichever was appropriate. She felt obliged to clarify this point because a group within the Labour Front, the National Association of Domestic Workers, had been trying to enlist full-time housewives as members. Now, in July 1936, Frau Scholtz-Klink banned such activity, and announced that where the interests of housewives and domestic employees coincided, provision would be made for joint meetings to take place at the *Kreis* level, under the supervision of the NSF,[88] to ensure that her orders were observed.

The National Women's Leadership was not itself an organisation but rather the central administrative agency in which the various branches of women's activity were represented by 'experts'. Predictably, Ilse Eben-Servaes became the authority on legal matters, while Auguste Reber-Gruber was the adviser on education. There were also experts on foreign affairs, nursing, the Labour Service, 'Mother and Child', and the radio, for propaganda.[89]   These officials, along with other general assistants, were appointed to enable Frau Scholtz-Klink to discharge her many duties in a vast number of organisations, in a wide variety of fields. The office evolved during the 1930s, but although modifications and extensions were made after 1936 it had by then developed its essential form. Its nine sections were divided into two groups, with those responsible for culture and education, national and domestic economy, foreign activity, social assistance, and training for motherhood coming into being in the years 1934-6, to co-ordinate the DFW's activity in the same areas. The other four sections dealt with purely organisational matters, including finance, personnel, information collation, and press and propaganda, which included radio, films and exhibitions.[90]

The propaganda network of the National Women's Leadership was modelled on the propaganda machine of the NSDAP. Within its jurisdiction came the publications of both the NSF and the DFW, including the *NS-Frauenwarte*, the NSF's official magazine. In addition, there were pamphlets, newsletters, and films and radio broadcasts directed specifically at women.[91] The radio programmes reinforced the DFW's sectional work, consisting chiefly of cookery hints, including the skilful use of cheaper foodstuffs, and 'cultural' items concerned with German literature and music; in keeping with the Party's view that women were first and foremost the mothers of the nation, there was also a regular 'Listen with Mother' feature for small children.[92] Propaganda included the staging of exhibitions, at both the national and local level; these were generally on the theme of 'Woman and Nation', the title of a national exhibition held in May-June 1935, or 'The Contribution of Women in the Community', the title of the women's exhibition held during the 1937 Party Congress.[93] These tended to consist of tableaux depicting women's role, the products of the DFW's sewing bees and illustrated records of the work of NSF and DFW women at home and abroad. In 1937 there were altogether 3,000 such exhibitions, visited by a million and a half people, while in 1938 there were almost 3,600 exhibitions – this time, however, visited by the smaller number of 1.1 million people. In addition, there were fêtes, sales of work and meetings; in 1937, almost 1.4 million women attended the 16,330 events of this nature, while in 1938 both these figures were nearly doubled.[94] But figures recorded in thousands and millions always sound impressive in themselves. Here, they appear extremely modest when set alongside the individual membership claimed for the NSF and DFW at this time – approximately three million in total[95] – and suggest that the level of activity and enthusiasm even among the organised was unremarkable, to say the least.

The contrast between real activity and membership of the NSF and DFW is even more marked when the corporate membership of the DFW is taken into account. The Party's statistical records show that in 1935 eighty-seven groups in this category provided 2.7 million extra members[96] who were at least nominally involved in the work of the DFW. And in spite of the dissolution of several of these groups subsequently,[97] a corporate membership of 'about four million' was claimed for the DFW in 1938; this, of course, included new groups from Austria.[98] By the beginning of 1939 the individual membership of the NSF and DFW together – now augmented by almost 470,000 from Austria and 300,000 from the Sudetenland – totalled 4.3 million[99] out of a population of some 30 million adult females. And the four million women under the supervision of the Women's Office of the Labour Front[100] were also counted as belonging to the women's organisation, so that Frau Scholtz-Klink felt confident in claiming, in April 1939, that '12 million women are daily under the influence of the leadership of the *NS-Frauenschaft*'.[101] This boast was inflated, not to say spurious. It is very clear that, at best, by 1939 the Nazi women's organisations could count on four million or so activists, the individual members of the NSF and DFW in Greater Germany. The connection of the eight million others with the Nazi organisations lay in the monopolising of all communal activity by the Party and its affiliates, so that   women had no option but to be corporate members of the DFW if they wished to engage in any degree of organised social, sporting or cultural life, and to belong to the Labour Front if they wanted to be secure in a job in a factory or an office.

The difficulty faced by Frau Scholtz-Klink's organisations was partly of the Nazis' own making: the full-time housewife – nominally, at least, the Nazi ideal as far as women were concerned – was potentially the least easy member of the community to organise. Special propaganda was therefore directed at her, to encourage her to accept her duty to be – ironically enough – 'politically aware' of her role in the life of the community, and to be involved in activities outside the home, to make contact with her fellow citizens.[102]   No doubt for some women who felt isolated as housebound wives, and who had perhaps felt threatened and uneasy in the relatively feminist atmosphere of the 1920s, the social intercourse and sense of importance provided by the Nazi women's organisations gave a new lease of life.[103]   But to many, it is clear, the organisational activity was exhaustingly overdone. In December 1935, the Party's agent in Bad Kreuznach, near Mainz, reported that the recruiting drives, cultural evenings, assemblies and Christmas festivities conducted by the Party and its affiliates had been so intensive and persistent that the local population was beginning to sigh, 'We're being organised to death!' The net results of this energetic activity were, accordingly, disappointing the only new recruits won for the women's organisations had been from among the wives of Party members and civil servants.[104]   Clearly, resistance to involvement could be the result of saturation by propaganda in favour of it. But it could also be the result of deliberate activity by the few agencies outside the NSDAP and its affiliates which

continued to exist; with most sources of actual and potential
opposition quickly eliminated in 1933, the largest ones remaining
thereafter were the Churches. Both the Evangelical and the Roman
Catholic Churches offered resistance to Nazi monopolisation of
organisational activity, since it was bound to encroach on their own
territory. The degree of obstructiveness was at times such that the
Party's local representative had to report, as in the case of Neuwied,
near Koblenz, in 1935, that

> it is not possible to form an NSF group in parish D. The lack of
> success is attributed to the women's association, which is under the
> influence and leadership of the parson's wife.[105]

As late as February 1938, it was reported from a district in the Trier
area that it had still not been possible to form an NSF group because
of the opposition of the priest.[106]

Much has been made of the blind and often hysterical enthusiasm
for Hitler and the Nazis manifested by some women.[107] But it ought
also to be stressed that in the day-to-day opposition and passive
resistance offered by the Churches in the Third Reich, women were
often in the forefront.[108] If it can be argued from this that women
were denying the claims of one ideology and its apparatus because
of their attachment to another, it is nevertheless true that there was
considerable resistance to Nazi organising drives among women at the
local, often parochial, level.

The *Reichsfrauenführerin* and her colleagues were, however, alive
to some of the potential difficulties in a large organisation claiming to
represent all members of one sex. Mindful that a conflict between
generations had been a major problem for the feminist organisations in
the later 1920s,[109] they were determined that no such difficulties
should upset the harmony of the Nazi women's organisation. Clearly,
eighteen or twenty-one-year-old girls coming straight from the BdM
into the NSF or the DFW, would have to be provided with interesting
activities; otherwise, they might feel that they were being submerged in
a housewives' club run by middle-aged matrons, and subside into
apathy or disaffection. The tactic adopted to try to avoid this, and to
encourage new recruits for the DFW and groom potential NSF members
and leaders, was the creation of 'youth groups' within both the NSF
and the DFW, in 1936, for the eighteen to thirty age-group. The official
regulations for the youth groups stated that their purpose was primarily
to bring young women together and to provide the opportunity for

them to do the things people of their age liked to do; these were deemed to include singing and dancing, with a high content of physical exercise, including hill-walking. But there were special 'education' – political indoctrination – courses as well, which were vital to the Nazi scheme given that young women had, in the Party's view, constantly to be reminded that their destiny lay in marrying and starting a family – or adding to a family they might already have. To emphasise this, the girls were also expected to take an active part in the DFW's sectional work, particularly in the realm of domestic management and child-care.[110]

In order to keep young women in this important age-group as much under Party surveillance as possible, a vast array of activities was designated as desirable, including training with the Red Cross and voluntary assistance in first-aid and welfare work, training in air-raid protection, and, for the more energetic, reaching a standard of proficiency in physical pursuits to win the women's National Sport Badge.[111] But in spite of the barrage of propaganda directed at attracting young women to the youth groups, recruitment here – as to the DFW generally – was disappointing. Perhaps the Nazis had, after all, misjudged the tastes of young women; or perhaps they had simply overestimated the extent to which they could, in a one-party State, with a monopoly of propaganda, mould the disposition and desires of groups of Germans, according to the role they were assigned in Nazi plans. At any rate, by the beginning of 1939 the youth groups had a modest membership of 168,533, while, it was observed, there were nearly 400,000 women between eighteen and thirty in the NSF alone, with a considerable number in the DFW in addition. It was, however, felt to be encouraging that the year 1938 had seen an increase of 48 per cent in the membership;[112] there was to be a further rise to 292,000 by September 1939, and the achievement of a membership of over 400,000 in August 1942. But these last figures apply to the Greater German Reich,[113] and are therefore not directly comparable with the 1938 figures, which apply to Germany within its 1937 borders.

Again and again, concrete information belies the proud boasts made by Frau Scholtz-Klink, her staff and her propaganda network that the Nazi-directed activity of women in the Third Reich was energetic, all-embracing and performed with enthusiasm by vast numbers of German women. There was certainly an impression of industry and large-scale participation, chiefly because the Party's press generally, and the women's press in particular, gave comprehensive coverage of events of even the most minor significance, exaggerating their scope and importance. In this context, the example of press circulation is itself instructive: the National Women's Leadership published its own newsletter (*Nachrichtendienst der Reichsfrauenführung*), the official magazines of both the NSF and the DFW, and two other magazines designed to interest women, *Mutter und Volk* (Mother and Nation) and *Deutsche Hauswirtschaft* (German Housekeeping). In 1938, when there were over two million NSF members, the *NS-Frauenwarte*, the official magazine of the NSF, had a circulation of 1.2 million; if this was perhaps respectable, it nevertheless meant that only just over half of the Party's élite organisation of women subscribed to their own magazine, which hardly indicates real enthusiasm. Also in 1938, when the DFW's individual membership reached 1.1 million in Germany alone, a mere 23,000 women took the DFW's magazine, *Frauenkultur im Deutschen Frauenwerk*; and only 76,000 subscribed to the *Nachrichtendienst*. The other two magazines together attracted about 300,000 readers between them, on a roughly half-and-half basis.[114] Thus the success of Frau Scholtz-Klink's office in promoting its publications — and two of its three official ones, particularly — was limited, not to say poor. The women's organisation was doubtless not exceptional in this, but the result nevertheless was that the barrage of propaganda put out by the women's organisations did not reach even all the women who had chosen to join an organisation, let alone the vast majority who had not.

If it is true that the housewife in any community is the most difficult member of it to organise, this is not particularly alarming in a liberal democracy or even an old-fashioned conservative autocracy. But in a modern dictatorship which aspires to be totalitarian it must be a source of concern, since it means that a whole category of citizens cannot be controlled and, of even greater importance, this is the category which influences and controls the youth of the nation in its earliest years. Their obsession with uniformity and control, and their deep concern for the upbringing of future generations of Germans, made the Nazis try continuously, by flattery and by appeals, to attract women to organisations under the supervision of the Party. They had some success with employed women, who at least had to pay lip-service to the Nazi system to feel secure in a job, but these tended to join specialist groups for both sexes rather than a group composed exclusively of women. For example, the records kept about women civil servants show that members of a group employed in the Chancellery itself chose — in addition to the *Reichsbund der Deutschen Beamten*, their occupational group — the National Air-Raid Protection Society, the NSV and the Colonial Society regularly, but the DFW

seldom.[115]   It can hardly be surprising that, in a society where such
stress was laid on the comradeship of men and women and the necessity
of raising the birth rate, the women gravitated — as most women
normally do — into mixed rather than segregated groups, thus
confounding the other, at times contradictory, Nazi preoccupation that
the functions of the two sexes should, on the whole, be kept separate.

The NSF was indeed a well-organised, élite, leadership group, as had
been intended, 'to educate in the spirit of community life through the
union of women from all sections of the population in the service of
the National Socialist idea.'[116]   But its 'followers' remained dispersed,
and to a large extent apathetic. It was loudly boasted that the DFW was
successfully cutting across the barriers of class and occupation, with
'the housewife and the employed woman, the domestic servant and the
professional woman, the unskilled woman worker and the artist' all
finding common ground in the activities of the *Frauenwerk*.[117]   But the
herding of as many women as could be persuaded into a segregated
organisation was an essentially artificial manoeuvre, for, as Ley himself
observed,

> The DFW cannot, in my opinion, be termed a 'National Socialist
> community' . . . The name 'community' can only be applied where
> there is a gathering of people from all sections of the nation. The
> organisation of members of one sex can therefore not be termed a
> community.[118]

Even the streamlining of the DFW, and its closer association with the
Party from 1936 could not disguise the fact that it was still basically
the product of the nationalisation of groups which had existed before
1933. Certainly, much of the activity, especially in terms of child-care,
homecraft and first-aid, was set on a more systematic footing, and the
organisations which were dissolved after the initial purge were either
not relevant to the sectional work of the DFW or else absorbed into
larger units. Thus, the corporate membership of the DFW continued
largely to consist of women who would have previously chosen to join a
group for specifically women's interests, while the individual members
were either genuine enthusiasts — like the NSF members — or else
trimmers, since coercion was not used. Coercion would not have been
practicable, since it would have been difficult to impose sanctions on
full-time housewives, who had no outside job to be dismissed from, and
who were in the delicate position of bringing up the nation's children.
This latter function created a real need to make these women well-

disposed towards the regime, so that threats were out of the question. To this extent, perhaps, the Nazis succeeded: if there was little positive enthusiasm on the part of women for Party activities, there was no organised opposition either. The resistance that manifested itself was resistance to involvement; as long as the Nazis allowed the mass of women to opt out of the Party's organisational activities, German women gave at least passive acquiescence to the regime. This was, of course, of incalculable value, but it was nevertheless a poor return for the incessant propaganda, the recruiting drives and the organisation of social activities. To the extent that the Nazis, and Frau Scholtz-Klink and the NSF leadership in particular, tried hard consistently to organise women and to mobilise positive support among full-time housewives for the women's organisations and their activities, they must be deemed to have failed.

Notes

1. G. Franz-Willing, *Die Hitlerbewegung* (Hamburg, 1962), p. 82.
2. Hitler's *Table-Talk*, no. 126, 26 January 1942, p. 252.
3. Basic coverage of the women's organisations associated with the NSDAP in the pre-1933 period may be found in A. Jill R. Stephenson, 'Women in German Society, 1930-40', Edinburgh University PhD. thesis, 1974 (hereafter Stephenson thesis). pp. 331-47.
4. Institut für Zeitgeschichte archive (hereafter IfZ), MA 253, frames 649-54, 'Der Einsatz der NSF/DFW im Kriegsjahr 1940'. There is a considerable amount of documentation for the activities of the NSF in the Second World War, in IfZ, MA 138, MA 225, MA 341, MA 441/8, and in the Bundesarchiv (hereafter BA) NS 22 files.
5. c.f. Richard Grunberger, *A Social History of the Third Reich* (London, 1974), p. 329.
6. 'Nationalsozialistische Frauenarbeit', *Frauenkultur im Deutschen Frauenwerk* (hereafter *FK*), April 1937, p. 8.
7. Jill Stephenson, *Women in Nazi Society* (London, 1975), pp. 27-30.
8. Stephenson thesis, pp. 333-47. There is substantial documentation of these events in the BA, NS 22 files, particularly in vorl. 348, vorl. 349, vorl. 355, vorl.357, and also in *Sammlung Schumacher* (hereafter *Slg.Sch.*), 230.
9. Born in 1902, married, had four children, joined NSDAP in 1929 or 1930. Berlin Document Center (hereafter BDC), her Party membership card and 'Lebenslauf', 16 February 1938.
10. BA, NS 22/10441, letter of 29 July 1931, and programme of 'Baden Gauparteitag 23.-27.9.31', Richard J. Evans, *The Feminist Movement in Germany 1894-1933* (London, 1976), p. 256.
11. BA, *Slg.Sch.*, 262, 'Neuordnung des weiblichen Arbeitsdienstes', 23 January 1934.
12. Stephenson thesis, pp. 347-64 gives an account of this. See also *Das Archiv*, 1933, pp. 270, 498, 854.
13. '5 Jahre Reichsfrauenführung', *FK*, February 1939, p. 3.
14. BA, op.cit., 230, 'Gau-Verordnungsblatt 2/34', Altona, 1 March 1934.
15. Ibid., 'Einrichtung eines Frauenamtes in der DAF, 12.7.34',

NS-Korrespondenz, no. 162, 13 July 1934.
16. BDC, Partei-Kanzlei Korrespondenz, letter to Gertrud Scholtz-Klink, 28 August 1934.
17. For examples, see *FK*, op.cit., pp. 3-5.
18. 'Einsatz der Frau in der Nation', speech by Gertrud Scholtz-Klink at the 1937 Party Congress, published by the DFW; Trude Bürkner, quoted in *Die Frau,* April 1937, p.402.
19. BDC, op.cit., 'Rundschreiben nr. 128/37', 6 October 1937.
20. BA, R43 II/427, letter from Gertrud Scholtz-Klink to Bormann, 24 January 1938.
21. Several examples of this may be found in IfZ, MA 253, *Rosenberg-Akten.*
22. BDC, Party Census of 1939 and a letter from Hess, 9 October 1936.
23. ibid., Party Census of 1939 and a statement by Dora Hein, 28 July 1939.
24. ibid., Anne-Marie Koeppen's file, 'Lebenslauf', 12 May 1938.
25. ibid., Party Census of 1939.
26. 'Nachrichten aus der Reichsfrauenführung. Januar-März 1939', *FK*, May 1939, inside of title page.
27. NSDAP Hauptarchiv (hereafter HA), Reel 13, folder 254, 'Partei Archiv', November 1936.
28. BDC, Ilse Eben-Servaes's file, answers to a questionnaire for the NSDAP leadership, 2 October 1939.
29. HA, loc. cit.
30. BA, R61/168, letter from Ilse Eben-Servaes to Loyal, at the Academy of German Law, 12 December 1938.
31. BA, *Slg.Sch.*, 230, 'Stab des Hauptamtes NS-F und DFW', n.d.
32. BDC, Ilse Eben-Servaes's file, letter of 22 January 1942.
33. Jill Stephenson, *Women in Nazi Society*, pp. 27-30.
34. ibid., pp. 159-60, 165.
35. BA, op.cit., 'Information (6) Nr. 0.18/35', 27 February 1935.
36. 'Zum Organisationsplan der NS-Frauenschaft/Deutsches Frauenwerk', *Deutsches Frauenschaffen*, 1939, p. 12.
37. Martin Broszat, *Der Staat Hitlers* (Munich, 1969), p. 253.
38. BA, op.cit., letter from Friedrichs, in Hess's office, to Ley, 17 January 1936.
39. Ibid., notice from Trude Bürkner to the Reich Youth Leadership and the *Gau* BdM leaders, 17 October 1936.
40. *Deutsches Frauenschaffen*, op.cit., p. 11.
41. BA, op.cit., 'Anordnung nr. 2/39', 25 October 1939, issued by Gertrud Scholtz-Klink.
42. *FK*, loc. cit.
43. BA, NSD 3/5, 'Aufgaben der NS-Frauenschaft', 16 July 1940, p. 659.
44. Figure calculated from information in BA, *Slg.Sch.*, 230, *Reichsfrauenführung Jahresbericht 1938*, pp. 11 and 14.
45. 'NS-Frauenschaft und Deutsches Frauenwerk', *Führerlexikon* 1934/35, p. 93.
46. IfZ, MA 609, frames 56489-92, 'Amt für wissenschaftlicher Arbeit', n.d.
47. BA, NS 15/15, frame 56526, Else Petri, 'Ziel und Aufgabe des Seminars', *Seminar für die NS-Frauenschaft an der Hochschule für Politik*, Winter 1939/40.
48. IfZ, op.cit., frames 56477-84, 'Bericht über die bisherige Tätigkeit des Seminars . . . 1935-39'.
49. ibid., MA 130, frame 86493, 'Pgn. Scholtz-Klink: Die NS-Frauenschaft', 17 April 1939.
50. BA, *Slg.Sch.*, 230, op.cit., pp. I-II.
51. Evans, op.cit., pp. 212-13, 240-2, 250-2.

52. Organisations appearing in reports in *Die Bayerische Frau* under 'Aus unseren Vereinen und Verbänden' between October 1931 and May 1933 also appear in BA, op.cit., 'Liste dem DFW angeschlossenen Reichsspitzenverbände, April 1935'. This also applies to some groups mentioned in BA, *Nachlass* Katharina von Kardorff, no. 28, 'Der XI. Frauencongress in Berlin, 17.-22.6.1929: Ehrenbeirat der Verbände'.
53. Reichsfrauenführung (ed.), *NS-Frauenschaft* (Berlin, 1937) p. 16.
54. 'Das Deutsche Frauenwerk über die Eingliederung der Verbände', *Die Frau*, April 1934, pp. 506-7.
55. *FK*, loc. cit.
56. Quoted from *NS-Mädchenbildung* in 'Zur politischen Schulung im Reichsmütterdienst', *Die Frau*, November 1936, p. 108.
57. E.g., *FK*, May 1939, loc. cit; 'Die kameradschaftliche Volksmutter', *NS-Frauenwarte*, May 1936, pp. 774-75 and p. 778.
58. BA, op.cit., pp. 8 and 37.
59. BA, R2/12771, letter from the *Deutscher Gemeindetag* to Rust, 20 October 1937; IfZ, MA 388, frame 726440, 'Die Gaubräuteschule des Deutschen Frauenwerkes Mütterdienst, Brüggen/Niederrhein', n.d. (?early 1939).
60. 'Frau Scholtz-Klink über: Die Mitarbeit der deutschen Frau im neuen Staat – Der Sinn des Muttertages', *Völkischer Beobachter*, 8 May 1935.
61. 'Arbeit des Reichsmütterdienstes, 1934-37', *Deutsches Frauenschaffen*, 1938, pp. 36-7.
62. BA, loc. cit.
63. HA, Reel 13, folder 253: order by *Brigadeführer* Giesler of SA *Gruppe Hochland*, 1 October 1937; order by *Gruppenführer* Günther of SA *Gruppe Thüringen*, n.d. (? October 1937). Report in *Frankfurter Zeitung*, 9 February 1938.
64. ' "Die Hausfrau der Zukunft", Schulung aller SS-Bräute durch den Reichsmütterdienst', *Frankfurter Zeitung*, 2 December 1936.
65. 'Bevölkerungspolitik', *Die Deutsche Sozialpolitik*, July 1944, p. 63.
66. HA, op.cit., Reichsfrauenführung 'Rundschreiben FW Nr. 48/37', n.d. (?June 1937).
67. ibid., folder 254, Reichsfrauenführung 'Rundschreiben FW Nr. 94/37', 14 October 1937.
68. 'Die Aufgaben der Bräuteschulen', *Frankfurter Zeitung*, 30 December 1937.
69. IfZ, op.cit., frames 726440-41. For discussion of the marriage loan scheme, see Stephenson, op.cit., pp. 46-7, 54, 86-8, 99-100.
70. 'Organisationsplan der Reichsfrauenführung', *Deutsches Frauenschaffen*, 1939, p. 8.
71. 'Die Arbeit der NS-Frauenschaft und des Deutschen Frauenwerks im Jahre 1935', *NS-Frauenwarte*, March 1936, p. 613.
72. BA, *Slg.Sch.*, 230, op.cit., p. 32.
73. ibid., p. 15.
74. ibid., pp. V-VI. Reichsfrauenführung, op.cit., pp. 28-9.
75. ibid., pp. 24-5.
76. BA, op.cit., pp. 55-6.
77. BDC, AOPG 2684/34, letter from Paula Siber to Bormann, 22 May 1934.
78. *Führerlexikon*, loc. cit.
79. *Die Frau*, April 1934, loc. cit.
80. BA, op.cit., letter from Sommer, in Hess's office, to Ley, 28 August 1935; ibid., letter from Ley to Hess, 8 October 1935.
81. ibid., 'Satzung des Deutschen Frauenwerks', *Der Führerorden*, 11 April 1936.

82. BA, R22/24, letter from Stuckart to Hess, 14 December 1936.
83. *FK*, April 1937, op.cit., p. 9.
84. *FK*, February 1939, op.cit., pp. 3-4.
85. Wolfgang Schäfer, *NSDAP. Entwicklung und Struktur der Staatspartei des Dritten Reiches* (Hanover and Frankfurt am Main, 1956), p. 63.
86. BA, *Slg.Sch.*, 230, 'Rundschreiben nr. 1/34', 5 January 1934, issued by Ley.
87. Stephenson, op.cit., pp. 164-5, 174-5.
88. ibid., NSF information leaflet, 'Zugehörigkeit der Hausfrauen zum DFW bzw. zur DAF', signed by Gertrud Scholtz-Klink, July 1936.
89. ibid., *Reichsfrauenführung Jahresbericht 1938*, 'Stab des Hauptamtes NS-Frauenschaft und Deutsches Frauenwerk', n.d. (? 1935).
90. *FK*, April 1937, loc. cit.
91. *Deutsches Frauenschaffen*, loc. cit.
92. HA, op.cit., 'Der Frauenfunk der Woche, 21.3-27.3.1937', pp. 1-6.
93. *FK*, February 1939, op.cit., pp. 3, 5.
94. BA, op.cit., pp. 28-9.
95. *Deutsches Frauenschaffen*, 1939, pp. 12-13.
96. NSDAP *Partei-Statistik*, 1935, Vol. III, p. 58.
97. Chiefly the conservative and nationalist organisations. See Stephenson, op.cit., p. 29.
98. BA, op.cit., p. I.
99. ibid., p. 15.
100. ibid., p. I.
101. IfZ, MA 130, loc. cit.
102. Lore Bauer, 'Die "politische" Frau', *Völkischer Beobachter*, 6 September 1935; 'Erziehung zur politischen Verantwortung: Die Frau, die Erzieherin der Jugend, muss teilnehmen an der Entwicklung des staatlichen Lebens', *Völkischer Beobachter*, 27 September 1935.
103. This, at any rate, was what the Nazis claimed to have achieved, and there was clearly some truth in it. This was confirmed by a former minor official of the NSF in Munich, in conversation; she seemed sufficiently uninhibited and free from a guilt complex to be credible.
104. F. J. Heyen, *Nationalsozialismus im Alltag*, Boppard am Rhein, 1967, 'Aus dem Lagebericht des Landrates von Bad Kreuznach über den Monat Dezember 1935', no. 164, pp. 291-2.
105. ibid., 'Aus dem Lagebericht des Landrats von Neuwied über den Monat 12.1935', no. 89, p. 179.
106. ibid., 'Politische Beurteilungen der einzelnen Ortsgruppen des Kreises Trier-Land-West, vom 1. Februar 1938', no. 200, p. 341.
107. L.P. Lochner (ed.), *The Goebbels Diaries 1942/43* (London,1949), entry for 12 September 1943, p. 358; Douglas L. Kelley, *Twenty-Two Cells in Nuremberg* (London, 1947), p. 60; Heinrich Fraenkel, *German People versus Hitler* (London, 1940), pp. 222 and 227; W. L. Shirer, *Berlin Diary 1934-41* (London, 1941), entries for 4 September 1934, pp. 22-3, and 4-5 September (3 am), 1940, p. 389.
108. Heyen, op.cit., 'Aus dem Lagebericht des Landrates von Bad Kreuznach über den Monat Januar 1936', no. 90, p. 180; ibid., from answers to a questionnaire in Koblenz, August 1938, no. 93, p. 185; BA, *Slg.Sch.*, 243/II, vol. 2, 'Demonstration kath. Frauen in Beulich', 2 May 1939. I am most grateful to Dr J.S. Conway of the University of British Columbia for generously sending me a copy of this document.
109. Stephenson, op.cit., p. 26.
110. BA, *Slg.Sch.*, 230, 'Anordnung Nr. 2/37', issued by Gertrud

Scholtz-Klink, 12 February 1937.
111. Dorothea Thimme, 'Die Jugendgruppen des Deutschen Frauenwerkes bekennen sich zur Leistung', *FK*, September 1938, p. 5.
112. BA, op.cit., *Reichsfrauenführung Jahresbericht 1938*, pp. 19-20.
113. BA, NSD 3/5, 'Jugendgruppen der NS-Frauenschaft/Deutsches Frauenwerk', 13 October 1942, p. 660.
114. BA, *Slg.Sch.*, 230, op.cit., p. 28.
115. BA, R 431I/1091c, information from personal records kept in the Reich Chancellery about its employees, compiled between March and May 1939.
116. Reichsfrauenführung, op.cit., p. 14.
117. ibid., p. 20.
118. BA, *Slg.Sch.*, 230, letter from Ley to Hess, 8 October 1935.

7 THE OLDENBURG CRUCIFIX STRUGGLE OF NOVEMBER 1936: A CASE STUDY OF OPPOSITION IN THE THIRD REICH*

Jeremy Noakes

While there were fairly numerous examples of small-scale resistance to specific measures of the regime, instances of public disaffection on a relatively large scale were rare in the Third Reich. Perhaps the best known is the protest movement which resisted the policy of so-called euthanasia for the handicapped, carried out during the first year of the war, a movement which eventually helped to force the shelving of that policy, at least officially.[1] Another far less well-known case was the Oldenburg crucifix struggle of November 1936. Although it was admittedly more limited in its extent and in its significance than the euthanasia protest, nevertheless a study of this particular conflict may provide an insight into the possibilities and also the limits of opposition to the regime. It may also throw some light on the relations between one particular section of the population and the Nazi state.

Work on public opinion in the Third Reich, on the attitude of the population to policies and practices of the regime has not proceeded very far. We already have numerous analyses of various organisations — the party apparatus, the *Gauleiter,* the SS and so on. We also have several accounts of specific policies, notably of course foreign policy but also such areas as Jewish policy and aspects of economic policy. Yet we know very little about how the population regarded the regime and about how it reacted to particular policies. We do not really have any clear idea of the composition of the bases of support for, or more negatively, acquiescence in the regime among the people, the balance between such ingredients as intimidation, the satisfaction of material wants such as full employment and welfare measures, and the satisfaction of psychological and emotional needs such as personal or group status through office, the flattery of propaganda, or foreign policy successes. In seeking to understand this aspect of National Socialism, it is important to be as specific as possible, to define support or opposition concretely: support for what and from which

* I would like to acknowledge my gratitude to the Alexander von Humboldt Stiftung for financing the research on which this article is based.

210

group? Similarly, what does one mean by opposition? Which particular aspect or policy of the regime was being opposed and how significant was this opposition for those involved? It was after all possible to oppose some aspects while supporting others. Moreover, in a regime such as that in Nazi Germany one cannot expect much *political* opposition from either groups or individuals. Even in a democracy the majority of people are not politically active; in a dictatorship, where the channels of communication are controlled by the government and where fear of denunciation is all-pervasive, it is even more difficult for ordinary people to develop, let alone express, political opinions which deviate from the official line. A few activists will try and maintain a presence for their particular group and rather more will go into 'inner emigration'. But, as far as the majority is concerned, their attitudes to the regime will be determined largely by what they experience in their daily lives — at work and in their families. To some extent, the regime can shape the way they interpret their experience by providing a framework of explanation — in the most general terms through an ideology and more specifically through day-to-day propaganda. But, in order to remain effective, ideology and propaganda must provide a means of enabling people to come to terms with or understand the concrete realities in which they find themselves. Where economic and social realities conflict with such an ideology it will increasingly lose its appeal and the effects of propaganda will be blunted. Moreover, attitudes to the regime will also be determined by the extent to which its measures and its propaganda conflict with existing norms and values. Where such values are deeply rooted and strongly held resistance to the regime is likely to prove strongest. With public means of expression closed by the agencies of repression, discontent tends to take the form of passive resistance to the fulfilment of obligations towards the regime — absenteeism or low productivity,[2] attempts to avoid participation in rallies or collections, ostentatious attendance at church services or ceremonies, or political jokes passed on surreptitiously by word of mouth. It is in such apparently unpolitical gestures that one can sometimes trace the articulation of discontent. For in a regime where no sphere is considered to be outside the realm of politics, every action assumes, at least potentially, a political significance.

Given the nature of the Third Reich, lack of knowledge about the relations between the state and its population is not of course surprising. The cloud of propaganda and fear concealed much. Yet, despite the official claim that Germany was a happy and contented *Volksgemeinschaft* under the joyfully accepted leadership of the Führer and his representatives, there were agencies which made it their business to keep a very close watch on the mood of public opinion and, as a result, there was undoubtedly an element of feedback into the system. The Party, the Propaganda Ministry, the Gestapo, the SD, the *Generalstaatsanwälte* and *Oberlandesgerichtspräsidenten* and through them the Reich Ministry of Justice, and for a time the Reich Ministry of the Interior through its field agencies, the *Regierungspräsidenten* and *Oberbürgermeister,* all these received regular reports on the state of public opinion throughout Germany. This material, some of which has survived, including detailed local reports for some areas, will provide scholars with an often unreliable, but nevertheless invaluable basis on which to build up a picture of public opinion in the Third Reich.[3] In seeking to assess public attitudes both in terms of support and of opposition, it will be essential to take account of the sectional character of German society. For, partly as a result of the lateness of national unification and partly as a result of the rapid but far from uniform industrialisation which coincided with it, Germany contained a large number of subcultures based on regional, religious and occupational lines. There existed communities with a great sense of cohesion based on common regional traditions, religion, occupation and sometimes on a sense of isolation or even alienation from the rest of the community. One of the main objectives of the Nazis had been to overcome such sectional loyalties. They projected themselves as a party representing all regions, all classes, all occupational groups and all religious denominations. And, to some extent, they were successful in overcoming some sectional barriers. The sons of the Guelph farmers of Hanover, for example, marched side by side in the ranks of the SA with the sons of their National Liberal opponents. But it may be argued that, at any rate before 1933, this only occurred where the basis of sectional division was already in an advanced state of decay, as indeed with the Guelph tradition of Hanoverian independence. How far the Third Reich was succeeding in breaking down sectional cleavages and forcing all Germans into a common mould is obviously difficult to assess, given the upheavals of the war and post-war period with their massive population movements. We cannot, for example, draw many conclusions about the continuity or discontinuity of political opinion from a comparison of pre- Nazi and post-Nazi electoral statistics.[4] The two sectional groups which proved most resistant to the penetration of Nazism before 1933 were the industrial working class and the Roman Catholic population.[5] Moreover, where these two groups were present in what one might describe as their purest form, on the one hand, employed in large factories in big cities where socialist organisations and traditions were most deep rooted, and, on the other hand, employed in agriculture in overwhelmingly rural areas, where their simple piety was least exposed to the corrosion of secular influences, under these conditions their resistance proved strongest.

What seems clear is that where groups existed with strong ties and deeply held beliefs of whatever kind, resistance to the regime tended to be strongest — at least to those aspects of it which conflicted directly with their beliefs. Similarly, particular organisations such as the Army or the civil service, which possessed a highly developed *esprit de corps* and a strongly entrenched set of norms, were also capable of providing barriers to Nazi influence. In addition, such organisations had an independent structure through which they could promote opposition or resistance. The Roman Catholic Church not only had a social basis, which, particularly in rural areas, had shown great cohesion, it also had an organisation with which it could operate independently. Unlike the Army or the civil service, it was not essential to the functioning of the regime. On the other hand, to some extent it was shielded by its international position and above all by its support within the population and the fear of the Government of provoking discontent. The Roman Catholic Church, therefore, possessed unique possibilities for resistance to the regime. The limits of those possibilities were defined partly by the regime itself, but also by the Church's own conception of its role within society and by the attitudes of its adherents, and the extent to which they coincided with aspects of Nazism. These possibilities and limits became very apparent in the Oldenburg crucifix struggle of November 1936.

Between 1918 and 1945 the state of Oldenburg consisted of an electorate of some 265,000 people (the 1926 figure) divided into nine electoral districts or *Kreise:* the urban *Kreise* of Delmenhorst town, Oldenburg town, and Wilhelmshaven town, and the rural districts of Ammerland, Cloppenburg, Friesland, Oldenburg county district, Vechta and Wesermarsch.[6] Of the population of Oldenburg, 25.4 per cent was Catholic in 1939 and they were concentrated in Delmenhorst, where they made up 18.5 per cent of the population, and particularly in the two *Kreise* of southern Oldenburg — Cloppenburg with 86.6 per cent of the population and Vechta with 92 per cent.[7] Catholics in Oldenburg tended to be particularly pious, perhaps because they bordered on solidly Protestant areas in the North. Whereas in the Reich as a whole 81 per cent of Catholics had fulfilled their minimum duty of attending mass on Easter Sunday in 1924, in Oldenburg the figure was 87.9 per cent.[8] Catholics in Oldenburg also tended to be much more loyal to the Centre Party than elsewhere in the Reich. In fact, Oldenburg had the highest percentage of Catholics voting for the Centre of any area in Germany.[9] For example, whereas in Bavaria only slightly more than 40 per cent of Catholics voted for the Centre Party's Bavarian cousin, the Bavarian People's Party, in the mid-1920s, in Oldenburg 89 per cent voted for the Centre Party.[10] To what extent did the Nazis succeed in eroding the electoral support for the Centre Party in Oldenburg compared with elsewhere?

Reichstag Election of 31 July 1932[11]

	Reich	Cloppenburg	Vechta
% of Catholics voting Centre	48.4	78.9	89.5
% of Centre Party vote	15.7	67.4	82.3
% of NSDAP vote	37.2	18.9	8.7

Reichstag Election of 5 March 1933

	Reich	Cloppenburg	Vechta
% of Catholics voting Centre	42.9	67.1	83.9
% of Centre Party vote	14	58.1	77.2
% of NSDAP vote	43.9	29.4	13.1

So that although the March 1933 election saw a drop of approximately 10 per cent in the number of Catholics voting Centre and in the percentage of the Centre Party vote in Cloppenburg compared with July 1932 and a drop of approximately 5 per cent in Vechta, the two *Kreise* still had majorities for the Centre Party over the Nazis of 2-1 in Cloppenburg and 6-1 in Vechta.

What then was the social structure of these two Catholic *Kreise*?[12] In 1930 the area of the *Arbeitsamt* Vechta, which contained the Oldenburg administrative districts (*Amtsbezirke*) of Cloppenburg, Wildeshausen and Vechta and which corresponded more or less exactly with the two *electoral* districts of Cloppenburg and Vechta, had a total population of 96,000 with a population density of only 48 inhabitants per square kilometre. In the Lower Saxony area this low density of population was matched only by the equally sparsely populated Lüneburg Heath districts. Of the population, 74.2 per cent were engaged in agriculture, the highest percentage of all the 28 *Arbeitsamt* districts in Lower Saxony. The farms were large (over 25ha), medium (5-25 ha) and small (under 5 ha) in more or less equal proportions; there were no large estates. There was slightly more arable than pasture with grain production predominating. Of the population, 12.8 per cent was engaged in industry and handicrafts, mainly connected with the processing of wood in various ways, but with a scattering of other light industry such as cigar manufacturing, agricultural machinery and the ubiquitous brick factories. The remaining 13 per cent were engaged in commerce, services and administration.

To sum up, then, the *Kreise* of Cloppenburg and Vechta were thinly populated, predominantly agricultural, with no very wide differences in the ownership of property, overwhelmingly Catholic and notably pious. The vast majority supported the Centre Party and had continued to do so even under the pressures characteristic of the March 1933 election. The political, economic and social homogeneity of these *Kreise* distinguished them from most of the rest of Oldenburg and indeed from most of Germany.

The Nazis had come to power in Oldenburg before Hitler took over the national government. In the state election of 16 June 1932 they had won an overall majority and had formed an all-Nazi government with their *Gauleiter*, Carl Röver, as Minister-President.[13] Part of their propaganda in this election had been geared to exploit the resentment of some of the Protestant population who felt that the Catholics, who were virtually united in support of the Centre Party, had managed in the past to secure an undue amount of influence in the state compared with themselves, whose political loyalties had been divided among a number of different and competing parties. Indeed, to some extent the Nazis had come to represent the party of Protestant north Oldenburg. While the Centre was gaining 70 or 80 per cent of the vote in the south, the Nazis were gaining 60 or 70 per cent in the rural areas of the north. One must not of course take this explanation too far. Hostility towards the Left was undoubtedly an even more important reason for the high Nazi vote. Moreover, there is no evidence that the Nazi leadership in Oldenburg had any more respect for the Protestants than for the Catholics. In fact, no sooner had they come to power than they were engaged in an acrimonious dispute with the Protestant Church.

In the March 1933 election, as we have seen, the Nazis gained only 29.4 and 13.1 per cent in Cloppenburg and Vechta respectively, well below the Reich average of 43.9 per cent, though a marked improvement on the figures for July and November 1932. The question was, then, what was to be done about 'Black Münsterland' as the Nazis dubbed the two *Kreise?* The dissolution of the Centre Party in July solved the overt political problem. But a far more intractable problem was posed by what one might call the infrastructure of Catholicism — the existence of the

Catholic youth clubs and, above all, the religious denominational
structure of education within the state, the monopoly of the so-called
'confessional schools'. These issues had been dealt with in the
Concordat ratified by the Reich and the Vatican on 10 September
1933.[14] Section 2 of Article 31 had covered those Catholic organisations
having social or professional purposes, affording them protection
'provided they guarantee to develop their activities outside political
parties'. Section 3 empowered the Reich Government and the German
episcopate 'to determine by mutual agreement, the organisations and
associations which fall within the provisions of this article'.
Unfortunately, however, the Vatican had dropped its attempt to get
agreement on a list of Catholic organisations to be protected under these
clauses and to get an agreed definition on party politics prior to
ratification of the Concordat. As a result, the future of the Church's
non-religious organisations, including its youth movement, had been left
unresolved.[15] Although from now onwards increasing pressure was
applied to the Catholic youth organisations in Oldenburg, it was clear
to the authorities that any attempt to enforce the ban on dual
membership of the Hitler Youth and denominational youth groups
imposed by Schirach on 29 July 1933 would be at the expense of the
Nazi youth organisations; in other words, faced with the choice of
joining the Hitler Youth or remaining in their Catholic organisations,
they would do the latter.[16] So that it was not until the decree of
1 December 1936 making the Hitler Youth the official state youth
organisation and the enforcement of the ban on dual membership which
followed it, that this issue was finally resolved by the Catholic youth
organisations being gradually forced into dissolution by 1939.

Even more significant both to the Nazis and to the Church than the
question of youth organisations was that of education. This too had
been defined in the Concordat.[17] Article 23 had guaranteed 'the
maintenance of the existing Catholic denominational schools and the
establishment of new ones wherever parents requested it and where the
number of prospective pupils was sufficiently large. This clause was
regarded by the Church as the most significant concession made by the
Nazi state. It soon became clear, however, that the Oldenburg
government was determined to limit as far as possible the influence of
the churches over education.

With the reorganisation of the government following the appointment
of Carl Röver as *Reichsstatthalter* of Oldenburg-Bremen in April 1933,
the Ministry of Churches and Schools passed into the hands of Julius
Pauly.[18] Pauly had joined the Party in 1931 and was a typical Nazi

recruit of the early 1930s, a 30-year-old lawyer on the make who
endeavoured to compensate for his relatively late adherence to the movement
by proving his commitment with tough speeches. Pauly was a Protestant
from the Oldenburg enclave of Birkenfeld in the Rhineland who, according
to rumour had repudiated his religion with the adolescent gesture of
scribbling ribald comments on the school bible. The key civil servant
recently appointed to the ministry, Anton Kohnen, was also a dedicated
Nazi and a fanatical opponent of the churches.

During the spring and summer of 1933, Pauly made it clear to the
Oldenburg teachers in a number of decrees that they were expected to
demonstrate their loyalty to the new state by becoming members of
Nazi organisations.[19] Initially, this seemed to pose few problems. In fact,
at a general meeting on 24 April, the Catholic Teachers' Association in
Oldenburg had declared its unqualified support for the 'government of
the national movement under the Chancellorship of Adolf Hitler' and
had joined the Nazi teachers' organisation, the NSLB, en bloc.[20] This was
of course part of the process of *Gleichschaltung* or coordination which
swept through Germany during the spring of 1933. It was reflected at
national level by a similar declaration from the national headquarters of
the Catholic Teachers' Association and there seems good reason to
believe that the sentiments behind it were for the most part genuine.[21]
Nevertheless, the Nazi authorities continued to regard the Münsterland
with suspicion. During 1934, Pauly sent round inspectors to discover
'whether the teachers really are National Socialists and are instructing
their pupils accordingly'.[22] And, indeed, it was not long before the
enthusiasm of the period of 'national uprising' gave way to a process
of disillusionment, which was answered by further decrees during 1935.[23]

The first big bone of contention came over Alfred Rosenberg and
his anti-Christian writings, which met with stiff opposition from
Catholic teachers. As a result of this, on 27 July 1935, Pauly felt obliged
to hold a meeting in the Assembly Hall of the Cloppenburg High School
for all teachers in the *Kreise* of Cloppenburg and Vechta.[24] He claimed
that while he did not demand that they should teach Rosenberg's
opinions in school, Rosenberg should be treated with the respect due to
a leading National Socialist. In the course of his speech he put his finger
on one of the weaknesses of Nazi education policy at that time:
'Unfortunately,' he said, 'at the moment we still lack suitable text
books. If we had them, everything would be much simpler. I can't write
all the text books myself. But I expect you to come and see me if you
are unable to teach in the way which I have requested and laid down in
my decrees'. In view of the acute shortage of teachers, however,

dismissal was not an easy remedy. One way round the problem was to transfer teachers from north to south Oldenburg and vice versa. On 2 October 1933, a law was passed to the effect that teachers of either denomination could be employed in all state high schools.[25] Thus, recalcitrant Catholic teachers could be transferred to the north and replaced by Protestants. But although such transfers could be and to some extent were carried out in the secondary schools in the few towns such as Cloppenburg, they caused far more problems in the much more numerous village *Volksschulen*. Here a Protestant teacher would be liable to feel very isolated and to meet with serious difficulties from the parents and the local priest.

Initially, it appeared as if the Government would act against the influence of religion in schools by a gradual process of piecemeal attrition, concentrating to start with on the less sensitive areas. Thus, in 1935 religious instruction was ended in all further education colleges (*Berufsschulen*) and agricultural colleges.[26] Moreover, on 11 June 1936, Pauly issued a new school law which, while confirming the denominational character of the Oldenburg education system, at the same time removed the right of the local priests or pastors to supervise religious instruction in the schools, restricted the amount of religious education and switched it to the last hour of the school day.[27] These measures had met with only a few isolated protests and it appeared as if the policy of avoiding confrontation by a piecemeal approach was achieving success. Five months later, however, the Government met with a massive setback.

The issue which provoked the trouble was in itself a relatively minor affair. On 24 October 1936, a new school building was officially opened in the village of Bösel in Cloppenburg with a ceremony at which Pauly himself was present.[28] The local priest did not attend the ceremony which was held on a Saturday, but on the following day held a consecration ceremony of his own in the school attended by the whole village. News of this event appears to have reached *Reichsstatthalter/ Gauleiter* Röver who promptly took Pauly to task for permitting such behaviour.[29] Pauly responded by issuing a decree dated 4 November.[30]

The decree began by banning the religious consecration of school buildings on the grounds that as public buildings they belonged to the whole Germen nation irrespective of their religious affiliations. But the decree went on to argue that, for the same reason, denominational symbols such as crucifixes or portraits of Luther should also not be hung in public buildings. It concluded: 'in future, ecclesiastical and other religious symbols of the kind mentioned above or of an official character may not be displayed in state, municipal, and parish buildings and those which are already in place must be removed. A report on the steps which have been taken to implement this decree is required by 15 December'. The decree was addressed to the headmasters of all Oldenburg schools, to the school inspector, and to the state authorities in the field — the *Amtshauptmänner* and *Bürgermeister* — and it was not published.

The authorities in the Münsterland were appalled by the decree.[31] The senior government official in Cloppenburg, *Amtshauptmann* Münzebrock, immediately contacted Pauly and tried to persuade him to revoke it on the grounds that it would provoke strong resistance from the population. Pauly replied that the Church authorities might encourage discontent for a time, but that 'grass would soon grow over it again'. Having failed to persuade the minister, Münzebrock contacted the district leader of the Party, *Kreisleiter* Meyer. Meyer had lived in the village of Essen in Cloppenburg since 1922. He had joined the Party rather late — in 1932 — and because of the dearth of Nazis in the area had been appointed local branch leader and was then promoted to *Kreisleiter* in October 1934. He had a good knowledge of conditions in the area and had apparently developed a reasonably good relationship with the local priest in Essen, Kaplan Niermann. Meyer shared Münzebrock's concern and, together with his colleague *Kreisleiter* Voss of Vechta, tried to persuade Röver in his capacity as *Reichsstatthalter* to overrule Pauly and revoke the decree — but to no avail.

On 10 November, a copy of the decree was leaked to the senior Catholic official in Oldenburg, the *Bischöflichen Offizial* in Vechta, Franz Vorwerk.[32] At the same time, Vorwerk was informed that the decree had not yet been sent out to the *Bürgermeister* or the schools by the *Amtshauptmänner,* who were, as we have seen, trying to have it withdrawn. Three days later, however, he received word that the decree had been sent to headmasters in north Oldenburg — a step which had clearly committed the government to the decree. On the following day, the fourteenth, he drafted a declaration to be read from the pulpits of all Catholic churches in Oldenburg on Sunday 15 November and distributed it by courier. The declaration concluded as follows: 'We can never give our consent to the banishment of the crucifix from the place of instruction of our children. We must do everything to prevent this. Join and help us and support the retention of the crucifix in our schools.'[33] At the same time, the clergy preached on the significance of the issue and referred to the relevant article of the

Concordat which confirmed the legality of denominational education. In other words, they claimed that the state decree was contrary to Reich Law and therefore that opposition to it was justified. Then, on 16 November, Vorwerk sent off a letter of protest to Pauly claiming that the decree was aimed against the denominational schools.[34] On the twentieth, Pauly replied with the argument that children of another denomination might be offended by the public display of denominational symbols.[35] He denied that the decree represented a step in the gradual abolition of denominational schools and suggested as a compromise that the crucifix could be used during the periods of religious education as educational material. Vorwerk replied at once that this suggestion was unacceptable and indeed represented an intolerable disparagement of the crucifix.[36] The Protestants also expressed objections to the decree. On 19 November the Praesidium of the Confessional Synod of Wilhelmshaven-Rüstringen complained in a letter to Pauly about an attack on the Christian faith.[37] And in letters dated 22 November and 2 December, the chairman of the *Hauptverein der Gustav Adolf Stiftung* protested against the decree and pointed out that their association's valuable work for the German cause abroad, particularly in the educational field, could be jeopardised if news of the government's action became known.[38] The school authorities in the Protestant area, however, generally obeyed the instructions to remove the portraits of Luther.[39] But, in the meantime, the dispute had moved beyond the official channels. It had produced an eruption of public protest of a kind that was almost unique in the Third Reich.

The wave of protest in south Oldenburg which followed the news of the decree took a very wide variety of forms.[40] At the beginning of the week following Vorwerk's announcement, meetings of clergy were held in all the deaneries to discuss the situation and to lay down guidelines. On Wednesday, 10 November, which was Remembrance Day, sermons were given in all the churches on the crucifix issue. At one of these services held at Bethen, a place of pilgrimage, and attended by some 3,000 ex-servicemen, there occurred what was virtually a mass demonstration against the decree.[41] In his address the priest adopted a very militant line which met with tremendous enthusiasm from the congregation who, according to an eyewitness, listened enthralled, oblivious to the pouring rain:

Our comrades died and we fought and bled for our fatherland on earth, so that we will be even more determined to fight and bleed, and if necessary to die for Christ and his kingdom and for the symbol of

Christianity, the crucifix. Someone, who has never smelt the smell of
cordite, who has never heard bullets whistling overhead [and here he
was clearly referring to Pauly] may be incapable of understanding this.
But we war veterans will make him aware that we still know how to
fight and if it comes to it to die . . . If anyone now wants to take the
crucifix out of our schools . . . the answer is we will never, never,
never accept it. That is our final word.[42]

A flood of protest letters and petitions was sent to the Ministry in
Oldenburg.[43] They came from both individuals and groups. There were
letters from simple farmers; a group of fifty women from the town of
Cloppenburg signed a petition; and 139 Catholic young men from
Dincklage in Vechta reminded the Ministry that the Nationalists in
Spain were ceremoniously bringing back the crucifix after a bloodbath.
Beginning on the 21 November a string of deputations began to arrive
at the Ministry from numerous parishes.[44] The cars bringing them lined
up outside the building and gave vent to their protest in rhythmical
hooting of their horns. The climax came on 24 November when some
75 cars were lined up outside having brought around 200 people
from the Münsterland. The protest also took more symbolic forms.[45]
In every parish the church bells were rung between 8.00 and 8.30 each
evening; in the larger parishes services of prayer were held. The crosses
on the farm houses, on the field paths, and on the by-roads were
decorated with greenery and people even broke into the schools at
night and decorated the crucifix. A large cross was put up on the church
tower in Dincklage and illuminated with electric light bulbs so that it
could be seen for miles around and later the church in Mühlen followed
suit. Women wore jewelry crucifixes prominently displayed.

It was not long before the authorities began to report back to the
Ministry in perplexed despair at the deterioration in the situation. Not
only had the majority of the teachers refused to remove the crucifixes,[46]
but the *Bürgermeister* were also unwilling to take the risk. On 20
November, the *Bürgermeister* in Lastrup wrote to the *Amtshauptmann*
in Cloppenburg complaining that 'a completely untenable situation has
arisen for the lower levels of the administration. If the decree were to
be implemented all contact with the population would be lost. Trust in
the state has been as seriously shaken by this decree as one can possibly
imagine. For the time being I am not in a position and am not prepared
to carry out the decree and request instructions.'[47] His opinion was
echoed by other *Bürgermeister*. Thus the *Bürgermeister* in Friesoy the
wrote that 'whoever is instructed to remove the crucifix will require a
strong police escort since if the action is carried out, it will inevitably

lead to open rebellion'.[48]

What was particularly serious from the point of view of the authorities was the fact that the whole Party apparatus in the two *Kreise* appeared to be in the process of disintegration. As Vorwerk reported later to his bishop: 'What was particularly gratifying was the number of old Party members who participated. The most faithful supporter of the crucifix was a Party member with a gold Party badge.'[49] His observation was confirmed in the later report of the *Kreisleitung* in Vechta which wrote: 'It is an only too regrettable fact that there were going to be many resignations from the rural local branches if the decree was not revoked.'[50] Indeed, in one branch the propaganda chief had made himself the spokesman of all the political and SA leaders and declared 'they would let themselves be beaten to death for their crucifix'. Reports began to come in of farmers refusing to cooperate with the 'production battle' and the Winter Aid programme.[51] People began to resign their offices on the parish councils. The SA in the village of Dümmerlohausen disbanded itself. Only 50 per cent of the *Jungvolk* in Daume turned up on parade. The problem was particularly serious because, as the *Bürgermeister* of Essen (Cloppenburg) pointed out, it had been extremely difficult to set up a Party organisation in this area because of people's suspicion of the anti-Christian elements of Nazism.[52] The whole crisis was summed up in a letter from *Amtshauptmann* Münzebrock of Cloppenburg to the Ministry of the Interior in Oldenburg dated 20 November: 'Everybody is furious and this anger is by no means confined to opponents of the Party or particularly pious people, but has also seized those who are normally co-operative and do not blindly follow the priests. With one blow a united front of the whole population has been created, which clearly is directed solely against National Socialism.'[53] Although, on 19 November, the legal department of the Labour Front in Cloppenburg telegraphed its support to the Minister and urged on him a policy of ruthless severity,[54] the two *Kreisleiter*, Meyer of Cloppenburg and Voss of Vechta, appealed in desperation to the *Gauleiter* to intervene and save the situation.[55]

To start with Röver resisted their appeal. The Party held meetings at which the decree was defended and, at a big meeting in Löningen in Cloppenburg on 17 November, he declared that the decree would not be revoked.[56] By the twenty-fourth, however, the pressure had clearly become irresistible. On that day, Münzebrock was informed that the *Gauleiter* had decided that the Pauly decree should be withdrawn.[57] He was ordered to arrange a mass meeting in the Münsterlandhalle in the town of Cloppenburg where Röver would make a speech, at the end of which he would announce its withdrawal. *Kreisleiter* Meyer strongly advised against this course of action and suggested that a brief statement should be issued instead. Röver, however, insisted that the public would then believe that he was too cowardly to face them.

The meeting was, therefore, arranged for 4.15 on the afternoon of 25 November. Attendance at the meeting was made compulsory for the Party organisations and state officials in the town. But in fact over 7,000 people packed into the hall to hear the speech and the vast majority were ordinary members of the public from the two *Kreise*. According to an eye-witness, as the official party — which consisted of Röver, Minister-President Joel and many other officials, though not including Pauly — entered the hall, they were met by an icy silence.[58] It was broken only when they neared the platform by rather hesitant applause from the ranks of the Party formations and *Arbeitsdienst*. They were followed by a detachment of SA which, significantly, had been brought in from Leer in East Friesland and which was also greeted with silence.

Kreisleiter Meyer had tried to persuade Röver to keep the speech brief and to the point but the *Gauleiter* had replied that in that case 'the audience would go home thinking that they had forced something out of me and I don't want that'.[59] He evidently hoped somehow to win the respect of the crowd — a reflection of his sublime self-confidence , his overestimation of his powers of leadership, and his ignorance of the feelings of his subjects. He began his speech by declaring that they should follow the lessons of history.[60] He then rambled on about how God had created various races each with its own particular characteristics and that the Germans should stick together and not get involved in bickering since they stood alone facing great difficulties. But before he had gone very far he was interrupted by shouts of 'We don't want to hear about that. Get to the point, the decree'. Soon there was chanting of 'Get to the point' and 'the crucifix'. Desperately, Röver began again and started talking about his life as a young business man in Africa before the war where he had learnt the importance of racial purity. But again he was interrupted with shouts of 'You should have stayed there. What do we want with Africa? We are in Cloppenburg. Get to the point, the crucifix'. The SA was sent to the rear of the hall and a young farmer was led outside. A policeman tried to take his name and address, but he was immediately surrounded by a crowd of young farmers who said: 'Hier giff et nix to schrieven! Das Notieren mackt wi', which can be freely translated: 'keep out of it. We'll do the note-taking around here'. Whereupon, the policeman pocketed his notebook and slunk away.

Meanwhile, in desperation Röver had finally come to the point. He admitted that 'perhaps it would have been better if the Ministry's decree had not been issued'. He went on: ' *Kreisleiter* Meyer and *Kreisleiter* Voss came to me and told me: "Gauleiter, you must come to the Münsterland immediately. You must help us". I told them: "My dear friends, I have been to Löningen and believe that everything is all right there . . ." In the final analysis it must be regarded as a purely educational matter . . . I don't think Pauly realized what effects it would have. If we make a mistake we have the courage to admit it'. Finally, he pulled a piece of paper out of his pocket and read out a decree which restored the crucifixes and Luther pictures.[61] The crowd burst into tremendous applause and pressed for the exit, bringing the proceedings to an abrupt end. That evening, church bells rang all over the Münsterland.

On the following day, the Cloppenburg meeting was reported in the local press as 'an impressive demonstration of confidence in the *Gauleiter* by the people of the Münsterland'.[62] His speech was 'repeatedly interrupted by loud applause and expressions of agreement'. The Münsterland, of course, knew better. But the authorities were determined to try and prevent the truth from becoming known. Ten days after the Cloppenburg meeting, on 5 December, Vorwerk was invited to a meeting with the *Gauleiter*.[63] A recording of Röver's speech was played back to him on which all background noise had been eliminated. He was then invited to sign a declaration to be read in all churches to the effect that the official recording had convinced him that Röver's speech had *not* been interrupted and that all reports to the contrary were false.[64] The aim was clearly also to publish such a declaration in the press. The *Offizial*, however, refused. Then, at the beginning of January 1937, Röver wrote to Vorwerk endeavouring to play down the whole issue and inviting him to another meeting which he duly attended on 5 January. Röver once more tried to persuade him to sign the declaration and, on his refusal, alleged that he had promised to do so and accused him of going back on his word. A Party campaign was then initiated in which Vorwerk was accused of failing to keep his word and of misinforming the Bishop of Münster. On 29 January, the *Offizial* rejected these accusations in a pulpit declaration.

In the meantime, on the Sunday after the lifting of the decree, services of thanksgiving were held throughout Oldenburg. In a letter to all Catholics the *Offizial* thanked them for defending the cross and warned of further threats to Christianity.[65] On 27 November, Bishop Galen of Münster also sent a pastoral letter to be read out in all the

churches of his diocese on the following Sunday together with a report
of the events of November, so that knowledge of these events spread
far wider than Oldenburg itself.[66] Indeed copies of the report were
sent to other dioceses.[67] In his letter Galen tried to build on the loyalty
of the Catholics which had been mobilised by the crucifix issue and to
encourage resistance to any further anti-Christian or anti-Catholic
measures:

> We will avoid all companionship with those who are enemies of the
> Cross of Christ; we will read no books or papers which disgrace the
> Cross of Christ and we will not tolerate them in our houses, in shop
> windows or in show-cases. And if, for the sake of the Cross, it
> becomes our fate to suffer disgrace or persecution with Christ the
> crucified, then we do not want to be cowardly or shrink. For we shall
> think of Him who, by dying on the Cross, won for us eternal life.

The crucifix struggle had ended in a dramatic victory for the Catholics
of Oldenburg. The Nazi authorities had been publicly humiliated. Indeed,
the report of the NSDAP *Kreisleitung* in Vechta to the *Gauleitung*
described it aptly as 'a road to Canossa for the NSDAP' and concluded
that the self-confidence and prestige of the clergy had increased to a
colossal extent.[68] To illustrate this, it quoted a remark made to a Labour
Service official: 'We Christians say "good morning" [i.e. not "Heil
Hitler"] because we won'.[69] Yet the drama of the occasion was liable
to disguise the very limited nature of what had been achieved.
This became clearer during the following months and years. Thus, Pauly's
ministry successfully resisted attempts to have the Luther portraits rehung
in the schools from which they had already been removed.[70] Protests
about the exclusion of parish priests from schools and about the lack of
religious instruction in the colleges of agriculture and further education
and about the transfer of religious instruction to the last hour in the
school day were all ignored.[71] The only concession made was to permit
two lectures a week in religion at the new teachers' training college in
Oldenburg.[72] Otherwise, the main effect of the affair was a delaying
one. Thus, whereas in Munich, Württemberg, the Saar-Palatinate and
Rhineland areas denominational schools were abolished during 1936 and
1937 by means of referenda held under conditions of intimidation, in
Oldenburg the authorities evidently felt obliged to move more
circumspectly and waited until 1938.[73] But the end result was the same
and by then the authorities clearly felt sufficiently strong to dispense
with rigged elections. Thus, at the end of April 1938, Pauly simply

ordered the suppression of small confessional schools and then later moved on to the larger ones.[74] This time attempts by parents to resist were quickly crushed by the Gestapo. Thus protests at the introduction of a non-denominational school (*Deutsche Volksschule*) in the village of Goldenstedt in Vechta at the beginning of May 1938, which took the form of a school strike by the parents, were met by 30 Gestapo officials and the whole gendarmerie of the *Amtsbezirk*; twelve of those arrested were sent to concentration camps and the two curates were banished from Oldenburg.[75] Finally, on 30 June 1938, the *Offizial* in Vechta, Franz Vorwerk, was banished by the police from Oldenburg, and the offices of his *Offizialat* were occupied. Whereas previously they had been caught off balance by the Catholics' reaction, now the authorities were clearly taking no more chances; and the fact that they were now following a piecemeal tactic of closing down the schools one by one enabled them to isolate pockets of resistance. They were also careful to mount a propaganda campaign claiming that denominational schools were divisive and liable to undermine national unity.[76] The fact that these measures coincided with a period of maximum diplomatic prestige for the regime with the recent successful conclusion of the *Anschluss* fresh in people's minds may also have helped to defuse hostility.

How should one assess the more general significance of the Oldenburg crucifix struggle? In a speech to a conference of deans on 28 October 1935 Bishop Galen of Münster had raised the question of 'whether the faithful would be prepared in case of need to "obey God rather than man". I cannot help feeling that many will weaken in their faith and loyalty and that the strength of the Church will be impaired'.[77] Galen believed that 'most of the faithful were not capable of engaging in an all-out fight'. A year later, a large section of his own diocese had apparently proved him wrong. Yet it would be dangerous to generalise from such a particular case. In trying to remove the crucifix from the schools of southern Oldenburg, the Nazi authorities had chosen the worst possible ground on which to fight. In the first place, the crucifix represented a symbol which the simplest person could understand, identify with and unite behind.[78] It was capable of generating a charge of emotional commitment which the more abstract issue of denominational schools was less able to achieve. The continual chant 'das Kreuz' in the Cloppenburg meeting of Gauleiter Röver and the propaganda use of the cross by ordinary people illustrates this. In effect, the Nazis had been beaten at the propaganda game of which they thought they were the masters. This was ruefully admitted by the *Kreisleitung* in Vechta who reported: 'the blacks* really understand propaganda'.[79]

But secondly, Cloppenburg and Vechta were exceptional in their degree of social and ideological homogeneity. They were a community with strong ties of solidarity and with a tradition of resisting the dominance of Protestant north Oldenburg now controlled by the Nazis. Finally, as far as the Reich authorities were concerned, the religious question was, for the time being at any rate, of secondary importance. The conflict fell within the period of July 1936 to March 1937 when, for both domestic and diplomatic reasons, Hitler had postponed the series of trials of Rhineland priests and lay brothers for homosexual offences and had sought a rapprochement with the Catholic Church.[80] At this time, a campaign against the crucifix would not fit in very well with the image of Germany as a bastion of Western cultural values against the Bolshevik threat, an image which the regime was assiduously cultivating for diplomatic reasons. It seems, however, unlikely that Hitler himself intervened in this particular dispute — there is no evidence for it. And although there is some evidence that Goebbels strongly criticised the measure and demanded Pauly's dismissal — which was refused by Röver [81] — it seems probable that the issue was decided at *Gau* level. Here there were hotheads who wished to pursue the Church more vigorously, but by this time the Party was coming to see its main function as ensuring a loyal and contented population. Measures which provoked widespread discontent would have to have a very good justification. The issue of whether or not crucifixes should hang in schools was not one of vital importance in 1936 and therefore the substance of the matter did not place any difficulties in the way of reversing the policy.

A more serious problem, of course, was the loss of face by the authorities, who were being forced to reverse a policy under pressure from public opinion. It is a striking example of the fact for which recent research is providing more and more evidence that the Nazi regime, despite its totalitarian claims and apparatus, was acutely sensitive to any large scale discontent expressed by those sections of the population whose loyalty it had good reason to doubt.[82] The crucifix issue in particular continued to remain a sensitive one. In 1937 there were protest demonstrations against the removal of crucifixes from schools in Kleve and Bislich in the Rhineland and the Reich Minister of the Interior was obliged to issue an order banning the arbitrary removal of crucifixes from schools by subordinate authorities.[83]

* A pejorative term for Catholics (= Black International).

Finally, in 1941, the Munich *Gauleiter* and Bavarian Minister of the Interior, Adolf Wagner, endeavoured to remove crucifixes from the schools in Bavaria. But he too was met by similar resistance and on 28 August, like Röver he was forced to revoke this order, though on this occasion Bormann intervened directly.[84]

What can we learn from this conflict about the attitude of the Catholic population towards the regime? Hostility towards the regime among Catholics even in Cloppenburg and Vechta appears to have been largely confined to those spheres in which the policies of the authorities interfered directly with their religious beliefs and practices – in particular, the role of the Hitler Youth and the influence of Rosenberg and his followers in the education of their children. In this sphere, as the crucifix conflict demonstrates, considerable discontent could be generated by tactically inept actions. Such discontent, focusing round a particular issue, could lead to more generalised opposition to the regime. In this connection a comparison between the *Reichstag* election results on 29 March 1936 and those of 10 April 1938 is illuminating. In 1936 in *Kreis* Cloppenburg out of a 99.1 per cent vote the NSDAP gained 98.72 per cent and there were 456 no votes or invalid votes of which 50 came from the town of Cloppenburg. In 1938 on the other hand, with a 98.24 per cent vote the NSDAP gained only 92.33 per cent and there were 2,696 no votes or invalid votes of which 325 came from the town of Cloppenburg.[85] It would seem plausible to attribute this decline in the percentage of the NSDAP vote to some degree at any rate to the experience of the crucifix conflict, since in the electoral district of Weser-Ems as a whole, which embraced both the state of Oldenburg and the Prussian *Regierungsbezirke* of Aurich and Osnabrück, with a 99.30 per cent vote the percentage in favour of the NSDAP was 97.86 per cent.[86]

Nevertheless it would be a mistake to make too much of this generalised hostility. For, although of course ultimately there could not be compromise between Nazi ideology and Christian beliefs, at this stage the two could coexist side by side without too much friction. On the whole, the church authorities themselves were anxious to emphasise the areas of agreement and to minimise those of friction.[87] Indeed, the fact that Cloppenburg and Vechta came under the diocese of the uncompromising Bishop Galen of Münster rather than that of their more immediate neighbour, the much more pliable Bishop Berning of Osnabrück, may even have contributed to the forcefulness of the confrontation to the extent that the *Offizial* could feel sure of firm support from his superior. Apart from the questions of youth organisations and education, it is doubtful that the regime provoked too much active hostility, though much more research would be necessary to assert this with any degree of confidence. In part this was a result of the nature of the Catholic sub-culture in Germany.[88] Like that of the nation as a whole its value system gave priority to what have been described as 'secondary virtues' such as loyalty, punctuality, cleanliness, conscientiousness in the performance of duty and hard work. These virtues are empty ones in the sense that they lack any moral content; they can be employed to any end. For example, it was characteristic that the SS motto was 'My honour is loyalty'. Such virtues do not involve commitments to deeper human values. For most German Catholics their religion had been subsumed into the system of secondary virtues by becoming identified as a series of very specific duties and rituals. These were affirmations of membership of a particular community but had no wider social relevance. This restricted outlook was partly a consequence of the semi-pariah position of Catholics in Germany since the *Kulturkampf*. But it was reinforced by the fact that in all religious and moral questions it was customary for Catholics to follow the lead of the Church and its hierarchy rather than feeling an obligation to follow their own consciences. Insofar as the Nazis, therefore, did not interfere with the performance of these rituals and duties, they were unlikely to provoke discontent. Indeed, to the extent that they went out of their way to stress the importance of the traditional German 'secondary virtues' they could expect, and for the most part received, the approval of both the Catholic Church authorities and the laity. Finally, Catholics did not possess an alternative political ideology which could provide them with a basis from which to criticise the regime in political terms. What political conceptions they possessed – an amalgam of corporatist, nationalist, anti-liberal and anti-Marxist values and attitudes – were sufficiently close to aspects of Nazism to make a clear-cut differentiation, let alone a fundamental critique, difficult if not impossible. Moreover, the political expression of Catholicism prior to 1933 had tended to take the form of relatively narrow pressure group activity on behalf of Catholic interests. As a result, with a few notable exceptions, Catholic opposition to Nazism tended to be provoked by injury to their interests or religious beliefs, and remain restricted to that; it did not become a general attack on the regime as a whole.

In analysing people's response to the regime at the grass roots it is clearly important to assess in what ways its policies and actions impinged upon people at this level and, in particular, to assess the role

of the Party. There is a clue to this in a letter from the *Bürgermeister*
and Party branch leader in Essen (Cloppenburg) to Pauly in which he
complained that the crucifix issue had ruined all his previous efforts:

> It was very difficult to get the right people to co-operate in Essen.
> For one reason only: they said, 'I don't want to have anything to do
> with the NSDAP, they are trying to take our faith away from us.'
> Through personal contacts with individual Party members the
> demands and requests of Party and state have been completely
> fulfilled. I can point in particular to the collections for the Winter
> Aid programme, the delegations to Nuremberg and Bückeberg, the
> celebration of the 1 May, and the National Day of Wine. And what
> particularly important for the Production Battle, the sowing of flax
> has been carried out in Essen.[89]

In other words, the role of the Party at this level appears primarily as a
propaganda one and, apart from the Hitler Youth, the impact of the
Party was felt in terms of the obligation to make periodic gestures of
loyalty either of a practical kind through collections or of a
demonstrative kind through attendance at particular ceremonies.
Although the collections may have become irksome, there was little
in these matters to provoke serious discontent.

It seems conceivable that the majority of Catholics respected the
leadership of Hitler, whose rule had apparently brought economic
recovery and diplomatic successes, while deploring the activities of
some of the organisations and representatives of the regime. They did
not appear to associate the objectionable features with the *Führer*.
According to the Bürgermeister of Molbergen: "The peasants declared:
'We have been born Catholics and wish for our own sakes and those of
our children to stay Catholics while being followers of the Führer Adolf
Hitler.'"[90] Indeed, it is possible that the key to the legitimacy of the
regime in the eyes of the majority of the people lies in Hitler's success
in acquiring a status which put him above day-to-day domestic politics,
so that he and the regime as such, which was identified with him, were
immune from criticism, unlike specific policies and actions which were
identified with other individuals or particular organisations and which it
was assumed he would have disapproved of had he had knowledge of
them.

Notes

1. For the euthanasia programme and resistance to it see Alexander
    Mitscherlich u. Fred. Mielke, *Wissenschaft ohne Menschlichkeit.*
    Medizinische und eugenische Irrwege unter Diktatur, Bürokratie und
    Krieg (Heidelberg, 1949), pp. 176 ff; L. Gruchmann, 'Euthanasie und
    Justiz im Dritten Reich' in *Vierteljahrshefte für Zeitgeschichte* 20. 1972,
    pp. 235-79 and G. Lewy, *The Catholic Church and Nazi Germany*
    (London, 1964), pp. 263-67.
2. cf. T.W. Mason, *Arbeiterklasse und Volksgemeinschaft* (Opladen, 1975),
    pp. 123 ff, 152, 801.
3. There are files containing such reports in many state archives, particularly
    those in Bavaria. A collection of these focusing primarily on the position
    of the churches is in the process of publication in several volumes: *Die*
    Kirchliche Lage in Bayern nach den Regierungspräsidentenberichten
    1933-1943, vols. 1-3, ed. Helmut Witetschek, vol.4 ed. Walter Ziegler
    (Mainz,1966-73). Dr Ian Kershaw of the University of Manchester is at
    present engaged on a study of public opinion in Bavaria during the Third
    Reich and I am grateful to him for a number of helpful comments. For
    the wartime period in Germany as a whole see the collection of SD
    reports in H. Boberach,*Meldungen aus dem Reich* (Neuwied, 1965) and
    the study based on them by M. Steinert, *Hitlers Krieg und die Deutschen:*
    Stimmung und Haltung der Deutschen Bevölkerung im Zweiten Weltkrieg
    (Düsseldorf, 1970). See also the collection of *Regierungspräsidenten*
    reports for the Aachen area in B. Vollmer,*Volks-opposition im Polizeistaat.*
    Gestapo und Regierungspräsidentenberichte 1934 bis 1936 (Stuttgart,
    1957); the Gestapo reports for Baden in Jörg Schadt,(ed.),*Verfolgung*
    und Widerstand unter dem Nationalsozialismus in Baden (Stuttgart,
    1975) and the miscellaneous collection of material in F.B. Heyen(ed.),
    Nationalsozialismus im Alltag (Boppard, 1967).
4. For an interesting attempt at such a comparison see T.H. Tilton, *Nazism,*
    Neo-Nazism and the Peasantry (Bloomington, 1975).
5. For an analysis of electoral support for the resistance to Nazism see the
    maps and figures in A. Milatz, *Wähler und Wahlen in der Weimarer*
    Republik (Bonn, 1965).
6. cf. G. Franz,*Die Politischen Wahlen in Niedersachsen 1867 bis 1949*
    (Bremen, 1957), p. 40.
7. ibid. p. 104.
8. ibid. p. 44.
9. ibid. pp. 44-5.
10. ibid.
11. ibid. pp. 104-5, 264 and 270.
12. For the following see *Die Wirtschaftsstruktur im Bezirk des*
    Landesarbeitsamtes Niedersachsen. Bearbeitet im Landesarbeitsamt
    Niedersachsen (Hannover, 1930), pp. 1, 4-5, 80.
13. cf. J. Noakes, *The Nazi Party in Lower Saxony 1921-1933* (London,
    1971), pp. 222 ff.
14. cf. L. Volk, *Das Reichskonkordat vom 20. Juli 1933. Von den Ansätzen in*
    der Weimarer Republik zur Ratifizierung am 10. September 1933 (Mainz,
    1972), pp. 153 ff., and G. Lewy, op.cit. pp. 79 ff.
15. For a study of Catholic youth organisations in the Third Reich which
    concentrates mainly on the Rhineland see Barbara Schellenberger,
    Katholische Jugend und Drittes Reich (Mainz, 1975).
16. See the correspondence in Niedersächsiches Staatsarchiv Oldenburg

(NStAO) 134/1158.

17.   cf. Lewy, *op.cit.*, pp. 82-3.
18.   cf. J. Göken, *Der Kampf um das Kreuz in der Schule. Eine Volkserhebung in Südoldenburg im Jahre 1936* (Herausgegeben vom Kulturausschuss der Deutschen Zentrumspartei im Lande Niedersachsen, 1948), p. 5.
19.   ibid. p. 6.
20.   cf. A. Münzebrock, *Amtshauptmann in Cloppenburg 1933-1945* (Cloppenburg, 1962), p. 30.
21.   cf. H. Müller, *Katholische Kirche und Nationalsozialismus* (Munich, 1965), pp. 99-100.
22.   cf. Münzebrock *op.cit.*, p. 53.
23.   cf. Göken *op.cit.*, pp. 9 ff.
24.   cf. ibid. pp. 19 ff.
25.   cf. Münzebrock *op.cit.*, p. 58.
26.   cf. Göken *op.cit.* p. 18.
27.   ibid. p. 25.
28.   For the report on these events by Anton Kohnen, the top civil servant in Pauly's ministry, dated 5 November see NStAO 134/1232.
29.   cf. Münzebrock *op.cit.,* p. 63.
30.   A copy is in NStAO 134/1232.
31.   For the following see Münzebrock *op.cit.* pp. 55 ff.
32.   See the Bericht der Bischöflichen Commissariat an den Bischof in Münster. Copy in Bundesarchiv (BA) NS8/256.
33.   cf. Göken, *op.cit.* pp. 35-6.
34.   Vorwerk to Pauly 16.11. 1936 NStAO 134/1232.
35.   ibid.
36.   Vorwerk to Pauly 25.11.1936, ibid.
37.   ibid.
38.   ibid.
39.   See the correspondence of the headmasters of Oldenburg schools in ibid.
40.   For the following see: Bericht der Bischöflichen Commissariat an den Bischof in Münster. Abschrift in BA NS 8/256, and Göken *op.cit.* pp. 42 ff.
41.   cf. the article 'Die Hände weg vom Kreuz' in the *Münsterländische Tageszeitung*, 23.11.1967, and Göken *op.cit.* pp. 37 ff.
42.   Göken *op.cit.* pp. 38 ff.
43.   They are contained in NStAO 134/1232.
44.   cf. Bericht *op.cit.* and Göken *op.cit.* pp. 53 ff.
45.   For the following see ibid.
46.   cf. Bericht *op.cit.*
47.   NStAO 134/1232.
48.   Der Bürgermeister der Stadt Friesoy to the Amtshauptmann in Cloppenburg 21.11.1936 in ibid.
49.   cf. Bericht *op.cit.*
50.   Kreisleitung Vechta: Zur weltanschaulichen Lage im November 1936, 4.12.36 in BA NS 8/256.
51.   These and the following reports are contained in NStAO 134/1232.
52.   The Bürgermeister of Gemeinde Essen to the Minister der Kirchen und Schulen durch den Herrn Amtshauptmann des Amts Cloppenburg 20.11.1936 in ibid.
53.   NStAO 134/1232.
54.   NStAO 134/1232.
55.   cf. Röver speech in Cloppenburg on 25 November in BA NS 8/256.
56.   cf. Bericht *op.cit.*, Göken *op.cit.*, p. 61, and the article 'Der Gauleiter sprach in Löningen' in *Nachrichten für Stadt und Land*, 19.11.1936.

57. cf. Münzebrock *op.cit.* p. 60.
58. For descriptions of the meeting see Göken *op.cit.* pp. 61 ff., Münzebrock, *op.cit.* pp. 61-2, and the report of an eye-witness in BA NS 8/256.
59. cf. Münzebrock *op.cit.* p. 61.
60. Copy of Röver's speech in BA NS 8/256.
61. Copy of decree in NStAO 134/1232.
62. See the article 'Gauleiter Carl Röver spricht in zwei eindrucksvollen Versammlungen' in *Nachrichten für Stadt und Land*, 26.11.1936.
63. For the following see Göken, *op.cit.*, pp. 74 ff.
64. An unsigned copy of the declaration is in BA NS 8/152.
65. cf. Göken, *op.cit.*, pp. 77 ff.
66. Copy of the pastoral letter in BA NS 8/152 and in *The Persecution of the Catholic Church in the Third Reich: Facts and Documents* (London, 1940), pp. 124-5.
67. cf. Lewy *op.cit.* p. 314 fn.14. News of the crucifix struggle appears to have had a considerable impact in Bavaria. Cf. *Kirchliche Lage in Bayern op.cit.* i pp. 183, 185, ii p. 134, iv p. 115, 119.
68. Kreisleitung Vechta: Zur weltanschaulichen Lage im November 1936 4.12.36 in BA NS 8/256.
69. ibid.
70. See Pauly's minute dated 4.2.1937 in NStAO 134/1232.
71. See Pauly's minute on a petition received on 19.12.1936 in ibid.
72. cf. Göken, *op.cit.*, p. 83.
73. cf. *The Persecution of the Catholic Church in the Third Reich, op.cit.*, pp. 143 ff.
74. ibid., p. 158 and Münzebrock *op.cit.* pp. 49 ff.
75. ibid.
76. cf. *The Persecution of the Catholic Church in the Third Reich,op.cit.* pp. 43-44.
77. cf. Lewy, *op.cit.*, p. 174.
78. Göken, *op.cit.*, p. 80.
79. cf. Kreisleitung Vechta, *op.cit.*
80. cf. H.G. Hockerts, *Die Sittlichkeitsprozesse gegen katholische Ordensangehörige und Priester 1936/37* (Mainz, 1971), pp. 65 ff.
81. cf. Münzebrock, *op.cit.*, p. 64.
82. See for example the sensitivity of the regime towards working-class discontent as described in T.W. Mason, 'Labour in the Third Reich 1933-1939', *Past and Present*, XXIV, 1964, pp. 139-41.
83. cf. Göken, *op.cit.*, pp. 86 ff. and Frick to the Oberpräsidenten etc., 26.6.1937 in NStAO 134/1232.
84. cf. Lewy, *op.cit.*, p. 315; E. Peterson, *The Limits of Hitler's Power* (Princeton, 1971), pp. 216-21, and Bormann to Rosenberg 15.1.42, BA NS 8/187.
85. cf. Münzebrock, *op.cit.*, p. 94.
86. ibid. p. 95.
87. cf. Lewy, *op.cit.*, pp. 160 ff.
88. For the following see the very suggestive analysis in Carl Amery, *Die Kapitulation oder Deutscher Katholizismus heute* (Reinbeck b. Hamburg, 1963) pp. 20 ff.
89. Dated 20.11.1936, in NStAO 134/1232.
90. Bürgermeister Prüllage to the Amtshauptmann in Cloppenburg 19.11.1936 in ibid.

8 BUREAUCRACY, POLITICS AND THE NATIONAL SOCIALIST STATE

Jane Caplan

I

Rival hierarchies, competing agencies, uncertain chains of command, duplication of responsibilities, reluctant pooling of information, inadequate machinery for co-ordination — these are typical symptoms of the administrative incoherence which now constitutes the most familiar picture of government in the Third Reich. The contribution of much recent empirical work on the structure of the state and the processes of government in Nazi Germany has been to refine and differentiate this image of pervasive institutional confusion, an image which is sustained by sound documentation from a wide variety of sources.[1] It is hardly surprising that one of these sources should be the experience of the civil service during the Third Reich. The civil service is, after all, an institution which might almost be seen as a synonym for the very principle of orderly administration, and hence peculiarly sensitive to the shock-waves of any procedural disturbance. On top of this, it offers ample scope for charting the effects of such disturbances, since ultimately all policy ends up in the executive hands of the administrative personnel.

A confirmation of the crucial importance of the bureaucracy as an index for the progressive decomposition of the Nazi state also seems to emerge directly from the contemporary sources themselves, although in two contradictory versions. On the one hand there is, roughly speaking, the claim that the civil service was the perpetrator of the confusion — a claim most commonly associated with Hitler himself, and at a more general level purveyed publicly by some *Gauleiters* and certain sections of the Party press, as well as by rank-and-file stalwarts. Hitler's long-standing contempt for the legal profession in which senior civil servants were trained was signalled privately in remarks such as that 'Every jurist is either born defective or becomes so';[2] or more openly in his general neglect of civil service questions in his decisions and speeches — a neglect punctuated by occasional unpredictable intrusions into details of policy.[3] At the lower level, the civil service was undoubtedly subject throughout the Nazi period to public attacks varying from crude ridicule to quite virulent verbal vilification. The SS newspaper,

Schwarze Korps, was a notorious offender in this sense, and the tone was picked up by the local press in particular, as well as by individual propagandists.[4]

This background of an apparently semi-official toleration in some quarters of abusive criticism of civil servants was in part responsible for the emergence of the alternative image of them which developed at the same time – the image of civil servants as the victims of administrative chaos. This image was especially (though not exclusively) cultivated in the Reich Interior Ministry, for reasons which will largely form the subject of this essay. It can be read in the cumulative evidence of a deep crisis in the civil service that was collected and retailed in the course of the ministry's policy development: this included the growing official concern at the rate and quality of recruitment into the senior ranks of the service, the allegations of a widespread collapse of morale and of the eclipse of the traditional qualities and virtues of the German civil servant, and the attempts to stem the tide of obloquy allegedly engulfing the civil service. The most familiar and revealing statement of the ministry's claims is an appeal drafted by state secretary Pfundtner in August 1941 for submission by his minister, Frick, to the Führer himself:

> I implore you, my Führer, to heed the moral distress of the civil servant in Greater Germany. Give him a word of thanks and recognition for all that he has accomplished since 1933, particularly during the war; let him be accorded the public honour and estimation he deserves; prove your confidence in him by entrusting him with new important tasks. Two million of Germany's best sons will thank you, my Führer, by mastering these tasks with the traditional loyalty and exemplary strength of character in which the civil service has been nurtured, with the expertise acquired by an incomparable training, and with selfless devotion and ready sacrifice.[5]

The sting of this rambling document lay in its claim – a threat almost – that if nothing were done, then tottering morale and crumbling recruitment would between them destroy the administration of the Reich – and with the administration, of course, the regime itself. It is evident, then, that the image of the bureaucrat-as-victim not only countered the attacks on the civil service, but also offered a potentially valuable lever for certain governmental interests.

In this essay, I propose to examine those interests and explain their use of civil service policy in the context of determinate political

236 Bureaucracy, Politics and the National Socialist State

schemes for governmental reconstruction after 1933. In this sense, the essay will be taking issue with a certain interpretation of the Nazi regime which sees it broadly as a field for a conflict between a rational authoritarian bureaucracy, and an irrational totalitarian political movement – an interpretation which, it will be apparent, takes more or less at face value the image of bureaucracy as victim. Interpretations of this kind have figured in the literature on Nazi Germany for many years, in a number of guises. One subtle version is to be found, for example, in Ernst Fraenkel's stimulating work *The Dual State*; it is echoed in Hannah Arendt's assertion that 'the principle of authority in all important respects is diametrically opposed to that of totalitarian domination'. If authors such as these have provided the theoretical framework for a particular kind of political interpretation of the regime, historians have in some cases applied it directly to their empirical observations. Thus, Hans Buchheim has made use of a concept of this kind in his attempt to derive an explanation of the Third Reich's political structure from the organisational values of the civil service:

> The relationship between the party and the state was originally conceived in the sense that the party would have the political leadership and initiative, while it would be up to the state to carry out the details of the policies ordered by the party. This conception was shipwrecked, however, by the independence of the bureaucracy, which was not as the Nazis thought simply a machine for the execution of any old orders, but in fact showed itself to be a system of ordered rule tailored in the minutest fashion to an administrative practice based on the rule of law. The more obvious this fact became, the less the National Socialist movement confined itself to reserving to itself the politically important decisions, and the more it began to take on the functions of the civil state [*staatliche Hoheitsfunktionen*]. It established executive organs outside the state administration, which were aligned from the start in accord with Hitler's methods and aims.[6]

The bureaucracy's commitment to 'a system of ordered rule' is thus advanced as the underlying explanation of the entire process of the political distortion of the German state under the Nazis.[7]

More recent research has tended to retreat from this fundamental contrast between party and state, but without finally evicting the dualism inherent in the rational bureaucracy-irrational movement pair, with serious consequences for the explanatory capacity of the interpretations proposed. The most important of these consequences is that the empirical identification of the Nazi regime as a system of institutional antagonism is simultaneously invoked as its own explanation: in other words, an effect is reduced to its own cause, and the result is not an explanation but a tautology. Thus Hans Mommsen's interpretation of the structure of the regime, which avoids the obvious party-state dualism, still falls victim to this unresolved feedback:

> The inner structure of the National Socialist state system cannot, however, be grasped as if it were a power structure established once and for all or securely based in an attachment to one particular form. The permanent remodelling of social and state institutions, and the constant foundation of sovereign agencies whose own arbitrarily defined spheres of competence were not properly demarcated from the existing state apparatus, allow of no generally valid answer to the question of what the 'state' was in the National Socialist era, nor of how far the typical characteristics of the modern institutional state disappeared in the unregulated pluralism of newly founded or remodelled state and political agencies. One of the essential and defining characteristics of the Third Reich seems to us to lie pre- cisely in the fact that its development rested on a progressive parasi- tical dissolution of an inherited authoritarian state [Obrigkeitsstaat] , and that consequently it was bound to collapse internally in the same way that the over-expansion of foreign policy objectives, to the extent of bidding for a European Greater Empire 'of Germanic nation', led simultaneously to external catastrophe.[8]

The strength of this passage is that it accurately identifies the prob- lem of the reproduction of the state apparatus as the crucial weakness of the Third Reich. Yet it is evident that the explanatory power of the interpretation is allowed to rest on the assertion that the regime was caught up in a restless 'parasitical' dynamism: and this is taken as the excuse for abandoning the search for a Nazi 'state'. The further ques- tion as to the origins of this dynamism is not answered, though reference is made to a comment about Nazism's 'urge to movement' (Bewegungsbedürfnis) in Gerhard Schulz's important study of the Nazi seizure of power.[9] Thus the explanatory quest seems to have been stopped short as the Weberian canon — planning, priority, rational choice — is permitted to swallow an entire political system.

Two defects are evident in this approach. First, it implies that in some essential sense Nazism remained a distinct element within the state after 1933, and that it was the sole or at least principal source of the regime's dynamism, and hence of its confusions. This essential Nazism is liable to be specified as an ideological content, which can then be given certain institutional locations – the party leadership, the *Gauleiters*, and so forth.[10] From this it follows, secondly, that the other components of the state, especially the bureaucracy, have to be seen as the defenders of an institutional status quo, that they have by definition a conservative rationality. The rival images of bureaucracy as perpetrator and as victim of governmental bad practice are thus purged of their older polemical content, to be reinstated as monuments of value-free political sociology. It is scarcely surprising that 'dynamism' or 'parasitism' are left hanging as the ultimate explanations.

It is not, of course, my contention that we should make do with the polemic contemporary image of the bureaucracy. But in stripping it of its polemical content, we should perhaps be more wary of throwing away the political aspects altogether, for this will leave us again at the mercy of a no less contingent ideology. In other words, the rival images of the bureaucracy ought to be viewed as evidence of a determinate political conflict, and not judged from some *a priori* assignation of the bureaucracy to a category of administration and order, and of the Nazi movement or party (however defined) to a category of politics and disorder. A distinction of some kind may well be validly drawn, but it ought to be sustained by theoretical clarity and historical evidence, not by the weight of pre-given assumptions. Only in this way will it be possible to achieve a comprehensive analysis of the Nazi state.

My objectives in this essay are, however, initially more modest. Administrative structure and civil service policy in the Third Reich are my stalking horses for a preliminary skirmish with the problem of the political structure of the Nazi state, but chosen advisedly in view of the tendency to underrate their significant content. An essay of this length demands a highly selective handling of the issues and the evidence, and in that sense the text that follows is intended more as an invitation to debate than as anything approaching a satisfactory account of the subject. Accordingly, I have chosen to concentrate on one particular group of problems – those connected with the centralisation of administration – and have approached them through one active agent, the Reich Interior Ministry, for reasons which will become clear.

II

It is easy enough to see the organisational continuity in the state apparatus that spanned the dividing line of 1933 – the extent to which particular offices, procedures, personnel and so on remained stable. This, of course, is the perspective from which the Nazi era can be viewed primarily as a collision between these survivals and the dissolving processes of the new regime. However, another thread of continuity which tends to be less emphasised in the administrative context is the persistence of attempts to solve the fundamental structural problems of the German state, especially the central problem of federalism and administrative decentralisation. The handling of these issues after 1933 – and particularly the apparent paradox that the concentration of political power under the Nazis was associated with such a degree of administrative incoherence – can hardly be understood without some grasp of their prior status. The intercalation is therefore more than just residual, and the question of continuity must accordingly be faced not as a matter of mere survival, but as a structurally integrated complex.

The general line of argument here is that the tendency for administrative and political issues of state organisation to converge during the republic lent the bureaucracy a curiously ambiguous weight: it was an institution which was under great pressure, as will be seen, but in some respects it was also being thrust into a more eminent political role. This tension was not resolved before 1933, but the advent of Nazis in the government – among them, most significantly, Wilhelm Frick as Interior Minister – offered a new opportunity for building on the 'positive' side of the bureaucracy's experience. Frick and his officials, backed initially by support from other ministries, took this opportunity to try to insert the bureaucracy more firmly into the political equation of state and government. Theirs was a dynamic intervention which needs to be considered in the light of the specific pre-1933 mix of political and professional expectation and frustration within the German bureaucracy.[11]

A number of themes can be identified here: firstly, the basic problem of the federal structure of Weimar Germany; secondly, the place within the republic of the civil service as a historic institution; and thirdly, the political disposition of the senior ministerial bureaucracy of the Reich – the point at which, in a sense, the other two themes intersect. Although these cannot be dealt with fully here, a number of general observations may be made.

As far as the fundamental federal problem was concerned, the constitution (though not of course itself the source of the strains) embodied a certain contradiction between federal sovereignty and a potentially more unified state, which expressed itself in the persistent

high level of constitutional debate throughout the period.[12] Behind it
lay the concrete fact that the constitution was papering over the
shaky fabric of a particularist state system which, in the political tensions of Weimar, threatened to come apart altogether. Any issue of
administration which touched upon Reich-*Land* relations was thus
liable to become the focus for political conflict, which again helped to
ensure that the constitution itself remained at the centre of public
controversy. The major political issues, such as for example the
problem of Bavarian particularism, are familiar enough;[13] and the
eventual destruction of Prussia in 1932 offered in a sense the most vivid
illustration of the delicate colligation of constitutional, political and
administrative threads that made up the republican Reich.[14] At any
rate, it is from this perspective of deep and sometimes crippling intra-
Reich tension that the unitarist strategies of the Nazi regime must be
evaluated. The political methods used and the solutions proposed by
the regime were certainly crude in the extreme; but the problem, with
its specific interweaving of constitutional and administrative issues, had
already been put on the agenda before 1933.

The strain of keeping the Reich together as a political unit, solved so
brutally after 1933, was also reflected at the level of the personnel who
staffed the administration – another aspect of unitarism that was to be
pursued with equal vigour under the Nazi regime. Stresemann, receiving
a deputation from the civil service staff associations in November 1923,
was making more than just a conciliatory declaration when he told
them that 'Now that, of the three traditions that held the Reich together, two – the monarchy and the army – have already disappeared,
the professional civil service is the last clamp that is holding the Reich
together'.[15] Here again political and organisational issues were closely
intertwined, against a complex background provided by the German
civil service's historic role in the state. The Weimar constitution's
guarantee of inviolability to the 'traditional prerogatives' (*wohlerworbene Rechte*) of the civil service ideologically anchored an imperial
institution into the republican state, while simultaneously making these
practical issues – rights of tenure, salaries, pensions – into fully-fledged
constitutional matters.[16] The implications of this were duly exploited
both by the staff associations (of all political complexions) and by
political parties. Indeed, it has been argued with some force that the
massive reduction of civil servants' salaries, enforced in 1930/1 as part
of Brüning's deflation programme, constituted a final crucial alienation
of the civil service, turning them away in bitterness from the republic:
for not only was it a harsh material blow, but it was experienced as the

culmination to a longer process of erosion of civil servants' status.[17]

There is undoubtedly much truth in these general claims, but a precise picture of civil servants' political attitudes to the republic would demand a much more careful specification, taking into account age, grade and location, as well as the long-term process of functional and political differentiation that had been affecting the bureaucracy since well before the First World War. There is no space to go into these questions in detail here, but some of the main points can be indicated.[18] In principle, the civil service in imperial Germany had already been undergoing the major structural changes associated with the growth of state activity, and with the development of a political pluralism. Precise figures for its numerical growth are hard to calculate, since the statistics available tend to aggregate them at different times according to different criteria; but the pattern that emerges indicates, firstly, that state employment was growing since the 1880s at a disproportionately high rate compared with all employment, and secondly, that this growth was mainly concentrated in the technical (and educational) sectors.[19] The functional association of the civil service with the sovereign state in the strict sense was rapidly becoming inappropriate; correspondingly, its status as a *Stand* or estate was also dissolving: corporate integrity was hardly a material actuality any longer, but had at most an ideological existence (though it was not necessarily less powerful an image for that). But the actual process of differentiation was reflected or accompanied by the development − slow at first − of sectional and political affiliations among civil servants, from consumer co-operatives and electoral associations in the later decades of the nineteenth century, to professional and proto-union groupings in the early twentieth century. These tendencies were strengthened and accelerated during the war and revolution, so that by 1920 the overwhelming majority of civil servants were affiliated to one or other of the government-recognised professional associations (quite apart from their continued high level of representation in the *Reichstag*).[20] Through these channels, civil servants of all grades played an active role in governmental deliberations over the whole range of administrative issues: they were in this sense a powerful pressure group.

Professional association or unionisation was thus the necessary counterpart to the dissolution of an older corporate status, but it was limited both by the practical constraints on civil servants' political activity, and by the residual reluctance of an ex-élite of senior civil servants to co-operate in their own demotion from an earlier role of considerable objective authority, and even greater subjective self-estimation.[21] The interplay of ideology and actuality is complex here: compressing the strands, it might be argued that the institution of the republic — replacing the emperor or monarch to whom a profoundly symbolic oath of loyalty had been given — provided an ideologically convincing excuse for not coming to terms with the real structural changes that were in fact re-shaping the civil service. For, in other contexts too, the republic was identified *tout court* with politically unwelcome developments of which it was more of a symptom than an embodiment (let alone a cause) — a form of reductionism which was a no inconsiderable source of the republic's weakness. Some senior civil servants thus found themselves unable to take the oath of loyalty to the new republic, and resigned; others were forced from office for political reasons; others still — and this is the group that can never be counted — took the oath reluctantly and with reservations, perhaps fortified by a commitment to a supra-constitutional concept of state and nation far removed from its actuality.[22]

Civil service 'alienation' in the republic was therefore a complex and variegated phenomenon, spanning a range of provocations from the material disappointments referred to earlier, to the more complicated disaffection of a beleaguered élite. On some issues, to be sure, defensive self-interest converged from a number of these positions. Salary cuts, for example, could mean many things: a material loss, a threat to status, an assault on civil servants' privileged rights, a betrayal of the constitution. The effect could be one of broad hostility to government policy, as voiced in the universally critical representations made to the government by the civil service associations in 1930/1 and taken up across the political spectrum; but behind this lay the sectional divisions that were the evidence of the civil service's troubled passage from *Stand* to profession.

Only to some civil servants, and to other entrenched defenders of an idealised notion of the *Stand*, were these divisions themselves a cause for concern, as a symptom of the deep decay of the German body politic. Significantly, the statements emanating from the official association of senior civil servants, the *Reichsbund der höheren Beamten*, were remarkably free of the conventional rhetoric of organic and *ständisch* integrity; the *Reichsbund* had found a mode of discourse which allowed a realistic defence of members' interests without directly conflating these with older role models. The self-conscious defence of tradition is to be found, rather, in the writings of academic commentators on administrative history and politics, such as Arnold Köttgen and Hans Gerber, who sought to expose and analyse the ideological or ethical integrity of civil service history.[23] Similarly, among the ministerial bureaucracy whose political disposition forms the third and final point for discussion here, there was less a self-conscious pursuit of a role formed in ideology, than a practical adaptation to objective circumstances, viz. a growing inclination towards an executive solution to the governmental problems of Weimar Germany.

The growth of that commitment in all arms of government is well documented,[24] and the point to be emphasised here is simply the continuity of its development, from the turbulence of the post-revolutionary period, through the 1920s and into the more familiarly tense reaches of the Brüning years and after. Of the middle years, the era of so-called fulfilment and stability, it has been said that 'they saw no strengthening of parliamentary government, but on the contrary the increasingly absolute validation of an inherited appreciation of the qualities of experts and bureaucrats [*fachmännisch-bürokratischer Leistungen*].'[25] In other words, the same price was paid both for securing and for maintaining governmental stability: a reliance on a political and institutional structure which was by definition non-parliamentary, and whose representatives were esteemed for the very fact of their 'technical' and 'non-partisan' capacities. Added weight was given to this system of values by the implications of federal administrative policy, especially the schemes explored after 1923 by the 'Spardiktator' Saemisch in his pursuit of retrenchment – the administrative equivalent of industrial rationalisation. Saemisch's concept of a streamlined administration harked back to the image of the 'liberal *Beamtenstaat*', with its looked-for incorporation of political relations into the administrative structure of the state.[26] Moreover, the retrenchment schemes actually adopted were characteristically divisive at the lower levels of the civil service, pruning its establishment by up to twenty-five per cent, and sowing the seeds of a discontent that was to be harvested by the Nazi party in the early 1930s.[27] Characteristic too was the fact that federal intervention of this kind in civil service affairs was experienced as profoundly disruptive, while the government's potentially more positive attempts to achieve greater uniformity in civil service law throughout Germany came to nothing.[28] The Weimar constitution had strongly implied that a new civil service code would be issued, to replace that in force since 1907 and to act as a framework for *Land* legislation. A major field thus stood open for comprehensive legislation by 1933; and the laws that were subsequently issued were in important respects the direct descendants of the inconclusive discussions of the 1920s and early 1930s.

The picture of the administration and civil service under the republic is, therefore, not a simple one, but reflects the full range of political and ideological currents that eddied through the state apparatus as a whole. The basic problems of federalism and of administrative reorganisation acted as channels through which controversial political issues were fed into apparently technical questions, such as, for example, the siting of field offices, or the assessment of civil service salaries. Evidently, the tendency to try to reduce a wider range of issues to their technical solutions again was a response to this pressure, an attempt to close the contradiction. The civil service itself was in the throes of an adaptation to its own changed circumstances as well as those presented by the republic: the terms in which it was renegotiating its relationship to the state included its own numerical growth and functional differentiation, as well as the governmentally-directed policies of democratisation in recruitment, training and so on. These were processes which disturbed certain traditionalists, but which were also realistically assessed and accepted by other more numerous officials, at least as represented by their professional associations. At the same time, the pursuit of their interests was blocked for civil servants, as for other economically active groups, in the early 1930s: and it can be argued that it was this fact, and not the rhetoric of *Stand* and state, which drove large numbers of lower-ranking civil servants into the arms of the NSDAP, as members or as voters.[29]

A simple equation of civil service and corporatist conservatism is therefore illegitimate at the level of practice, even though this perspective did exist in rhetoric. But the more complex truth is constituted by the fact of the tensions between a rhetoric of integrity and an objective diversity, between the responses of adaptation and of resistance, between the reform of civil service law in some areas and the persistence of pre-republican law and practice in others, between the assaults on the *wohlerworbene Rechte* on the one hand and the potential for a relocation of civil authority on to the administrative apparatus on the other. These positions were, moreover, combined in various permutations whose relations cannot be extrapolated from ideological assumptions alone, but have to be evaluated in determinate political contexts. This is as true for the period after 1933 as it is for the republic; and it is to this that the essay now turns.

III

In our context, the coalition cabinet that took office on 30 January 1933 was as significant for the fact that it contained Wilhelm Frick as

Interior Minister as it was for Hitler's Chancellorship. For the next ten years, until his replacement by Himmler, Frick was to lead a dogged campaign for administrative reform, in which his objectives were to expand the power of his ministry and to consolidate it on a base of civil service strength. His initial lever in this programme was the need, acknowledged within the Nazi leadership though interpreted in different ways, for a secure political base; but eventually, as the depth of the political cross-currents within the regime was revealed, Frick was to make increasing use of arguments about administrative disintegration and civil service demoralisation. His claims on this score were certainly not without foundation, for similar symptoms were noted by all the major agencies of civil administration. However, the origin of these problems, the strategic deployment of them by Frick, and the hardening of his official stance, can be appreciated only in the light of the wider context explored in the previous section. For Frick's policies must be understood as active interventions into a situation that pre-dated the coming to power of the Nazi regime, and not simply as responses to pressures that developed after 1933. His ministry played an important part in the process of the regime's consolidation, helping to define and execute policy in the early crucial stages. When the Interior Ministry found itself pushed on to the defensive, as was increasingly the case after about 1935, it was as the result of the defeat of particular concepts and programmes, and not simply the unspecified effect of comprehensive governmental confusion.

Evidence for such an interpretation rests in a close examination of the evolution of policy within the Interior Ministry, in the analysis of its connections with the other major arms of the civil administration (the judicial and financial systems), and in its relations with the other governmental agencies, including those thrown up from within the NSDAP. Space does not permit a lengthy account of this kind here,[30] but the central links in the argument, and especially the crucial relationships with pre-1933 issues, can be broadly described.

The structure of government in the Third Reich was characterised as much by the dissolution of Germany's federal constitution as by the erection of a one-party state, and the two processes developed side by side. Defederalisation thus realised on a permanent scale the implications of the emergency powers in Article 48 of the Weimar constitution, with its association of centralised with executive authority, by concentrating and relocating the political and administrative powers gathered in from the *Länder*. It was the Reich Interior Ministry that initially was able to capitalise on the need for an immediate programme of constitutional and administrative reform, building on its objective importance in the first weeks after 30 January 1933 as the only agency competent and in a position to handle the programme.[31] In this process, Frick was ably assisted by his state secretary Hans Pfundtner — who a year earlier had already drafted an administrative action programme[32] — and by a highly experienced group of civil servants in the ministry who were strongly committed to the construction of an executive state on the lines canvassed before 1933.

The package of reforms carried out from 1933 to 1934, and culminating provisionally in the *Neuaufbaugesetz* of 30 January 1934, was thus the source of a vast accumulation of new powers by the Interior Ministry. From being in the republic a small supervisory ministry without a field machinery, it had acquired by 1934 direct authority over the huge Prussian interior administration, plus indirect control, through the *Reichsstatthalter,* over the interior administration throughout the whole of Germany. The exclusion of the *Reichstag* from the political process was not only the necessary base for the development of these powers, but also of course considerably enhanced the independent authority of the ministry: if in the republic it had had departmental responsibility for constitutional issues, now it was on the way to becoming the constitutional office itself. Even more than Krosigk's Finance Ministry, Lammers's *Reichskanzlei*, and Gürtner's Justice Ministry — the major governmental agencies in the administrative policy sphere — the Interior Ministry seemed in many respects to be a favoured heir of the Nazi revolution. Yet it was to become apparent that, as its administrative authority expanded, so its political power waned. The turning point occurred at the latest in 1935, with the reduction of *Reichsstatthalter* dependence on the ministry,[33] and the evidence of progressive defeat in a range of areas began to accumulate more thickly after 1937.

In terms of organisational capacity, Frick had in fact overreached himself, acquiring for his ministry powers which it was unable to deploy successfully. His entire policy, indeed, was based on a precept of administrative unity — 'Einheit der Verwaltung' — which looked to the concentration of all government field tasks on a single administrative machine. The specialist agencies (e.g. postal, fiscal, judicial) were to be reduced to an absolute minimum, and ought if possible to be co-ordinated — for example, in terms of their territorial structure — with the interior administration. Thus the interior administration was set to become both the 'backbone of the administration' and the standard for all other field systems. Frick remained deeply committed to these principles, despite their profoundly controversial implications. On a purely ideological basis, of course, it was easy enough to argue that the *Führerprinzip* implied a system of strict hierarchy, and indeed it was on the crest of this initial wave that Frick was able to embark on his plans in 1933. But the ideological declarations, to which anyone could pay lip service, concealed a set of political conflicts which by the end of 1935 had shattered any likelihood that Frick could pursue his aims to their logical – though in terms of organisational rationality highly dubious –political end.

At the end of 1935, Hitler ruled that 'all questions relating to constitutional and territorial reform [*Reichsreform*] are to be left alone for the time being'.[34] His decision came after more than a year of increasingly bitter dispute between the Interior Ministry, and the *Reichsreform* department established in May 1934 in Hess's *Stab des Stellvertreters des Führers*, and headed by the Bavarian *Gauleiter* Robert Wagner. If in this period of controversy Interior Ministry officials had been driven to voice deep frustration at the impossibility of carrying on ordinary business while basic questions of administrative structure remained unanswered,[35] after 1935 the situation worsened still further, as the half-finished structure, no longer powered by any political authority on Frick's part, drifted into the shoals. Frick's response to this problem was to redouble his efforts to achieve further fundamental reform, especially when the outbreak of the war seemed to offer further opportunities for advance.[36] He could hardly fail to be aware that his reputation, as well as his ambition, was at stake by this time: his close colleagues, especially Lammers and Krosigk, themselves threatened by shifts in the political spectrum of the regime, found it impossible to support Frick, while acknowledged enemies such as Goebbels and Bormann kept up a running critique of Interior Ministry policies. And of course the more Frick referred to the evidence of confusion, the more he was accused of having brought it upon himself.[37]

As we saw at the beginning of this essay, one of Frick's levers in his battle for political recovery was the civil service itself. From the earliest legislation of 1933 – the 'Law to restore a professional civil service' adopted in April[38] – the Interior Ministry had pursued an active policy of civil service reconstruction, which increasingly revealed a highly ambiguous ancestry. Laws on training, on appointment and promotion procedures, provisional legislation on a great range of urgent organisational matters, ultimately in 1937 a new civil service code and disciplinary law – the catalogue indicates a coherent scheme of reform, which was intended to be co-ordinated with the overall plans for

Reichsreform.[39] The protracted negotiations over these laws between the ministry and other interested parties – including of course Hess's staff – revealed evidence of much pressure on Frick's conception of the civil service as the integrated institutional counterpart to his projected system of unified administration. From Hess's staff, and from other sources within the party organisation, came persistent, though tactically varied, attempts to establish a secure foothold in civil service organisation. The efforts stemmed from the party's initial interest in the civil service purge that accompanied the seizure of power, and in manipulative control over access to jobs for deserving party members; but they subsequently developed, under Bormann's influence in particular, into a more comprehensive campaign to resist Frick's plans. To some extent, therefore, the various laws as finally promulgated did reflect quite directly defeats or compromises on sensitive issues – such as the allocation of authority to monitor the political behaviour of civil servants, or the introduction of exceptional promotion opportunities for politically reliable officials. However, it would be a mistake to conclude that the entire programme of legislation devised in the Interior Ministry was merely a contingent response to NSDAP pressure. On the contrary, it represented a relatively orderly attempt at building the civil service predicated by the ministry's own administrative strategies – and this was itself the source of some of the hostility shown by other politically interested agencies.

On the civil service front, the major setbacks began to be experienced after 1937, the year of the new civil service code; the code was a considerable paper achievement, but left scope for adverse political maneouvring in practice. Little further advance on this measure was possible, for the schemes of which it was a part had reached an impasse: only a major new initiative would have a chance of loosening the blockage. The outbreak of war, as already suggested, seemed to provide one such opportunity. Apart from the immediate organisational and procedural simplifications that were adopted, the course of the war up to 1941/2 offered prospects for what might become a thorough-going post-war settlement of all the administrative anomalies arising from the accumulation of new territory – a process which had of course been going on since 1938, and which had already been the field for struggles over administrative control in which the Interior Ministry risked being totally outflanked.[40] However, Frick's main attempts to use the exigencies of wartime administration, or the promise of victory, as the springboard for further progress, were largely unsuccessful; nor was his ministry much more fortunate in the later years of the war, when the deepening demand for labour power stimulated bitter competition both for personnel and for powers of control. Once again, his ministry's discomfiture was registered in the acquisition of responsibilities without the necessary powers of co-ordination.

Both of these two periods — 1937/8 to 1941/2 and 1942 to 1945 — were notable for the new prominence in debate of problems concerning the civil service salary system: in the first period it was the level of pay that was brought into the open, while in the second the structure and organisation of the system itself was the focus of attention. The first question was relatively simple: civil servants had suffered pay cuts of up to twenty-five per cent in 1930/1, and these had not subsequently been restituted despite the rise in the cost of living and the alleged advance of other wages. The Interior Ministry in 1937 initiated what was to be a sustained campaign for the restoration of full salaries, building it up through a series of major policy statements by Frick in which he did not hesitate to paint the alleged destitution of the civil service in alarming colours, nor fail to draw out its inferences for the future of a stable administration.[41] Undoubtedly much of the information he deployed to such great effect was accurate, for civil servants *were* increasingly badly off by most standards of comparison, and their morale was, according to all reports, showing signs of great strain. Yet it is hard to escape the conclusion that the prominence given to the issue by Frick was determined by other motives than a disinterested concern for the civil service. By elevating civil service troubles to the status of a national crisis, he was providing himself with extra ammunition in his strategic policy battles.

Similar conclusions can be drawn from the case of the salary system itself, which featured prominently in administrative policy debates after about 1941. The problems were in part highly technical and complex, but a couple of general points can be made here. Firstly, piecemeal amendments to the salary code (a total of thirty-six were issued between 1933 and 1943) had made a shambles of what in theory was the backbone of civil service structure, in that the salary system expressed in practice the organisationally necessary principles of hierarchy and institutional coherence. Its confused state by the late 1930s thus embodied a further aspect of the impasse reached by the Interior Ministry, insofar as its policy objectives depended upon the security of its authority over civil service organisation. But secondly, the ministry was not itself above exploiting the confusion for its own purposes (as other ministries did, for example, by demanding special salary supplements for their staff, or additional supernumerary posts), nor did it shy away from using the pretext of reform to advance the status of its own officials.[42] In this sense, it was once again the co-author of its own troubles.

The context in which Pfundtner drafted his abject appeal to Hitler, with which this essay began, had thus been formed as much by his own ministry's aggressive but unsuccessful policies, as by its attempts to deflect encroachments (from whatever source) upon its field of responsibility. In declaring a crisis in the civil service, Pfundtner (echoing his minister) was also describing his ministry's loss of control in administrative policy, a defeat which could also be measured in other aspects of policy such as the controversial problem of civil servants' membership of the NSDAP, or in the broader developments in relations between the Interior Ministry and the department of Hess's office run by Bormann.[43] A retreat which had begun around 1937 was gathering speed by these early war years, and the acceleration it eventually achieved was enough to throw Frick and Pfundtner out of their seats in 1943, and to lift Himmler into office as Interior Minister. Yet the fact that the retreat became a rout should not encourage too ready an assumption that the ministry's movement had always been in that single unfortunate direction; nor — and this is more important — should it lead to an over-simplified or superficial conclusion about who was routing whom. After all, only a deep eclecticism could generate the idea that Himmler's administrative pedigree was less formalistic than that of the bureaucracy he was supposedly engulfing.[44] Indeed, it is primarily the identity of the SS as an undoubtedly bureaucratic organisation that has sustained the appeal of 'dual state' theories. The fact is that in the discourse on the modern state, 'bureaucracy' arrived freighted with values derived from a belief in the rationality of the capitalist system in which it played a part: any rival organisation which impugned the core rationality thus had to be divested of its essential identity, so that it could be made incommensurable with the true institution.[45] This does not mean that there are no differences to be discerned in this case between the civil administration under Frick, and the SS under Himmler: but ultimately these will have to be expressed in their political base, and not in their institutional appearance.

IV

It has already been observed above that the central problem of the Nazi state was its inability to reproduce itself as a functioning political system.[46] In concurring with this now orthodox interpretation, this essay has also tried to reach beyond an essentially taxonomic account of this failure, and to enquire more searchingly into the concrete practices that make up the process of reproduction. In formal terms, its conclusion is that the reproduction of the state must be grasped as a process of the continual renegotiation of relations between its constituent institutions or apparatuses, a process which also comprehends the internal reproduction of the institutions themselves, whether these be political parties, representative bodies, bureaucracies or whatever. This proposition must necessarily be advanced at a fairly high level of abstraction, but there need be no difficulty in locating it concretely in the empirical material examined here.

If the reproduction of the state is conceived in this way, then it is clear that a dualist model of the Nazi state will not be adequate to comprehend the process. Neither the chronological opposition between the pre-Nazi and the Nazi state, nor the structural opposition between stability and dynamism, takes account of the fact that the civil service, like other constituents of the state, was engaged in a permanent round of adaptative reproduction. Thus, for example, we noted contradictory responses to the civil service's changing terms of operation since the end of the nineteenth century: its numerical growth and functional diversification were indices of the scope and the need for a renegotiated place and identity, while the protective provisions of the Weimar constitution represented the strength of a conservative stability. Similarly, the thrust of civil service policy after 1933 can be read as a bid to construct a new place for the institution, by means of a decisive intervention into the process of negotiation. The legislative initiatives of the 1930s are a clear mark of this process; later, in the war years, schemes for a fundamental reform of training procedures indicate a retreat from the open arena of political initiative to a more closed world of ideological image-building, an attempt to generate on paper the institution that had been blocked in practice.[47]

The self-destructive capacity of the Nazi state thus makes sense only if the process of reproduction is recognised as a perpetual one, in which the institutions and their relationships are constantly in motion. Unless this point is made, the identity of the Nazi state is both underplayed and oversold: underplayed, in the sense that the contingent appearances of this process are substituted for its structural origination, but oversold in the sense that these appearances take over the whole task of representing the state as such. Thus, as we noted at the beginning of this essay, the institutional confusion of the Nazi state becomes both its essential identity, and the explanation of its downfall.

In bare outline, this is the kind of interpretative apparatus which is

needed to rescue analysis of the Nazi state – or of those aspects discussed here – from a mere reflex of its organisational incongruities. But
ultimately, the bones of this theoretical skeleton must be fleshed out
with a comprehensive analysis of the structural crisis which buckled
and stretched the state apparatus into so many unfamiliar forms, a
crisis of class representation whose subtleties are only beginning to be
explored.[48] This project extends beyond the scope of the present essay,
which, conscious of its own limitations and its narrow focus, has raised
many more questions than it has answered, and left some of the most
important questions untouched. But the posing of questions, however
awkward and unformed, to a rapidly congealing orthodoxy remains its
own permanent imperative.

Notes

1. Monographic studies of the Nazi regime are now too numerous to be listed
    in full here. Recent publications in the field of government and administra-
    tion include Peter Diehl-Thiele, *Partei und Staat im Dritten Reich: Unter-
    suchungen zum Verhältnis von NSDAP und allgemeiner innerer Staatsver-
    waltung* (Munich, 1969); Peter Hüttenberger, *Die Gauleiter. Studie zum
    Wandel des Machtgefüges in der NSDAP* (Stuttgart, 1969); H. Matzerath,
    Nationalsozialismus und kommunale Selbstverwaltung (Stuttgart/Berlin/
    Cologne/Mainz, 1970); H. Mommsen, *Beamtentum im Dritten Reich*
    (Stuttgart, 1966); E.N. Peterson, *The Limits of Hitler's Power* (Princeton,
    1969). Martin Broszat, *Der Staat Hitlers* (Munich, 1969) is a highly
    perceptive general account.
2. H. Picker, *Hitlers Tischgespräche im Führerhauptquartier 1941-1942*, edited
    A. Hillgrüber (Munich, 1968), p. 69.
3. e.g. when he intervened to forestall moves to review the position of divorced
    civil servants early in 1937 (documentation in Bundesarchiv, Koblenz (=BA)
    R 43 II/443); a similar example relating to women civil servants with
    illegitimate children is cited in D. Schoenbaum, *Hitler's Social Revolution.
    Class and Status in Nazi Germany 1933-1939* (New York, 1966), p. 280.
    More seriously, Hitler enforced a personal interpretation of a clause in the
    1937 civil service code relating to guarantees of political reliability, which
    went well beyond the law's intent; cf. J. Caplan, 'The Civil Servant in the
    Third Reich' (Oxford D.Phil. thesis, 1973), pp. 171-2.
4. The style can be judged from an article in the Essen *Nationalzeitung*, 2
    November 1941, which satirised an imaginary *Obersekretär* Kleinhirn and
    Amtmann Erstkommich; other evidence, including more serious attacks,
    discussed in Caplan, op. cit., pp. 335-7.
5. Reprinted in full in Mommsen, op. cit., pp. 200-2.
6. Hans Buchheim, *Das Dritte Reich. Grundlagen und politische Entwicklung*
    (Munich, 1958), pp. 50-1.
7. A more deliberate apologetic attempt is apparent in some postwar writing,
    e.g. Gottfried Neesse, *Staatsdienst und Staatsschicksal* (Hamburg, 1955),
    which purported to demonstrate that the professional civil service (*Berufs-
    beamtentum*) was in principle the strongest bulwark against totalitarianism.

8. Mommsen, op. cit., p. 13.
9. Gerhard Schulz, 'Die Anfänge des totalitären Massnahmenstaates', in K.D. Bracher, W. Sauer and G. Schulz, *Die nationalsozialistische Machtergreifung. Studien zur Errichtung des totalitären Herrschaftssystems in Deutschland 1933/34* (Cologne/Opladen, 1962), p. 512. Schulz's own discussion of Nazi totalitarianism is also somewhat unsatisfactory in its reduction of Nazi 'irrationality' to the pursuit of 'die jeweils nächsten Zwecke' – a constant succession of immediate aims (p. 376). His handling of administrative and bureaucratic tendencies is, however, extremely sensitive (e.g. his chapter 4, on *Reichsreform*): it is to be regretted that this, like many of the book's other qualities, lies buried in such an unwieldy work.
10. cf. Diehl-Thiele, *op. cit.*, p. 32: 'Party and state, totalitarian movement and rational administrative apparatus, remained antinomies.' A similar opposition is set up in Hans Buchheim's contributions to the symposium *Anatomie des SS-Staates* (Munich, 1967), e.g. vol. i, pp. 28-9. Cf. also Caplan, op. cit., *passim*. Evidently, the sheer contradiction between two such antagonists can be made to explain a great deal.
11. The best existing accounts in this respect are Schulz, op. cit., *loc. cit.*, and Broszat, op. cit., chapter 7 especially.
12. For the problem in general, see Herbert Jacob, *German Administration since Bismarck. Central Authority versus Local Autonomy* (New Haven and London, 1963) and references therein. A detailed and deeply revealing treatment in Gerhard Schulz, *Zwischen Demokratie und Diktatur. Verfassungspolitik und Reichsreform in der Weimarer Republik*, vol. i, 'Die Periode der Konsolidierung und der Revision des Bismarckschen Reichssaufbaus 1919-1930' (Berlin, 1963) – an indispensable book for the period.
13. cf. Franz Menges, *Reichsreform und Finanzpolitik. Die Aushöhlung der Eigenstaatlichkeit Bayerns auf finanzpolitischem Wege in der Zeit der Weimarer Republik* (Berlin, 1971).
14. cf. Werner Braatz, 'Franz von Papen and the *Preussenschlag*, 20 July 1932: a move by the "New State" toward *Reichsreform*', *European Studies Review* iii (1973), pp. 157-80. See also Arnold Brecht, *Federalism and Regionalism in Germany: the Division of Prussia* (New York, 1945), as well as his more general statement of the problem in *Reichsreform – Warum und Wie?* (Berlin, 1931).
15. Minute of a discussion with the governmentally-recognised civil service associations (*Spitzenverbände*) about the *Personalabbauverordnung*, 14 November 1923 (BA R 43 I/2612).
16. For the adoption of these guarantees in the Weimar constitution, see Lothar Albertin, *Liberalismus und Demokratie am Anfang der Weimarer Republik* (Düsseldorf, 1972), pp. 131-3; also A. Falkenberg, *Die deutsche Beamtenbewegung nach der Revolution* (Berlin, 1920), pp. 51 ff. According to Gerhard Anschütz's standard commentary on the constitution, *Die Verfassung des Deutschen Reiches* (Bad Homburg, 1961; first published 1921), the relevant articles (129-131) 'guarantee the persistence of the German professional civil service [*Berufsbeamtentum*] in its traditional legal form, and are therefore an institutional guarantee'; also 'the guarantee of the "wohlerworbene Rechte" is not a guideline for future legislation, but is directly valid law' (pp. 591-2).
It must be remembered that German law and practice distinguish between two principal categories of public official: the *Beamte* or civil servant proper, whose legal status is the subject of a special corpus of public law; and the *Angestellter* (salaried employee) and *Arbeiter* (wage-worker), whose different positions are regulated in ordinary contract and labour law. It was the *Beamten* whose status was covered by the constitution, and who form

the subject of the present article. Their legal situation in Weimar is summarised in Gerhard Anschütz and Richard Thoma (eds.), *Handbuch des Deutschen Staatsrechts* (Tübingen, 1932), vol. ii; see also the regular reports of current legislation in the *Jahrbuch des öffentlichen Rechts* for the relevant inter-war years. Arnold Köttgen, *Das deutsche Berufsbeamtentum und die parlamentarische Demokratie* (Berlin/Leipzig, 1928) is the most important contemporary analysis. A more recent survey in Hans Fenske, 'Monarchisches Beamtentum und demokratischer Staat', in *Demokratie und Verwaltung. 25 Jahre Hochschule für Verwaltung Speyer* (Schriftenreihe der Hochschule Speyer Band 50, Berlin, 1972), pp. 117-36.5.

17. This build-up of tension is charted by Hans Mommsen, 'Die Stellung der Beamtenschaft in Reich, Ländern und Gemeinden in der Ära Brüning', *Vierteljahrshefte für Zeitgeschichte* xxi (1973), pp. 151-65. Wolfgang Runge, *Politik und Beamtentum im Parteienstaat* (Stuttgart, 1964) is an account of Prussian civil service policy in the republic which also sheds some light on the political effects of reformist policies.
    On the constitutional status of the salary system, see Anschütz, *Die Verfassung des Deutschen Reiches*, pp. 592-5; and Carl Schmitt, 'Wohlerworbene Rechte und Gehaltskürzungen' in his *Verfassungsrechtliche Aufsätze* (Berlin, 1958), pp. 174-80.

18. These aspects have in any case been less researched than the problem of the continuity of the élite, sometimes with the implication that the entire civil service is reducible to that section alone. Falkenberg, op. cit., contains some general information, as also Albert Lotz, *Geschichte des Deutschen Beamtentums* (Berlin, 1914). Peter-Christian Witt, 'Der preussische Landrat als Steuerbeamte 1891-1918. Bemerkungen zur politischen und sozialen Funkiton des deutschen Beamtentums', in I. Geiss and B.J. Wendt (eds.), *Deutschland in der Weltpolitik des 19. und 20. Jahrhunderts* (Düsseldorf, 1973), pp. 205-19, is a meticulous exposé of the realities behind the virtuous ethical image of senior civil servants. Jürgen Kocka, *Klassengesellschaft im Krieg* (Göttingen, 1973), pp. 82-4, charts the wartime experience; and Georg Kalmer, 'Beamtenschaft und Revolution. Eine sozialgeschichtliche Studie über die Voraussetzungen und Wirklichkeit des Problems', in K. Bosl (ed.), *Bayern im Umbruch* (Munich, 1969), pp. 201-61, is an important study of the political transition.

19. Statistical information assembled and reviewed by John P. Cullity, 'The Growth of Governmental Employment in Germany, 1882-1950', *Zeitschrift für die gesamte Staatswissenschaft*, 1967, pp. 201-17.

20. For civil servants in the *Reichstag*, cf. P. Molt, *Der Reichstag vor der improvisierten Revolution* (Cologne/Opladen, 1963), pp. 139-56; Fritz Poetzsch-Heffter, 'Vom Staatsleben unter der Weimarer Verfassung', *Jahrbuch des öffentlichen Rechts* xvii (1929), p. 71. For the development of civil service associations, see Falkenberg, op. cit.; a publication of the West German Deutscher Beamtenbund, *Deutscher Beamtenbund. Ursprung. Weg. Ziele* (Bad Godesberg, 1968), is a useful historical survey, though written from the standpoint of one association only. Contemporary publications of the associations are an important source for their policy, e.g. Heinz Potthoff, *Grundfragen des künftigen Beamtenrechts* (Berlin, 1923), a publication by the social-democrat oriented Allgemeiner Deutscher Beamtenbund. Copies of the associations' submissions to the government can be found in the files of the *Reichskanzlei* (BA R 43 I), as also protocols of negotiation meetings etc.

21. Full references on this in Caplan, op. cit., chapter 1; cf. e.g. Otto Hintze, *Der Beamtenstand* (Leipzig/Dresden, 1911), and for a critique Eckart Kehr, 'Zur Genesis der preussischen Bürokratie und des Rechtsstaats' in Hans-

Ulrich Wehler (ed.), *Der Primat der Innenpolitik. Gesammelte Aufsätze zur preussisch-deutschen Sozialgeschichte im 19. und 20. Jahrhundert* (Berlin, 1965), pp. 31-52.
22. The significance of the oath is discussed in Köttgen, op. cit., pp. 115-20; see also Runge, op. cit., chapter 4 especially.
23. Köttgen, op. cit.; Hans Gerber, 'Vom Begriff und Wesen des Beamtentums', *Archiv des öffentlichen Rechts* N.F. xviii (1930), pp. 1-85; see also Theodor Wilhelm, *Die Idee des Berufsbeamtentums* (Tübingen, 1933).
24. For the political developments, see principally Wolfgang Runge, op. cit., chapters 5 and 6 especially; Peter Hauungs, *Reichspräsident und parlamentarische Kabinettsregierung. Eine Studie zum Regierungssystem der Weimarer Republik in den Jahren 1924 bis 1929* (Cologne/Opladen, 1968), pp. 264-94 especially; Karl Dietrich Bracher, *Die Auflösung der Weimarer Republik* (Villingen, 1960); Gotthard Jasper, *Der Schutz der Republik. Studien zur staatlichen Sicherung der Demokratie in der Weimarer Republik* (Tübingen, 1965); also Schulz, *Zwischen Demokratie und Diktatur*, chapters 1, 11 and 13 especially. The background in juridical and political theory is discussed in Kurt Sontheimer, *Antidemokratisches Denken in der Weimarer Republik* (Munich, 1962).
25. Hauungs, op. cit., p. 269.
26. Schulz, *Zwischen Demokratie und Diktatur*, pp. 516-63.
27. See the lengthy documentation on the 1923 *Personalabbauverordnung* (Reichsgesetzblatt (=RGB1) 1923, I, p. 999) in BA R 43 I/2612 to 2614. For its later exploitation by NSDAP propaganda, see Caplan, op. cit., pp. 69-71.
28. Discussions of new civil service legislation from 1924 to 1931 documented in BA R 43 I/2553 to 2556.
29. By 1930, according to the *Partei-Statistik* (issued in 1935), civil servants were as a profession over-represented in the NSDAP — they were about 7.7 per cent of membership, compared with about five per cent of employment; figures discussed in Caplan, op. cit., pp. 79-85.
30. See Jane Caplan, 'The Politics of Administration: the Reich Interior Ministry and the German Civil Service 1933-1943', *Historical Journal* (1977); also Caplan, 'The Civil Servant in the Third Reich', chapters 3-6.
31. See principally Schulz, 'Die Anfänge des totalitären Massnahmenstaates', chapter 4; also Broszat, op. cit., chapters 4 and 7.
32. Reprinted in Mommsen, *Beamtentum im Dritten Reich*, pp. 128-35.
33. Details discussed in Diehl-Thiele, op. cit., pp. 37-73.
34. Internal note (*Vermerk*) in Reich Interior Ministry, 27 December 1935 (BA R 18/373).
35. Cf. for example an internal note by Franz Medicus, *Referent* with sub-departmental responsibility for *Reichsreform* in the Interior Ministry, 14 May 1935: 'Questions of administrative reform are being foiled or frustrated on all corners by the fact that up till now any basis for *Reichsreform* — whether for organisational or regional reconstruction — is lacking. In today's post alone there are three important questions which we are unable to reply to with any certainty, because even the barest outlines of reconstruction plans have not been settled. The consequence is that partial measures are being adopted without regard to a general line, but according to the narrow viewpoints of the individual ministries.' (BA R18/373)
36. See for example the Interior Ministry's attempts to recoup its position after the passage of the 'Law on the unification [*Vereinheitlichung*] of the state apparatus [*Behördenaufbau*]', 5 May 1939 (RGB1 1939, I, p. 1197), a measure which in the process of drafting had weakened the ministry's hold

256   Bureaucracy, Politics and the National Socialist State

over the internal administrative apparatus: for months thereafter, the
ministry sought to recommend new legislation that would finally destroy
the remnants of *Land* administrative autonomy, and subject them wholly to
the Reich Interior Ministry (documentation in BA R 19/5450).
Similarly, the ministry used the information on administrative problems
collected from the *Reichsstatthalter* in spring 1941 (documentation in BA
R 43 II/1394, 1394a and 1394b) as a basis for a further bid for massive
administrative concentration: but the single decree drafted in the ministry
was forcibly broken up into six separate regulations, issued in March 1942,
which effectively thwarted the ministry's own ambitions (documentation
to be found in BA R 43 II/707a, and in R 18/5450 and 5451).

37. Goebbels was a particularly virulent critic of Frick; cf. Louis P. Lochner
(ed.), *The Goebbels Diaries* (London, 1948), pp. 40, 99, 108, 180 etc.;
also Diehl-Thiele, op. cit., pp. 196-7.
For the critical state of relations between Frick and Krosigk and Lammers,
see for example documentation from 1942 on long-running disputes over
responsibility for civil service policy, in BA R 43 II/143.

38. RGB1 1933, I, p. 175; for details, see Caplan, 'The Civil Servant in the Third
Reich', pp. 122-39; Mommsen, *Beamtentum im Dritten Reich,* pp. 39-61,
151-65.

39. cf. report of state secretaries' meeting, 9 December 1936, to discuss relationship of four major civil service measures to *Reichsreform* (report in BA R
43 II/494); details of the full legislative programme in Caplan, op. cit.,
chapters 4 and 6 especially.

40. cf. Diehl-Thiele, op. cit., pp. 123ff.

41. Details discussed in Caplan, op. cit., pp. 173-219.

42. See for example Interior Ministry attempts to re-classify the salary scales of
key posts in the field administration, criticised in two *Reichskanzlei*
memoranda of 11 July and 19 September 1941 (BA R 43 II/429b).

43. For the issue of NSDAP membership, see Mommsen, *Beamtentum im
Dritten Reich,* chapter 4 especially; for the development of Bormann's
department and its relations with the Interior Ministry, see Caplan, 'The
Politics of Administration'.

44. A telling example of this is documented by Hans Mommsen, 'Ein Erlass
Himmlers zur Bekämpfung der Korruption in der inneren Verwaltung vom
Dezember 1944', *Vierteljahrshefte für Zeitgeschichte* xvi (1968), pp. 295-309

45. cf. in particular Buchheim, 'Die SS – das Herrschafts-instrument', in
Anatomie des SS-Staates, vol. i, pp. 15-30.

46. p. 237 above.

47. See Caplan, 'The Civil Servant in the Third Reich', pp. 273-302.

48. The most interesting discussion of these questions is Nicos Poulantzas,
Fascism and Dictatorship (London, 1974); see also Jane Caplan, 'Theories
of Fascism: Nicos Poulantzas as Historian', *History Workshop Journal* 3
(Spring 1977).

9 THE GERMAN FILM INDUSTRY AND THE NEW ORDER

Marcus Stuart Phillips

I

The New Order was Hitler's attempt to extend the National Socialist Revolution beyond the borders of Germany. Announced in 1940, when German military prestige was nearing its height, it proposed the reorganisation of the European economy with the aim of creating a self-sufficient, large scale, economic union (*Grossraumwirtschaft*) quarantined from the more materialistic systems of the rest of the world, especially the United States. This, however, was only a means to an end.[1] Within this area a programme would be introduced to restore the racial (*völkisch*) consciousness of the Nordic peoples by the removal of destructive elements and the restoration of a genuine *Kultur*. Put another way, for the last two hundred years liberalism and capitalism had been tending to develop a certain type of man. The National Socialist Revolution sought to change the course of European History by creating a new type of man.[2]

How seriously did the Nazis take the New Order? So far as it involved the elimination of Communists, Jews and other 'destructive elements', it seems obvious that they took it very seriously indeed. Finding evidence of a coherent policy of a constructive nature is more difficult. The New Order and its ramifications were discussed at length by Hitler in his 'Table Talk', in leading articles in newspapers (especially *Das Reich*), and in countless pamphlets, letters, memoranda and speeches, but it was never precisely defined. Hitler said little about the future of the so-called 'Germanic' peoples of Europe. He seems never to have made up his mind about the future of Britain and doubts about the role of France prevented the adoption of any consistent policy towards the richest of Germany's conquests. Indeed, taking Hitler's career as a whole he was diverted so often from his ideological course that many historians have regarded the whole programme of Nazi expansion and conquest as little more than a series of improvisations, forced on Hitler either by the tensions within Nazi society or simply by his dynamic nihilism; but not by his attempts to carry out a genuine revolutionary programme. It is true that coherent plans for the long term reorganisation of the European economy were devised by

257

various German industrialists but in practice these hardly differed from traditional closed-shop imperialism. This merely lends support to the view that the Nazis did have a coherent policy but it was identical to that of the capitalists they claimed to have supplanted.[3]

If the New Order was merely an empty phrase to cover the traditional short term exploitation of occupied territories it follows that efforts by the various Nazi agencies responsible for implementing the European 'cultural revolution' were merely propaganda aimed at reconciling the peoples of Western Europe to German political hegemony. The reverse of the argument is also true for, in the New Order, fascist ideological and economic imperialist motives were inextricably intertwined. Furthermore, if the Nazis did not take the New Order seriously the same is true for the revolution they claimed to have brought about in Germany, for, in the long run, the political and economic ideas of National Socialism made no sense if they were confined to Germany. Hitler's frequently voiced assertions about the superiority of German civilisation indicate that he thought Germany could do without the art and culture of other peoples. Hitler, however, can never have seriously believed that even 'Greater Germany' could be economically self sufficient.[4] The autarchic 1,000 year Reich could only be constituted on a European basis and this meant a Europe that included considerable areas of the Soviet Union.

In this paper I plan to examine the role of the German film industry in the years of German conquest and occupation of Europe. There are several reasons for supposing that this should throw light on the nature of the New Order and therefore on the basic character and ultimate aims of German National Socialism. The industry's staple product, the feature film (*Spielfilm*), was a major weapon of Nazi long term ideological indoctrination.[5] But more than any other artistic manifestation, the film was also international 'big business'. Commercial and artistic priorities had always been in conflict within its structure though the Nazis claimed to have resolved them. Lastly, this industry was under the direct control of the Propaganda Minister, Dr Joseph Goebbels, one of the most intelligent and clear sighted (though most fanatical and ruthless) of the Nazi leaders, who placed it very high on his own list of priorities.[6]

It was only to be expected that Goebbels would attempt to direct the output of the German film industry so that its films would contain an optimum of Nazi propaganda,[7] and that he would attempt to exhibit these films as widely as possible in occupied and neutral Europe. What needs to be ascertained is whether or not Goebbels seriously attempted

to reorganise the European film industry on a permanent basis and, if
this is so, the structure he envisaged the industry should have, the type
of film he encouraged, the priorities he followed and the success he
achieved. Before considering Goebbels' attempts to extend his 'film
revolution' abroad it is necessary briefly to sketch the 'revolution'
inside Germany.

II

Nazi policy towards the world of the cinema was initially directed
along three lines. Control over the content of individual films was
carried out by the Propaganda Ministry (RMVP). It chiefly took the
form of a compulsory (later voluntary) script censorship carried out by
a RMVP official, the *Reichsfilmdramaturg* (Reich Film Script Editor).
The RMVP also controlled the import of foreign films into Germany.

   Control over the careers of individual film makers was the responsibility of the 'Reich Film Chamber' (RFK), one of seven constituent
chambers of the 'Reich Culture Chamber' (RKK), a subordinate agency
of the RMVP. The RFK also directed the economic affairs of the
industry which in practice took the form of regulating seat prices,
distribution rentals, and running the *Filmkreditbank,* principally to
help finance the small independent producer. The general aim of RFK
policy being to preserve a healthy independent middle-class (*Mittelstand*)
element in the film industry.[8]

   By the end of 1936 the film industry was in a severe financial crisis.
Rising costs (due largely to the RMVP's interference during production),
combined with a sharp fall in exports,[9] had already virtually eliminated
the small producer and were now threatening the major production-
distribution combines. At this point, Goebbels and Walther Funk, who then
held the rank of Under Secretary at the RMVP, persuaded the Finance
Ministry (RFM) to advance money for the purchase of a controlling
interest in the two leading German film combines, Ufa[10] and Tobis.[11]
The government agent in these transactions was Max Winkler, owner of
the *Cautio Treuhand GmbH,* who had been involved in trustee work for
the governments of both Weimar and Nazi Germany, though hitherto he
had been of service to the Nazis chiefly in the acquisition of publishing
companies.[12] Later in 1937 Winkler obtained further loans from the
RFM to purchase control of the third largest Berlin film company,
Terra Film AG and the Munich *Bavaria Film AG.*[13] Goebbels made
Winkler responsible for the economic future of the 'state supported'
film industry, as it was now called, with the title 'Reich Delegate for the
German Film Economy'. After 1938 the RFK ceased to be of much

importance except in the exhibition sector.

The RFM had shown considerable reluctance to advance the necessary sums which by April 1938 amounted to RM 43,045,000.[14] They feared that once the industry was nationalised both the RMVP and the film artists would spend money regardless of whether it would ever be recouped and the industry would become a permanent drain on the budget. Winkler had other ideas. With Goebbels' full support he ran the industry as though it was a private enterprise, his immediate aim being to make it solvent. He diagnosed that the main problem was shortage of credit and arranged, via the *Reichskreditgesellschaft* (a bank established in 1924 to finance government industrial undertakings) for a new company, the *Film Finanz GmbH* to be set up which would supply credit for a whole year's production. Films were budgeted on the assumption that they would retrieve their costs within an average period of nine months. The *Film Finanz* was administered by a committee of representatives from the various government agencies involved and the film companies who all had one thing in common: they were financial experts and business men not artists.[15] In so far as he had control over selection of personnel, Winkler chose professionals rather than Nazis. As far as production was concerned, Winkler merely extended the system which had operated at Ufa since 1927 to the whole state industry. The individual companies co-operated in such matters as the utilisation of studios and expensive equipment, exports, programming of premiere cinemas and technical research, but in other respects they remained independent and competitive. In short, Winkler's programme was one of rationalisation not revolution.[16]

Goebbels' motives in supporting Winkler's orthodox profit making approach were largely tactical. He wanted to see the film industry working more efficiently and drawing good audiences. The financial state of the industry was a useful index as to how the industry was performing. Hitler, on the other hand, did not care whether the industry was profitable or not. Early in 1938 he ordered the reconstruction of a German film academy in Berlin and giant (and impractical) film studios in Munich. The initial outlay needed to start these projects was RM 20 million[17] and the final cost would have been much more.[18] The expenditure could not be justified in economic terms, but as far as Hitler was concerned, if it added significantly to the prestige of Nazism and German *Kultur* at home and abroad then it served its purpose.[19]

Goebbels had the same objectives but he had different priorities. As long as the state film industry owed money to the RFM then the RFM,

one of the most conservative of government departments, would
insist on having a say on how the money was spent.[20] As soon as the
industry was showing signs of recovery Winkler began to try and loosen
the RFM's control. In May 1939 he suddenly produced a scheme for
the state companies to form a profit sharing cartel. He argued that this
would simplify administration, though its main justification was that
the industry as a whole would pay 10 per cent less tax. The latter point,
however, cut no ice with the RFM since the tax was paid to them.
Furthermore, they had objections to the plan. Under the existing
arrangements losses by individual companies were covered through the
Film Finanz and this gave the RFM the opportunity to inspect loss
making companies and, if necessary, demand remedial action. If money
from profitable companies was merely transferred to unprofitable ones
both would lose incentive and the RFM would lose control. The probable result would be a general decline in profits. The only beneficiary
would be Winkler whose authority would be greatly augmented.

The RFM's argument was somewhat contradictory. The plan was
based on the assumption that the state industry would show at least an
overall profit as otherwise Winkler's authority would be diminished not
increased. Maybe they did not trust Winkler and Goebbels not to divert
profits from the film companies for unauthorised purposes. At all events,
the RFM vetoed the plan.[21]

This was only a temporary setback. The scheme was finally introduced in February 1942 as part of a more comprehensive reorganisation.
Meanwhile the film industry had become a very profitable investment.
These profits gave Winkler and Goebbels the chance to extend the state
film industry without consulting the RFM. The remaining independent
companies were absorbed into a single company, *Berlin Film GmbH*
(September 1941) and companies were formed for the production and
distribution of newsreels (*Deutsche Wochenschau GmbH* – November
1941) and animated films (*Deutsche Zeichenfilm GmbH* – July 1941).
The latter two companies were created to challenge American
supremacy in their respective fields by concentrating resources and
personnel.[22]

By the autumn of 1941, however, the industry, although financially
prosperous, was facing further difficulties. As the war went on fewer
films were being made and they were taking longer to make.[23] This was
partly due to shortages in material and manpower and general wartime
disruption but the RMVP itself was also to blame. Soon after the war
began, Goebbels redoubled his efforts to revolutionise the style and
content of the German film. This involved commissioning a number of

expensive prestige films and reintroducing the compulsory script censorship. The RMVP Film Department was enlarged and began interfering at every stage of the film production process. By 1941 their constant demands for alterations to films had led to the amount of negative exposed exceeding the length of the final cut by 25 times, in many cases, compared to an average of 11 times in 1939. By 1942 it had become clear that the war was going to continue for some time and there seemed every reason to suppose that shortages of labour and material would get worse. The principle of maximum studio utilisation, on which Winkler had based the film economy, had already been eroded and might soon collapse.

Film production could, of course, be continued on a reduced scale but that would be uneconomic and create difficulties after the war. In any case, Winkler and Goebbels insisted that the industry should be producing more films not less. German military success had given Germany the opportunity to establish itself as the leading film power on the continent. In order to consolidate this position it was necessary to produce more films and exploit the situation abroad in a systematic way. This could only be achieved if production was streamlined and administration and finance centralised so as to facilitate control over the European market. A necessary corollary was that the RMVP modify its policy and allow the production of more entertainment films which could be made with less supervision.[24]

This 'new order' of the film economy involved creating a single holding company with exclusive control over distribution of profits and future investment. Distribution and exhibition were 'neutralised' that is carried on by separate non-profit making companies. The existing state film companies were broken up and re-formed to function solely as production units. Studio utilisation both in Germany and the occupied West (the studio situation in the East was regarded as too uncertain to enable any concrete plans to be made) was centrally organised so as to make maximum use of foreign studios and imported labour. This arrangement appealed rather more to the RFM which was offered representation on the governing boards (*Aufsichtsräte*) of the key companies. The splitting of production and distribution simplified auditing and made it easier to spot over-expenditure. Winkler, for his part, claimed that he needed the participation of the RFM to 'stop the RMVP forming unsound companies.' It was also agreed that after a further loan of RM 120 million to buy cinemas in the occupied West, no more money would be provided by the RFM for the nationalised film industry. The new holding company, called *Ufa-Film GmbH* (Ufi) on Hitler's orders, was founded on 10 January 1942. The changes were announced by Goebbels in a speech on 28 February.

III

The speech in which Goebbels announced the formation of the Ufi was given to a selected audience of film makers and he spoke more frankly than usual.[25] Part of the speech consisted of the customary harangue against the prevalence of rumours and general irresponsibility in the film world together with exhortations to greater performance, but the core of the speech was a remarkable exposé on the programme of the New Order and its relevance to film making.[26]

Goebbels' basic theme was that the Ufi was the final realisation of National Socialist ideas in relation to film making. Instead of selfish competition for money and prestige the new system would encourage competition for the benefit of the community. It had been created at this juncture because it was only now that the film industry was being confronted with the real task imposed upon it by the National Socialist revolution. All that had gone before was merely the overture. Germany had temporary military control of most of Europe but in the long run this was meaningless unless a permanent cultural revolution was instituted in Europe similar to that instituted in Germany. This would involve deploying all the resources at Germany's disposal.

> I believe I can say with confidence that after the war we will be the richest nation on earth, and that it will at last be possible for us in our development to solve all the problems which have always frustrated us in the past, because our mental and geographical perspectives were simply too narrow and could not comprehend everything.
>
>   These problems arise, of course, in every area of life and do not just apply to the chemical industry, coal mining, or the iron and steel industry. It goes without saying that we cannot rule Europe economically if we do not also make ourselves supreme in the cultural field. Cultural hegemony, however, can only be achieved with the help of a large number of technical aids. And, in this respect, film is one of our major resources.

The first part of the above passage is a striking demonstration of how permanent and immutable the Nazi revolution was intended to be. Goebbels went on to demonstrate the scope of the revolution in which film had such an important part to play. It aimed to transform the language and consciousness of Europe and ultimately the world. Germany could not claim to be a world power until German had become an international language and the best propagators of the German language were radio and film.

This did not mean that the particular demands of Germany were to be ignored. At the end of 1941 Goebbels had been one of the first Nazi leaders to realise that the only chance of winning the war lay in the full scale mobilisation of Germany's resources. This would mean increasing hardship in the civilian sector. It would also mean that the average German would, for the first time, be 'living' the ideology of National Socialism. Consequently, there was less need to express that ideology in films. On the contrary, ordinary entertainment films, provided they were well made, would further the National Socialist revolution by providing relaxation and renewed strength for the workers who were a part of that revolution.

During the first two years of war resources had been concentrated on producing elaborate political films which had helped cement the Nazi revolution in Germany and gained prestige abroad. Now priorities had been changed. Production which had fallen to 60 films a year, was to be raised to 110 even though this would involve a reduction in the number of prestige films. This was the course dictated by circumstances inside Germany and in Europe as a whole.

Why was it so urgently necessary to establish a hold over the European film market at this stage? The impregnation of other European peoples with Nazi ideas must, of necessity, be a long term process; why not wait until after the war? Goebbels feared that the opportunity might not last. Throughout history, he claimed, the Germans had been chronically unable to use the opportunities which their natural virtues had won for them. One of the axioms of the leadership of the Third Reich was that it would not make the same mistakes as its predecessors.

The enemy against whom preparation had to be made was Hollywood. American films were just as effective propagators of American *Unkultur* as German films were of German *Kultur*. The previous summer Goebbels had seen some alarming evidence of the power of American *Unkultur* to corrupt even the indoctrinated youth of Germany.[27] Its influence over the youth of other European countries would be still more potent.

Goebbels naturally claimed that German films were superior to American but insisted that this meant little as long as the Germans were unable to match the Americans' technical, financial and industrial resources. He also pointed out that technological advance might lead to all kinds of problems which, at the moment, could not be foreseen. American films might be banned from countries controlled by Germany but they still circulated in neutral countries and could only be driven from these by superior business organisation and marketing methods backed up, of course, by a supply of suitable films. There was no question of forcing the peoples of Europe to live entirely on a diet of German films. After the war even small countries would have their own national cinemas but only German films would receive international distribution. The Ufi was the instrument with which German resources were to be co-ordinated with a view to building up such tight control over the European market that American films would be permanently excluded.

> Unknown to the public we are now building a film market in Europe so that when the decisive hour comes after the war we can confidently take up the struggle with America ... For this purpose I must naturally centralise resources for it is just as necessary in the development of films as in the military and other economic sectors.

IV

Goebbels' attempts to influence, and ultimately control, the European film market did not begin with the creation of the Ufi. Indeed they dated back to before the nationalisation of Ufa. The German film industry had always had an international outlook and it was not the Nazis who invented the idea that German films had a mission to foster a European film art distinct from that of Hollywood. Even when the cinema was at a comparatively primitive stage, German industrialists had tried to use films as cultural propaganda abroad.[28] In the 1920s Ufa had brought itself to the verge of ruin by over-straining its resources trying to gain too big a share in the American distribution market.[29] The arrival of the sound film, which confined film making in Scandinavia and Eastern Europe to small scale production for the domestic market, furthered Germany's international position because of German control of the *Tobis-Klangfilm* sound film patents.[30] Indeed, before 1933 one of the Nazis' main criticisms of German films was that they pandered too much to international taste.

In 1933 Goebbels, in one of his early speeches to the film makers, told them that they had been making a mistake trying to produce 'international' films. Instead they should give their films as strong a Germanic flavour as possible, since foreign audiences did not want to see mere imitations of their own films.[31] He was proved wrong

since German film exports declined after 1933. This was partly due to
the unpopularity of the Nazi regime abroad but it also reflected the fact
that Germany was becoming increasingly isolated both commercially and
artistically. Before 1933 the artistic world of Berlin had a highly international character. Artists from all over the world came to work in the
Berlin film studios. This was killed by the Third Reich. Business and
intellectual contacts were lost. The rate of emigration was highest
among German artists who had an international reputation. As a result,
German film making became inbred and lost touch with international
tastes and fashions.

   As compensation Goebbels undertook a programme of organisation
at the international level. In 1935 he staged an elaborate International
Film Congress in Berlin and proposed the formation of an International
Film Chamber whose primary task would be to develop the role of film
as a means of increasing international understanding. The Chamber was
inaugurated two years later in Paris with representatives from every
European country except Britain.[32] It did not, however, achieve a
great deal mainly because other European countries resented the fact
that it was all too clearly under German and Italian domination. The
Germans, however, did succeed in persuading the international federation of professional film writers (Fipresci) to accept a resolution not to
collaborate on films (especially newsreels) liable to prejudice international understanding (*Hetzfilme*). The point of this was that the
resolution only applied to member countries and, since the USSR was
not a member of Fipresci, did not apply to anti-communist films.[33] On
a more clandestine level, agents of the RFK attempted to interfere in
production in both Austria and Czechoslovakia before these countries
were physically occupied. This interference chiefly took the form of
organising, with the aid of local Nazis, boycotts of Jewish producers
and artists, especially those who had recently emigrated from Germany.
In the case of Austria, the Cautio obtained control of the Viennese
Tobis by their acquisition of shares in the parent company (Intertobis)
early in 1935.

   Following the *Anschluss*, the Austrian film industry was rapidly
incorporated into that of Germany. The German film censorship laws
and the RKK law became valid in Austria on 11 June 1938, and the
Viennese production companies were bought out and centralised into
another state film company, *Wien Film GmbH* by November 1938. A
similar state controlled German film company in Bohemia, *Prag Film
AG*, was established in November 1941.[34] The integration of the
Austrian film economy into that of Germany did not take place without

some disagreement. The trouble arose over the 'Aryanisation' of Austrian cinemas and is worth considering in some detail as it shows how Winkler's plans to run the expanding industry on a sound capitalist footing could clash with the atavistic ideas (and greed) of various Nazis, and also how the absorption of foreign film economies involved something more comprehensive and complicated than merely extending the censorship and nationalising and centralising production and distribution.

Austria was a special case in that it was intended to become a permanent part of Germany and one would expect its economy to have been as closely integrated as possible with that of the *Altreich*. On the other hand, Winkler's policy towards the Austrian cinemas was the same, in principle, as that which he adopted in all other countries occupied by Germany. In Germany the première cinemas were all owned by distributors but smaller cinemas were in private ownership and there was a general feeling that they should remain part of the independent, middle-class (*Mittelstand*) economy. Winkler therefore followed the policy in occupied countries (and where possible in neutral countries as well) of buying up key cinemas and either leaving the smaller ones in the possession of their original owners, or (as was generally the case in the occupied East) handing them over to trustees or 'commissars' with the ultimate intention of using them to provide a livelihood for disabled ex-servicemen. When the Ufi was formed, a new company, *Deutsche Filmtheatre GmbH* was created to expedite the buying up of key foreign cinemas and also run those cinemas in Germany which had belonged to the nationalised combines.

The Austrian film industry had never been able to produce more than a fraction of the number of films required for the Austrian market and consequently there had never been any attempt to restrict the number of foreign films which appeared on Austrian screens. Ever since 1933 it had been government policy in Germany to reduce the frequency with which exhibitors changed their programmes. The aim was to reach a point where German production could supply all the films required by the German market so as to make it possible to eliminate foreign films. By 1938 the ordinary German cinema changed its programme once a week. Many smaller Austrian cinemas changed theirs every two days. These relied on cheap, old, American films and could not afford to hire new German films. The 'Aryanisation' programme in Austria amounted at first to little more than 'smash and grab' by the local Nazis. This threatened to do serious harm to the Austrian economy as a whole but order was restored following the ap-

pointment of *Gauleiter* Josef Bürckel as 'Reich Commissar for the
Reintegration of Austria' (*Reichskommissar für die Wiedervereinigung
Österreichs*).

Bürckel, a veteran Nazi, considered himself responsible solely to
Hitler and paid little attention to the opinions of government bureaucrats in Berlin. In this respect he was typical of the people chosen by
Hitler to administer newly occupied territory. He introduced an 'Aryanisation' procedure for cinemas which was consistent with Nazi doctrine
but had little appeal for Winkler. The cinema was taken over by a Nazi
commissar who paid the former owner the site value of the property
and then sold it to a member of the Austrian NSDAP for its real value
based on an estimate of the cinema's annual turnover. The proceeds
from the sale went to a fund for financing Jewish emigration (!)[35] The
more powerful Nazis,including Bürckel and August Eigruber, the
Gauleiter of *Oberdonau*, earmarked the better cinemas for themselves
and even had plans to start their own distribution network.

This situation was potentially serious. Important cinemas were
passing into the hands of people who possessed neither experience nor
collateral. They would naturally demand that in view of local circumstances they should be allowed to hire films at reduced rates. If this
happened not only would the financial yield for the distribution
companies in Berlin be less than expected, but other *Gauleiter* in
Germany might imitate their Austrian colleagues. On the other hand,if
they were forced to pay the same rates as German exhibitors,the
majority of Austrian cinemas might well go bankrupt. Winkler, however,
had one important card. A number of première cinemas in the centre of
Vienna formed a company called the *Kino Betriebs Anstalt* (Kiba)
which was owned by the Viennese municipal authorities. These were not
involved in the 'Aryanisation ' programme but they were affected by
the laws of the RFK which prohibited the ownership of cinemas by
municipalities. Accordingly, Winkler urgently demanded money from
the RFM to buy these cinemas. His aim was then to buy, or exchange,
other cinemas so as to gain control of all the leading cinemas in
Vienna and other major Austrian towns. These cinemas would be able
to afford German rentals while the smaller cinemas would be thinned
out leaving only the more efficient ones in operation.

It was not until August 1938 that Winkler was able to persuade the
RFM to provide the necessary funds for the purchase of Kiba cinemas.[36]
As soon as this was agreed the Kiba was transformed into the Cautio-
owned *Ostmärkische Film Theaterbetriebs GmbH* (OFB),and on the
same day new RFK regulations on the hiring of films in Austria were

published.[37] These allowed Austrian cinemas to rent films at slightly
lower rates than those in Germany. Two weeks later the RFM advanced
further funds to enable the OFB to purchase cinemas outside Vienna.[38]
Complaints were soon received from Vienna which accused Winkler's
agents of trying to disrupt the whole 'Aryanisation' programme.[39]
Winkler replied that 'Aryanisation' did not mean the wholesale
looting of Jewish property.[40] Its real purpose was to replace an in-
efficient Jewish system with one that was efficient and 'culture worthy'
(*kulturwürdig*). In this case the leading cinemas were best managed by
experienced professionals with sufficient credit to see them through a
difficult period of transition. In March 1939 the 'cinema aryanisation'
programme in Austria was brought to a halt.[41] The Austrian NSDAP
was obliged to subsidise small cinemas that remained in Nazi hands
while the remainder were handed over to agents of the RFK.

Winkler and the RFK did not, however, enjoy a total victory. In
July 1943 Bürckel succeeded in creating his own cinema company in
Lothringen, former French territory, which he was responsible for
integrating into Germany. The cinemas were jointly owned by the
Gau and the local authorities and hence Bürckel's action was illegal. The
RFK does not, however, appear to have taken any action.[42] Austria was
exceptional in that Winkler had to contend with a strong, established,
local Nazi Party but the same kind of dispute occurred in Poland where
his policy as head of the *Haupttreuhandstelle Ost* [43] brought him into
conflict with the SS; and in occupied Russia, where Rosenberg's Ministry
for the Occupied Eastern Territories (RMbO) claimed responsibility for
cultural and propaganda matters. As far as the film industry was
concerned, Winkler's experience and the support he enjoyed from
Goebbels and Goering ensured that his views generally prevailed.

Apart from the aforementioned policy of buying up key cinemas,
policy towards the occupied countries in the East varied, partly for
ideological reasons, and partly because the countries had different assets.
In the Protectorate considerable use was made of the well appointed
Prague film studios which, until the creation of *Prag Film*, were used for
overspill production by the German state companies. Czech films
continued to be made by native companies though their numbers
dwindled. A Slovak film company was set up in Bratislava but it was
unable to begin serious production owing to lack of equipment.

In Poland, on the other hand, a determined attempt was made to
wipe out the Polish intelligentsia and in accordance with this, Polish film
production was stopped, cinemas confiscated, and admission to them
increasingly restricted to Germans.[44] Those cinemas which remained

open to the Poles showed German propaganda shorts, entertainment films, and the occasional pre-war Polish film. In Warsaw, considerable use was made of printing laboratories which supplied dubbed prints not merely for Poland, but subsequently, the whole occupied East. In order to minimise the risk of sabotage these remained under Polish management.[45]

The territories occupied following the invasion of the USSR were treated in much the same manner as Poland. In November 1941 Winkler formed yet another company, the *Zentralfilmgesellschaft Ost GmbH* (ZFO) to purchase cinemas, and take charge of studios in Riga, Reval and Kiev. Two subsidiary companies, *Ostland Film GmbH* and *Ukraine Film GmbH* distributed German films in their respective areas. There was some delay before the companies began to operate owing to disagreements between the RMbO and RMVP over how they should be administered. The Cautio eventually secured total ownership of the ZFO though the RMbO continued to be represented on the ZFO governing board.

Even after this differences of opinion continued. At a board meeting of *Ostland Film* in April 1942 Winkler's policy in the East was attacked by the RMVP representative, Eberhard Taubert, as too 'mercantile'. As far as Winkler was concerned the principal task in the East was to build up an efficient distribution and exhibition system whereas Taubert insisted on the 'primacy of the political task.'[46] In 1943 Taubert and the RMbO representatives at the ZFO initiated the production of a series of short anti-communist films.[47] These were primarily intended for Russian audiences though attempts were made to extend their distribution to neutral Europe. The films lost money and Winkler did everything in his power to have them stopped. He eventually succeeded by a somewhat roundabout method in March 1944 though shortly after this the Russian advances obliged the ZFO to suspend its operations.[48] In view of the circumstances prevailing in these areas the overall profits obtained from Eastern Europe were surprisingly high. In Poland, annual cinema attendance during the years of German occupation averaged 20 million. In 1942/3 ZFO receipts totalled RM 6.5 million and the total value of confiscated equipment was estimated at RM 7 million.[49]

German economic policy in the occupied West differed radically from that in the East. The peoples of France, Belgium, Holland and, especially, Scandinavia were thought to be racially superior to the Slav populations of the East and their economies were more sophisticated. In contrast to the wholesale confiscations which took place in the East, economic assets in the West were usually left in the possession of their owners, unless they were Jewish, with the intention that after the war they should continue to operate in a kind of 'common market' that was heavily biased in Germany's favour. This, at least, was how many German economists saw the situation and, as far as one can tell, Winkler thought along similar lines.

The occupied West offered greater opportunities to the German film industry than the East though there were difficulties involved in exploiting them. The regime imposed by the Germans varied from country to country: a military governor in France and Belgium, Reichscommissars in the Netherlands and Norway, a Reichsplenipotentiary in Denmark. The film markets of these countries also varied. France had the largest number of cinemas but many of these were rather primitive. There was a large film production centre in Paris, but there were also film studios in Nice and Marseilles. If French film production were to continue under German auspices it would be necessary to convince at least some of France's leading film makers that they would be better off working in Paris than in the unoccupied South. Belgium and Norway, by contrast, had no film industries of any significance apart from cinemas. The Netherlands, despite having fewer cinemas than Belgium, supported a thriving industry. This was already linked with Germany through the Tobis syndicate, and studios in Amsterdam and The Hague were frequently used by German companies before 1939. The Danish film industry which had once exercised great influence on Germany had declined since the coming of sound. Few Danish films had been shown abroad in the Thirties and the tastes of Danish audiences had grown out of touch with the rest of Europe. The neutral markets of Spain and Sweden, where German films had still to compete with American ones, contained more cinemas than any of the occupied countries except France.

In contrast to the East, where native film production was normally stopped, film production in Western occupied countries was allowed to continue, so it was necessary to introduce Nazi censorship and RKK legislation. The RMVP was, however, unable to introduce the script censorship in occupied France because the military governor demanded the final say in all matters of censorship. In the Netherlands, on the other hand, a 'Central Office for Public Enlightenment and Art' attached to the Reichscommissar was established as early as the end of May 1940. Comprehensive film censorship legislation based on that of Germany was enacted in August 1941.[50]

The RMVP had an easier time establishing organisations analogous to the RFK. Agents from the RFK were at work in Paris by the end of

June and in Amsterdam by the end of July 1940.[51] The idea of creating a French RFK had been gaining ground in France as a result of the missionary activities of the International Film Chamber. On 2 December 1940 the Vichy government set up the 'Organisation Committee for the Film Industry' (*Comité d'organisation de l'industrie cinématographique* (COIC). This was one of the Organisation Committees which had been formed in the Summer of 1940 to administer the economy in the unoccupied zone. The COIC was controlled by the Vichy government and had powers similar to the RFK including a script censorship.[52] Film production in the occupied zone remained subject to the military authorities who concerned themselves only with the finished film. In the Netherlands a 'Dutch Culture Chamber' was established on 25 September 1941 though it did not have such wide powers as the RKK.[53]

Winkler decided to leave Scandinavia to one side and concentrate on establishing German control as unobtrusively as possible in France, Belgium and Holland. As his agent he appointed the producer Alfred Greven who was entrusted with some RM 15.5 million to build up a camouflaged production and distribution network in this area. Greven based himself in Paris where in October 1940 he founded *Continental Film srl*. This company produced 30 feature films during the occupation[54] and by 1942 controlled some 60 cinemas. By 1943 Greven had invested RM 12.5 million in France and RM 2.8 million in Belgium and Holland in the purchasing of studios and cinemas.[55]

It seems that Greven's activities were intended as a stopgap measure to facilitate long term capital penetration of the West by the other state companies.[56] After 1940 Ufa began to reactivate their foreign subsidiaries, many of which had been dormant for several years, and Tobis founded a string of subsidiaries in both occupied and neutral Europe.[57] It was hardly practical to have the companies competing against each other so when the Ufi was formed the whole export programme was placed under the control of Ufa. The only exception were the studios in Holland which were placed at the disposal of the new *Berlin Film* and studios and cinemas in Paris which remained the responsibility of *Continental Film*.

The German film industry's investments in the occupied West recorded an overall loss in the early years of operation. This was regarded as temporary and it was assumed that in time the tendency of occupied peoples to boycott German films would be overcome. A report compiled in January 1945 estimated the loss in audience receipts caused by the Allied advance in the West to be RM 30 million.[58]

V

The 'new order' in the German film economy marked by the formation
of the Ufi lasted barely two and a half years. The demands of the war
economy had already curtailed production before August 1944 when
Goebbels' 'Total War' measures led to an even sharper cut back.
Initially, however, Winkler did succeed in increasing production though
not as much as he had hoped. This was largely because neither
the utilisation of foreign studios nor the importation of foreign labour
proved as effective as anticipated.[59] Even so, in January 1943, it was
planned to produce 120 films in the coming year[60] though this was later
recognised as unrealistic. As late as November 1944 it was still thought
feasible to produce 46 feature films in 1945 and at that stage there were
enough new films in various stages of completion to ensure a satisfactory supply to German cinemas.[61]

Looked at purely from the point of view of production output and
turnover there seems little doubt that Goebbels' and Winkler's plans
proved quite successful in the short time in which they were allowed to
function. The success of Nazi film policy cannot, however, be evaluated
solely in these terms. The purpose of building up a film monopoly in
Europe was to further the National Socialist revolution, not to make
money. It was easy enough to build up a European 'following' for
German films, audiences would see them since there was no alternative.
The real aim, however, was to make films which would both appeal to
foreign audiences who would see them in preference to others, and
make propaganda for the New Order.

At a conference in January 1944 a report was submitted by Fritz
Kaelber, General Manager of Ufa, which showed that Goebbels' dreams
were far from being realised.[62] On the credit side, Kaelber was able to
report that new German showpiece cinemas had opened at either end of
the Mediterranean, in Lisbon and Istanbul. German films were at last
making headway against American competition in certain important
neutral markets. Especially good progress had been recorded in Spain
and Portugal where the Americans had made the mistake of distri-
buting too many war films which were not popular in these countries.
In Zurich the Agfacolour film *Immensee* had broken all records by
running continuously for four months.

On the debit side too, few of Germany's new films were being
accepted for export by the censorship. Between 1 April 1943 and 6
January 1944, 54 new films had been submitted to the Ufa export
department. Of these, only six had been considered suitable for

universal international distribution. Eighteen had been passed for exhibition in certain countries, twenty had been considered 'usable under
certain conditions' and the remaining ten were thought to be totally
unsuitable for exhibition outside Germany.

Behind these disappointing figures lay the familiar story of departmental antagonisms and conflicting priorities. In 1940 the larger
cinemas in newly occupied territories were forced to show propaganda
films such as *Jud Süss* (anti-Semitic), *Ohm Krüger* (anti-British) and
Feuertaufe (*Luftwaffe* propaganda). This was criticised as premature
by Karl Hartle chief of production at *Wien Film*. He argued that it was
better to concentrate on building up a mass following for German films by
initially showing only the best available entertainment films and introducing the more tendentious products at a later stage.[63] The *Wehrmacht*
and the foreign office, Goebbels' arch enemies, endorsed Hartl's view,
though from different motives. The fact that screenings of *Jud Süss* led to
anti-semitic riots and lynchings in newly occupied territories was no
doubt gratifying to the RMVP but less welcome to the German
occupying authorities who were concerned to avoid civil disturbances
and diplomatic incidents. They naturally preferred that only the most
innocuous films should be shown until the situation had become more
stabilised. Goebbels was prepared to compromise to some extent but he
still preferred to show the more 'revolutionary' Nazi films whenever
possible. Consequently, he was often in dispute with the Foreign Office
whose cultural attachés in German embassies abroad claimed the right
to censor German films before they were exhibited in the country in
question. In the occupied East, the power of the SS presented a further
complication. Their representatives could take exception to films on
abstruse racial and ideological grounds which ordinary film makers
must have found difficult to comprehend let alone anticipate.[64]

The result was that the films chosen for unrestricted export were not
necessarily the best available but simply films to which no one was
likely to raise any objection. This at least is the most plausible explanation for the six titles thus chosen. The films in question were:

Das Lied der Nachtigall (The Song of the Nightingale)
Der weisse Traum (The White Dream)
Immensee
Titanic
Tonelli
Zwischen Nacht und Morgen (Between Night and Morning)

The strangest feature of this list is that two of the films (*Titanic* and

Zwischen Nacht und Morgen) had been banned from exhibition inside
Germany! Goebbels had found both of them too depressing.[65] It also
emerged that two of the films (*Das Lied der Nachtigall* and *Tonelli*) had
been made against the wishes of the official script editor (*Reichsfilmdramaturg*). Indeed these two films and *Der weisse Traum* were all
set in an artists' milieu, an escapist setting often used by scenarists of
the period because it minimised the risk of political complications.[66]

The report also indicated the type of films which were popular and
unpopular with foreign audiences. The popular films included any film
with a well known star, musical films, especially Viennese operettas, and
large scale fantasy pictures. The unpopular subjects included biographies
of obscure German heroes, peasant farces (bavarian style), *Heimat* (i.e.
'local colour') films, films dealing with politically sensitive subjects and
(especially) historical costume films.[67] With the exception of *Heimat*
films these were equally disliked by German audiences.

The report also listed the most popular stars. Here too there was
little discrepancy between foreign and domestic preferences though
foreign audiences tended to be more critical of the fact that too many
male leads were being played by actors who were much too old for
them. It was also thought to be a matter for concern that of the German cinema's six most popular female stars only one was German, and
she had been born in Austria.[68] Kaelber concluded by suggesting that
more attention should be paid to these points during the planning and
casting of new films. No one disagreed, although a plea that some young
male actors might be released from active service was turned down as
being totally impossible at the present time.

This report indicates very clearly how Winkler and his colleagues
viewed the subject of film exports and how far their ideas differed from
the official policy of the RMVP. There was nothing in any of Kaelber's
assumptions and conclusions that would have been out of place in a
report by a Ufa executive of 1917 or 1929. Successful exporting was a
matter of finding out what was in demand and adjusting output accordingly, even if that involved filling the vacuum left by the withdrawal
of American films by producing German films which might equally well
have been made in Hollywood. It is clear that Goebbels' ideas on the
subject had proved to be misconceived. In 1933 he had argued that the
key to international success was to develop a cinema with a characteristic national identity. In February 1942 he had predicted that the
German film would play its part in the spiritual rebirth of Europe by
replacing the alien, Jewish, products of Hollywood by films that would
be both grounded in the spirit of European civilisation and be popular

with mass audiences. In the event, the only successful types of film which had come to be associated with Germany were those for which the German cinema had established a reputation before 1933. Considering Goebbels' predilection for didactic costume pictures it was rather ironical that the only costume films which had proved popular were Viennese operettas – a 'bourgeois' genre *par excellence* which Goebbels, by all accounts, detested.[69]

It would perhaps be unwise to exaggerate the extent to which Goebbels' policies had been repudiated. He was a realist who must have been aware that there was no point in trying to force people to attend films they found distasteful and that the creation of German supremacy over the European film market must, of necessity, be a long term process. He also had to contend with serious practical difficulties: opposition from within the NSDAP and certain government departments, the unpopularity of the Nazi regime abroad, and the difficulties of producing any films at all under wartime conditions. If Germany's political and military control over Europe had been sustained then it may well be that Nazi style films would have found a wider acceptance. All the same, if one judges purely on results one can only conclude that Goebbels had been much too optimistic about the conquest of the European film market and that the predictions he made in 1933 and 1942 had not been fulfilled.

What light does this throw on the nature of the New Order? There seems little doubt that Goebbels' plans for the domination of the European film market were comprehensive and intended to be permanent. His priorities are less obvious because, like Hitler, he was obliged by circumstances to adjust his policies. It is simplistic to conclude that just because the economic imperialist aspect of Nazi film policy was successful and its ideological programme a failure, Nazism was simply monopoly capitalism under a new name and Goebbels' revolutionary pretensions merely a sham. Just as early in 1942 the long term policies of the New Order of the European economy were increasingly subordinated to the short term demands of the German war economy so Goebbels, at roughly the same time, was compelled to place his 'film revolution' in cold storage and allow the production of routine entertainment films to become a priority. The evidence, however, is that this was merely temporary. His diary shows that he was unhappy about the extent to which capitalist practices flourished in the state film industry[70] and after July 1944 he at last allowed the RMVP Film Department to virtually destroy Winkler's system in favour of one that was considered more in the spirit of

National Socialism.[71]

It seems more correct to say that Goebbels made use of Winkler because he wanted quick results and that the success of Winkler's methods obscured the antithesis between the capitalist and revolutionary fascist aspects of Nazi policy towards the film industry. In this respect the state film industry reflected the tensions of the Third Reich as a whole.

Notes

1. As Tim Mason has pointed out it was a cardinal tenet of Nazi ideology to assert the primacy of politics over that of economics. See T. Mason, 'Der Primat der Politik – Politik und Wirtschaft im Nationalsozialismus', *Das Argument* 41 (8 Jahrgang, Heft 6, December 1966), pp. 473-4. Whether this was true in reality is, of course, another matter. See the discussion in *Das Argument* 47 (10 Jahrgang, Heft 3, July 1968): Eberhard Czichon, 'Der Primat der Industrie im Kartell der nationalsozialistischen Macht, ' pp. 168-92: Tim Mason, 'Primat der Industrie? Eine Erwiderung', pp. 193-209; and Dietrich Eichholtz and Kurt Gossweiler, 'Noch einmal Politik und Wirtschaft 1933-1945', pp. 210-27. It has to be borne in mind that Hitler understood 'politics' to include artistic and cultural matters.
2. cf. A.S. Milward, *The Fascist Economy in Norway* (Oxford, 1972), p. 291.
3. The significance of the New Order for the various theories of fascism has been comprehensively discussed by Milward, op. cit., pp. 290 ff., though he concentrates on economic factors.
4. Hitler acknowledged this on the eve of the invasion of the USSR saying that the striving for German autarky had gone too far. A.S. Milward, *The New Order and the French Economy* (Oxford, 1970), p. 31.
5. The aspects of National Socialist ideology which determined the Third Reich's policy towards the feature film (as distinct from the short film and newsreel) are discussed in M.S.Phillips, *The German Film Industry and the Third Reich*, unpublished PhD thesis, University of East Anglia, 1974, pp. vii-xxv.
6. It was on Goebbels' orders that film production continued in Germany into 1945. He insisted on allocating scarce war materials priority so that the Agfacolour film *Kolberg* could be completed.
7. This is the formulation of Gerd Albrecht, *Nationalsozialistische Filmpolitik. Eine soziologische Untersuchung über die Spielfilme des Dritten Reiches* (Stuttgart, 1969), p. 303. It takes account of the fact that the overt propaganda content of feature films produced in the Third Reich varied greatly from film to film and from year to year.
8. Details of the various organisational measures of the RMVP and RFK can be found in W. Becker, *Film und Herrschaft. Organisationsprinzipien und Organisationsstrukturen der nationalsozialistischen Filmpropaganda* (West Berlin, 1973) and its companion volume, J. Spiker, *Film und Kapital. Der Weg der deutschen Filmwirtschaft zum nationalsozialistischen Einheitskonzern* (West Berlin, 1975).
9. The proportion of total income which Ufa derived from film exports declined from 30 per cent in 1932/3 to 10 per cent in 1935/6 and 5 per cent in 1938/9. Bundesarchiv Koblenz (BA), R2 (*Akten des Reichsfinanz-*

278 The German Film Industry and the New Order

ministeriums) /4799, *Denkschrift über die Notwendigkeit steuerfreier Sonderrücklagen in der Filmwirtschaft* (October 1939).

10. Ufa (Universum Film AG) had been founded in November 1917 on the initiative of Ludendorff as a distribution combine incorporating most of the leading German film companies and the Danish Nordisk Film. The Cautio purchased control of the company from Hugenberg who had owned it since April 1927.

11. Tobis (Tobis Tonbild Syndikat AG) was the German subsidiary of the Dutch International Tobis Matschappij nV (Intertobis). Originally a cartel of sound film patent holders, by 1936 Tobis distributed more films in Germany than Ufa though it was unwieldy and undercapitalised. The Cautio had held a controlling interest in Intertobis since 1935.

12. For Winkler's career see the works of Becker and Spiker cited above. Also O.J. Hale, *The Captive Press in the Third Reich* (Princeton, 1964), pp. 127 ff.

13. Tobis, Terra and Bavaria were transformed into private companies and reorganised.

14. BA R2/4790, *RFM Aktenvermerk*, 25 April 1938.

15. Thus the RMVP was represented by the Budget Department not the Film Department.

16. The RMVP Film Department and the various NSDAP film organisations wanted the film industry to be organised on totally different lines. For a summary of their ideas see Phillips, op. cit., pp. 166-7.

17. Hitler later decided that the studio should include a hall with an area of 20,000 square metres which would have been the largest film studio ever built. Goebbels objected, claiming that a studio of 2,000 square metres was the largest size compatible with efficiency. Hitler overrode these objections so Winkler tried to persuade him that if such a construction had to be built it made better sense to site it in Berlin. Hitler insisted that the studio be built in Munich but added that he had no objection if Winkler wanted to build one of equal proportions in Berlin! BA R2/4281, *Niederschrift der Bavaria Filmkunst Aufsichtsratssitzung*, 4 October 1938.

18. The outbreak of war stopped the building programme though Hitler did not forget his projects. In March 1941 he ordered that plans for the première cinema be redesigned so as to include a bomb proof auditorium capable of seating 3,600 people. BA R2/4826, *Geschäftsbericht der Deutsche Lichtspielbau GmbH*, 23 May 1941.

19. According to Speer, Hitler thought his building projects would ultimately pay for themselves by attracting tourists. A. Speer, *Inside the Third Reich* (London, 1970), pp. 140-1.

20. Even after the Cautio had acquired a substantial majority holding in the film companies Winkler still insisted on buying every possible share out of private ownership.

21. For details see Becker, op. cit., pp. 176-9.

22. BA R109 (Akten der Ufa-Film GmbH in Liquidation) 431, *Die Reichsbeteiligung in der deutschen Filmwirtschaft, Rechnungshofbericht X2-5/44*, Potsdam, 8.V.1943), p. 17, also BA R2/4809, *Bericht für den Tobis Filmkunst Aufsichtsrat*, 3 December 1940, p. 16.

23. Feature film production in 1940/1 declined by 29 per cent compared to 1939/40. Average preparation and shooting time increased by 170 per cent. BA R2/4792, *RFM Vermerk (11.V.1942) über die Winklerische Ausarbeitung 'Die deutsche Filmwirtschaft im Kriege.'* This has served as a basis for the following paragraph.

24. BA R2/4792, *RFM Aktenvermerk über eine Besprechung in Filmfragen*, 21

October 1941. For further details of the negotiations leading up to the creation of Ufi and the final structure of the company see Becker, op. cit., pp. 184 ff., and Spiker, op. cit., pp. 200 ff.

25. This does not prove that the views expounded in the speech necessarily represent Goebbels' real opinions at the time. They seem, however, to correspond with those expressed in his diary. See Phillips, op. cit., pp. 307-15.

26. The full text of the speech (reproduced from an original *Führermaschine* copy in the Deutsches Institut für Filmkunde, Wiesbaden) was first published by Albrecht, op. cit., pp. 484-500. Only a very brief summary was published at the time.

27. See H.P. Bleuel, *Das saubere Reich* (Bern & Munich, 1972), pp. 279-80.

28. A curious, not to say cynical, example of how German industrialists hoped to benefit from *Kulturpropaganda* was the suggestion, in 1914, by Ludwig Klitzsch (later General Manager of Ufa) that films publicising German social welfare schemes should be made for distribution in America. He thought this would encourage American workers to demand similar benefits from their employers thereby undermining the capacity of American industry to compete with Germany for world markets! Spiker, op. cit., p. 249, note 43.

29. Via the 'Parufamet' contracts, ibid., pp. 42-3.

30. Tobis patents covered the production of sound film, Klangfilm patents its reproduction. The latter were owned by German electrical firms and remained in private ownership after Tobis was nationalised. In 1930 representatives of the American and German/Dutch sound film patent holders met in Paris and agreed to divide the world (!) into two zones in which each would have monopoly rights with a third zone open to competition. The so-called 'Paris Agreements' gave the German-Dutch cartel a monopoly in Eastern Europe and Scandinavia.

31. 'If an American sees a German film he doesn't want to see a film that could equally well have been made in America. If he sees a German film he wants to see something typically German.' From a speech on 20 May 1933, reproduced in Albrecht, op. cit., pp. 442-7.

32. The Americans objected to the *International Film Kammer* on the grounds that it was an attempt to block the free distribution of American films in Europe. Events showed that their suspicions were justified. The official reason for Britain's refusal to join was that the British industry had closer links with America than Europe. *Kinematograph Weekly*, 8 July 1937, p.16.

33. BA R56 VI (*Akten der RFK*)/15, *Olimsky to Weidemann: Bericht über die Wiener Tagung der Fipresci*, 20 January 1937.

34. For details see Becker, op. cit., pp. 168-70.

35. BA R2/4825, *RFM Aktenvermerk*, 29 August 1938.

36. Ibid., 22 August 1938.

37. H. Tackmann (ed.), *Filmhandbuch als ergänzbare Sammlung herausgeben von der RFK (Loseblattausgabe)* (Berlin, 1938 ff.), VI C 2a *Anordnung zur Regelung der Filmvermietung im Lande Oesterreich für die Übergangszeit Verleihjahr 38/39*, 4 August 1938.

38. BA R2/4825, RFM *Aktenvermerk,* 29 August 1938.

39. ibid., *Der Staatskommissar in der Privatwirtschaft und Leiter der Vermögensverkehrsstelle . . . in Wien to Winkler*, 17 November 1938.

40. ibid., *Winkler to Staatskommissar . . . in Wien*, 24 November 1938.

41. ibid., *Lehnich (RFK President) to Bürckel*, 14 March 1939.

42. BA R2/4792, *RFM Aktenvermerk*, 5 July 1943. Cf. also *The Goebbels Diaries* (London, 1948), p. 127: diary entry for 19 April 1942.

43. The *Haupttreuhandstelle Ost* was a subordinate agency of the Four Year Plan organisation and responsible for the administration of confiscated

Jewish and Polish property.

44. Czech film production in Prague declined from 41 feature films in 1939 to 31 in 1940, 21 in 1941 and 11 in 1942. J. Havelka, *Filmwirtschaft in Böhmen und Mahren* (Prague, 1943).
45. For further details see Becker, op. cit., pp. 213 ff.
46. ibid., p. 217. On the career of Taubert see J.W. Baird, *The Mythical World of Nazi War Propaganda* (University of Minnesota Press, 1974), p. 21.
47. cf. J. Wulf, *Theater und Film im Dritten Reich* (Gütersloh, 1964), p. 318.
48. The film production unit of the ZFO was transferred to the *Ufa Sonderproduktion GmbH* over which Winkler had closer control. See Becker, op. cit., pp. 122 and 217.
49. Becker, op. cit., p. 217.
50. G. Hoffmann, *NS – Propaganda in den Niederlanden* (Munich and West Berlin, 1972), pp. 241-6.
51. BA R56 VI/2, *RFK Fachgruppenleitersitzungen*, 24 June 1940 and 29 July 1940.
52. Of the 220 feature films made in France during the occupation only 3 were banned after the war as Nazi propaganda. See 'Le cinéma des années noires' in L'Avant-Scène: Cinéma, Nos. 127/8, pp. 81-6.
53. Hoffmann, op. cit., pp. 180 ff.
54. Greven tried to initiate a more 'nationalist' type of film. This met with Goebbels' disapproval. See Goebbels' Diary entries for 15 May 1942 and 19 May 1942, op. cit., pp. 160 and 165.
55. Becker, op. cit., p. 219.
56. In 1943 Winkler tried unsuccessfully to purchase control of the two leading French film companies, Gaumont and Pathé.
57. Between June 1940 and June 1941 Tobis liquidated their subsidiary in Warsaw and founded new ones in Amsterdam, Brussels, Zurich, Madrid, Bucharest and Zagreb. Between June 1942 and March 1942 they founded further subsidiaries in Stockholm, Copenhagen and Sofia.
59. The reasons for this are discussed in Phillips, op. cit., pp. 370-3.
60. BA R109/9, *Ufi Firmen- und Produktionschefssitzung*, 22 January 1943.
61. Phillips, op. cit., p. 400.
62. Privatarchiv Dr Gerd Albrecht, Cologne: *Niederschrift über die von dem Reichsbeauftragten für die deutsche Filmwirtschaft einberufene Sitzung vom 14 Januar 1944: Punkt 1 der Tagesordnung 'Auslandsfilme', Berichter: Generaldirektor Kaelber.*
63. BA R2/4817, *Wien-Film Aufsichtsratssitzung*, 28 November 1940.
64. For example see the SS objections to *Die goldene Stadt* reproduced in Wulf, op. cit., p. 317.
65. *Titanic,* an anti-British (and anti-capitalist) film on the sinking of the 'Titanic' was apparently banned because it was feared that German audiences would see a parallel between the fate of the liner and the Third Reich. This view had some justification since in March 1945 a current joke likened the Propaganda Ministry to the orchestra of a sinking ship.

Goebbels' comments on *Zwischen Nacht und Morgen* (unpublished diary entry for 2 November 1943) are of interest since they show that (at this stage of the war at least) he did not personally approve the script of every film as some writers have claimed!

This evening I saw a new Ufa film *Zwischen Nacht und Morgen*, which deals almost entirely with the psychology of a blind person. The film is horrible – three quarters of the scenes are in hospital wards and operating theatres. I have warned the Production Chiefs time and time again to avoid this kind of setting.

66. At a meeting of the chiefs of the Ufi production companies in January 1943, Hippler, the head of the RMVP Film Department complained that, 'Granted that political considerations limit the choice of subject, that is no reason to set every other film in the milieu of artists, doctors, circuses and rich business men.' He recommended that writers should concentrate on hitherto neglected subjects such as 'radio, journalism and family stories.' BA R109/9, *Ufi Firmen- und Produktionschefssitzung*, 22 January 1943.

67. 'Historical and costume films such as *Der liebe Augustine, Kameraden, Komödianten, Paracelsus*, have been resounding failures.'

68. Viz: Jenny Jugo. The other five were Marika Rökk (Hungarian), Ilse Werner (Dutch), Zarah Leander and Kristina Söderbaum (Swedish) and Hilde Krahl (Yugoslav).

69. In 1940-2 a large proportion of the resources of the state companies had been lavished on the production of elaborate costume films in which the heroes had been diverse historical characters (Schiller, Carola Neuber, Paracelsus, Frederick the Great, Rembrandt) portrayed as genii who perceived that they were living at a time when one age was giving way to another. The overall implication of these films was that historical progress only comes about through the visions of such people for whom the normal laws of human conduct do not apply. The relevance to Hitler and the New Order was obvious enough. It was this type of film which Kaelber dismissed as 'resounding failures.'

70. cf. his (unpublished) diary entry for 13 April 1942, 'We have been too timid in our approach to the cinema and have allowed the difficulties made by the film capitalists to hinder us from taking the necessary measures.'

71. See Becker, op. cit., pp. 222-6.

GLOSSARY AND ABBREVIATIONS

ADGB	Allgemeiner Deutscher Gewerkschafts-bund – General Federation of German Trade Unions
AG	Arbeitsgemeinschaft der nord-und westdeutschen Gauleiter der NSDAP – Working Group of the Northern and Western German Gauleiter of the NSDAP (1925-26)
AG	Aktiengesellschaft – Joint stock company whose shares are publicly transacted
Altherrenverband	Alumni association
Altreich	The territory of the German Reich prior to the annexation of Austria in 1938
Amtmann	Middle-ranking civil service official
Amtsbezirk	An administrative unit, and the Oldenburg equivalent of the Prussian Regierungsbezirk – see below
Amtshauptmann	The senior administrative official of an Amtsbezirk (see above), and the Oldenburg equivalent of a Regierungs-präsident in Prussia
Der Angriff	Goebbels' Party newspaper in Berlin – founded in 1927
Anschluss	The incorporation of Austria into the German Reich in 1938
ANSt	Arbeitsgemeinschaft nationalsozialisti-scher Studentinnen – Working Group of National Socialist Girl Students
Arbeitsamt	Employment Office
Arbeitsbeschaffung	Work Creation
Arbeitsdienst	The National Labour Service (Reichs-arbeitsdienst) headed by Konstantin Hierl
AStA	Allgemeiner Studenten-Ausschuss –

	General Students' Union Council of which there was a branch at every German university
Aufbau	Munich-based society dedicated to fostering Russo-German relations in the early 1920s
Auf gut Deutsch	An extreme, anti-semitic Munich newspaper of the early 1920s and edited by Dietrich Eckart
BA	Bundesarchiv (Koblenz)
Bavarian People's Party	Bayerische Volkspartei (BVP) – the main party in Bavaria before 1933 and closely linked to the Centre Party (see below)
Bay. HSA:ASA	Bayerisches Hauptstaatsarchiv: Allgemeines Staatsarchiv
Bay. HSA:GSA	Bayerisches Hauptstaatsarchiv: Geheimes Staatsarchiv
Bay. HSA:SAM	Bayerisches Hauptstaatsarchiv: Staatsarchiv München
BDC	Berlin Document Center
Beamte	The term used to distinguish the civil servant proper
Beamtenstaat	The concept of a highly structured civil service integrated with the political orientation of the state
Berliner Arbeiterzeitung	One of the principal newspapers published by the Kampfverlag (see below)
Berliner Börsenzeitung	Right-wing, pro-business newspaper
Berufsbeamtentum	Professional civil service
Bezirksführer	District leader of the NSDAP
Bischöflichen Offizial	A senior official of the Catholic Church, and the representative of the Bishop in a particular area
Black Front	Popular name for Otto Strasser's Kampfgemeinschaft revolutionärer Nationalsozialisten (Combat Group of Revolutionary National Socialists)
Black Reichswehr	Illegal army formations of the early 1920s

Bodenpolitik	Territorial policy; the policy of territorial aggrandisement pursued by Hitler
Brechung der Zinsknechtschaft des Geldes	Breaking of Interest Slavery; a theory popularised by Gottfried Feder
Brigadeführer (SS)	The SS equivalent of a Brigadier in the British Army
Bund Bayerischer Kapitalklein-Rentner	Association of Bavarian Small Savers
Bund deutscher Mädel (BdM)	League of German Girls; the girls' branch of the Hitler Youth
Bund Oberland	Right-wing, paramilitary organisation in pre-1923 Bavaria
Bund Reichskreigsflagge	Bavarian rightist paramilitary group which was banned at the same time as the NSDAP after the 1923 Putsch
Bürgerbräukeller	The famous Munich beer hall from which the 'National Revolution' was launched by Hitler in November 1923
Bürgermeister	Mayor of a medium-sized town or smaller community
Centre Party	The main Catholic party of the Weimar era
COIC	Comité d'organisation de l'industrie cinématographique – Organisation Committee for the Film Industry
DAF	Deutsche Arbeitsfront – German Labour Front, established in 1933 following the Nazi dissolution of the trade union movement. Dr Robert Ley headed the DAF
DAP	Deutsche Arbeiterpartei – German Workers' Party, the immediate predecessor of the NSDAP
Der Deutsche	Christian trade union newspaper
Deutsches Frauenschaffen	Nazi women's publication (post-1933)
Deutsches Frauenwerk (DFW)	German Women's Service – the national women's organisation in the Third Reich
Deutsche Hauswirtschaft	'German Housekeeping'; women's magazine published by the Reichs-

	frauenführung (see below)
Deutscher Kampfbund zur	German Combat Association for the
Brechung der Zinsknechtschaft	Breaking of Interest Slavery, set up by
	Gottfried Feder in 1920
Deutscher Sozialist	Nuremberg-based organ of the DSP
	(see below)
Deutsch-Sozialistische Partei	German Socialist Party; an early rival
(DSP)	of the NSDAP with which it event-
	ually merged at the end of 1922
Deutschvölkischer Schutz-und	German Racist-Nationalist Protective
Trutzbund	and Offensive Association; large anti-
	semitic organisation (1918-22)
Deutsche Volksschule	Non-denominational state school in
	the Third Reich
Deutschlands Erneuerung	Racist and Pan-German periodical of
DHV	the 1920s Deutschnationaler Hand-
	lungsgehilfenverband – German Nation-
	al Union of Commercial Employees.
DNVP	Deutschnationale Volkspartei –
	German National People's Party – the
	main political organisation of the
	conservative-nationalist right until
	decimated by the NSDAP
DSt	Deutsche Studentenschaft – German
	National Students' Union
DVFP	Deutschvölkische Freiheitspartei –
	German Racist-Nationalist Freedom
	Party; leading völkisch political
	organisation (1922-8)
Ellenbogenraum	'Elbowroom'; a slogan used by the
	Pan-German League
Feme	Term applied to the murderous
	activities of right-wing extremists in
	early Weimar who took the law into
	their own hands in punishing alleged
	'traitors' who had informed on
	German violations of the Versailles
	Treaty's disarmament clauses
Fipresci	Fédération internationale de la presse
	cinématographique – International
	Federation of Professional Film

	writers
Frankfurter Zeitung	The leading liberal newspaper of the Weimar era
Franz Eher Verlag	The official publishing house of the NSDAP
Frauenkultur im Deutschen Frauenwerk (FK)	Women's magazine
Führer	Leader. Hitler's title as head of the National Socialist Movement
Führerprinzip	Leader-principle
Gau	The main regional administrative unit of the NSDAP party organisation
Gauleiter	Regional Leader of the NSDAP
Gauleitung	Regional headquarters of the NSDAP
Gemeindewahl	Municipal election
Generalstaatsanwälte	Public Prosecutors
Gereke-Circle	Headed by Dr Günther Gereke, the group promoted reformist-conservative economic ideas in 1932 and was closely identified with General von Schleicher's politics
Gestapo	Geheime Staatspolizei – Secret State Police
GLAK	Generallandesarchiv Karlsruhe
Gleichschaltung	'Co-ordination'; the term applied to the destruction of oppositional and non-National Socialist groups after 1933, and the subsequent institution of a National Socialist monopoly in German organisational life
GmbH	Gesellschaft mit beschränkter Haftung – Limited liability company
Grossdeutsche Volksgemeinschaft	Greater German People's Community – one of the National Socialist splinter groups in 1924/5
Grossrussland	A 'Greater Russia', comprising non-Russian as well as Russian peoples
Gruppe (SA)	Administrative or territorial unit
Gruppenführer (SA)	Rank equivalent to a Major-General in the British Army
Guelph	Term descriptive of the movement for the restoration of the Guelph dynasty

	and independence for Hanover. The Deutsch-Hannoversche Partei (DHP) was popularly known as the 'Guelphs'
HA – Hauptarchiv der NSDAP	Nazi Party archives
Hauptamtsleiter	Leader of a Main Department in the NSDAP party organisation
Hauptverein der Gustav-Adolf-Stiftung	The main German Protestant missionary association
Hessenhammer	NSDAP newspaper of Gau Hesse-Darmstadt
HHW	Hessisches Hauptstaatsarchiv Wiesbaden
Hitler Youth (HJ)	The youth group of the NSDAP, and later the official youth organisation of the Third Reich
HStAD	Hauptstaatsarchiv Düsseldorf
IfZ	Institut für Zeitgeschichte (Munich)
International Film Kammer	International Film Chamber
Jungvolk	Deutsches Jungvolk – German Young Folk, the junior branch of the Hitler Youth
Kamaradschaft	Political training cell of the NSDStB (see below)
Kampfbund	Deutscher Kampfbund – German Combat League; an association of Bavarian right-wing extremist organisations set up in autumn 1923
Kampfverlag	The radical NSDAP publishing house in Berlin owned by the Strasser brothers
Kampfzeit	The 'period of struggle' before the NSDAP came to power in 1933
Kiba	Kino Betriebs Anstalt (Vienna)
KPD	Kommunistische Partei Deutschlands – German Communist Party
Kreis	Administrative unit of the NSDAP; the principal sub-division of a Gau. Also denotes an electoral district
Kreisleiter	District leader of the NSDAP responsible for the administration of a Kreis (see above)
Kreisleitung	District headquarters of the NSDAP
Kultur	civilisation
Kultur-Erziehung-Schulung	The name of a section of the DFW (see

	above) with responsibility for cultural-educational training
Kulturkampf	'Clash of Civilisations'; the struggle between the Catholic Church and the Bismarckian state during the 1870s and 1880s
KVP	Konservative Volkspartei – Conservative People's Party
Labour Front	See under DAF
Labour Service	See under Arbeitsdienst
Land (pl. Länder)	Province or state – there were fifteen German Länder 1918-33
Landesinspekteur	Provincial Inspector; the new administrative post created by Gregor Strasser in 1932
Landtag	State legislature
LAS	Landesarchiv Speyer
LC	Library of Congress, Washington DC
Lebensraum	'Living Space'. Denotes National Socialist expansionist policies in Eastern Europe, primarily at Russia's expense
Luftwaffe	German Air Force
Machtpolitik	Power Politics; a policy based on strategic considerations, or a policy of inflexibility
Machtübernahme	'Assumption of Power' by the NSDAP in 1933. This term was generally preferred by the National Socialists to 'Machtergreifung', or 'seizure of power'
Mic. Alex.	Microfilm collection at Alexandria, Virginia
Mittelstand	Traditional, independent middle class
Münchener Neueste Nachrichten	The leading liberal Munich daily newspaper before 1933
Münchener Post	Influential Social Democratic daily newspaper in Munich (pre-1933)
Mutter und Volk	'Mother and Nation' – women's magazine published by the Reichsfrauenführung (see below)
Nachrichtendienst der	The official newsletter of that organ-

Reichsfrauenführung	isation and an official magazine of both the NSF (see below) and the DFW (see above)
Der Nationale Sozialist	Newspaper published by the Kampfverlag
Nationalsozialistische Briefe	'National Socialist Letters', established by Gregor Strasser in 1925 as the organ of the Arbeitsgemeinschaft der nord-und westdeutschen Gauleiter der NSDAP
Nationalsozialer Volksbund (NSVB)	National Social People's Association; founded by Anton Drexler following his separation from Hitler in 1925
Neuaufbaugesetz	Important legislative measure relating to the civil service (1934)
NHStA	Niedersächsisches Hauptstaatsarchiv, Hannover & Pattensen
NSBO	Nationalsozialistische Betriebszellen-organisation – National Socialist Factory Cell Organisation
NSDAP	Nationalsozialistische Deutsche Arbeiterpartei – National Socialist German Workers' Party (Nazi Party)
NSDStB	Nationalsozialistischer Deutscher Studentenbund – National Socialist German Students' Association
NSF	NS-Frauenschaft – National Socialist Women's League – the élite women's organisation in the Third Reich
NS-Frauenwarte	The official magazine of the NSF (see above)
NS-Korrespondenz	Official NSDAP publication
NSLB	Nationalsozialistischer Lehrerbund – National Socialist Teachers' Association
NS-Schwesternschaft	National Socialist Sisterhood; the Nazi nursing corps, and commonly referred to as the 'Brown Sisters'
NS-Studentenkampfhilfe	National Socialist Students' Combat Auxiliary; a fund-raising association of university alumni supporting the NSDStB set up in 1931

NStAO	Niedersächsisches Staatsarchiv Oldenburg
NSV	Nationalsozialistische Volkswohlfahrt — National Socialist Public Welfare Organisation led by Erich Hilgenfeldt
Oberbürgermeister	Lord Mayor (of a large town or city)
Oberlandesgerichtspräsident	The senior judge of a regional court of appeal
Oberleutnant	First Lieutenant
Obersekretär	Principal secretary (civil service rank)
Oberstleutnant	Lieutenant-Colonel (British Army equivalent)
Oberste Parteirichter	Supreme Party Judge; the title given to the head of the Oberste Parteigericht — the Supreme Party Court (successor to Uschla — see below)
Obersturmbannführer (SS)	SS equivalent of a Lieutenant-Colonel in the British Army
OFB	Ostmärkische Film Theaterbetriebs GmbH
Offizial	See under Bischöflichen Offizial
Ortsgruppe	Local branch of the NSDAP
Ostmark	Old Germanic name for Austria
Ostpolitik	'Eastern Policy'; a term which became current during the First World War, denoting German diplomatic strategy in Eastern Europe
Ostsiedlung	'Settlement in the East'; the policy of settling Germans in Eastern Europe
Personalunion	The holding of positions of a similar nature in different organisations to provide continuity and uniformity of policy
PO	Politische Organisation — Political Organisation. The general term for the NSDAP's party administration after the Strasser affair in December 1932
PRO	Public Record Office (London)
Programmatiker	Ideologist/thinker
Promi	The customary National Socialist abbreviation for the RMVP (see below)

Raumpolitik	National Socialist policy of territorial expansion
Regierungsbezirk	The administrative sub-division of a Prussian province
Regierungspräsident	Rank of the senior administrative official in a Regierungsbezirk
Das Reich	A leading newspaper of the Third Reich
Reichsbank	Imperial Central Bank (Berlin)
Reichsbanner	Reichsbanner Schwarz-Rot-Gold; set up in 1924 as the paramilitary organisation of the SPD, Centre and Democratic Parties. By the early 1930s, however, it was more closely identified with the SPD
Reichsbund der Deutschen Beamten	National Association of German Civil Servants — the official civil servants' organisation in the Third Reich
Reichsbund der höheren Beamten	National Association of Senior Civil Servants
Reichsfrauenführerin	National Women's Leader, the title conferred on Gertrud Scholtz-Klink in November 1934
Reichsfrauenführung	National Women's Leadership, set up in 1936
Reichsführer-SS	Reich Leader of the SS; Himmler's title as head of the SS
Reichskanzlei	The chancery of the Reich Chancellor of which Heinrich Lammers was head
Reichsleitung der NSDAP	The National Directorate of the NSDAP
Reichsministerium für Wissenschaft, Erziehung und Volksbildung	Reich Ministry for Knowledge, Education and Popular Enlightenment
Reichsmütterdienst	National Mothers' Service — a section of the Reichsfrauenführung
Reichsorganisationsleiter der NSDAP	National Organisation Leader of the NSDAP
Reichsparteitag	National Party Rally (of the NSDAP)
Reichspropagandatagung	National Propaganda Meeting
Reichsreform	The term given to matters concerning constitutional and territorial reform
Reichsstatthalter	The Reich Governor of a German state,

	a new post created by Hitler in April 1933. With the exception of Bavaria and Prussia, all the posts were allotted to NSDAP Gauleiter
Reichsstudentenführer	National Student Leader; Gustav Adolf Scheel's title as head of the Reichsstudentenführung after 1936
RSF (Reichsstudentenführung)	National Student Leadership, established in 1936
Reichstag	German Parliament
Reichswehr	The army in the Weimar Republic
RFK	Reichsfilmkammer — Reich Film Chamber
RFM	Reichsfinanzministerium — Reich Ministry of Finance
RGB1	Reichsgesetzblatt; the official legal gazette issued by the Ministry of the Interior
Rhenisch-Westfälischen Wirtschaftsdienstes	A principal organ of Ruhr Industrial interests
RJF	Reichsjugendführung — National Youth Leadership, the central administration of the Hitler Youth
RKK	Reichskulturkammer — Reich Chamber of Culture
RM	Reichsmark
RMbO	Reichsministerium für die besetzten Ostgebiete — Reich Ministry for the Occupied Eastern Territories, established in 1941 under Alfred Rosenberg
RMVP	Reichsministerium für Volksaufklärung und Propaganda — Reich Ministry for Popular Enlightenment and Propaganda
ROL	Reichsorganisationsleitung der NSDAP — Central Party Organisation
RSFWü	Archiv der ehemaligen Reichsstudentenführung und des NSDStB, Würzburg
RWR	Reichswirtschaftsrat der NSDAP — Reich Economic Council, established in 1931
SA	Sturmabteilungen — Storm Troopers,

	the paramilitary formation of the NSDAP
SAG	Staatliches Archivlager in Göttingen
SAK	Staatsarchiv Koblenz
Scharführer (SA)	Commander of the smallest SA formation (Schar) which had about twelve members
Die Schwarze Front	Principal organ of Otto Strasser's Black Front
Das Schwarze Korps	Main SS newspaper
SD	Sicherheitsdienst – the Security Service of the SS formed in 1932 under Heydrich
Slg.Sch.	Sammlung Schumacher
SPD	Sozialdemokratische Partei Deutschlands – The Social Democratic Party
srl.	société à responsibilité limitée
SS	Schutzstaffel – Protection Squads, the élite National Socialist formation in the Third Reich
Stab des Stellvertreters des Führers	Office of the Deputy to the Führer (under Rudolf Hess)
Stahlhelm (Bund der Frontsoldaten)	Conservative-nationalist ex-soldiers organisation (1918-35)
Stand	Estate (as in class)
Studentenbund	See NSDStB
Sturm (SA)	Company unit of about 150 members
Sturmbann (SA)	Battalion of about 600 members
Sturmführer (SA)	Company Commander, the lowest commissioned SA rank
Süddeutsche Monatshefte	Important, right-wing Munich newspaper
Tägliche Rundschau	Gained prominence in 1932 as the mouthpiece of the Tatkreis/Schleicher grouping
Technische Hochschule	Technological university where the emphasis is on the sciences and engineering (roughly equivalent to a Polytechnic)
Thule Society	Munich-based anti-semitic organisation of the early 1920s

TLS	Times Literary Supplement
Tobis	Tobis-Tonbild-Syndikat AG
Truppführer (SA)	Troop Commander (of approximately forty men organised in a 'Trupp')
Ufa	Universum Film AG
Ufi	Ufa-Film GmbH
UniHH	Hamburg University Archives
Unkultur	Derogatory term for alleged 'inferior' civilisation or cultural development
Untergruppe (SA)	Sub-Group. SA formation with up to 15,000 members
Uschla	Untersuchungs-und Schlichtungs-ausschuss – Investigation and Arbitration Committee; Nazi Party Court
Verbände	National associations of student fraternities
VfZG	Vierteljahrshefte für Zeitgeschichte
VKV	Volkskonservative Vereinigung – People's Conservative Union
völkisch	racist-nationalist
Völkisch-Sozialer Block (V-S-B)	Extreme right-wing amalgam which contested the Reichstag elections in 1924 as well as local elections
Völkischer Beobachter (VB)	The main newspaper of the National Socialist Movement
Völkischer Kurier	Racist publication 1924-5
Volksgemeinschaft	People's Community
Volkspolitiker	A politician who is prepared to cut across party lines
Volksschule	Primary and junior secondary school. Attendance at this type of school between the ages of six and fourteen years constituted the minimum full-time educational requirement in pre-1933 Germany
Volkssturm	Home Guard, established towards the end of the Second World War as Germany's last military defence
Vorwärts	Main newspaper of the SPD
Wehrmacht	German Armed Forces; the term

	replaced 'Reichswehr' in May 1935
Weltanschauung	'World view'; ideology or philosophy
Wirtschaftliches Sofort-programm der NSDAP	Emergency Economic Programme of the NSDAP
Wohlerworbene Rechte	Traditional prerogatives of civil servants
WPA	Wirtschaftspolitische Abteilung – Economic Policy Department of the NSDAP Reichsleitung created in December 1930. Dissolved in September 1932
ZFO	Zentralfilmgesellschaft Ost GmbH
ZStA	Zentrales Staatsarchiv Potsdam

CONTRIBUTORS

Jane Caplan is a Research Fellow at Newnham College, Cambridge. She has published articles in *History Workshop* and the *Historical Journal*, and is currently writing a book on the bureaucracy and the state in the Third Reich.

Conan J. Fischer is Lecturer in German Studies at the University of Aston in Birmingham. He is completing a doctoral dissertation on the social history of the SA 1929-35.

Geoffrey J. Giles is a Research Associate at the Institution for Social and Policy Studies, Yale University. He has published a number of papers on the Nazi student movement as well as on university development in Germany from 1933 to the present. He is now working on a study of the Nazi student organisation, and a further study on the structure of higher education in the German Democratic Republic.

Jeremy Noakes is a Lecturer in Modern European History at the University of Exeter. He has contributed to the *Journal of Contemporary History*, and is the author of *The Nazi Party in Lower Saxony 1921-1933* (1971), and co-editor (with G. Pridham) of *Documents on Nazism 1919-1945* (1974). He is at present writing a book on the political structure of Nazi Germany.

Marcus S. Phillips teaches at an Inner London Comprehensive school. He wrote his doctoral thesis on 'The German Film Industry and the Third Reich' (University of East Anglia, 1974), and is presently researching into the role of the cinema during the German Revolution (1918-20).

Peter D. Stachura is Lecturer in History at the University of Stirling. He has published articles in the *Journal of Contemporary History*, *Journal of European Studies*, *European Studies Review*, and the *Vierteljahrshefte für Zeitgeschichte*. He is the author of *Nazi Youth in the Weimar Republic* (1975), and *The Weimar Era and Hitler, 1918-1933 : A Critical Bibliography* (1977). Currently, he is writing a history of the German Youth Movement 1918-1945, and a study of Gregor Strasser.

Jill Stephenson is Lecturer in History at the University of Edinburgh. She has published in the *Journal of Contemporary History* and in the anthology, *German Democracy and the Triumph of Hitler*, eds. A.J. Nicholls and E. Matthias (1971). She is also author of *Women in Nazi Society* (1975), and is writing a book on the Nazi organisation of women.

Geoffrey Stoakes is Lecturer in History at the College of Ripon and York St. John, York. His doctoral thesis on the development of Nazi foreign policy ideas in the 1920s is nearing completion.

Albrecht Tyrell is a member of the staff engaged on the 'Dokumente zur Deutschlandpolitik' series under the auspices of the Federal Ministry for Intra-German Relations, Bonn. He has published in the *Vierteljahrshefte für Zeitgeschichte*, and is the author of *Führer befiehl. . . Selbstzeugnisse aus der 'Kampfzeit' der NSDAP. Dokumentation und Analyse* (1969), and *Vom 'Trommler' zum 'Führer.' Der Wandel von Hitlers Selbstverständnis zwischen 1919 und 1924 und die Entwicklung der NSDAP* (1975). He is also a co-editor of *Bibliographie zur Deutschlandpolitik 1941-1974* (1975).

INDEX

AG *see* Working Group of the North
    and West German *Gaue*
Allgemeiner Studenten-Ausschuss
    162-3
Alumni associations 172, 176-7
Anrich, Ernst 164
anti-semitism 23, 24, 25; among
    students 163-4
Arbeitsgemeinschaft National-
    sozialistischer Studentinnen
    (ANSt) see Group of Nazi Girl
    Students
Arendt, Hannah 236
Auf gut deutsch 54
Aufbau 42
Austrian film companies: *Kino*
    Betriebs Anstalt (Kiba) 268
Austrian film industry 266-9; and
    'Aryanization' 267-9; and Josef
    Bürkell 268-9; developments
    following Anschluss 266-7;
    Winkler's plans for 267

Balfour Declaration (1917) 25, 26
Bayer, Alois 92
Belgian film industry 270, 271, 272
Berlin Document Center 141-2
Berliner Börsenzeitung 95
Bolsheviks, Bolshevism 31, 32, 38, 39;
    Hitler's opinion of 24
bookburning 169
Bothmer, Karl v. 55, 59, 60
Bredow, Colonel von 103
Brest-Litovsk, treaty of 37-8
Brüning, Heinrich 240; friendship
    with Gregor Strasser 101-2
Buchheim, Hans 236
Bund deutscher Mädel (BdM) 188;
    and NSF membership 191
Bürgerbräukeller putsch 64, 66
Bürkner, Trude 191

Capitalism 25
Churches, passive resistance of to
    NSDAP 201
civil servants: and oath of loyalty
    242; professional associations of
241; salary cuts 240-1, 242,
    249
civil service: adaptation to changing
    situation in Weimar republic 244;
    alienation of 242; as perpetrator
    of confusion in Third Reich
    234-5; as victims of administrative
    chaos 235; experts and bureaucrats
    in 243; growth of 241;
    reconstruction of in Interior
    Ministry 247-8; reforms of in
    early war years 248; reproduction
    of the State 250-1; retrenchment
    of by Saemich 243; salaries
    249-50; setbacks to after 1937
    248; situation in from 1880s to
    1933 241-4
Coburg, Prince Cyril of 42, 43
Cordemann, Reinhold 100
Cuno, Wilhelm (Reich Chancellor)
    34
Czech film industry 269

Daitz, Werner 100
Danat Bank collapse 166
Darré, R.W. 74
Das Schwarze Korps 174
Derichsweiler, Albert, leader of
    NSDStB: attempts to control
    student fraternities 170-3; seeks
    control of NSDStB for DSt 173-4
Deutsch-Sozialistische Partei (DSP)
    59
Deutsche Arbeiterpartei (DAP) 55
Deutsche Studentenschaft (DSt) 162;
    disputes student leadership with
    NSDStB 169-70, 173-7; loses
    government income 163-4;
    NSDStB gains control of 166-7
Deutscher Kampfbund zur Brechung
    der Zinsknechtschaft 33, 58, 60
Deutscher Sozialist 58
Deutsches Frauenwerk (DFW):
    absorption of existing women's
    organizations 190-1, 193-4,
    197-8; beginnings of 188, 193;
    control of by NSF 196-7;
    exhibitions, fêtes, meetings 199;
    membership of 199-200;
    propaganda function of 195-6;
    streamlining of 196, 204; youth
    groups in 201-2
Deutschnationaler Handlungsgehilfen-
    Verband (DHV) and Gregor
    Strasser 97-9

Deutschvölkischer Freiheitspartei
(DVFP) 67, 68, 107
*Deutschvölkischer Schutz-und
Trutzbund* 52; banning of 61
Dräger, Heinrich 100
Drexler, Anton 55, 56; and *NS-
Volksbund* 68; and twenty-five
point programme 56; and
Völkischer Beobachter incident
59-61
Dutch film industry 270, 271, 272

Eben-Servaes, Dr Ilse 190, 198
Eckart, Dietrich 24, 54, 55
Egger, Wilhelm 100
Eisner, Kurt, Prime Minister 53
Elbrechter, Dr Hellmuth, and Gregor
Strasser 97
Ellenbogenraum 36
Engelbrecht, Otto 57
England 28, 33, 39; Alfred
Rosenberg's animosity towards
26; and Jewish subversion 26-7;
Anglo-French friction 28, 30;
Hitler's opinion of 1919-20,23
English Alliance 25-30, 35
'Erfurt Agreement' 165-6
Esser, Hermann 55, 68

Factory Cell Organisation (NSBO)
97, 131
Feder, Gottfried 90, 95, 109; and
AG 68-70; and *Bürgerbräukeller*
putsch 66; and DSP 59; and Hitler
64-5; and journalism 53, 54; and
Kampfbund 58; and Marxism 52;
and NSDAP 'left wing' 72-3; and
Organisation Department II 74-5;
and Reich Economic Council
(RWR) 75-7; and twenty-five
point programme 56; and
Völkischer Beobachter incident
59-61; and Walther Funk 76; anti-
semitism of 52; as 'the Ideologist'
of NSDAP 70-2; attempt to
establish Party power base 73-6;
career 1932-41 78-9; claims
creation of new political dogma
52; disagreement with Alfred
Rosenberg 72; disgust at
materialism 51; early career 49;
early loose connection with
NSDAP 55, 59-61; elected to
Reichstag 66-7; fails to secure
Party posts 73; formulates 'breaking
of interest' theory 49-50; high

self-opinion of 62-3; hopes to heal
class divisions 51-2; in ROL 76-7;
joins DAP/NSDAP 55; lectures to
Reichswehr 55-6; made Finance
Minister in provisional government
64; NSDAP career 55, 62, 70-2,
77, 79; origin of theories 50;
protests to Hitler about
Chancellorship 78; puts his
theories to government 53;
strengthens ties with NSDAP
61-2; supports refounded NSDAP
67-8; takes up financial theory
49-50; turns to political right for
help 53-4; views on capital 51
Feickert, Andreas, leader of DSt 170,
171; seeks control of DSt for
NSDStB 173-4
film industry *see* Austrian, Belgian,
Czech, Dutch, French, German,
Polish, Scandinavian film
industries
Finance Ministry (RFM) 259; and
Austrian film industry 260, 261,
262
Fraenkel, Ernst 236
France 28, 33; Anglo-French friction
28,30
French film industry 270, 271, 272
Freyberg, Dr Alfred 69
Frick, Wilhelm: and civil service
salaries 249-50; and Interior
Ministry 235; as Interior Minister
239, 244-5; dismissed from
Interior Ministry 250; policies of
246-7
Funk, Walther 76, 95

Gaue 68
Gerber, Hans 242
Gereke, Dr Günther 100
German film companies: Bavaria
Film AG 259; Berlin Film 272;
Cautio Treuhand GmbH 259,
266, 268; Continental Film srl.
272; Deutsche Filmtheater
GmbH 267; Film Finanz GmbH
260; Ostland Film GmbH 270;
Ostmärkische FilmTheaterbetriebs
GmbH (OfB) 268, 269; Prag Film
AG 266, 269; Terra Film AG 259;
Tobis 259, 265, 266, 271, 272,
278nll, 279n30; Ufa 259, 260, 272,
273, 277n9, 278n10; Ufa-Film
GmbH (Ufi) 262-3, 265, 272; Wien
Film GmbH 266; Zentralfilmgesel-

lschaft Ost GmbH (ZFO) 270
German film industry: as propaganda
weapon 258; competition with
Hollywood 264-5; difficulties of
261-2; early attempts to use films
as cultural propaganda abroad
265, 179n28; New Order in
273-7; NSDAP policies for 259-63
German films 273-5, 280n65,
281n66, 281n69; censorship in
films for export 273-5; popularity
of 275
German Girls' League 131; *see also*
Bund deutscher Mädel
Germany: and reparation payments
28, 30; bourgeoisie of 50-1;
overpopulation of 36-7;
unemployment in 147; working
class of 136-7
Gesell, Silvio 59, 61
Glaser, Alexander 107, 129n217
Goebbels, Dr Joseph: aims for
German film industry 258-9, 260;
and creation of Ufi 263-4; and
films for foreign audiences 265-6;
and German film exports 273,
274, 275-6; and role of films in
Germany 264; and role of films in
Nazi revolution abroad 263-4;
efforts to revolutionise German
films 261-2; organisation of
international film industry 266;
plans for domination of European
film industry 264-6, 276-7
Gottschewski, Lydia 188
Grossrussland 32
Group of Nazi Girl Students (ANSt)
191, 197

Habermann, Max 98-9
Harrer, Karl 55
Haushofer, Prof. Karl 36, 40-1
Hein, Dora 190
Hess, Rudolf 36, 61, 170
Hierl, Konstantin 73-4, 104
Himmler, Heinrich 175; as Interior
Minister 250
Hildebrand, Klaus 23, 36
Hitler, Adolf 30, 48; aims for Ger-
man film industry 260; and a
'national' Russia 32-3; and AG
69-70; and alliance with 'nationa-
list' Russia 31; and anti-semitism
36, 64; and 'border policy' 40-1;
and 'breaking of interest' theory 64;

and *Bürgerbräukeller* putsch 63,
64; and business interests 75, 77;
and DHV 98; and English alliance
33-4; and Gottfried Feder 64-6,
70, 71, 76; and Gregor S rasser
104-5, 109; and *Kameradschaft*
houses 171; and Ring Movement
37; and Ruhr crisis 28; and the
New Order 257; and twenty-five
point programme 56-8, 64-5; and
Völkischer Beobachter incident
59-61; approach to foreign affairs
33-4; attitude to civil service 234;
belief in Jewish subversion of
English policy 27; denounces
Gregor Strasser 112; deprecates
student fraternities 173;
establishes himself as NSDAP
leader 63; fails to gain chancellorship 97; forbids Gregor Strasser
to deal with General Schleicher
106-7; foreign policy programme
41-4; foreign policy views (1919-
20) 23-4, (1922) 34-5; has chance
to be Chancellor 77-8; his
territorial imperialism 36-41; joins
DAP/NSDAP 55-6; method of
handling partisan pressures in
NSDAP 65, 70; opinions on
Russian alliance 24; opposition
to coalition front 102; political
strategy 77; refounds NSDAP 67;
rejects idea of Russian alliance
30-1; supports English alliance 28;
views on Bolshevism 24; views on
England and English alliance 25-6,
27-8, 34
Hitler Youth 131
Horn, Dr Curt 110

ideology, Nazi 22-3; importance of
'Jewish conspiracy' to 24-5
independents 139, 140
industrialists 113; and NSDAP 94-5
Interior Ministry 235, 238, 245-50;
civil service reconstruction in
247-8; confusion and controversy
in 247; Frick's policies in 246-7;
growth of power of 245-6;
Himmler appointed to 250

Jewish state 25
Jews 35; 'world conspiracy' of 23-5
Jung, Rudolf, Sudeten German NS
leader 90, 92

Kameradschaft houses 170-3
Kameradschaften: and RSF 177-8;
 effect of war on 178-80; failure of
 leadership 174-6; lack of guidelines
 for 175-6, 179; membership, not
 possible to enforce, 180-1;
 membership, numbers of 177-8
Kampfbund see *Deutscher Kampfbund
 zur Brechung der Zinsknechtschaft*
Kampfverlag 91-2
Keppler, Wilhelm 95
Klagges, Dietrich 72
Klasse an sich/Klasse für sich notion
 136, 137
Koeppen, Anne-Marie 190
Konservative Volkspartei (KVP) 98
Körner, Oskar 60
Köttgen, Arnold 242
Krebs, Albert 98
Krüger, Gerhard, Nazi Leader of
 DSt 169
Krummacher, Dr Gottfried Adolf 188
Kube, Wilhelm 107
Kuhn, Axel 29, 34
Kultur-Erziehung-Schulung (KES):
 tasks of 195; courses 195

Labour Front 191, 198, 200
Latvia 38
Lebensraum doctrine 36, 37
Leipart, Theodor (1867-1947) 99-
 100
Lenin 24, 37
Lloyd George, David 26; and Upper
 Silesia 27; resignation of 28-9
Lossow, Lt.-Gen. von 65
Lubbert, Dr Erich 95, 100
Lüdendorff, General Erich von 33,
 38, 41
'Lumpenproletarian' 134, 138

'Manifesto for the Breaking of
 Interest Slavery' 50, 54
Marxism 25
Mayr, Captain Karl 55
Mein Kampf 23, 33, 35, 36, 39, 42,43
military training 167-8
Ministry for the Occupied Eastern
 Territories (RMbO) 269, 270
Mommsen, Hans 237
Müller, K.A. von 54
Münchener Neueste Nachrichten 34

National Women's Association of the

German Red Cross 189
National Women's Leadership: as
 central administrative agency
 198-9; creation of 197; failure to
 activate support among fulltime
 housewives 199, 200-1, 202-5;
 magazines of 203; propaganda
 functions of 199, 202
nationalism 25
Nationalsozialer Volksbund 57
*Nationalsozialistische Deutsche
 Arbeiterpartei* (NSDAP) 131; after
 Gregor Strasser's resignation
 111-12, 113; and AG 68-70; and
 alliance with 'nationalist' Russia
 31-5; and Brüning government
 101-2; and industrialists 94-5;
 and 1928 *Reichstag* election 90-1;
 and 1932 election 102-4; and
 NSDStB 160-1; and Paul Schulz
 93-4; and trade unions 99-101;
 and *Völkischer Beobachter*
 incident 59-61; attempts to
 establish theoretical base 73-5;
 early ideological weakness of 61-2;
 Economic Policy Department
 (WPA) of 74-5; foreign policy of
 41-4; Gregor Strasser's role in
 building up 88; interest in raising
 birth rate 195; 'left wing' of 89,
 107; Organisation Departments in
 73-5; Otto Strasser secedes from
 91-2; policies for German film
 industry 259-63; refounding of
 67-8; twenty-five point programme
 of 56-8, 68-71; *see also* Feder,
 Gottfried
Nationalsozialistische Völkswohlfahrt
 (NSV) 191, 194, 197
*Nationalsozialistischer Deutscher
 Studentenbund* (NSDStB):
 activities of 166-7; and Baldur
 von Schirach 163-5; and 'Erfurt
 Agreement' 165-6; anti-semitism
 of 163-4; attempts to clarify aims
 of 161; attempts to seize control
 of DSt 162; becomes mass
 organisation 168-9; becomes RSF
 174; decline in support for 167-8;
 disputes student leadership with
 DSt 169-70, 173-7; élitism in
 161-2; founding of 160; gain
 control of AStA 162-3; gain
 control of DSt 166-7; introduce

302 *Index*

Führerprinzip 167; lack of
ideology 168-9; membership
figures 168; membership figures,
effect of war on 178-80; NSDAP's
doubts about value of 161;
political vigour of 162-3; reasons
for students' apathy towards
180-1; small early groups of 160;
unable to produce constructive
measures 180; *see also
Reichsstudentenführung* (RSF)
Nationalsozialistischer Frauenschaft
(NSF): as an élite organisation
191-2; creation of 187; early
changes in leadership 188;
membership of 181-2, 199-200;
official task of 1933-9 187, 192;
propaganda function of 193;
seminars of 192; use of
professional staff 192-3; use of
volunteer workers 192; youth
groups 201-2
*Nationalsozialistischer-Schwestern-
schaft* 197
*Nationalsozialistischer Student-
enkampfhilfe* 176-7
Nazi Lawyers' Association 190
Nazi Teachers' League 190, 191, 197
New Order, the: cultural aims of
257-8; economic aims of 257-8
North Rhineland 141-2
numerus clausus 163

Oertzen, Friedrich Wilhelm von 97
Ostpolitik 38, 39
Ostsiedlung 38

Pan-German League 37
Paul, Else 190
Pfundtner, State Secretary 235, 250
Polish film industry 269-70
Propaganda Ministry (RMVP): and
German film industry 261, 262;
and Winkler's policy in the East
270; responsibilities of in relation
to film industry 259
Protocols of the Elders of Zion 23,25

Rapallo agreement 31, 32
Reber-Gruber, Auguste 189-90, 198
Red Army 38
Reich Culture Chamber (RKK): and
Austrian film industry 266
Reich Economic Council (RWR) 75,
76-7
Reich Film Chamber (RFK): and
Austrian film industry 268, 269;
interference in foreign film
industries 266; responsibilities of
259
Reichsfrauenführung see National
Women's Leadership
Reichsmütterdienst: courses 194-5;
staff of 194; tasks of 193-4
Reichsstudentenführung (RSF) 174;
and enlistment 178; and
Kameradschaften 177-8; effect
of war on 178-80
Reichswehr in Bavaria 54-5
Reusch, Paul 95
Reventlow, Count Ernst zu 107
Rosenberg, Alfred 22, 41, 109; and a
'national' Russia 32-3; and
English alliance 35; and European
balance of power 27; animosity to
England 26; anti-semitism of 24-5;
belief in European balance of
power 28-9; belief in Jewish
subversion of English policy 26-7;
views on England and English
alliance 27-8, 29-30; views on
Russia 24-5
Ruhr crisis 28
Russia 31, 35, 36, 37-9; Alfred
Rosenberg's views on 24-5; Hitler
rejects alliance with 30-1; Hitler's
opinion of 1919-20 23-4
Russian alliance 31-4, 35; Hitler
rejects 30-1
Russian émigrés 31, 42
Rust, Bernhard, *Reich* Minister of
Education 169-70, 173

Scandinavian film industry 270, 271,
272
Schacht, Hjalmar, President of *Reich*
Bank 78, 79, 95
Scharrer, Eduard 39, 41; report on his
interview with Hitler 34-5
Scheel, Gustav Adolf 178, 179; and
alumni association 176-7; and
Kameradschaft leadership failure
174-6; career of 184; unable to
enforce compulsory membership
of NSDStB 180-1
Scheubner-Richter, Dr Max von 33, 38,
39, 42
Schleicher, General Kurt von 88, 96, 97

99, 103; and Gregor Strasser 105-6; attempts to split NSDAP 93; plans after Gregor Strasser's resignation 112-13

Scholtz-Klink, Gertrud: and membership of NSF 191; and National Women's Leadership 197, 198; and propaganda network of NWL 200, 202; and *Reichsmütterdienst* 193; appointment of 188; as 'token woman' 189; as unifier and co-ordinator 196, 197-8; career and appointments of 189; qualities of 188-9; tactics adopted towards women 201-2

schoolboys 139

Schubert, Günther 23

Schulz, Gerhard 237

Schulz, Paul 93-4, 97, 129n217

Schüssler, Rudolf 57

Schutzstaffel (SS) 131

Siber, Paula 188, 193

Sicherheitsdienst des Reichsführers-SS (SD), students in 174

Silverberg, Paul 95

Spengler, Oswald 90, 97

Springorum, Fritz 95

Stäbel, Oskar, leader of NSDStB 169

'State Bankruptcy – the Salvation' 54

Stinnes, Hugo 95, 97

Stöhr, Franz 98, 107

Strasser, Gregor 43, 57, 68, 69, 73, 75, 78; ambitions of 105; and *Deutschnationaler Handlungsgehilfen-Verband* 97-9; and Dr Hellmuth Elbrechter 97; and friendship with Heinrich Brüning 101-2; and Hans Zehrer's *Tatkreis* 96-7; and his brother Otto 91-2; and Hitler myth 104-5, 111; and 'left-wing faction' 89; and neo-conservatives 96-9; and 1932 election 102-4; and Oswald Spengler 97; and Otto Wagener; and Paul Schulz 93-4; and SA 108; and General Schleicher 105-6; and trade union movement 99-101; and Walther Funk 95; as *Reichsorganisationsleiter* 88; breaks with Hitler 109-110; changes views after 1928 election 90-1; conflicting evidence about his motives 89; cooperation with industrialists 94-6; creation of NSF 187; criticises Hitler 128n204; cultivates contacts outside NSDAP 93; denounced after

resignation 112; differences with Hitler defined 126n152; estrangement from Hitler 102, 105; his character analysed 111; his letter of resignation 113-16; his socialism becomes blunted 91; Hitler's position in Party too strong for 109; leaves politics 111; loyalty to Hitler 111; need for historians to study 88-9; NSDAP support for 107-9; reasons for resigning 110; receives money from mining industry 94-5; relations with Hitler 91-2; resignation of 88, 109-10; should be viewed as Weimar politician 89; socialism of 90, 92-3; supports coalition front 102-4; writes to Dr Curt Horn 110

Strasser, Otto 90: attempts to capitalise on brother's resignation 111-12; secedes from NSDAP 91

Streicher, Julius 59

student fraternities 162; and 'Erfurt Agreement' 165-6; and Hitler 173; loose control of DStB 166-7; NSDStB attempt to control houses of 170-3

students 139; and military training 167-8; and *numerus clausus* question 163-4; apathy towards NSDStB, reasons for 180-1; in SS 174; rights of movement curtailed 174

Sturmabteilungen (SA) 108, 131; and army 132; assumptions over social background of 133; command structure analysed by age and social class 151-2; disagreement over class and occupation background of 133-4; disagreement over social and economic history of 132-3; general concern over 131; leaders of 131-2; numerical strength of 132; official records of 137, 138-40, 141; purge of leadership 132; violence of 104; workers in, proportion of 140-1; works on discussed 132

SA membership: age structure of 145, 149-51; by class 137-9; by employment 141-2; by occupational group 137-44; by social background 140; by workplace 143-4; depended on nature of local economies 143; documentary sources available for 135; occupational structure, terminology of 135-7; social background of as reported by

primary 134-5; social mobility of
144-7; unemployment among 147-9
Süddeutsche Monatshefte 54
Sunkel Reinhard 164

Tatkreis 96-7; and Gregor Strasser 96-7
Tempel, Wilhelm 160, 162
Third Reich: administrative incoherence
in 234; conflict between rational
bureaucracy and irrational political
movement 236; contradictions
between federal sovereignty and
unified state 239-40
Thyssen, Fritz 95
trade union movement and Gregor
Strasser 99-101
training camps 172

unemployment 147-9
USSR film industry 270

Versailles, treaty of 26, 28, 40; and
Upper Silesia 27
Vögler, Albert 95
Völkisch movement 50, 51, 54, 56, 58,
59, 66-7
Völkischer Beobachter 41, 57, 59-61, 72,
98
Volkskonservative Vereinigung (VKV) 98
Volkssturm units 180

Wagener, Dr Otto 74-5, 100; and Gregor
Strasser 95
Weimar era, occupational structure of
135-6
Winkler, Max: activities in Western
Europe through agency of Alfred

Greven 272; and Austrian film
industry 267, 268-9; and German
film exports 275; and German film
industry 273, 277; as 'Reich Delegate
for the German Film Economy' 259;
plans for profit-sharing cartel 261;
policy for Eastern European film
industries 270; policy for German
film industry 260; policy for Western
European film industries 270-1, 272;
reorganisation of German film
industry 261, 262-3
Winnig, August, Reich Plenipotentiary
for the East 38, 97
Wolff, Otto 95, 100
women: efforts by NSDAP to secure
goodwill and cooperation of 203,
204-5; *see also* National Women's
Leadership
Women's Labour Service 189, 191
Women's Office of the German Labour
Front 189
women's organisations: changing role of
186-7
women's role: functions of women's
organisations 186; in NSDAP
organisation 186; Nazi view of 186
'workers': definitions of 136-7; social
mobility of 144-6; training of 144
working class 136-7
Working Group of the North and West
German *Gaue* (AG) 68, 69

Zander, Elsbeth 187-8
Zehrer, Hans 96-7

DD
249
S43

The Shaping of the Nazi state / edited
  by Peter D. Stachura. -- London :
Croom Helm ; New York : Barnes &
Noble Books, 1978.
  304 p. ; 22 cm.
  Includes bibliographical references
and index.
  ISBN 0-06-496492-2

  1. Germany--Politics and
government--1918-1933. 2. Germany--
Politics and government--1933-1945.
3. National socialism. I. Stachura,
Peter D.

DD249.S43   320.9/43/085
                          77-10038

SUPA   B/NA A D1-186581   08/23/78